# LightWave® v9 Texturing

## Angel Nieves

**Technical review by William "Proton" Vaughan, NewTek's LightWave evangelist**

**Wordware Publishing, Inc.**

**Library of Congress Cataloging-in-Publication Data**

Nieves, Angel
    LightWave v9 texturing / by Angel Nieves.
        p.   cm.
    Includes index.
    ISBN-13: 978-1-59822-029-2
    ISBN-10: 1-59822-029-2 (pbk., companion cd-rom)
    1. Computer animation.  2. Computer graphics.  3. LightWave 3D.  I. Title.
    TR897.7.N54 2007
    006.6'96—dc22                                    2006101143
                                                         CIP

© 2007, Wordware Publishing, Inc.

All Rights Reserved

1100 Summit Ave., Suite 102
Plano, Texas 75074

Printed in the United States of America

ISBN-13: 978-1-59822-029-2
ISBN-10: 1-59822-029-2

10  9  8  7  6  5  4  3  2  1
0702

All inquiries for volume purchases of this book should be addressed to Wordware
Publishing, Inc., at the above address. Telephone inquiries may be made by calling:

(972) 423-0090

This book is dedicated...

To my wife, Marilyn, and my two kids,
Andy and Jazzy, the source of inspiration in my life.

# Contents

Contents . . . . . . . . . . . . . . . . . . . . . . . . . . . . . . . . . . . . . . . . . .

# Acknowledgments

I'd like to thank the following people who have given me so much support over the course of writing this book.

To my family, my wife, Marilyn, who supported me all the way through, during the good times and the not-so-good times where I wasn't in my best of moods. To my kids, Andy and Jazzy, for understanding why Daddy couldn't play with them all the time. I love you all.

To all my friends who have given me input, support, and have helped me stay sane: Eric Hartz, Edwin Sumilave, Cesar Montero, Annie Stegg, Brandon Wheeler, Ramon Garcia, and Tim Dunn.

To Werner Ziemerink, Brendon Goosen, and David Mass for the cool models.

Special thanks to Leon Harmon (http://www.thewayisleon.com) who provided me with the awesome concept for the cover, even during tough times.

To all the cool friends at SpinQuad and CGTalk for their daily inspiration and support.

Jamie from Pixologic for the very cool software! Without Jamie, the LightWave/ZBrush workflow chapter would have never been possible. To Richard Jennings from The Graphics Factory for providing the awesome IFW2 demos.

And, of course, to all the great people at Wordware Publishing, especially Tim, Beth, Martha, and Denise, who have made the process of writing this book so easy and so much fun.

And lastly a huge thanks to William "Proton" Vaughan for all the help, input, and support.

# PART I

# The Art and Science of Texturing

# CHAPTER 1

# Observing the World Around Us

## Looking at the World a Little Differently

Before we begin to explore all the theory and techniques that are involved in the process of texturing, it is vital to observe the world around you in such a way as to enable you to understand exactly what you need to create within the computer-generated environment in which you work. Merely observing the world on a superficial level is not sufficient. Take a look around you. What do you see? Naturally, you see the world that you have been looking at every single day of your life.

Now take another look around you. This time, concentrate on every different surface that you see and describe to yourself exactly what the surface looks like. When you begin to describe what you see, you will realize that every surface is comprised of many different qualities.

Concentrate on one particular surface. What colors are in the surface? Are there any scratches, fingerprints, or other blemishes or imperfections in it? Is it reflective? Does any light penetrate the surface? Answering questions such as these will help you to understand exactly what you need to know in order to recreate a surface such as the one that you are examining.

Look at the photo of a dusty electric guitar in Figure 1-1 on the following page. The fingerprints in the dust tell us that someone has recently touched it. However, the heavy layer of dust tells us that the guitar has probably been sitting unused for some time.

Touch the surface. Is it hot or is it cold? Smooth or rough? The actual tactile quality of the surface is very important. To make a texture believable, you have to be able to convey to viewers exactly what the surface would feel like if they were to reach out and touch it. The art of creating textures is so much more than just defining the colors of surfaces; it is about creating the quality and tangibility of them too.

Figure 1-1

To become a texturing artist, one needs to observe and experience the world in this manner. Make a habit of noticing all the tiny details in everything, and how they alter the way in which you perceive the actual surfaces. These are the details that you have to create in order to make interesting and believable textures.

As crazy as it sounds, I often find myself looking around and noticing, and subsequently admiring, one particular aspect of a surface. I may be sitting in traffic, carefully studying the specular properties of the back of a garbage truck, or sitting in a movie theater, closely examining the unusual and fascinating falloff of light on the plush cushioning of theater seating. In Figure 1-2 we can see a nice example of the lovely way in which light falls onto velvet. This broad falloff is very different from the falloff of light from plastic or metal.

Figure 1-2

Developing a keen, perhaps almost rabid, fascination with such detail is the key to becoming a great texturing artist, as it equips you with an excellent understanding of how things look in the real world.

The next time you see an old metal water tank with amazing rusty streaks all the way down the sides, don't be too embarrassed to run frantically up to it, practically foaming at the mouth, so you can have a closer look at those incredible orange drips and smudges that form after years of sun and storms. Touch it, study it, even smell it! Explore every inch of the surface so that you can see exactly what colors and details are in the rust, thereby forming an excellent mental reference for any instance in the future in which you may have to create a rust texture.

Just ignore the people who are staring at you as if you are some kind of weirdo.

Figure 1-3 shows some rust that has been building up on the lower tray of a little portable barbeque that lives outside on a third-story balcony. Notice all the different tones within the rust (it is not a single color), and notice also how the rust has formed in the bottom of the tray, where water gathers, and not on the sides of it.

Figure 1-3

I cannot emphasize enough the importance of this kind of attitude. You have to become excited about the way things look. That way, you will find the process of recreating them exciting and enjoyable too.

By the time you have finished reading this book, you will be well versed in the knowledge of all the different attributes and qualities of which surfaces in this world are comprised. Once you are armed with all that knowledge, identifying and examining these properties will be very easy for you to do, and will greatly aid you in the process of observing things in a manner benefiting your texturing skills.

## The Effects of Time and Weather

It is safe to say that nothing in this world remains untouched by time or weather. One of the biggest mistakes made by texturing artists is overlooking, and consequently excluding, the effects that the world, as well as just the mere existence of the object in question within the dimension of time, has on any surface. All too often we see things created in 3D that are just too clean. I am not suggesting that everything needs to look completely wrecked and ancient, but it is important to show some weathering in your textures, however subtle.

When texturing things that generally remain outdoors, as opposed to things that are usually sheltered, you have to consider how the weather will have affected it over time. A house in a nice, quiet, sunny suburb is going to show some form of aging and damage, no matter how often the loving homeowner sprays the structure down with the garden hose. The sun, rain, and wind affect everything they touch to some degree, regardless of whether these things are manmade or natural.

The two most damaging aspects of weather are the sun and wind. Rain does have a considerable impact on things, but since there are no places on earth where it rains every single day, its effect is not as consistently damaging as the other two, but rather plays a slightly different role, which we discuss in a moment.

Take a walk outside, and notice the way in which the weather has affected everything.

The sun dries things out, causing colors to fade and substances like paint or mud to become brittle and crack (see Figure 1-4, which is a photo of a balcony wall), while the wind blows minute particles of sand and other debris around, gradually causing minute erosion on everything.

The wind can also create very tiny and subtle details, such as grains of sand in paint and varnish that may have become stuck in the coating while it was drying. The wind also, obviously, carries dust and other dirt around, causing it to become lodged in cracks, scratches, joins, and any other abrasions or irregularities on surfaces. Another detail to note is that if the wind has been blowing in only one direction, the dust will all lie on the same side of things too.

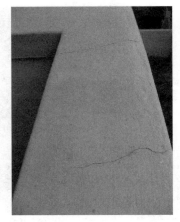

Figure 1-4

The effects of rain can have quite an impact on the appearance of things. Apart from the obvious examples such as streaking paint and dirt, it also causes streaks of rust to form over time, as shown in Figure 1-5.

Areas that experience a fair amount of rain will generally produce foliage that is far more lush and green than areas that do not. It is essentially, and in most cases, not

Figure 1-5

so much a damaging effect but a nourishing one.

Of course it can also be a destructive force, as in the examples of cyclones and other tropical storms, but since water is, for the most part, one of the main sources of life on this planet, its effect is usually a more appealing and welcome one. Areas that have a lot of moisture present, and especially if they also have less intrusion from the sun, tend to allow the growth of molds, moss, and lichens, which are subtle yet interesting and important details that convey to the viewer what the environment feels like.

Notice the manner in which all these weather elements affect different substances in different ways. Bricks weather in a different fashion than wood. Depending on their construction or the substance from which they are made, some surfaces are able to withstand these effects better than others. For instance, car paint is covered in a special lacquer that protects it from the sun and prevents things from sticking to it, whereas a metal mailbox will rust and gather dirt, even if the two are positioned right alongside one another in a scene. It is essential that you do not weather everything in one scene equally, but rather treat each individual surface in the unique manner that suits it.

The effect of time is easy to observe. The longer something exists in this world, the more wear and tear it will have. An old building is not going to look as clean and perfect as a newly built one. Even if an old building is still in good condition, structurally speaking, its walls and windows are going to show some form of aging. These marks could come not only from the weather but also from interaction with people.

## The Effects of Human Interaction

Humans have a remarkable effect on their surroundings. Every single day of our lives, we go about from place to place, leaving our mark on everything that we touch. This goes beyond just mere fingerprints and footprints. The way in which we handle items that we use determines, to a large degree, the manner in which they gather dust and grime and develop telltale signs of wear and tear.

Take, for instance, the example of a light switch. Sure, after many years of use, the entire switch and mounting will become somewhat grubby and worn, but if you were to examine it very closely, you would notice areas where the plastic has become worn in a more specific manner. You do not even have to actually examine a light switch to know that the actual switch part will have developed streaks from fingers being dragged over it every time a person has used it. These streaks become so worn into the plastic that eventually it becomes impossible to completely remove every trace of them. It is almost as if they become a part of the plastic itself. Even if the actual streaks are not brown and dirty, there is still a trace of them that cannot be erased.

Figure 1-6

This sort of specific, localized mark is a typical example of human interaction and how we affect the surfaces of the items around us.

Let us consider another example: your computer mouse. No matter how much you clean your mouse, you will never completely remove the marks that you leave on the buttons. As I mentioned before, these marks do not have to be literal streaks of grime. No matter how faint the marks are, they are there to stay. The same goes for your computer keyboard. Eventually, the buttons are going to develop a slightly worn appearance.

When texturing anything, you have to consider what manner of human interaction affects the object. Consider not only the actual manner of interaction, but also the frequency and purpose of such use.

## Every Surface Tells a Story

Now that we have discussed the effects of time, weather, and human interaction on the surfaces of all items that we find in the world around us, we can begin to put all of these surface effects together and start adding further unique details to each texture to create, for the viewers, a sense of history for the surface that you are making. This makes the textures not only far more interesting to look at, but also much more believable. The key to believability lies in convincing the viewer that the object has some sort of purpose and conveying the manner of that purpose by creating subtle details on its surface that give an indication as to what function the item may have.

Creating a texture for something is so much more than just defining the colors, light reflection and absorbance properties, and other properties of an object or character. It is about creating a sense of identity for it and giving the viewers an idea of where this item or character has been and what it has been doing.

For example, if you were making textures for a soldier or warrior type character, you would add things like small scars and such, because a character that has been involved in fighting or aggressive training would most definitely acquire a few marks on his body along the way. His clothing and weapons would also show battle scars of some sort, perhaps scrapes from shrapnel or even actual rips, tears, or gouges from hand-to-hand combat. However, it would be easy to get a bit carried away with all this and just end up adding loads of details that just result in a really disheveled and messed-up looking individual. Sure, a soldier who has just been fighting is going to look a bit messed up, but the kinds of details that tell a story are the very specific, unique little ones. Perhaps, if the warrior is wearing armor, there might be one deep gouge in the metal that has tiny flecks of copper in it. A tiny, almost indiscernible detail such as this would indicate that the weapon that had caused that particular cut in the armor was made of copper. If his armor has been pierced, then perhaps it would be a nice idea to add tiny shards of wood around the puncture to indicate that the damage had been caused by a wooden arrow or bolt. Details like these add a certain element of richness to the character, and to the world that you have created for him, by creating a sense of where he has been and what he has encountered.

Let's take another example: an old softcover book. If you were to create textures for an old book with a soft cover that has been read many times, what sorts of details could you add to it that could make it look unique?

What details could you include that might give you some indication of who has been reading the book?

Perhaps you could add an old ring-shaped stain from the bottom of a coffee mug to the cover. Or maybe one of the corners of the book has become dog-eared and bent, as happens with many softcover books. These details could tell the viewer that perhaps the reader of the book is not very careful when reading, or does not particularly care about keeping the books he owns in good condition.

You could even add a detail such as a person's name or a small doodle drawn on the soft, lacquer-coated cover, done by a person who may have been bored. Or perhaps, at one point, somebody accidentally tore the cover very slightly, and then mended it using a piece of tape.

Very well-read books also tend to develop wrinkles or creases in their spines. If you wanted to indicate the book has been read many times, you would not only make the cover a bit grubby, but you should also add things like creases along the spine or slightly dog-eared pages.

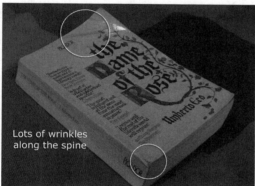

Lots of wrinkles along the spine

Figure 1-7

Details like these are not merely examples of basic human interaction because they are not universally common to all objects of the same type. Not all books are going to wear the same way and some books are more carefully looked after than others.

For example, if you were to create a book that belonged to a small child, you could add elements such as old food spills or even crayon pictures scrawled on the pages.

Looking at details such as these, especially a detail such as childish scribbles, the viewer would immediately be able to conclude that the book had, in fact, belonged to a child.

Let's explore another example of this. Imagine that you were to create textures for a car. How could you add details to the texture that would give the viewer an idea of the history of the vehicle? First, you should indicate what sort of person owns the car. To give a clue as to the nature of the vehicle's owner, we should decide on an appropriate color for the car. A bright red car with yellow racing stripes may indicate that the owner is young and bold and outgoing, whereas a plain white or black car may belong to a more sophisticated and possibly more conservative owner.

The condition of the car can give us further clues as to the nature of the owner. If a reckless teenager, or perhaps an old person with somewhat impaired senses, owns the car, then it is more than likely the car will have bumps and scratches on its front and back fenders from clumsy parking, or scratches on its body from scraping against walls or barriers. Figure 1-8 shows a car that could belong to ... a hippie perhaps?

Figure 1-8

If the car has been in a serious accident, perhaps some minor details might still be visible despite any repairs that may have taken place. There could be signs of welding repair work, or perhaps one of the side mirrors is still broken from the impact, having yet to be replaced.

Decorations can say a lot too. A teenager might also have lots of stickers on the bumpers and rear window, whereas an older, more responsible person might just have an auto club decal on the window.

Perhaps the person who owns the car likes to take trips, in which case he may have collected many decals from his various destinations that he has stuck on his rear window. People who travel across country borders in their vehicles often display a decal with their own country's flag on it.

Second, what sort of environment is it in on a daily basis? And where has the car been? If the car is kept outside, then it will have become more damaged from the weather than one that is kept inside a garage. If the car is used in heavy traffic on a daily basis, it will probably be slightly grubbier than one that is not, due to all the road grime.

If the car has been taken out for a drive in the country recently, it may have slight traces of mud splattered above the wheels or dried mud caked between the tire treads.

Or perhaps the car has just been through a car wash and still shows traces of the cleaning mechanisms on its body. The circular motion of the brushes inside some car washes leave spirals on the car paint that can be seen at certain angles.

Maybe the vehicle has just been stolen, in which case the door locks may show signs of tampering, such as deep scratches around the keyhole where a piece of wire may have been used to pick the lock.

Third, what is the vehicle used for? A 4x4 pickup truck is likely to be used for safari trips and off-road adventures, which means that the actual body of the truck will probably show signs of such activity. Details could include mud that has sprayed up from the road and dried along the base of the truck's body, scratches in the paintwork from low, overhanging tree branches, and perhaps even tufts of animal fur on the front grille where the truck tragically collided with some kind of wildlife. At the other end of the scale, a car that is only used for shopping trips and picking the kids up from school is likely to be clean and in good order. If the car has a trunk for carrying goods, and the vehicle is used very frequently for conveying cargo of any sort, the keyhole on the trunk is going to show a lot of use, and perhaps the paintwork around the trunk could show slight scratches or smears from cargo that may have been clumsily placed in it. Perhaps the owner of the 4x4 sells firewood that he delivers to customers, in which case the paint around the truck's bed could become very scratched from logs hitting it.

All these examples illustrate the details that we need to include in our textures to create a sense of identity, purpose, and history for the objects we are texturing. Remember, in order to enthrall your audience and capture their attention, you need to give them something that they can identify with, and therefore believe. So when you are creating textures, always begin by building up some kind of visual story to communicate to your audience some of the details of the life thus far of your objects and characters.

## Gathering References

An absolutely essential tool for any texturing artist is an excellent library of references. Whenever you come across a great picture of any kind of substance or surface, scan it into your computer and stash it away for future reference.

This will help you enormously, as you should never work without some idea of what you are going to create. Although many details like those we have discussed can be created straight from your imagination, the actual qualities of a surface, in terms of its physical properties, are usually best created using a number of good reference images to ensure that you establish all your main settings quickly and efficiently.

It is also a good idea to have an extensive library of images for when you are trying to give your client an idea of what kind of look you will be creating for a certain object. This saves a lot of time, especially since it is always annoying when you work for a few days on something only to find that the client had envisioned a slightly different look for it. There is no point in wasting time trying to guess what your client has in mind when you could instead show him a bunch of images demonstrating different variations of whatever it is he wants you to make. He can then choose the look that he wants, thus giving you a perfect starting point of reference for your own creation.

Building up a library of images is pretty easy. You can obtain thousands of reference pictures from the Internet, using image search engines (such as Google), or you can get your own pictures by scanning actual materials using a normal computer scanner or by taking photographs yourself, or you can buy images from stock photo libraries on CD.

As we will discuss a bit later, photographs can also be used as a base for your actual texture maps, so having a large collection of high-quality photographs can be extraordinarily useful. It is important, however, to bear in mind that only high-quality images should be used for your texture maps. Although this may seem like common sense, you often find people using low-resolution images as texture maps, which result in unsightly, blotchy surfaces when rendered. This is usually a result of people using images that they have gotten from the Internet, as most images found on the web are highly compressed and low resolution. Although the images can be fine for reference, they should not be used to create actual textures.

Building up your reference library should be an ongoing process. You can never have enough reference, so add to your library any picture that may prove to be of some use, even if you have 100 images of the same type of thing already.

It is very useful to obtain an image browser (such as Deep Exploration, IrfanView, or ACDSee) to manage your library. Most browsers include thumbnail preview options that make navigating the folders within your collection much quicker and more efficient. Of course, assembling your library using a logical and specific naming format is also essential for ease of use. Create a folder for each different type of image, such as metal, wood, fabric, etc. This also helps you to find what you are looking for more quickly.

Now that we have prepared ourselves for the texturing process, we can begin to delve into the exciting world of creating surfaces and textures in LightWave!

**NOTE:** Please see the companion CD for images of all the figures in the book, many of which are in color.

# CHAPTER 2

# Lighting Basics

## Observing Light and Its Effects

Essentially, what we are doing when we create surfaces for objects is defining the manner in which light will affect the surface. This is because everything that we see, we are able to see because of light. Without sufficient light, we are unable to see colors and details on things because that information is carried to our brains via waves (and particles) of light. Light bounces off objects and those rays then enter our eyes, transmitting the information about what those surfaces look like to our brains. Therefore, when we are setting up the surface of an object, we are actually defining the information that will be carried to the brains of the viewers by providing the surface colors and details to transmit via rays of light.

Because of this, as texture artists we need to have a basic understanding of light and how it affects surfaces that it touches. We also need to have an idea of basic lighting setups within LightWave so that we can render our textured models and show off our textures to their full potential.

> **NOTE:** *LightWave v9 Lighting* by Nicholas Boughen (1-59822-039-X) covers this topic in depth. I will only briefly cover the subject of lighting for the purposes of this book, and recommend reading Nicholas's book for more information.

The properties of surfaces in the real world that pertain most directly to light are color, diffuseness, specularity, glossiness, reflection (in the real world the last three are the same thing, although they are split up in the world of computer graphics), and luminosity. You can read about each of these in Chapter 4, "Surface Attributes." LightWave obviously offers a number of other surface attributes to play with, but these particular properties of a surface are the ones that are most affected by the lighting in your LightWave scene since they essentially shade the surface. By *shading* I mean that these attributes will determine the manner in which the lighting in your scene will affect your surface most noticeably, and will thereby essentially create the tangible quality of the surface as we see it.

It is important to have a good understanding of how these surface properties work so that you can shade your surface correctly, making it act more realistic in regard to its environment and therefore more believable.

# Basic Light Options in LightWave

LightWave offers a nice toolset of options for setting up lights and lighting environments in Layout.

There are five different types of lights that you can create in LightWave, each having its own specific characteristics and effects. The different types are distant lights, spotlights, point lights, area lights, and linear lights. You can create these from your Items menu in Layout.

Figure 2-1

## Distant Lights

By default, whenever you create a scene in Layout, a distant light is created within the scene. Distant lights are supposed to simulate sunlight in LightWave, as they project infinite parallel rays of light that have no falloff in whichever direction they are facing.

Figure 2-2: Scene lit with distant light

Distant lights have sharp-edged shadows and the light has no set radius, so it essentially lights everything that lies in its path equally, unlike a spotlight that has a cone radius that will only light objects where the actual beam of light within that cone lies.

The position of the light is irrelevant, so you can place it anywhere in your scene. It is only the direction of the light that matters. The light also has no defined origin, as the direction simply focuses the rays from an infinite source.

The advantages that distant lights offer is that they do a relatively decent simulation of sunlight and they render quickly. The drawback, however, is that they only offer sharp-edged shadows (as opposed to fuzzy-edged shadow maps), and if you study sunlight, you'll see that the shadows become softer farther away from the object casting them. Also, because the rays coming from the light are all parallel, the shadows cast by objects will remain exactly the same size and shape, regardless of how far from the object the shadow falls. This is not technically accurate (in terms of real sunlight), although it isn't always noticeable in shots, especially when the shadows are mostly in the background.

## Spotlights

The second type of light that we have is the highly versatile spotlight. These lights are extremely useful as they can be used to create a number of effects, and they can imitate other lights such as area lights and point lights (discussed in a moment) and even distant lights with a few tweaks of their settings.

A spotlight creates a cone of light that emanates from a single point and casts a circle of light onto subjects in the scene.

One of the most useful things about spotlights is that they can produce both sharp-edged shadows as well as soft, fuzzy shadow maps, as shown in Figure 2-4.

Figure 2-3: Spotlight

Figure 2-4: Spotlight with fuzzy shadows

Figure 2-5: Spotlight with gobo effect

By experimenting with the cone angle and the shadow settings, you can simulate the effects of using point lights, distant lights, or area lights. You can also project images through spotlights for creating what are known as gobo lighting effects. A *gobo* lighting effect is a method used predominantly in theater and film where plates that have shapes cut into them are placed in front of the light so that the projected light can appear to, for example, be coming through a canopy of leaves in a forest, as shown in Figure 2-5.

Aside from these advantages and uses, spotlights are relatively fast to render, especially when using shadow maps, since this requires no ray tracing. One disadvantage to using these lights is that when using them with ray tracing, their shadows can be extremely hard (like distant lights). Another disadvantage of spotlights is that their shadow maps are physically inaccurate and can sometimes look very strange, especially with high fuzziness settings, which can often give the illusion that the shadows are not properly "attached" to the objects that are casting them.

## Point Lights

Point lights, often also called omni lights, cast light in all directions (omnidirectionally) from a single, nondimensional point in 3D space. They are technically inaccurate in the sense that all lights in the real world have physical dimension, whether it is the sun or the filament of a lightbulb. Not having any real dimension means that the light appears to have no scale, which makes it impractical for creating the lighting of something as large as

a lightbulb, although it can be useful for creating quick illumination for things like LED lights on a VCR since the scale of such an item is so small anyway.

Point lights have ray-traced shadows, which create hard shadows with no softening whatsoever.

The most common use of point lights is simply for creating some ambient illumination in your scene, usually with the shadows switched off.

Figure 2-6: Scene lit with point light

## Area Lights

Area lights look great and they create very cool-looking shadows. As they are more physically accurate than any of the other light types in LightWave, they are capable of producing very realistic lighting.

One of the best things about area lights is that their size is adjustable, which makes them extremely useful for any type of

Figure 2-7: Scene lit with area light

lighting source that needs physical dimension. Because the light has a dimension, it is capable of producing realistic shadows that are hard near the source and gradually grow softer as the shadow falls farther from the object. The only drawback to using area lights is that they take much longer to render than other light types. However, this price may be worth the effect that they create.

## Linear Lights

Lastly, we have linear lights, which are similar to area lights in the sense that they appear to have dimension. While an area light is essentially like a two-dimensional rectangular array of ray-traced point lights, a linear light is like an adjustable one-dimensional row of point lights. This creates a lighting

effect that casts shadows along the axis on which the light lies.

Linear lights are useful for things such as fluorescent lighting tubes, since they have the same shape. However, their shadows can sometimes be a bit strange, and are often best left turned off.

Figure 2-8: Scene lit with linear light

## Creating Basic Lighting Setups

While we are in the process of creating textures and setting up surfaces on our objects, we ideally need to be able to view those surfaces in the best possible way so that we can keep track of how the surfaces look.

The best way to ensure that your textures look the way that they should is to light them in such a way as to illuminate the entire model so that all the surfaces are totally visible and not hidden or obscured in any way by shadow.

Even if your final lighting setup is going to be dim or colored in some way, it is best to set up the textures with a relatively neutral lighting setup, as this gives us the best indication of the "natural" look of the surfaces. If the surfaces look right under neutral lighting, then chances are they will work well under any other type of lighting (as this is how things work in reality) with minimal tweaking.

One of the most neutral and efficient lighting setups for this process is a studio style setup, such as would be used in any photographic studio. This type of lighting rig is often called "three-point lighting," as it usually consists of three lights, or three areas of illumination: the key light, fill light, and backlight. This lighting is great because it ensures the subject is totally illuminated from all angles without looking too unnatural.

Nicholas Boughen, the author of *LightWave v9 Lighting*, totally hates three-point lighting, but I have to recommend this type of setup because it really is efficient when setting up texturing!

Let's take a look at each of the three lighting sources and examine their purpose.

## The Key Light

The key light is the primary source of illumination. It can consist of a single light or a number of lights, depending on your scene. This light is usually placed above your subject (although it can actually be placed anywhere — there is no hard-and-fast rule about its placement in a scene), and generally provides illumination for approximately three-quarters of your subject. This light is typically the brightest point of illumination in the scene.

Figure 2-9 shows some crates being lit by a key light only, in this case an area light.

Figure 2-9: Scene lit with key light only

## The Fill Light

The purpose of the fill light is to provide illumination in the shadow areas not illuminated by the key light, so that there are no areas that are totally black (as this is not possible in the real world, unless your scene takes place in a black hole!). As with the key light, your fill light does not necessarily have to be an actual light. It can be created using radiosity, a sky dome, or anything else that provides a secondary source of illumination in your scene. Generally the fill lighting is of a fairly low intensity.

Figure 2-10 shows our crates being illuminated by both the key light and the fill light, which is positioned off to one side of the objects.

Figure 2-10: Scene lit with key light and fill light

## The Backlight

Also called a rim light, a kicker light, the highlight, and a variety of other names, the backlight is simply there to create highlights on a surface so that the object stands out from its background. This light often casts no shadows.

Figure 2-11 shows our lovely little crates being lit by all three lights. The backlight is positioned directly behind the crates in the scene. Notice how it catches the specularity along the edges of the crates, making them stand out slightly from their surroundings.

Figure 2-11: Scene lit with key light, fill light, and backlight

Starting off your scene with just a basic three-point lighting setup using these elements generally provides a decent starting environment for creating your surfaces.

These are really just the basics, and I would highly recommend doing some further reading on the subject of lighting, especially if you would like to specialize in the areas of shading and texturing, as a solid knowledge of lighting can benefit you greatly in this regard.

# PART 2

# The Surface Editor

# CHAPTER 3

# Introduction to the Surface Editor

Just as a quick note before we delve into the mysteries of the Surface Editor, I want to point out that in order to set up surfaces for your objects, you will need to have assigned appropriate surfaces to your model in Modeler. This may seem a pretty obvious thing to do, but I want to ensure that I mention every step of the process, and assigning surfaces to the model is naturally the first step. And because a lot of surface creation is best done within Layout, remembering to assign surfaces may have slipped your mind!

To assign a surface to an object in Modeler, simply select the polygons that you want to apply the surface to and press "q." The Change Surface dialog pops up with a number of basic options, including a space to enter the name of the surface. Set these up as you wish, bearing in mind that you can change these settings later.

Figure 3-1

## Opening the Surface Editor

Once you have all your various surfaces assigned to your object, you are ready to begin using the Surface Editor, which is the place where you assemble all your textures and create all your surfaces.

To open the Surface Editor, you can press Ctrl+F3, the default keyboard shortcut, or press the Surface Editor button just below the top of your toolbar.

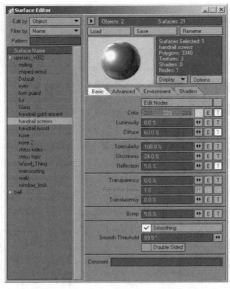

Figure 3-2: LightWave's Surface Editor panel

Notice that any objects you currently have open or that are within your scene are listed on the left side in the Surface Name list. This list displays every surface assigned to each different object file. You can collapse this list by clicking the arrow button above the Load button on the right side of the panel. If you do this, a drop-down list labeled Surface appears, from which you can select the surface you wish to work on. For ease of use, let's just keep the panel the way it is for now. You can click on the little white triangle next to each object name in the Surface Name list to expand and display all the surfaces assigned to that particular object.

## Edit Modes

At the top-left corner of the Surface Editor is the Edit by button. There are two edit modes available for the Surface Editor: Object and Scene.

The Object editing mode is a "discrete" editing mode, in that it allows you to work on each surface individually, regardless of whether there are multiple surfaces that share the same name in the scene. This pertains particularly to when you are working in Layout with a number of different objects, some of which have surfaces with the same names. Using the Object editing mode will ensure that each surface is treated individually and that no global changes are accidentally made. Object is the default editing mode.

Whereas Object edit mode allows you to keep surfaces completely separate, Scene edit mode applies changes globally. This means that if you are working with a number of different objects in your scene, the scene editor condenses all the surfaces that share names and treats them as single surfaces. In other words, if you have two different objects, each of which has a surface named "black plastic," selecting the surface and making changes to it will affect both surfaces with that name. This is particularly useful when you have a lot of objects that you want to share surfaces, and eliminates the hassle of copying and pasting surfaces from file to file. When using Scene edit mode, notice that the list of surfaces in the Surface Editor is much shorter and does not list the surfaces according to the object they are on.

> **NOTE:** The edit mode that you use is saved from session to session. Consequently, if you are using Scene mode, when you load up your scene again, LightWave will apply the settings of the last object loaded to the others sharing that surface name.

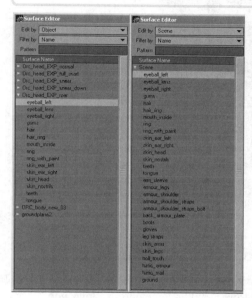

Figure 3-3: Object edit mode (left) and Scene edit mode (right). Notice the way in which Scene edit mode condenses all surfaces with the same name to a single surface.

# Filtering Options

Below the Edit by button you will see the Filter by button, which basically allows you to control what surfaces are shown in the Surface Editor. By default, the Name option is active. This option shows all the surfaces within the scene (in Layout) or on the object (in Modeler) in alphabetical order.

The next filter option is Texture. Selecting this will display only surfaces that use procedural textures.

Similarly, the Shaders option displays only surfaces that use shaders.

The Preview option will display all surfaces that are currently included within the image in the render buffer, on a pixel-by-pixel basis. Of course this means that you will have to render a frame first, and naturally, this option can only be used in Layout.

Below the Filter by button is the Pattern field. This is simply an extension of the Filter by button. Entering any text that appears in any surface name into the Pattern field will display those surfaces in the Surface Editor. For example, if you have a few surfaces that have names that include the word "skin," you can type the word into the Pattern field and the Surface Editor will only display surfaces containing the word "skin."

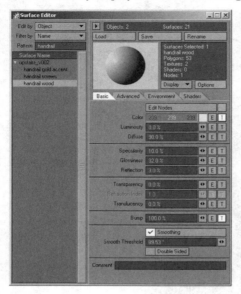

Figure 3-4: Using the Pattern field to filter surfaces displayed in the Surface Editor

# Loading, Saving, and Renaming Surfaces

On the top-right side of the Surface Editor we find a few basic file options, namely Load, Save, and Rename. The Save option allows you to save the surface you have currently selected to an external surface file (.srf file), while the Load function simply loads a surface (.srf) file into the currently selected surface. The Rename option allows to rename your surfaces.

> **NOTE:** You can also right-click on any surface name, which gives you options for copying and pasting entire surfaces from one to another.

# The Preview Window

Directly below your file and surface name options is the preview window. This little window gives you an idea of what your current surface looks like.

Clicking the Options button gives you a few customizable options for how the preview window displays your previews (see Figure 3-6).

Figure 3-5: The preview window

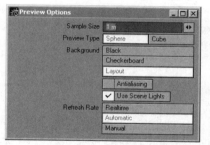

Figure 3-6: The Preview Options panel

The Sample Size option allows you to set the surface area size of the little sphere shown within the preview window. Ideally, one should set the sample size close to the actual physical size of the area to which the surface is applied; however, it is also useful to check very tiny details you may be adding to your surface by changing this value to a rather small one. Preview Type allows you to change your preview object to a sphere or a cube.

> **NOTE:** Unfortunately, if you are working with UV maps, this preview window cannot display them, no matter what you set these options to.

Background gives you a couple of options to choose for the backdrop behind the preview sample. Black is obviously plain, flat black. Checkerboard gives you a backdrop of little black and white checks. This option is particularly useful for checking transparency and refraction settings. Layout displays the backdrop settings that you have created for your scene in the Background settings panel found under Layout's Effects panel. This setting is only available in Layout.

Antialiasing activates or deactivates antialising in the preview window. Antialiasing gives you a smoother sample, but takes slightly longer to update within the window.

Activating the Use Scene Lights option uses the lighting setup in your scene instead of the default lighting to illuminate the sample in the preview window. This can be useful in determining how your color and other surface settings will react to your current lighting. This setting is also only available in Layout.

Refresh Rate sets the manner in which the preview window updates itself. Realtime updates the sample whenever you make any adjustments to interactive controls, such as adding texture layers or adjusting values. Automatic updates whenever you release your mouse button after making any changes or selecting a new surface. Manual updates only when the preview window is clicked. This last option is useful when you are working on complex scenes that are hogging your system memory.

To the left of the Options button is a button labeled Display. If you wish to concentrate on a particular surface channel, you can set your preview window to display only that channel by selecting it from the Display list. Render Output is the default setting, and displays the surface as it would appear when rendered.

**TIP:**   All of these options can also be quickly accessed by right-click-ing on the preview window itself.

# Edit Nodes

The first option under the Basic tab in the Surface Editor is a button called Edit Nodes along with a check box. This little button opens up a whole new world for texturing in LightWave. Node networks have been the norm in high-end 3D packages for a very good reason — flexibility. Now don't let this intimidate you; node texturing will be your best friend once you under-stand some things before you dive into creating shading networks. We discuss the Node Editor further in Chapter 14, "The Node Editor."

# Smoothing

Leaving the actual surface attributes themselves for the time being, we now look to the bottom of the Basic tab on the Surface Editor panel, where we find the Smoothing option.

Figure 3-7: The Smoothing option

Smoothing is a method that LightWave uses to create the effect of smooth surfaces when they are, in fact, made of loads of flat-faced polygons. If smoothing is not on, the polygons that make up your object are clearly visible. This is usually not the effect that you want, since it would result in your rendered model looking jagged (pixelated) and blocky across its sur-face. So LightWave uses a shading model called *Phong shading* to create the illusion of the model being smooth by taking the points where smoothed polygons meet and making them appear as if they are one continuous sur-face as opposed to separate polygons.

You can activate Smoothing by checking the little option box.

Smooth Threshold determines the angle limit at which LightWave ceases to smooth. If the angle between two joined polygons is equal to or greater than 90°, as it would be in the case of a shape such as a cube, LightWave will not, by default, create any smoothing, unless you adjust the Smooth Threshold setting. The default Smooth Threshold amount is 89.5°, which means that anything over that amount will not be smoothed unless you specify that it should be by changing this amount.

It is important, however, to note that smoothing does not affect the actual geometry of an object. Although the object may appear smooth when rendered, sometimes you may still be able to discern the individual poly-gons along the model's edge, especially when viewed up close. If you find this happening with your models, you will need to smooth your actual model by adding more geometry.

## Double Sided Surfaces

Below the Smoothing and Smooth Threshold options is the Double Sided option. You can activate it simply by checking the little box. Double Sided makes your polygons appear to be two-sided, which can be useful should you need to go inside the object or if you are working with an object that is very thin, such as a piece of paper or fabric, that has been modeled with only one-sided polygons.

Double Sided is also very useful for making glass surfaces or transparent plastics appear to have more thickness. These surfaces are explored in greater detail later in this book.

Be aware that using the Double Sided option does result in longer render times, since LightWave has more polygons to render.

## The Comment Field

Below the Double Sided check box is the Comment field.

Figure 3-8: The Comment field

You can enter notes or comments into this field if necessary. This is rather useful for leaving notes to any other texture artist who may have to work with surfaces that you have set up or for keeping track of changes that you have made in the particular surface.

# CHAPTER 4

# Surface Attributes

## Color

### What Is Color?

The first surface attribute that we encounter is that of color. Now, I know what you are thinking: "Oh, no, here comes the boring section on color theory." Don't be afraid; I won't delve into it for too long. While color theory might sound boring, to me it is a fascinating world that when studied and mastered can be used to help bring your messages across to your audience.

Color theory is more than just a bunch of color wheels with primary, secondary, and complementary colors; it is also about "perception," or how colors interact with each other and how they affect the human psyche. Temperature is a good example of color perception and how it affects the viewer. The brain will immediately interpret hot with reds and yellows and cold with blues and purples, for example. These colors can also be used to identify "good vs. evil." When you understand color theory, you can use it to your advantage and sort of "fool" the viewer's perception of things just by cleverly manipulating color and therefore provoking thought. We'll be exploring some of the basic concepts of color manipulation in the next couple of pages. There are several good publications about color theory if you would like to learn more about the topic. I personally like *The Elements of Color* by Johannes Itten. It is an old book, but it's great.

Absolutely everything that you model in LightWave will have color of some sort, so you will always use it in some way, no matter what you are working on.

To use color in LightWave, you can specify a base color for your surface by entering an appropriate RGB value in the Surface Editor or by assigning textures to the Color channel.

Figure 4-1

You can alter the RGB values by simply clicking on the little digits and dragging your mouse to increase or decrease each value.

Figure 4-2

You can also click on the little color swatch next to the values to bring up a color selection window, similar to the one you would find in any paint application.

This window contains a number of basic colors from which you can choose, as well as a full RGB spectrum for creating your own colors.

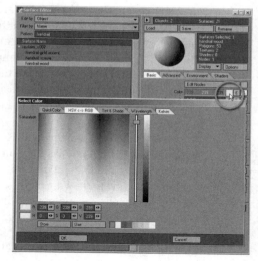

Figure 4-3

## Using Color

Color is used in texturing in two ways.

First, you use color simply because the object you are texturing is that particular color in real life. You wouldn't, for example, create bright blue textures for a human, since human skin is not blue. You would use flesh tones instead. So the first manner of color use would be purely using certain colors because that is what color the object is supposed to be.

The second use of color is more subjective and artistic. This comes into play when you are given artistic freedom to decide on the colors used for certain props and such in your work that are more flexible in terms of the colors you can use for them.

This artistic use of color can also overlap real-life color groups, subtly altering people's perceptions of things, even if the overall colors that you have used in the textures have been created simply as a recreation of how that object would appear in life.

An example of this would be perhaps if you were texturing an evil character, where you would be more likely to use a palette of darker, cooler colors like shades of blue, purple, or even browns and blacks to indicate a shady personality or darker agendas. On the other hand, if you were texturing an angelic character, you would be more inclined to use an array of dazzling, bright colors, such as white and gold. This sort of use of color is very subjective, and can help to convey ideas about your characters simply because of the colors that you have chosen and people's common mental associations with them.

This type of effect can also be achieved (often more effectively) through the use of colored lighting setups.

You may also have the need to alter what would otherwise be the more technically accurate colors for something else purely because it would suit your purposes more appropriately. An example of this would be in a situation in which your textures for a human character in certain lighting conditions within your scene make the realistic and accurate colors change and appear unnatural or even just plain nasty. You would then use a more artistic approach to alter the colors in your textures so that they look better in your lighting setup.

Color is the best starting point for texturing, in my opinion. By roughly sketching out the color ideas for your surface, you can easily begin to conceptualize what the final product will look like.

However, even knowing all this, no matter how much color theory you study or how well you understand the fundamentals behind the actual use of color, actually using it can be a tricky matter for many. Working effectively with color in order to recreate the correct, desired look for something is often no easy feat. It is easy to say, "Oh, just paint what you see," but recreating that color can sometimes be trickier than you imagined.

When working to recreate real-world objects, it is advisable to obtain good quality photographs of them and use the color picker of a paint program to copy the RGB values from the photographs. Even if you do not end up using those exact colors, using a color picker can be a good starting point.

## Ensuring Color Accuracy

Okay, I know I said that we would not delve much into color theory, but we do need to discuss some theory here for a moment. As you know, the colors that you create in LightWave (as well as in most paint packages) are created within the RGB color space. If you have studied design or have a good knowledge of programs like Adobe Photoshop, you know that the RGB color space is just one of a number of different color spaces. Another example of a color space is the CMYK color profile.

These color spaces are linear color spaces. *Linear* color space has regular tonal values as the brightness of the color increases. You no doubt remember learning in school about the primary colors, RYB (red, yellow, and blue), which also exist in linear color space, and existed long before we had computer monitors!

However, since the color values are computed within an application,

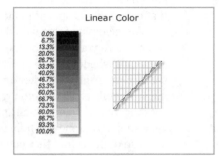

Figure 4-4

your actual perception of these colors can differ depending on the device on which the image is viewed. Unfortunately, this means that there can be major discrepancies between the actual computed color values and the perceived colors.

Although RGB is the only color space available for us to use within LightWave, we should know a little about *logarithmic* color space, commonly referred to as log color, especially when texturing for broadcast media. Log color differs from color spaces like RGB and CMYK in that it has weighted curve values that result from more steps in the lower tonal area, as opposed to being evenly spaced.

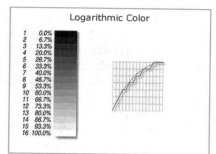

Figure 4-5

This type of color space is a far more accurate way of calculating color values. It correlates closely to the way in which humans perceive color, because the human eye is less sensitive to differences in tone as the brightness of color increases.

When texturing, we would ideally want to be able to view our textures within log color space, as we can then get a much better indication of how they will actually look on a film screen or television.

Many high-end programs, such as Flame, Shake, and Kodak Cineon, as well as more affordable packages like Adobe After Effects, have options for converting RGB content into log color space. If you have access to any of these, it is recommended that you check your content on them to ensure that your colors are going to be correct when they are viewed.

Another thing that you can do to ensure that your colors are as correct as possible is to make sure your computer monitor is correctly calibrated. This way you can be certain that your monitor is not set up totally wrong, resulting in colors that appear normal and correct to you being completely wrong and wacky to people viewing them elsewhere. For more information on monitor calibration, refer to your monitor documentation or use an application such as Adobe Gamma, included with Photoshop.

## Manipulating Color

When working with color, it's vital to understand how to manipulate it to suit your needs. Sure, painting in the colors that you want is usually the ideal course of action, but there will also be situations in which you will need to make color adjustments to your work, or even to photographs.

When working with color images, we need to have a good understanding of their different components so that we can manipulate them as necessary.

**33**

## Hue

Hue is basically the color of pixels within an image. When working with different images that you want to blend together seamlessly, adjusting the hues of the images can be a good way of getting them to mix. Making hue adjustments to images can subtly or drastically change the colors within the image, giving you control over the look of the image. When texturing, you will probably find yourself making many hue adjustments in your paint program, especially when you see what the image looks like when applied to your model and rendered, since the color in the paint application and the

color in the render can sometimes drastically differ. Sometimes this is not a problem, although there are times when it really is.

Figure 4-6 demonstrates this. The inset shows the painted color map, while the main image shows what it looks like when applied to the model and rendered. Notice how different the colors are when lit and rendered within LightWave.

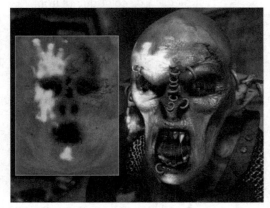

Figure 4-6

> **NOTE:** Please refer to the companion CD to see the images from this chapter in full color.

Very often, I have sat and painted really cool-looking color maps that look great just as images. However, once I have applied them to my model, lit the scene, and rendered it, the colors look completely different. To fix this, I just adjust the hues within the image, usually using Adobe Photoshop. One of the best ways of altering hue within Photoshop without risking messing up your image completely is by using Adjustment Layers. More information about Adjustment Layers is available in the Photoshop documentation.

Most decent painting packages allow you to independently adjust the individual hues within an image. So if, for instance, you just want to adjust the hue of the green parts of an image, you can do so.

The following image demonstrates this. I have adjusted the green hues in the image to be blue (actually, I have adjusted the green hues so that they become closer to blue hues).

Figure 4-7

Alternatively, you can use LightWave's own hue adjustment slider on the Image Editor to make hue changes in images. See Chapter 12 for more information on using the editing tools in LightWave's Image Editor.

Sometimes you may find that you will also need to make slight hue adjustments to your textures if you are working with a scene that has strongly colored lighting. In that case you would simply adjust the hues of your textures accordingly.

### Saturation

The saturation of an image is the amount of color that each pixel contains and the intensity of that color. If you remove all the saturation from an image, it becomes grayscale. Using saturation correctly is important because oversaturation of textures is a very common problem, especially among beginners, and looks really nasty.

The following image shows an example of oversaturation.

Figure 4-8

As you can see, this is quite an extreme example, but believe it or not, this kind of thing happens more often than you might think. Oversaturation can also occur from diffuse levels on your surface in LightWave being too high, but we discuss that matter in the section titled "Diffuse" in this chapter.

There is no foolproof way of ensuring that your images are not oversaturated, as it can be quite subjective. However, if your textures are looking really blown out, try decreasing the color saturation.

You can increase or decrease the saturation of images within LightWave's Image Editor (see Chapter 12) or within your paint package.

### Brightness

Brightness is easy to understand. We all know the difference between a bright image and a dark image, so no in-depth explanation is really necessary here. However, I often come across artists' images that are either too dark or too light. Sometimes this may be due to lousy lighting in their scenes, but often this can be because they have painted their images strangely.

The best way to check whether your images are too bright or too dark is to take a look at them on a different computer.

You can adjust the brightness of an image in LightWave's Image Editor or within your painting package. Don't go too wild with this setting though, as it can really ruin images, especially if you make them too bright. Making an image too bright washes all the color out of it, making it look rather awful, as in Figure 4-9.

When working within LightWave, you must be careful with your lighting, as this may also totally ruin the color in your textures, especially in terms of brightness, as well as saturation.

Figure 4-9

## Contrast

Sometimes you might paint a nice-looking color map, but when you look at it, it seems a little plain. Increasing the contrast of your image can sometimes help to push the colors out nicely by increasing the difference between the dark

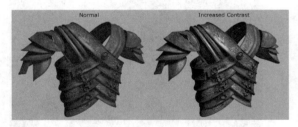

Figure 4-10

pixels and the light pixels. This can greatly improve colors that may be otherwise dull, and can also help to enhance details.

As with the aforementioned color adjustments, too much contrast can really ruin an image and make it appear totally overblown and ugly. So use it carefully.

• • •

Well, now that you have a basic understanding of the adjustment tools that you can use to manipulate color in images, go forth and experiment!

Painting programs such as Adobe Photoshop or Jasc Paint Shop Pro can be used for more than just painting. They can also be used for photograph and image manipulation and editing and simple hue and saturation adjustment. So next time you are having difficulty getting a color to work properly, remember that there are a lot of tools at your disposal for manipulating the colors within your images, and use them!

As I said before, I do not want to go into too much detail regarding color theory and whatnot, so this information should suffice. While all that stuff is extremely important in graphic design and the printing industry, when working as a texturing artist, you can get by with an intermediate knowledge of this type of thing. Just make sure that your images are not too dark, too light, too saturated, too desaturated, and are the right color, and you should get along just fine!

> **NOTE:** I have only really scratched the surface of color theory in this chapter. Writing more about the subject here would really be rewriting the vast tomes that have already been written about it. Nicholas Boughen's *LightWave v9 Lighting* (1-59822-039-X) covers the subject and makes an ideal companion for this book. I did think long and hard about putting in a lot of additional information on color theory, but since there is also such a vast wealth of information about it available freely on the web, I thought it better to devote the limited pages of this book to more practical (and popular!) topics.

## Diffuse

### What Is Diffuse?

Aaah, the diffuse value. A much debated surface property, this one. Many people disregard the need for diffuse when it is, in fact, rather important. What exactly is it? It is a strange property to explain, but basically diffuse determines how much of a surface's color we see by determining how much light is scattered (and reflected) and how much is absorbed (diffused) by the surface. If you have used any other 3D programs, you may have noticed that some of them label the color channel in their surface editors as diffuse, when in fact color and diffuse are different, even though they are inextricably linked.

The diffuse value (not to be confused with "diffusion") determines how much light is being reflected by the surface. The higher the diffuse value, the more light is being reflected by the surface; therefore the brighter the surface will appear. This is called "diffuse value" instead of reflection because a bumpy, rough, or uneven surface scatters the light when it is reflected so that no reflected image is discernable. A highly reflective surface does not scatter the light much at all, but reflects it back out much in the same pattern it had when it arrived. In fact, LightWave's "diffuse value" and reflection (and also specularity in CG) are the same thing in the real world. However, the nice people at NewTek have separated specularity, diffuse, and reflectivity into separately controllable channels so we can fiddle with them.

> **NOTE:**   "Diffusion," on the other hand, refers to light being scattered *through* something such as smoke, steam, a glass of milk, or a piece of paper. (Note one of the latest buzzwords in the CG world — *subsurface scattering*, or SSS.)

So, for starters, why is it important to use diffuse correctly? Well, the answer is simple. If you leave diffuse at 100% in the Surface Editor, and light up your scene and render it, the chances are very high that your surfaces are going to end up looking oversaturated and really not very nice because the diffuse is just too high. In reality, nothing has 100% diffuse, because everything scatters some light and absorbs some. There is no cut-and-dried value for calculating diffuse values in CG, so generally you just have to trust your own judgment and use your artistic sense to apply appropriate diffuse values to your surfaces.

If your diffuse setting is 100%, it means that your surface is reflecting all the light, and that is why the surface becomes oversaturated. This is a big problem, especially with colors that are bright, as in Figure 4-11.

**Figure 4-11**

If you lower your diffuse amount, you will notice that your surface will appear darker. If your diffuse amount is 0%, your surface will appear totally black. This is because a value of 0 allows none of the light to be reflected, resulting in a color-less (black) surface. You may think that this would be totally nonfunctional, but it does actually have its uses, which we examine in a moment. Different types of substances diffuse light differently, so it's up to you to ensure that you assign an appropriate diffuse value to your surface, depending on what sort of surface you are creating, and also what type of lighting you are using for it in some cases.

## Using Diffuse

So, how do we go about using this diffuse surface property properly? Well, the bad news is that there is no simple solution, as diffuse is not as straightforward an attribute as the others that we use. This is because the value can vary so drastically from surface to surface, and it is a difficult property to observe in real life, unlike properties like specularity, reflection, and bump mapping. One thing you can be sure of, however, is that nothing in real life is 100% diffuse.

The good news is that we do not always need to create actual diffuse maps for surfaces. In many cases, simply altering the overall value in the Surface Editor to an appropriate value or using a simple gradient instead can suffice.

With surfaces that are reflective, however, you may find that you need to create a diffuse map, especially if you have created a reflection texture as well. It is safe to say that the more reflective a surface is, the lower its diffuse value. Refer to the section "Diffuse Value and Reflection" later in this chapter for more information on this phenomenon. Essentially, if you have created a reflection map (an easier map to create than creating a diffuse map from scratch), you can generally get away with simply inverting the reflection map and using this image as your diffuse map. This helps to make the reflections crisper and more realistic. It also prevents your reflections from appearing milky, as demonstrated in Figure 4-12 (no pun on the word "milky" intended!).

Figure 4-12

The cow on the left has 100% reflection as well as 100% diffuse applied, whereas the cow on the right has 0% diffuse. Notice how the reflections in the cow on the right are more distinct and less washed out. This is a classic example of how effective lower values of diffuse are when used with anything that needs to be reflective, especially metals.

Of course, the problem with lowering your diffuse value is that it darkens the color. This is not always necessarily a problem, especially not in the case of anything that is reflective, but it can sometimes be an issue. To counteract this, you may find that you sometimes need to lighten your image map when you have lowered your diffuse value. If, for example, you are texturing a head and you lower your diffuse value to around 70% (a good diffuse value for skin generally), you might find that lightening your image map by 30% (in other words, the percentage value by which the diffuse value has been decreased from 100%) can improve the look of the texture. However, this is just a rough estimate, and often adjustments can be made on either side until the desired effect is achieved. The important issue with using diffuse correctly is that you use it to eliminate oversaturation, and this, as I mentioned earlier, can often rely partly on lighting situations as well. As a very rough guideline, for nonreflective surfaces that are placed in evenly lit scenes, you generally use diffuse values between 65% and 90%.

## Luminosity

### What Is Luminosity?

You know how when you go to raves, and you get all dressed up in luminous yellow and orange clothing so that you will look all cool under the UV lights on the dance floor?

That has nothing to do with luminosity.

So what is it then? Well, in a nutshell, luminosity makes things appear to be self-illuminated. It really is as simple as that. Nothing more, nothing less. Basically, it makes them luminous, in the sense that they appear to emit a light of their own.

Figure 4-13 shows the difference between using luminosity for the computer screen and little power lights, and not using it. Big difference.

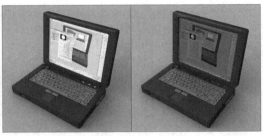

Figure 4-13

Need to make something look like it has a light of its own? You use luminosity to make things like LED displays, red-hot swords, glowing eyeballs, neon signage, flashing lights, and fluorescent tubes, to name just a few examples. It is perfect for lighting up those red eyes of your latest hideous demon model, boiling lava in a volcano, and the energy thrusters and lasers for your

Figure 4-14

spaceships, or for adding some electric power to your animé-style villain's oversized sword.

Luminosity, however, is not the same as using the glow effect found in LightWave. That is something separate, discussed in a moment, and can be very effective in enhancing the effect.

### Using Luminosity

To use luminosity on a surface, simply increase the value of the property in the Surface Editor, or add textures or images to its texture channel. Remember that the lighter the color of the texture in the channel, the stronger the luminosity will be.

Figure 4-15

Looking at Figure 4-15, we can see how the lighter areas of the image that I used as a luminosity map make the sphere more luminous, whereas the darker areas have a lesser effect. The actual use of images and gray values in texturing is discussed in Part 3 of this book.

Do take note that using luminosity on its own will *not* actually illuminate objects around it or actually emit light; it is merely the appearance of self-illumination.

However, using luminosity in conjunction with radiosity when rendering does cause luminous objects to illuminate their surroundings. This works best with very high luminous values.

> **NOTE:**  For more information on radiosity and its use in illumination, please refer to your LightWave manual. Or you can check out Nicholas Boughen's lighting techniques in *LightWave v9 Lighting*.

However, the drawback to using radiosity is that it can result in really long rendering times. Anyone who has worked with it before knows that radiosity looks fantastic when used properly, but can often result in unacceptable rendering times, especially when you are working on a deadline.

With a little cunning, we can create this effect using other methods. One way we could do this is by using gradients (discussed in greater depth in Chapter 9).

For example, if you were using that laptop shown earlier in a darkened scene, and had a character step close to the screen, you would want to illuminate his face slightly, as in reality this is what would happen. We can do this by using a Distance to Object type gradient on the character's face, with the input parameter of the gradient set to the laptop object. You could set up the gradient's parameters so that as the character comes within a certain radius of the laptop screen, his face would appear to become slightly illuminated.

The following image demonstrates this method, using a sphere to represent the character.

Figure 4-16

Figure 4-17

Using this method would have no severe impact on rendering times, and also, in some ways, gives you greater control in defining the effect and nature of the illumination.

Of course, another way of creating this effect would be to simply position a light by the luminous object and set it up so that it appears to illuminate its surroundings.

Figure 4-17 shows the laptop once again, this time with an area light, sized to the same dimensions as the screen and placed directly in front of the screen, at a fairly low intensity.

In this particular case, this latter method is probably a more realistic way of creating the effect than the gradient method, as the area light also illuminates the rest of the laptop itself.

As you can see, using a little creative thinking can solve problems like this, and can greatly enhance the effect of the object's self-illumination.

## Using Glow with Luminous Surfaces

If you look at the Advanced tab in the Surface Editor, you will find a setting called Glow Intensity.

Figure 4-18

Using glow is really cool for further enhancing the effect of luminosity. Of course, it is not really essential for everything that is luminous, such as an LED or a computer monitor, but for effects like lava or lasers, glow is really useful for adding more substance to the effect.

To use the glow option, simply enter an appropriate amount in the Glow Intensity field in your Surface Editor.

In order to have the glow render, you also need to activate it in your Image Processing options by clicking on the button under your Scene tab in Layout or by pressing Ctrl+F8.

Figure 4-19

Activate the glow by clicking on the Enable Glow check box. You can further control the intensity of the glow, and set its actual size in pixels for when it renders in the Glow Radius field. This radius setting determines the actual size of the glow surrounding the surface, so if, for example, you set it to 15, then you will have a 15-pixel thick glow surrounding the surface. Be conservative with the Intensity value, as it is very strong.

> **NOTE:** Both of these values can be animated by using the envelope function, represented by the "E" button. See Part 5 of this book for more information on envelopes. This can be really cool for creating flickering effects.

Let's explore a case of using glow, using an everyday lightbulb as an example. Take a look at Figure 4-20.

Sure, it's a lightbulb, but don't you think it would look a lot better if the filament of the bulb was glowing, as it would if it were switched on? Even though the surface of the filament in this example is set to 100% luminosity, the effect is not quite strong enough.

All we need to do is add some glow to the filament's surface, and immediately the bulb starts to come to life, as shown in Figure 4-21.

Figure 4-20

Figure 4-21

The settings used for the filament surface in this case were those shown in Figure 4-22, using 100% luminosity.

There are two processing filters within LightWave — Bloom and Corona — that you can use for similar effects. Corona can actually use textures for creating turbulence within the effect as

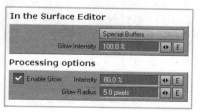

Figure 4-22

43

well, so you can use combinations of these options for creating some really cool stuff.

See Chapter 19 for more information on these filters.

## Specularity

### What Is Specularity?

Essentially, in real life, specularity is the reflection of any light sources that are illuminating the object, and is actually a shortened term, the full term being *specular reflection*. If we were to zoom in really closely on a highlight on a surface, we would find that the highlight is in fact simply a pure reflection of a local light source. However, in CG, specularity is really a cheat. Actually, specularity in many art forms is a cheat. In painting, the addition of specular highlights to a surface is often done solely for artistic reasons, and not because the surface actually had any highlights. And in graphic design, people often use effects like highlights on text and 2D logos and such to enhance them. It basically comes down to that little need for shine that we often feel the necessity to add it. It just looks cool.

In LightWave, this surface property determines how bright the reflective highlights on the surface appear to be when light shines onto it by lessening or increasing the strength of the highlights that the light creates on the surface. Pretty much everything in this world is shiny to some degree, so specularity, you will find, is used often when texturing. Without shininess, an object's surface appears flat, and does not really "react" to the light shining on it. (Of course, the fact that it has a color means that it is reacting in some way to the light, but I'm talking more in terms of visible "highlights" or "hotspots" here.)

Take a look at the following image. The sphere on the left has no specularity, whereas the one on the right does. Notice how the specularity not only makes the surface appear more interesting, but it also enhances the bump map rather nicely, giving it a little more definition.

Highlights on a surface give us an idea of how the surface feels — whether it is smooth or slightly rough (not in terms of the object's topography, which is generally defined by the bump map), hard or soft, dry or wet, old or new, greasy or slimy, etc.

Figure 4-23

Another extremely important thing detail relays to us is the object's everyday interaction with the world; by altering and breaking up the reflection of light on its surface, we can get clues as to how the object is handled by people or how it is used in the world. In other words, it shows us how the world and its inhabitants have left their mark on it, so to speak. For instance, a wine glass is never really 100% squeaky clean; look closely at it and you will see oily fingerprints, faint grime from general handling, smears from the last time it was washed, and an entire host of other greasy smudges, abrasions, and dusty marks.

Figure 4-24

All of these marks reduce the shininess of the object. On the other hand, sometimes certain interactions can increase the shininess; for instance, an apple that has just been polished will have brighter, shinier spots where it has been polished harder. It really depends upon the type of surface we are dealing with.

You may be wondering at this point why we would use specularity, which as mentioned earlier is really a cheat, when LightWave's Surface Editor also has a Reflection option. Surely, you may be thinking, we could just use the reflection properties of a surface to get highlights, and surely that would also be more realistic? Well, ideally it would be, but unfortunately, using reflection mapping often results in surfaces appearing overly mirrorlike, as opposed to simply shiny. Yes, we know that shininess on a surface in real life is due to the surface actually being reflective, but in CG reflection is often just too strong. That is why we use specularity to give highlights to a surface without it actually becoming mirrorlike in appearance. Sometimes some slight reflection mapping can enhance a surface very nicely, but once again, this really depends on the surface at hand.

Essentially, in the end it comes down to the fact that on most surfaces we create we need to add some level of shininess. And whether we use reflections or specularity, or a combination of both, we are going to be creating highlights on the surface.

Specularity is also separated out because it is much less CPU intensive to calculate just a "bright spot" based on angles of incidence and reflection than it is to actually calculate the real-world reflections that are involved in specularity.

## Using Specularity

Specularity is applied to a surface in much the same way as any of the other non-color surface attributes: by using either gradients, procedurals, or image maps that assign specular values using shades of gray. The lighter

**45**

shades of gray increase the specular value while darker values decrease it. Essentially this means that pure white in a specular map results in 100% specularity, while black areas have none.

Something that baffles many people is the process of creating a specular map by hand. For some reason, they find the idea of highlights on a surface a little confusing. This is because when we look at a photo, for example, of a person's face, we might find a nice streaky highlight on the person's nose, as in Figure 4-25.

However, the confusing part for some is that they now struggle to understand how to get that streak of light on the nose if they were to attempt to recreate the same head in CG. For many people, their first instinct is to create a specular map that has a bright spot right where that specular highlight is showing in the photograph. Perhaps their specular map would look something like Figure 4-26.

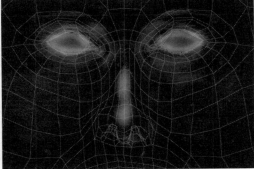

Figure 4-25                    Figure 4-26

Sure, if you use this texture on a model and light it, you might get something similar to the photograph, but essentially we need to consider why the nose was highlighted in the photograph and why the highlight was so strong in that area.

The fact is that the highlight on the nose is not there because the person's skin is ultra shiny along that narrow streak on the nose. This highlight is simply a reflection of a light in front of the person's face. The highlight is quite strong because the skin on a person's nose is often a bit shinier than the surrounding skin on the rest of the face, not just shinier along that streak but on the entire nose. So a more accurate way of creating a specular map in this instance would actually be to create something more along the lines of Figure 4-27, and then to place a light in front of the face and tweak the surface settings and light settings until the highlight is looking the way you want it.

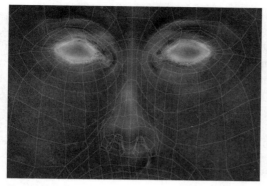

Figure 4-27

As you can see in this example, the entire nose has a slightly higher specularity than the immediately surrounding skin, resulting in brighter response to light. If you look at an average human face, you'll notice that generally a person's nose, forehead, and the areas under his eyes tend to be slightly shinier than the cheeks and chin. Sometimes the chin can also be a bit shinier, especially at the very tip, but not always.

So we create our specular maps to show the entire area that is shinier, not just the areas where we want to see highlights, since the position of highlights is really dependent on the actual positions of lights in your LightWave scene.

## Tinting Specular Highlights

By default, specular highlights in LightWave are white, and will take on the color characteristics of any colored lights that may be illuminating the surface as well. However, this is not always desired, since having bright white highlights on everything tends to make things look fake and plastic. While this is obviously fine for plastic objects, it may not work for other surfaces. So what we tend to do is tint our specularity. You can do this by using the Color Highlights option under the Advanced tab in the Surface Editor, shown in Figure 4-28.

Figure 4-28

The Color Highlights option basically adds the color of the surface itself to the specular color, the strength of which depends on the highlight's value. The higher the value, the more of the surface's color will appear in the specularity, as shown in Figure 4-29.

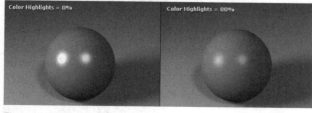

Figure 4-29

The Color Highlights option is very useful for surfaces like glass, as it prevents the surface from looking overblown when lit. It is also a great option for shading skin, as skin tends to have very muted highlights. Actually, you find most often that some tinting of the specular highlights is required for surfaces, at varying strengths.

**47**

You can also use shaders like the BRDF shader to add color to the specularity as well as specular shaders in the Node Editor. The BRDF shader actually allows you to define a color that you want to have in the highlights. See Chapter 14, "The Node Editor," and the section on the BRDF shader in Chapter 5 for more information.

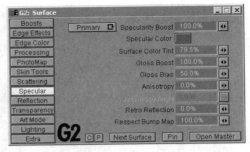

Figure 4-30: The G2 interface

Worley Labs' G2 shader also has the ability to tint specularity, as well as to define a color for it.

The G2 shader allows you to define a specific color for the highlights, using the Specular Color option, and then blend it with the color of the surface using the Surface Color Tint option.

## Anisotropic Specularity

Examine any stainless steel surface, and you'll find that there is something odd about the way that light reflects from it. Take a look at Figure 4-31, which shows a close-up of a stainless steel surface.

Notice how the reflection of light on the surface tends to run horizontally in this particular photograph. We see this phenomenon on surfaces that have been machined with tiny grooves across the surface, which are quite visible in this photograph. These parallel grooves cause the light to be spread out in one particular direction, an effect known as *anisotropy*.

Figure 4-31

We can see this same effect on the surfaces of compact discs, where the light causes lines of reflection that radiate from the center of the disc outward. This is because a CD surface has thousands of tiny grooves machined onto a thin metal disc, which is coated in plastic. These grooves are essentially cylindrical, in that they are etched in rings around the disc. This causes the light to be spread in a cylindrical fashion, producing these lines of light that emanate from the center.

Figure 4-32

As you can see in these two examples, the reflection of light occurs at an angle that is directly opposite from the angle of the grooves. In other words, the reflections occur at a right angle to the direction of the machining.

To create this effect in LightWave, you can use the BRDF shader (see Chapter 5 for more details), Worley Labs' G2 shader, or anisotropic shaders in the Node Editor (see Chapter 14 for more information), all of which have anisotropic options. You can use these shaders to define an angle of anisotropy to create this effect. The BRDF shader applies this effect to the specularity only, while the Node Editor and G2 allow you to have anisotropy in both your specularity and your reflection (which is more realistic).

Surfaces such as stainless steel (cooking pots, for example), wood fibers, and even fabrics like satin and silk have anisotropy.

## Glossiness

### What Is Glossiness?

Glossiness is a specular highlight caused by the reflection of light. The rougher a surface is, the more diffused the specular highlight becomes. The more diffuse the specular highlight is, the less "glossy" the surface appears. Therefore, smoother surfaces appear more "glossy" than rough surfaces.

We generally associate the word "gloss" with anything that is plastic or wet, and really, well, glossy.

When setting up surfaces, we use glossiness combined with specularity, which we explored in great detail in the previous section.

Specularity is like the glossiness intensity. The higher the specularity, the brighter the glossy highlight.

The way it works is that basically the higher the gloss amount, the tighter, or smaller, the highlights on the surface will be, as demonstrated in the following image.

| 0 % gloss 100% specularity | 50 % gloss 100% specularity | 80 % gloss 100% specularity | 100 % gloss 100% specularity |

Figure 4-33

This is not the only way that you can achieve a glossy look, though. You can also adjust the difference between the specularity amount and the gloss amount. This means that you can make a surface glossier not just by increasing the gloss amount, but also by reducing the difference between the gloss value and the specular value. Of course, you would do this in a case where you do not necessarily want the glossiness to be very strong.

Figure 4-34 shows how this relationship between the gloss value and the specular value can alter the highlights.

0 % gloss
50% specularity

20 % gloss
40% specularity

40 % gloss
40% specularity

40 % gloss
10% specularity

**Figure 4-34**

So essentially you could say that glossiness controls the spread of the specular highlight, thereby controlling the plastic look of the surface. A low gloss value gives a very broad highlight, whereas higher values make the highlight small and tight.

You should note that if you have no specularity on a surface at all, then you cannot assign a glossiness value, as glossiness is not available unless you have at least some fraction of specularity assigned to the surface.

## Using Glossiness

As explained before, we use glossiness to determine the spread of the specular highlight on the surface. It should be used quite carefully though, as one of the main things that make CG objects look CG is when they look like they are made out of plastic, which often results from using gloss values that are too high.

Glossiness can work really nicely in combination with reflection on certain types of surfaces, especially when you are trying to make something look slimy or wet.

Generally speaking, plastic and glass objects can have pretty high gloss amounts, whereas metals and untreated woods tend to have lower overall gloss amounts. Substances like skin and some fabrics can have widely varied gloss amounts, depending on their condition.

## Reflection

### What Is Reflection?

Let's start off by establishing right from the beginning that the Reflection option in the Surface Editor is *not* for creating what will be reflected in your surface, as many people seem to think at first. Instead, what reflection does is define what areas of your surface are reflective and how reflective those areas are. So by placing images, gradients, or procedural textures into your Reflection surface attribute, you control how reflective the surface is and if that reflectivity is constant or varied across the surface. Figure 4-35 shows some spheres with 100% reflectivity rendered in LightWave.

**Figure 4-35**

While specularity (which we discussed previously) fakes the reflection of light sources, using reflection mapping on your surface accurately reflects everything that is surrounding your surface, as if the surface were a mirror. Of course, the reflections need not be as strong as they would appear in a mirror, as you can easily control the amount of reflectivity. Therefore, using reflection mapping on your surfaces results in a high degree of realism when used correctly.

It is important to realize that adding reflection textures to your surface will not necessarily make your surface mirrorlike. This only occurs with higher levels of reflectivity, and is the reason why reflection mapping should be done carefully, as with many surfaces the reflectivity should actually be very subtle. Most surfaces that we encounter are reflective to some degree, with the exception of most fabrics, unfinished woods, and dry rock or stone.

## Creating an Environment for Reflections

First and foremost, when using reflection mapping, you have to give the surface something to reflect. It is of no use to assign a level of reflectivity to a surface if it is simply floating in black space, as all it will be reflecting is black.

This may sound stupidly simple, but it is actually the cause of much frustration for many people who are beginners to texturing and are trying to make their surfaces reflective!

The simplest ways to create an environment for the surface are either by placing it into an actual modeled environment or by using an image-based environment, which you can do by using an image in Image World or by using Textured Environment within Layout.

Another way of giving your surface an environment is to use one of the options under the Environment tab in the Surface Editor, the process of which is discussed in depth in Chapter 5.

### Using Image World

Image World is designed especially for use with HDR (High Dynamic Range) images (which can be either 360° environmental photos called *light probes* or any other HDR image) as spherical environments for your scenes. Although HDR images are most effective here, normal images can be used as well.

> **NOTE:** For a little more information on HDR images, please refer to Appendix B, "A Guide to Image Formats."

The image is then wrapped spherically in space and surrounds your entire scene, no matter how large the scene is.

To use Image World, simply load an image that you wish to use as an environment into Layout, and then open the Effects panel, which is located under the Window pull-down menu in Layout's left menu buttons (or use the Ctrl+F5 shortcut). In the Backdrop tab of the Effects panel, load the Image World environment from the Add Environment menu.

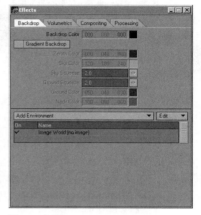

Double-click on the Image World name in the list to open its panel, and then load the image you want from the Light Probe Image drop-down menu. Note that you cannot load images

Figure 4-36

directly from within the Image World panel; you need to load them into the Image Editor first.

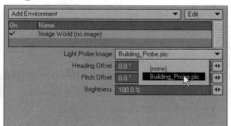

Figure 4-37

You can adjust the brightness of the image by adjusting the Brightness value, or adjust its rotation in space using the Heading Offset and Pitch Offset options.

When using Image World, the environment that it creates is not static, which means that as you move the camera, the image will appear to move with it. It is not stuck in space surrounding your scene like a physical environment, but acts more like a virtual environment that while it does show up in reflections is not regarded as actually being there.

## Using Textured Environment

Unlike Image World, which simply loads and uses images to create an environment around the scene, Textured Environment uses a Texture Editor (just like we find in the Surface Editor) to create this environment. You can use images, gradients, or procedural textures for this, just like you do when setting up surfaces.

Another way in which Textured Environment differs from Image World is that the environment it creates is static, so if you move the camera around, it will appear to pan around the environment.

To use Textured Environment, simply select it from the Environment list under the Backdrop tab in Layout's Effects panel (the same as loading Image World).

Double-click on its name to open up its control panel. From this panel you select the scale, offset (position), and projection of the texture, as well as open up the Texture Editor itself by clicking on the Texture button.

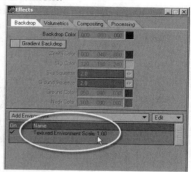

**Figure 4-38**

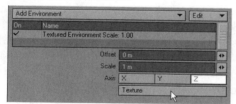

**Figure 4-39**

Note that the Scale, Offset, and Axis settings that you specify in this panel override any settings for these properties within the Texture Editor itself.

## Using Reflection

The simplest way to make an object reflective is to assign it any value of reflection in the Surface Editor, either by typing a value in the field or by using the

**Figure 4-40**

left or right arrows to decrease or increase this amount of reflectivity. By default, all surfaces have 0% Reflection.

Using just a basic value for your reflectivity suffices for some types of surfaces in certain instances, especially if you are short on time or are creating objects that will be far in the background of your scene. As you can see in Figure 4-41, lower levels of reflection allow more of the surface's own color (in this case, gray) to show through, while as the reflectivity increases, we see less of the surface's color and more of the reflected environment itself (which is an HDR image in this example).

However, for a high degree of realism, creating a texture for your reflection is a better idea. This is because, as we know, nothing in the real world has a constantly perfect surface. This means that even on a clean

**Figure 4-41**

mirror there are variations in the degree of reflectivity defined by the manner in which the mirror surface has
been touched. Even a cloth that has
been used to clean the mirror will
leave faint marks that lessen the
overall reflectivity. Yes, those marks
may be extremely faint, but they *are*
there. The photograph in Figure
4-42 shows a rather dusty hand mirror. Notice how the dust, smears,
and fingerprints alter the reflectivity
of the mirror by lessening it, especially at an angle like this.

Figure 4-42

Reflection, like all of the other
surface properties apart from color, works with gray values. The higher
(lighter) the gray value, the more reflective the surface is, whereas the
lower (darker) the value is, the less reflective it will be. Therefore, when
creating textures for your reflection, you use lighter tones for those areas
that you wish to be more reflective, and darker tones or black where you
want it less reflective, or not reflective at all, respectively.

Very rarely will you have areas in your textures that are 100% reflective
(pure white). This is because on any surface that has any variation in reflectivity, it is highly unlikely that you will have any areas that are perfectly
reflective. So try to avoid ending up with areas that are pure white, unless
you specifically need such a strong effect.

## Diffuse Value and Reflection

As mentioned earlier in the section on diffuse, the amount of reflectivity
should affect the amount of diffuse that you use on a surface.

This is because diffuse controls the amount of surface color that we see,
so naturally if an object is reflective, we see less of its own color, and instead
see the object's surroundings reflected in its surface.

If you leave the diffuse value in the Surface Editor at a high value when
you have a high value for reflection, your surface tends to end up looking
rather milky and strange, especially if the surface's color is quite light.

To counteract this, we lower
the diffuse amount according to
the reflection value. By lowering
the diffuse value, less of the surface's color shows through,
creating more realistic reflections.

Figure 4-43

The two different surface properties generally work together in direct proportions. For example, if you have 25% reflection, then your surface will probably look best with 75% diffuse. Or if you have 70% reflection, then you should have 30% diffuse.

Basically, the two values should be directly opposing, and together should add up to a value of 100%.

When using textures in reflection and diffuse, they should basically be direct opposites of each other, so essentially you could create one and simply invert it to create the other.

Naturally, this is not a hard-and-fast rule, as you may find yourself tweaking one or both of the values either way to get the desired effect, but this is a good general solution.

## Activating Reflections in Your Render Settings

In order for your reflective surfaces to correctly render surrounding objects reflected in them, you have to activate them in your Render Globals panel in Layout. This is because reflections need to be ray traced when rendered, and LightWave does not ray trace reflections by default.

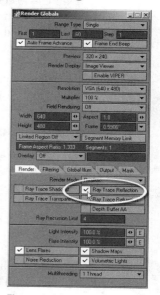

To activate reflections for rendering, open your Render Globals panel in Layout and check the box next to Ray Trace Reflection on the Render tab.

You can also set the Ray Recursion Limit option, located a little farther down on the panel. This value determines the number of times that a reflection will bounce between reflective surfaces.

In real life, if you were to place two mirrors opposite one another, they would reflect each other infinitely. However, when working in 3D this is highly impractical as it would take far too long to calculate when rendering. Setting the Ray Recursion Limit option appropriately controls the number of times that the reflection will bounce between two reflective surfaces that encounter one another, thereby saving on rendering time. The default value is 16, although you can go as high as 24. Using values lower than 4 will result in unrealistic reflections, while using a value of 0 will show no reflections at all.

Figure 4-44

If you have very complex scenes with a lot of reflections in them, try decreasing this value to save on rendering time. Values between 4 and 8 work well with large, complex scenes that require a fair amount of realism.

# Transparency and Refraction

## What Is Transparency?

Well, if you don't know what transparent means, then perhaps you should be reading a dictionary instead of this book! But just to make things absolutely clear, in LightWave, the Transparency surface option makes surfaces "see-through," whether they are clear or have color. Surfaces like glass,

water, most other liquids, and some types of plastics are all examples where you would use a certain degree of transparency in order to create the correct look for the surface.

Figure 4-45 shows a clear, glasslike surface made in LightWave.

As mentioned, a surface does not have to be clear (uncolored) in order to be transparent. You can make any surface of any color as transparent as you wish.

Figure 4-45: Transparency

## What Is Refraction?

Refraction is the bending of light that occurs when light rays travel at an angle through a substance of a different density. The light bends because the

speed at which it is traveling decreases due to the change in density, thus creating an illusion.

Take a look at the photograph in Figure 4-46.

Notice how the spoon appears distorted through the surface of the water. This is because of refraction. The light rays have bent through the water, creating the illusion that the spoon is split in two. Take a look through the water to the bottom of

Figure 4-46: Refraction

the counter, and see how the line running along the edge of the counter also appears distorted. As you can see, it is not only things that come into contact with a refractive surface that appear distorted; anything that you can see through the surface is shifted slightly as well. You can see how the glass itself has refracted light by seeing how the grout between the tiles, just above where the spoon enters the water, has become somewhat distorted as well.

Different substances refract in different amounts. This is because, in reality, refraction is a result of angled light passing from one medium to another, which causes it to change direction (bend). The density of the medium through which it is passing determines how much the light rays are bent and in what direction they are bent. As we saw in the previous photograph, the glass refracted slightly differently than the water, because they are of different densities.

We determine the amount of refraction of a surface in CG by assigning it an appropriate refraction index. The *refraction index* is a number (typically between 0.1 and 2.0, although some surfaces can exceed this) that determines how much refraction occurs in the surface. Lower values produce less distortion, while higher values produce more.

In other words, a value of 1.0 means there is no difference in density between the air and the material, and therefore no refraction will occur. A value above 1.0 means the material is more dense than air and will refract in one direction. A value below 1.0 means the material is less dense than air and refraction will occur in the other direction.

Refer to Appendix C of this book for a list of natural refraction indexes.

## Using Transparency and Refraction

One of the easiest ways to spot a transparent surface created by someone who doesn't quite know what he or she is doing is by looking to see if the artist has made the surface blue in an attempt to make it look transparent. This may seem strange, but it is actually very common, especially when beginners try to create clear glass or plastic surfaces.

Getting transparent surfaces to look decent is not always as easy as you may think, as it can be very tricky to get them to look solid, especially when creating surfaces like glass, which has almost 100% transparency. Some people like to create two layers of polygons, while others like to go even further and actually model the spaces (or air, in some cases) between the outer faces of the transparent surface, thereby physically modeling the actual volume of the object or substance.

However, strictly in terms of surfacing, you generally get better-looking results when using the Double Sided option in the Surface Editor as opposed to standard single-sided surfaces, and by setting up your reflections and tinting correctly, as we explore in a moment.

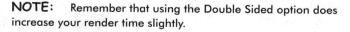

**NOTE:**   Remember that using the Double Sided option does increase your render time slightly.

Alternatively, you can copy your glass geometry to another layer, flip the polygons, and then paste it back into the original layer. This actually creates a more accurate model for the refraction.

When creating clear glass or plastic surfaces, you generally get the most realistic and eye-pleasing results from setting the Diffuse value to 0% and making the surface color black. This removes all color from the surface (as a clear surface essentially has no actual color), thereby making it clearer and less milky, and the black surface color allows us to effectively use settings like Color Highlights, discussed in a moment.

When creating transparent surfaces that do have color, try to keep the Diffuse value as low as possible (between 20% and 30%), and also ensure that your color is not too bright. This prevents the surface from becoming overblown when lit.

## Transparency, Reflection, and the Fresnel Effect

It is probably safe to say that pretty much any transparent surface is also reflective to some degree. However, when dealing with transparent surfaces, we encounter an effect called the *Fresnel effect*. Named after French physicist Augustin Jean Fresnel (pronounced "fra-nel"), this effect is the phenomenon that we observe in the real world whereby the amount of reflection and transparency that we see on a surface differs according to the angle at which it is viewed.

Let's examine again the image from the beginning of this section.

Notice the way in which the reflectivity of the surface increases as it slopes away from the camera along the edges of the object. This is the Fresnel effect in action. This effect causes the reflectivity to appear to increase as the angle at which we view the surface decreases. Take a look at Figure 4-48. The object is now viewed from an even narrower angle, which results in the surface appearing even more reflective.

Figure 4-47

Now, at the same time that the reflectivity is increasing, the transparency is appearing to decrease, because we are seeing more reflection and less through the surface itself. Ideally then, to create this effect, we need the Reflection attribute and the Transparency attribute to counteract one another. We can do this either by using opposing Incidence Angle gradients (a tutorial covers this process in Chapter

Figure 4-48

9, "Gradients") or by using one of LightWave's Fresnel shaders, namely Fast Fresnel or Real Fresnel. See Chapter 5 for more information on these shaders.

It is important to simulate this effect on your transparent surfaces so that the reflection does not overwhelm and interfere with the transparency, as this detracts somewhat from the transparent quality of the surface, making it appear more mirrorlike than necessary.

### Color Highlights and Color Filter

Looking under the Advanced tab in the Surface Editor in LightWave, we find a few options that we can use to enhance our transparent surfaces. While the details of these are covered in Chapter 5, it is worth mentioning them here as well.

Color Highlights is especially useful on transparent surfaces for reducing overblown specularity. The following image demonstrates the difference between a surface using 50% Color Highlights (left) and a surface without (right).

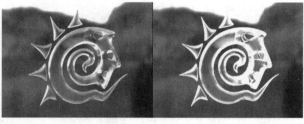

Figure 4-49

Using Color Highlights essentially tints the surface with the surface color, in this case black. This obviously results in the strength of the reflections and specular highlights becoming substantially lessened.

This option also works very well with surfaces that do have color, especially when used in conjunction with the Color Filter option, discussed next. The following image shows a colored surface with Color Highlights applied (left) and without (right).

Figure 4-50

The Color Filter option is specifically for transparent surfaces, and colored transparent surfaces in particular. It tints the entire surface with the surface color, which can otherwise be totally washed out and ineffective on transparent surfaces. Figure 4-51 shows a red surface that has no Color Filter applied (left) and the same surface with 79% Color Filter applied. Notice how even though the surface color in the Surface Editor is set to red, the color does not really show up much at all without Color Filter.

Figure 4-51

Values between 50% and 80% work the best in most cases, although this can, of course, vary.

### Ray Trace Transparency

Looking in your Render Globals window in Layout, you find an option called Ray Trace Transparency.

Select this option only when you have volumetric effects within a transparent object. There is no real need to activate it under any other circumstances. In older versions of LightWave, one had to set the Refraction index higher than 1.0 to be able to see HyperVoxels within transparent objects, so this setting eliminates that necessity.

### Ray Trace Refraction

In order for your refraction to be correctly rendered, you need to select the Ray Trace Refraction option in your Render Globals window. Without it activated, no refraction will be calculated.

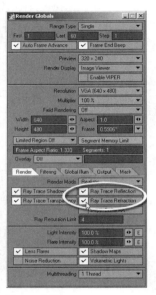

Figure 4-52

## Translucency

### What Is Translucency?

*Translucency* is the quality of a substance's surface that allows light to travel through it or to penetrate it to a certain degree, resulting in it appearing to be backlit or have some faint luminous quality of its own. This property can be seen with cloth materials or paper, skin (especially people's ears when they are lit from behind), and substances like wax and milk.

As we already know, when light hits surfaces in the real world, the light hits the surface at one angle and is reflected off at another, allowing us to see the surface the way we do. In the case of translucent surfaces, the light hits the surface, but then actually enters it before leaving it. This phenomenon occurs in most substances except metals and some woods, stones, and other very opaque materials.

Do this little experiment if you never have done so before: Go into a dark room and stretch your hand out while lighting it from beneath with a flashlight. You will notice that you can actually see the veins and hazy outlines of the bones in your hand. This is because skin is very translucent.

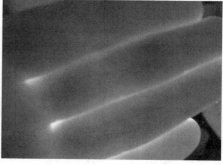

Figure 4-53

Another great example of translucency in real life is that of fabric. If you have ever gone to the theater you will know how the curtains on the stage can be lit from behind. People or objects that are behind the curtain cast their shadows onto the curtain when backlit, and because the fabric that the curtains are made of is translucent, we can see these shapes as they move around behind it. In much the same way, when a person stands in a sunny or otherwise brightly lit area and they are wearing loose-fitting clothing, it is easy to discern their body shape beneath their clothing.

Figure 4-54 shows how translucent paper is when lit from behind by a halogen lamp. As you can see, the ominous outline of a scary action figure lurks behind the paper, his entire profile cast directly onto, and through, the paper.

Figure 4-54

## Using Translucency

To use translucency on a surface we can simply shade it by assigning it a certain value of Translucency in the Surface Editor, or we can create a texture for it, using images, procedural textures, or even gradients to enhance the effect.

Assigning a basic value to the surface will naturally create a similar effect to what we saw in Figure 4-54 with the action figure and the piece of paper.

Figure 4-55 demonstrates a similar setup rendered from LightWave, with a large translucent plane (80% translucent) being lit from behind by a single spotlight. A character model standing behind the plane is clearly visible.

Figure 4-55

If we wish to add variation to the translucency in a surface, we can simply use a grayscale texture (image or procedural) to define these variations. The lighter gray areas of the texture increase translucency while the darker areas decrease the effect. Black areas will not be translucent at all while white areas will become 100% translucent.

Take a look at Figure 4-56, where we see a very simple translucency map created for a human head (I've colored the image red so that the details will be more apparent).

As you can see, I have created strong increases in translucency around the eyes and on the ears. When applied to a character's head, I get the effect shown in Figure 4-57.

Figure 4-56

Figure 4-57

Notice how the ears almost appear to glow because the light is penetrating them. This is exactly what people's ears look like in reality, so you can see how this is important for realism.

Of course, for absolute realism in an example like this (a human head) it would be necessary to create all the bones and muscle beneath the skin as well, but as with most things in CG, we generally tend to just cheat it. Of course, there is nothing wrong with modeling subdermal details, so if you have the patience to do so, by all means go ahead!

## Subsurface Scattering in Translucent Surfaces

Wherever we find translucency in a substance, we encounter a phenomenon called subsurface scattering. This term has become quite a buzzword in the last few years, and is actually often mistaken for translucency itself (in computer graphics the two are treated separately, although this will probably change in the future). In very simple terms, *subsurface scattering* is the effect that we see when light enters a substance and bounces around just beneath the surface, as opposed to light simply hitting a surface, being partially absorbed, and being reflected back, as we observe in non-translucent substances, demonstrated in Figure 4-58.

When light hits a very translucent substance like human skin, some light is reflected and some of it penetrates the skin layers and is consequently scattered around within the layers of skin, as shown in Figure 4-59.

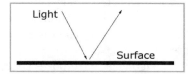

Figure 4-58

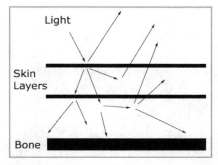

Figure 4-59

This causes the skin to appear almost as if it is somewhat illuminated from within. While a very subtle effect, it is extremely effective for creating realism in organic and other translucent surfaces.

While in the real world, subsurface scattering and translucency occur simultaneously (since they are essentially the same in real life), LightWave's native translucency does not act like subsurface scattering at all, as it has no scattering properties. However, LightWave now has built-in subsurface scattering in the form of nodes in the Node Editor. Kappa is what is called "fast SSS" in the industry, while Omega is an adaptation of a "physical" SSS shading model. See Chapter 14 for more information.

There are other subsurface scattering solutions for LightWave, such as Worley Labs' G2 Shading system, which includes subsurface scattering capabilities, and OGO_Hikari.

# Bump Mapping

## What Is Bump Mapping?

Probably the most commonly used surface property along with color, bump mapping is a method whereby you can create the illusion of irregularities, topical abrasions, and damage (e.g., scratches, dents, veins, or any kind of textural grain) to a surface without adding to or altering the geometry of the model in any way. Because no surface in this world is perfectly smooth, no matter how smooth it may appear, all surfaces you create will require some kind of bump mapping in order to create a sense of tangible texture or roughness to the object. Clever use of bump mapping conveys to the viewer an idea of what the surface would feel like to the touch.

Figure 4-60

It is important to note, however, that bump mapping does not affect the actual geometry of the object to which it is applied in any way. It is solely an illusion. This means that even if you have, for example, a bunch of grooves in your bump map that run around the entire surface of your object, the edges of the object will nevertheless appear ungrooved, as demonstrated in Figure 4-61.

Figure 4-61

Even though the grooves appear to create noticeable indentations along the surface, the edges of the sphere betray the fact that the surface is in fact completely flat when rendered. Because of this, bump mapping should be used with care, and only for minor topographical details.

The really great thing about bump mapping, as I just mentioned, is that you can use it for creating roughness on your surfaces. Even surfaces that appear very smooth, such as plastic, still have a certain degree of roughness on them if you look very closely. Adding this roughness to your surfaces greatly enhances their realism by giving the surface a tangible tactile quality and by breaking up the light upon the surface itself.

If you are creating surfaces for skin, you can use bump mapping to create the cellular texture that skin has, as well as wrinkles, pimples, moles, stubbly hair, and other irregularities like scars.

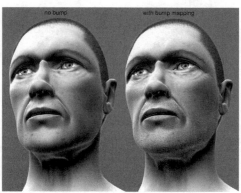

Figure 4-62

If you are working on surfaces such as rock and stone, you can use bump mapping to create the roughness that these substances have, as well as small holes or tiny cracks that may appear on the surface.

Figure 4-63

Figure 4-64

For metals, bump mapping can be used to show grooves from machining, irregularities from rusting, and any other scratches and abrasions. Figure 4-64 shows a bump map being used to create a machined (brushed) metal look.

These are obviously just a few examples. As I mentioned before, nothing in this world is perfectly smooth, so you will pretty much always be using bump mapping in some way or another to create details in your surfaces.

## Using Bump Mapping

The important rule that you must adhere to is that bump mapping should never be used to compensate for a lack of geometry that should actually be there. One often encounters beginners attempting to create details with bump mapping that should actually be modeled. Do not use bump mapping to create large canyons or eye sockets or anything like that, as the illusion simply does not go so far as to create actual structures.

When using bump maps, as with the other attributes that work with gray values, the lighter parts of a texture give the illusion of increased bump (raised areas), while the darker areas decrease the bump value, creating the illusion of indentations.

Take a look at the following image. I have used circles to indicate the placement of a particular area on the object itself so that you can see exactly how the image has affected the bump map.

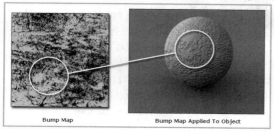

Figure 4-65

Remember that using values of pure white and pure black is not really advisable, since they create an effect that has no real variations, instead creating boring, harsh-edged effects that generally do not look very good. Use black and white only if you need a very plain yet strong effect, such as embossed letters or engravings.

**65**

The default value of bump within the Surface Editor is 100%.

Figure 4-66

You can obviously increase or decrease this value as you wish to alter the overall effect of the bump maps that you are using. Using a negative value will invert the bump maps that you are using.

When using images as bump maps, notice that upon loading them into your Texture Editor, there is a field for entering a Texture Amplitude value that is not found in the Texture Editor for any of the other surface attributes.

This value determines the actual strength of the individual bump maps; it is like height or depth, from the lowest valley in the bump map to the highest peak. The default value is 1, which should suffice for most cases, especially since we now know that bump mapping is really only for slight textural effects, not huge gaping holes and such. However,

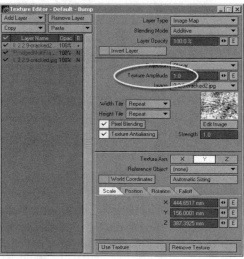

Figure 4-67

should you need to increase this value for any reason, it is not really advisable to use values higher than 4 or 5, as this will more than likely begin to look rather unsightly.

Figure 4-68

If you really need to increase the effect of your bump map, try increasing the contrast within the bump image itself.

It is important to note that where you have bump mapping details, you invariably have a change in the details of the other surface parameters. Although it is generally good practice to adopt this attitude when working with all the different surface attributes, it is almost more important in the case of bump maps, as details like scratches and dents and abrasions almost always affect all the other surface attributes in a very noticeable way.

For example, if you were texturing a car surface, and there was a scratch in the paint, the metal beneath the paint would show through. The metal would have different color, specularity, reflection, and diffuse properties than the outer layer of paint, and so it is therefore very important to ensure that the scratch in your bump map is included in your other maps as well. This is generally common sense, but with bump mapping, it is often overlooked for some reason.

Another example would be in the case of a brick or stone wall. People are quick to add a bump map to the wall to create the illusion of bricks or stone blocks, but don't bother to add the details of this type of bump map to the other maps used on the surface. So what you are left with is often this plain colored wall with a brick look to it, when, in fact, a brick wall would have mortar between the bricks, which is very different, not only in color, from the rest of the surface.

Figure 4-69

Figure 4-70

Lastly, a little tip for enhancing your bump maps is to ensure that your surface has at least a little bit of specularity. If you are having problems with seeing your bump map, or simply wish to enhance the effect of your bump map, try increasing your specular amount, as this can greatly add to the bump effect.

## Bump Mapping vs. Displacement

Okay, so we have discussed the fact that bump mapping should never be used to compensate for a lack of geometry. Well, have you ever wished that there was a way to create geometry using a bump map? There is a way to do that, and that method is called displacement.

Displacement basically takes a texture and deforms the geometry of an object according to the texture used, whether it is a procedural texture or an image map created in ZBrush, for example. Displacement is not really a texturing issue; however, sometimes it is completely necessary in order to complement the texturing job. Some examples of this relationship would be an ocean, a canyon, or models sculpted and textured in ZBrush; all of these examples are in Part 7, "Tutorials."

Something that we do need to consider is when to use just bump map texturing and when to use displacement. The tricky thing with displacement is that in order to get really great displacement, you need to have extremely high polygon counts on your models, and this can greatly increase rendering time. LightWave v9 aids you with this problem with the addition of a system called Adaptive Pixel Subdivision (or APS for short) where the objects, at render time, get subdivided per object level, polygon level, or pixels per polygon. These options can use weight maps, textures, or gradients (or a combination of the three) to drive where and how much the subdivision takes place, allowing you to render complex models with levels of detail that were previously impossible to render. For more information on APS, refer to Chapter 24, where it is covered in the ocean and canyon tutorials, and to Chapter 25, "LightWave/ZBrush Workflow."

Of course, having the actual details in the geometry itself does look fantastic, but for things like the coarseness of sand or the grain of skin (also referred to as "high-frequency details"), using displacements is slightly over the top. In cases such as those, you can get away with using only bump mapping. However, sometimes using displacement for details such as wrinkles in skin, which you can do with just bump mapping, can actually look a lot better when done with displacement. This is especially true for extreme close-ups, or when these details would be visible along the edges of your model when viewed from angles that would ordinarily reveal the fact that these details were nothing more than an illusion if they were done with a bump map. The trick is to find a good balance between "high-frequency details" and "low-frequency details," such as big bulges, which are considered major changes in the topology of the mesh.

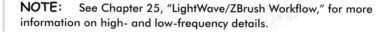

**NOTE:** See Chapter 25, "LightWave/ZBrush Workflow," for more information on high- and low-frequency details.

# CHAPTER 5

# Advanced Options in the Surface Editor

Apart from the different basic surface attributes, the Surface Editor also has a number of options for more advanced effects and settings, as well as quite a few shaders that you can use to enhance your surfaces. There are Advanced, Environment, and Shaders tabs, each containing various options for changing the appearance of your surface, as well as setting up environments.

## The Advanced Tab

### Alpha Channel Options for Surfaces

The Alpha Channel option allows you to set the values for the alpha of that surface. The alpha you set here will determine the final values that will apply to the surface in the alpha channel of the final render. Using alpha channels correctly in your renders is extremely important, since they are a vital element in the process of *compositing*, which is the process whereby elements that you create within LightWave are blended with any live action shots or other renders in order to create the final plates for an animation or image.

As compositing is really an entirely separate subject, I will not go into detail about it here. I recommend doing some research into compositing if you are not familiar with the process, as it is an extraordinarily important part of production.

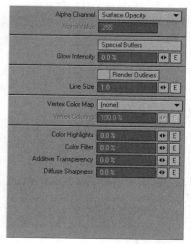

Figure 5-1

69

> **NOTE:** See Chapter 11 for more information about alpha channels.

There are four different options for setting the alpha for a surface.

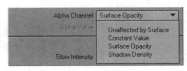

Figure 5-2

### Unaffected by Surface

Quite simply, this option causes the alpha
channel to be totally unaffected by the
object's surface. Note that selecting this option results in the renderer treat-
ing the surface as a transparent surface, and the object does not appear in
the alpha channel of the render at all.

Take a look at the following image. The glass surface of the lightbulb
has been set up with this alpha option, resulting in the entire surface being
excluded from the alpha channel.

In this example, the ground
plane object is also excluded
from the alpha channel (simply
because when it is included, the
entire alpha channel appears
white because of the position of
this object).

Figure 5-3

### Constant Value

This option allows you to enter your own value for the alpha. This value,
however, is a constant, flat value, not allowing for any variations across the
surface.

Even if the surface is totally transparent, if you set its alpha setting to
Constant Value with a value of 255, it will be solid in the alpha channel, as in
Figure 5-4.

Even though this object is
glass, and is therefore transparent, the alpha setting of 255 (in
other words, pure white) makes
it solid in the alpha channel of
the render.

Of course, you can set this
value to anything from 0 to 255.

Figure 5-4

## Surface Opacity

This is the default alpha setting. Surface Opacity basically takes all the information from the basic surface attribute settings of the transparency channel, and uses that to determine the values in the alpha channel. Any details that you have included in the Transparency Texture Editor that have variations in transparency will remain intact in your alpha channel as well, usually resulting in a more accurate channel for compositing.

In the following image, this setting is used on the bulb's glass. Because the transparency of the bulb is set up using gradients to create a Fresnel effect (gradients are discussed in Chapter 9), the transparency of the bulb lessens at the edges of the glass. As you can see, this effect is taken into account in the alpha channel.

Any detail in the transparency channel, regardless of whether it is a gradient, a procedural, or an image, will affect the surface opacity and therefore the alpha channel.

Figure 5-5

## Shadow Density

This alpha option is geared especially toward use in renders that will be composited with live action plates. Using Shadow Density will exclude the entire object from the alpha channel, *except* for areas where there is a shadow falling onto it.

So if, for example, you are working on an object that will be composited onto a surface on a live action plate, you could create a surface object that represents that surface in the filmed footage and use this alpha setting on it. That way, the object will not be included in the alpha channel, except for the areas where the object to be composited has cast a shadow on it. The following figure shows this option being used for the ground object. As you can see, the ground plane is not included in the alpha channel except for the area where the shadow from the bulb object is cast into it. The rest of the ground object is therefore ignored by the alpha channel.

Usually you would create a texture for the surface that is as closely matched as possible to the one in the filmed footage so that any colors that may be included in the shadow are carried over into the composited frames.

Figure 5-6

If we composite this render onto another image, we get the type of effect shown in Figure 5-7.

Although this is obviously a rough example, you can see how the shadow is then included when you composite using the alpha channel of the render.

## Special Buffers

This option is rather mysterious for even many seasoned LightWave users. Just what on earth are special buffers? Honestly, this one took me a while to figure out.

Figure 5-7

Special Buffers are basically there to let you enhance your surfaces using some of the image filters found in LightWave. Since I discovered how to use them properly, I use them all the time!

To use Special Buffers, you need to have some processing filters set up in the Processing tab (in the Effects panel) in Layout (press Ctrl+F8 to get the Effects panel), under the Image Filter heading. There are only four filters that work with Special Buffers: Render Buffer Export (called just Buffer Export when added to the filter list), Corona, Full Precision Blur (called FP Blur in the list), and Soften Reflections.

Usually when these filters are applied in Layout, they affect everything in the render. However, these four particular filters can be isolated to affect only surfaces that are using them through Special Buffers, using the individual options in each, as illustrated in Figure 5-9.

If you set these filters up as shown, they will not have a global effect when rendered.

Figure 5-8

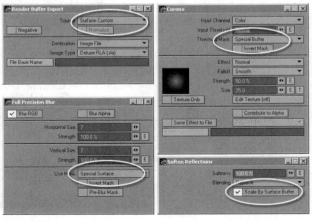

Figure 5-9

Instead, they will affect only those surfaces that are accessing them using Special Buffers.

Take a look at Figure 5-10. In this example, the Full Precision Blur filter has been added to the Effects panel, but has not been isolated to Special Buffers, as illustrated previously. As you can see, the blur is applied to the entire render.

Now, if we want to limit this blur to the logo at the back only, we can do so using Special Buffers.

Figure 5-10: Using Full Precision Blur filter

As you can see in Figure 5-11, the blur effect of the filter is applied only to the logo at the back because that one is using Special Buffers. Pretty useful, eh?

So how exactly do we use Special Buffers then?

Well, it is fairly simple. Go the Advanced tab in the Surface Editor and click on the Special Buffers button. The Special Buffers Options panel opens.

Figure 5-11: Using Full Precision Blur filter with Special Buffers

Figure 5-12

As you can see, there are four fields in this panel. Each of these fields corresponds directly to an image filter in the Effects panel. The first field in the Special Buffers Options panel works in conjunction with the first filter in the Image Filter list, the second field with the second image filter, and so on.

Obviously, since there are only four image filters that work with Special Buffers, there are only four fields. That is the simple part.

Actually using them properly requires a little bit of brain work. To best demonstrate how to use these buffers, let's examine each of the four filters individually.

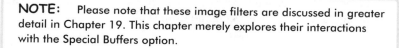

**NOTE:** Please note that these image filters are discussed in greater detail in Chapter 19. This chapter merely explores their interactions with the Special Buffers option.

## Corona

Corona can use Special Buffers to control its Input Channel and Threshold Mask settings.

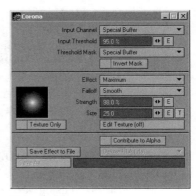

The Input Channel parameter in this particular filter determines what aspect of an object's surface triggers the Corona effect, which is basically a very strong bloom effect, such as you get from very strong light reflections of certain types of surfaces.

If you select to use Special Buffer as the Input Channel, then this obviously causes the effect to only work together with any surfaces using Special Buffers.

Figure 5-13

So, in this example, to get the Special Buffers to work with Corona, we will enter a value of 1 in the first field in the Special Buffers Options panel for this surface.

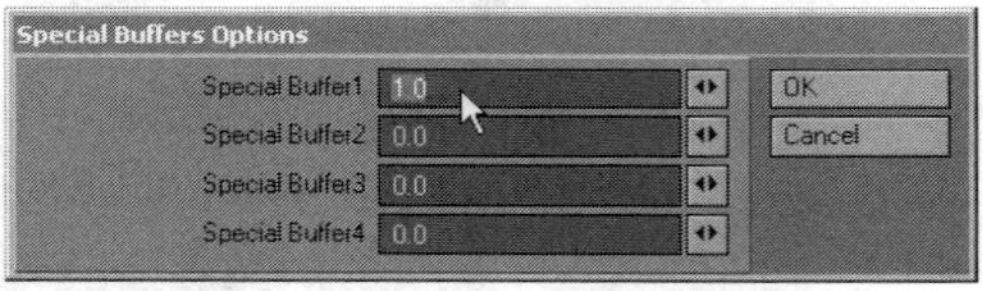

Figure 5-14

You may be wondering why a value of 1. Well, this is the part that gets a bit tricky, because this particular aspect of using Special Buffers is what differs from filter to filter.

When using Corona, using a value of 0 will obviously result in no effect from the filter, whereas a value of 1 basically activates the filter. This particular filter does not work with any values other than 1 and 0. Choose 0 to essentially switch the buffer off, and choose 1 to switch it on.

Figure 5-15 is a rather extreme example of using Corona on the surface, using Special Buffer as the Input Channel in the Corona filter.

As I mentioned a moment ago, Special Buffers can also be used to control the Threshold Mask setting for this filter. This particular setting is used to limit the effect of the filter by masking it out based on input determined by what is specified as the mask. In this case, using this setting basically works opposite of the Input Channel setting.

Figure 5-15: Using Corona filter with Special Buffers

Selecting Special Buffer as the Threshold Mask will exclude any surfaces using them from the effect of the Corona filter.

> **NOTE:** Using the Special Buffer option as both the Input Channel and the Threshold Mask will result in no Corona effect, as they effectively cancel each other out.

## Full Precision Blur

As we saw earlier, the Full Precision Blur effect can be controlled by Special Buffers simply to determine which surfaces it blurs. This is a pretty straightforward filter to use.

To use it, open up its panel by double-clicking on it in the Image Filter list in the Effects panel. Select Special Surface as the Use Mask option.

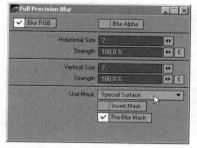

Figure 5-16

Using this filter with Special Buffers in the Surface Editor is a little different from the way that we used it with the Corona filter.

Take a look at the settings I have used in the blur. As you can see, I have used a value of 7 for both the horizontal and vertical blur.

To make sure that the surface blurs according to these values, we need to choose the correct Special Buffers value for it in the Surface Editor. In this case, I need to enter a value of 70.

Figure 5-17

You do not need to be a brain surgeon to understand how this works. In this case, I multiplied the value from the filter by 10 and entered the resulting value.

The funny thing is that even amounts like 20 look almost identical to this value, so entering a value of 70 was only really for absolute precision for the sake of an example. It is only when we start going down to values closer to 0 that we begin to see a noticeable difference.

Figure 5-18: Using Full Precision Blur filter with Special Buffers

Figure 5-19 shows a render using a Special Buffers value of 1.5.

You may be thinking at this point that perhaps merely using the same values in the filter and the Special Buffers (in other words, for this example, using a value of 7 for both) would create the effect with precision. Well, the difference between using a value of 7 and a value of 70 is almost imperceptible, but it *is* there.

Figure 5-19

## Render Buffer Export

This filter allows you to save images from LightWave's internal buffers, which you select from the Source list. To use this filter with Special Buffers, use the Surface Custom option.

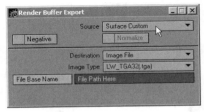

Figure 5-20

So what is this useful for? When used with the Destination option set to Rendered Alpha, you can use this filter, in conjunction with Special Buffers, to control the alpha values of different surfaces. Of course, the actual filter has other uses, but this is the only way that it can use Special Buffers. Not terribly exciting, but occasionally useful.

Although you can, of course, use your alpha setting in the Surface Editor to do this as well, using this filter to do this can be handy because it allows you to set up a save path to save the alpha channel separately. You control the actual gray value for this alpha with the Special Buffers amount in each surface.

Setting the actual value in Special Buffers for this filter, however, is not as simple as with the previous two filters that we have looked at.

As we all know, when dealing with gray values, 0 is black and 255 is white. However, despite this, the Special Buffers value in this case only ranges from 0 to 1. When entering values in this filter, 0 is black and 1 is pure white.

So, in order to enter the required amounts correctly, we need to do a little calculating. Luckily the calculation for this is not too complex. All we need to do is decide on a gray value from 0 to 255, as we usually would, and then figure out what percentage of 255 that value is and enter it into the Special Buffers field.

So if, for example, we wanted a gray value of 72, we would simply calculate it as follows: 72 / 255 = 0.28235.

We would therefore enter a value of approximately 0.28 in the Special Buffers field. This would result in the filter producing a render with the surface's alpha channel being roughly equal to a gray value of 72.

## Soften Reflections

Figure 5-21

The fourth and last image filter that works with Special Buffers is the Soften Reflections filter. Obviously this filter is for making reflections in surfaces appear softer, which is often a more realistic look, as we all know that really extreme, harsh reflections usually end up looking really fake.

To use Special Buffers with the Soften Reflections filter, simply select the Scale By Surface Buffer option in the filter's panel.

Figure 5-22

Using this filter in conjunction with Special Buffers is really straightforward. When using the Scale By Surface Buffer option, the amount you enter into the Surface Buffers field acts as a percentage of the value in the filter's options. A value of 1 in Special Buffers will be 100% of the filter's percentage; a value of 0 has no effect. Working out all the values in between is no major challenge, as they simply divide the filter percentage by 100.

Obviously, when using the Scale By Surface Buffer option, the filter affects only those surfaces that have a value entered into the corresponding Surface Buffer field. In Figure 5-23, the logo at the back is using its Surface Buffer to soften its reflections.

And that's it for Special Buffers!

Figure 5-23

## Glow

As the name suggests, this option is used to create a glowing effect on the surface to which it is applied.

To use it, simply enter a desired value for the glow.

Figure 5-24

This amount can be animated using envelopes, which is great for creating flickering glows. See Chapter 18 for more information on animating surface parameters.

In order for the glow effect to render, you have to activate it in your Processing options, found on the Effects panel in Layout (Ctrl+F8), by checking the little box labeled Enable Glow.

The Intensity setting determines how strong the effect will appear in the render, while the Glow Radius determines the size of the glow around the surface, in pixels.

You may wonder why there are settings for Glow Intensity on both the Surface Editor and the Effects panel. The answer is because the setting on the Surface Editor determines the percentage of the value on the Effects panel that the glow for that surface will have. In other words, if you have a Glow Intensity value of 50% on the Effects panel, and 100% in the Surface Editor, then that surface will glow at an intensity of 50%. If you set the value on the Surface Editor to 50% as well, the surface will glow with an intensity of 25% when rendered.

Using this option is great for making laser beams, evil glowing eyes, glowing skulls, and many other cool things.

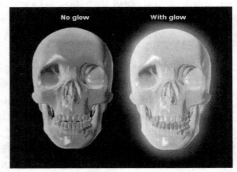

Due to the nature of this option, it obviously works best with surfaces that have some degree of luminosity applied to them. See the "Luminosity" section of Chapter 4 for more information about using glow in conjunction with luminous surfaces.

Figure 5-25

## Render Outlines

The next option we find on the Advanced tab is Render Outlines. When this option is selected, the surface will render showing the outlines of the polygons instead of a smoothed version. This is basically similar to rendering a wireframe of the surface.

To use it, simply activate the option by checking the little box, and select an appropriate pixel width for the lines to be rendered.

Figure 5-26

## Applying Vertex Color Maps

The Vertex Color Map option allows you to select and apply a vertex map that you may have made to the surface. Select the vertex color map that you wish to use from the drop-down list, and use the Vertex Coloring setting to determine the strength of the map. This amount can be animated.

Figure 5-27

See Chapter 7 for more information about creating and using vertex color maps.

## Color Highlights

You use this option to color highlights on a surface according to the color of the surface itself. By doing so, you can lessen the harshness of specular highlights on a surface by allowing the surface's color to essentially show through the highlights.

You can also use this option to tint reflections on a surface, which can be extremely useful for creating realistic reflections.

Using color highlights on glass is also great for lessening specular glare that can often ruin transparent surfaces.

This effect can be animated.

## Color Filter

This useful option is for tinting transparent surfaces, thereby making everything you see through the surface appear tinted by the color of the surface to which it is applied.

For example, if you make a glass orange, you can use this setting to make everything appear orange when you look through that glass. Obviously the Color Filter option only works on objects that are transparent to some degree. This effect can be animated.

## Additive Transparency

This setting can also only be used on transparent surfaces. It basically adds the color of the surface to which it is applied to the colors of objects that are seen through it, which creates the effect of the surface appearing much brighter by increasing its intensity. It is useful for creating surfaces that need to appear really blown out or overexposed, such as flames or other gaseous surfaces. This effect can be animated.

## Diffuse Sharpness

Use this option for making the falloff of light on your surface harsher. It basically increases the contrast between the illuminated part of your surface and the non-illuminated part. Some surfaces, such as certain fabrics, can have this effect to a small degree, although you usually use it on objects that are rather large, like a planet that is totally devoid of light on the side that faces away from the sun (provided, of course, that said planet is illuminated by only one sun). This effect can also be animated.

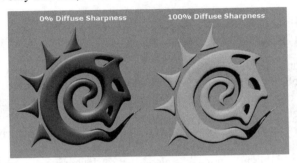

Figure 5-28

# The Environment Tab

## Setting Up Environments

The next tab that we encounter in the Surface Editor is the Environment tab. Using the options on this tab, we set up the reflection and refraction settings for your surfaces, as well as set up environments for those settings, should you require them.

Environments are basically there to give your reflective objects something to reflect if the actual environment in your scene is unsuitable or insufficient for any reason. You also use the Environment settings to specify how the reflective surfaces get their reflection when rendered.

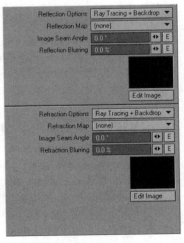

Figure 5-29

# Reflection and Refraction Options

## Choosing Reflection Settings

We have a number of different options for setting up the reflections of the surface. The first thing that we need to choose here are the Reflection Options, which you select from a drop-down list. This determines what your surface actually reflects. You have four options.

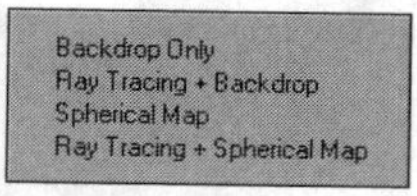

> Backdrop Only
> Ray Tracing + Backdrop
> Spherical Map
> Ray Tracing + Spherical Map

**Figure 5-30**

The first option, Backdrop Only, causes the surface to only reflect whatever is in the background in your scene (you set up the background in the Effects panel in Layout). Using this option will have the surface ignore any geometry around it in its reflections.

Figure 5-31 shows the result of this, using an HDR image as the background in the scene. As you can see, neither the red cubes nor the ground plane appear in the surface reflections.

The second option, Ray Tracing + Backdrop (which is the default), sets the surface to reflect everything that is around it (other models), as well as the background that you have set up in Layout. This usually gives the best results, as the entire scene is accurately reflected in the surface. See Figure 5-32.

**Figure 5-31: Backdrop Only reflection**

This option takes slightly longer to render since everything in the scene is taken into account.

The Spherical Map option uses an image, which you select from the Reflection Map drop-down list, as an environment that is invisibly "wrapped" spherically around the surface and then reflected in it.

**Figure 5-32: Ray Tracing + Backdrop reflection**

Using this option causes the surface to ignore any surrounding geometry (like the Backdrop Only option), as well as the background in the scene. The only thing that we see reflected in the surface is the image that we select as the reflection map. Figure 5-33 uses this setting, with the same HDR image applied as the reflection map.

When using a reflection map, we can control the rotation of this image by changing the Image Seam Angle setting.

Figure 5-33: Spherical Map reflection

Figure 5-34

You use this setting because when images are wrapped spherically, as is the case here, there is invariably a seam at some point where the two ends of the image meet. Of course, you can create seamless images (we explore this in Chapter 11), but if your image does have a visible seam, you can adjust this amount to rotate the seam out of sight in the render. This value can be animated.

The fourth choice for Reflection Options is Ray Tracing + Spherical Map, which allows both the reflection map that you have chosen, as well as any surrounding geometry, to show up in the surface's reflection.

As you can see in Figure 5-35, the image you are using as a spherical map acts in the same manner as a backdrop in the scene would work. When using this option, the surface totally ignores whatever the actual background is in the scene and instead uses the spherical image. However, you still retain control over the rotation of this image, just as with the normal Spherical Map option.

Figure 5-35: Ray Tracing + Spherical Map reflection

## Choosing Refraction Settings

When using transparent surfaces, we have to deal with refraction. Luckily, setting up the refraction options is pretty simple to explain because your options are exactly the same as those we just looked at for reflections.

Please note that the following images all have a certain degree of reflectivity to them as well as a refraction index of 1.2.

Backdrop Only causes the surface to refract the backdrop image only. Any objects seen through the object are not refracted. This creates a rather unrealistic look, although it can be useful when there is no other geometry and you are looking straight through the object to the background.

Figure 5-36: Backdrop Only refraction

Figure 5-37: Ray Tracing + Backdrop refraction

Figure 5-38: Spherical Map refraction

This option, like the Ray Tracing + Backdrop option, can cause your render times to increase rather dramatically.

Ray Tracing + Backdrop (which is the default) causes the surface to refract the backdrop as well as any surrounding geometry. Just as with your reflection settings, this option usually gives the best results, as the entire scene is accurately refracted through the surface; however, it also takes quite a while longer to render (refraction generally does take a long time to render anyway).

Spherical Map uses an image that is refracted inside the surface. This option causes the surface to ignore any surrounding geometry (like the Backdrop Only option) as well as the background in the scene, which are not refracted at all through the surface. Due to the nature of refraction, this option is an extremely unrealistic one.

You select the image from the Refraction Map list, and rotate it using Image Seam Angle just as you do with a reflection spherical map.

Ray Tracing + Spherical Map allows both the refraction map that you have chosen, as well as any surrounding geometry, to be refracted through the surface. Just as with your reflection option of the same name, the spherical map acts like a background image. Rays passing through the surface will bend and continue traveling until they hit any objects behind the refractive surface or the backdrop.

Figure 5-39: Ray Tracing + Spherical Map refraction

## Reflection and Refraction Blurring

Both your reflection and refraction settings panels have a Blurring option. Use this option with caution as it greatly increases render times. These values can be animated.

> **TIP:** If you want to blur your reflections, but do not have the time to sit and wait for really long renders, consider using the Special Buffers option in conjunction with the Full Precision Blur filter, as discussed in the Advanced Tab section of this chapter.

Don't forget that in order to have your reflections and refractions render correctly you need to activate Ray Trace Reflection and Ray Trace Refraction in your Render Globals panel in Layout.

Figure 5-40

## Shaders

Just what are shaders? This is a question that I get asked fairly often. I believe this is because this term is used in different ways from program to program. In some 3D packages, the term "shader" is used to describe any surface created and applied to a model, whereas in other programs, a shader is a special script written to give the surface certain qualities. Sometimes the term "shader" is confused with shading models, which are something else entirely. *Shading models* are basically mathematical models that determine how surfaces react to different lighting conditions. As LightWave users, we are generally not bothered by different shading models though, as LightWave only uses the Phong shading model.

In LightWave, a shader is a special plug-in that you add to your surface to give it certain properties, usually properties that define the manner in which light reacts to the surface, as opposed to actually adding details to the surface.

Just to clarify a bit further, the entire art of creating and setting up surfaces in CG involves two distinct steps: texturing and shading. Texturing encompasses all the processes of creating image maps, setting up procedural textures, and basically doing anything that creates details on the surface at hand.

Shading the surface is setting up the way that the surface reacts to light by defining the manner in which it reflects, absorbs, and scatters light. Sure, creating reflection maps and such can define where the surface is reflective, but the actual nature of that reflection (such as the tint of the reflection itself or the direction of that reflection, etc.) is controlled by the shading of the surface, which is set up separately. By using shaders in LightWave, we can apply global shading attributes to the surface as a whole without having to make changes in each of the surface's individual channels.

> **NOTE:** For more information on the difference between shading and texturing, refer to the end of this chapter.

While LightWave ships with a number of shaders included, there are also a large number of commercial shaders that one can purchase, as well as free shaders that you can download from various developers' sites on the web.

## Built-in LightWave Shaders

To add a shader to your surface, go to the Shaders tab in the Surface Editor and click on the Add Shader button. This presents you with a drop-down list showing all the shaders that you currently have installed in LightWave.

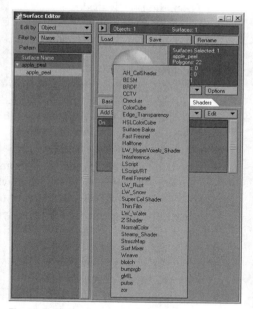

> **NOTE:** This image shows only standard shaders that come with LightWave. If you have other shaders, and wish to use them, simply add them to LightWave, and they will appear in this list along with the others. See your LightWave manual for information on adding plug-ins.

Figure 5-41

Selecting a shader from this drop-down list will add it to the shaders list in the Surface Editor. Within this shaders list, you can reorder, remove, copy, and paste shaders as you wish.

Double-clicking on a shader's name in the list opens up its command panels, if it has one (some shaders do not have panels).

## BRDF (Bidirectional Reflectance Distribution Function)

Yes, this shader has one of the most impressive names in the whole 3D field! Amaze your friends by dropping this term at important events, and then pretending that it is something really profound. Further amaze them with this really complex explanation:

> *The bidirectional reflectance distribution function gives the reflectance of a target as a function of illumination geometry and viewing geometry. The BRDF depends on wavelength and is determined by the structural and optical properties of the surface, such as shadow-casting, multiple scattering, mutual shadowing, transmission, reflection, absorption and emission by surface elements, facet orientation distribution, and facet density.*

Just make sure that you look like you know what you are talking about when you say all that.

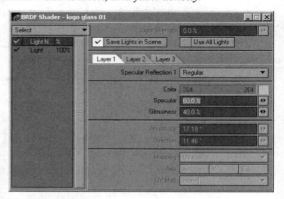

In terms of actual execution, the BRDF shader is actually quite simple. And the cool thing about this shader is that it can be used for a couple of different things.

Take a look at the shader's interface in Figure 5-42.

It looks a little complex, doesn't it?

**Figure 5-42**

First, and most simply, you can use this shader to exclude certain lights within the scene from the surface. Notice the list on the left-hand side of the panel where all the lights in the scene are listed. You can check or uncheck each light in this list, depending on whether or not you want it to affect the surface. Just click on the little check mark next to the light's name to disable it.

**Figure 5-43**

Selecting each light in the list also allows you to set values for the light's strength on the surface. You can enter this value in the field labeled Light Strength.

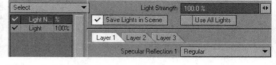

**Figure 5-44**

That is the first useful thing about this shader, although it is not the actual main intention of it. It is just one of those little things that you can use it for.

The main purpose of this shader lies in its ability to assign up to three different layers of specularity, each with different settings, onto the surface.

Why would we need to do this? Simple. Some surfaces have multiple layers of specularity, or at least appear to. Take a look at any lacquered surface, such as wood that has been varnished. How would you texture that? Sure, we could take a quick route and just make it nice and shiny, and a bit glossy as well. However, a more realistic approach would be to consider the properties of the wood and the properties of the varnish separately. Because surely, when you think about it in those terms, you realize that wood has a different specularity than varnish. In this case, you can use this shader to specify that the surface has a layer of low specularity (the wood), which is covered by a second layer that has a higher specularity (the varnish). Take a look at Figure 5-45.

Low specularity for wood    Higher specularity for varnish    BRDF shader using 2 levels of specularity, one for the wood, the other for the varnish

**Figure 5-45**

In this image, the first sphere shows the wood texture using just a normal low specular setting, as would be appropriate for wood. The second sphere shows a higher specularity and gloss setting, more suitable for varnish. The third sphere uses the BRDF shader to create two separate layers of specularity, each with specular and gloss settings appropriate for its substance.

Figure 5-46 shows the first layer of specularity. This is a broad highlight for the wood. I have used a color for the highlight here as well, as wood tends to have a lot of its own color in its specularity.

Figure 5-47 shows the settings for the second layer in the BRDF shader, the layer that gives the specular look to the varnish on the wood.

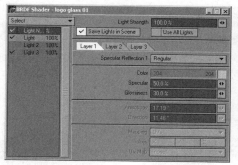

**Figure 5-46**

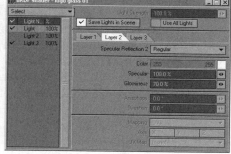

**Figure 5-47**

As you can see, this has higher specular and gloss settings and is set to pure white so that it is nice and shiny. In the render that we saw previously, this creates a nice glossy highlight on top of the broader, duller highlight, just as varnish on wood would do.

This example uses only two layers of specularity, but the shader does allow up to three layers that you can stack on your surface.

All these examples have used the Regular option of the Specular Reflection setting. Now let's delve into the other types.

The third use for this shader is for applying anisotropic shading to your surface's specularity. *Anisotropic* shading is useful for when you are creating surfaces such as brushed metal, where the surface is covered by tiny grooves that break up the light, consequently causing a distortion in the reflections and highlights on the surface.

The BRDF shader offers two types of aniso-tropy: Anisotropic (controlled by two angles of disturbance) and Anisotropic II (which uses map-ping coordinates to control the disturbance).

Figure 5-48

Anisotropy is defined with two values, Aniso-tropy and Direction, both of which are measured in degrees. The Anisotropy value sets the angle along which the "grooves" in the surface lie, while the Direction value determines the angle at which light will gather in these grooves.

Figure 5-49 shows a sphere with an Anisotropy set-ting of 0° and a Direction value of 90°. As you can see, this causes the light to gather perpendicular to the direc-tion of the Anisotropy.

This setting would be ideal for a brushed metal sur-face such as typically found on lava lamp bases or stainless steel kitchenware.

Figure 5-49

Figure 5-50 shows the same sphere with the settings switched around, so the Anisotropy value is now 90° and the Direction value is 0°.

As you can see, the results are rather different. This type of setting almost emulates a radial anisotropy such as you find on the knobs of a hi-fi system.

The Anisotropic II option allows you to use either Cylindrical, Cubic, or UV parameters to define the anisotropy.

Figure 5-50

The Cylindrical and Cubic mapping types are shown in Figure 5-51. The Cylindrical option allows you to select an axis along which the anisotropic effect will project.

The UV option allows you to use a selected UV

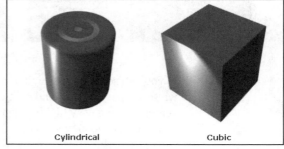

Cylindrical

Cubic

Figure 5-51

map as the method of defining the anisotropic effect. The way that this option works is that it looks at the way in which your UV map is constructed and determines the direction for the effect. You alter the effect and create patterns by flipping the points within your UV map in Modeler, using the Flip UV Point Map command, or by manually rotating parts of the map around.

Figure 5-52 demonstrates this. The cube has been UV mapped and every other block in the UV map has been rotated. As you can see, this forms a checkerboard type pattern where the light hits the surface, even though there is no such texture applied to the model. This is because the anisotropic effect is now defined by the coordinates of the UV map, and since some of those points have been flipped, the effect becomes flipped.

Figure 5-52

You may wonder how this could be useful. Well, you could use this to create iridescence in surfaces, or simply to create other unusual patterns of light.

### Edge Transparency

This particular shader is only for use with surfaces that are already transparent to some degree, as its purpose is to define the clarity of transparent edges. This is espe-cially useful for clear transparent surfaces that often tend to lose clarity when placed in front of other objects or a backdrop.

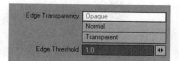

Figure 5-53

Take a look at Figure 5-54. The logo on the left is a simple transparent surface, while the logo on the right uses the Edge Transparency shader (with default settings). As you can see, the shader creates edges that appear solid to a certain degree, using the surface's color.

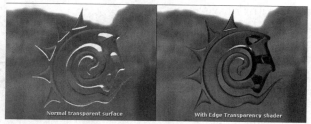

Figure 5-54

The shader gives you three different types of blending for the edges: Opaque (the default), Nor-mal, and Transparent.

The Opaque option (shown in Figure 5-54) creates an adjustable black semisolid-looking edge, while Normal subtly creates the appearance of a totally solid, hard edge. Transparent makes the edges blend completely away with no definition whatsoever. Both the Opaque and Transparent options have an Edge Threshold setting that you can adjust to vary the amount of blending between the surface's color and the transparency at the edges.

Figure 5-55 shows each of the types using default settings.

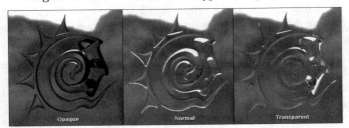

Figure 5-55

Use Edge Threshold to soften or harden the edges by increasing or decreasing the value, respectively. The following image shows a low value and a high value of Edge Threshold using the Transparent type.

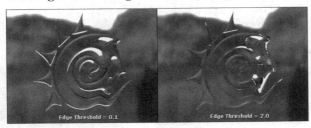

Figure 5-56

## Surface Baker

The Surface Baker shader is an extremely useful little thing. Have you ever created a really cool procedural texture in LightWave but wished you could somehow manually paint some more details into it? Or have you ever wanted to somehow add the highlights and shadows from your scene lighting into your textures for a game model? This is what the Surface Baker shader is for. You essentially bake your textures and/or lighting information (this includes all highlights and shadows, and even caustics and radiosity) to an image (using a UV map) or directly onto your object's vertices.

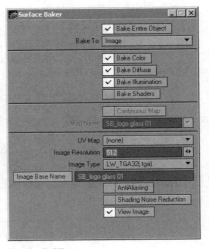

Figure 5-57

To use the Surface Baker, simply assign it to your surface, set it up as desired, and render your image. The image baking will occur before the camera rendering takes place. Once the baking is done, the image is saved to a selected destination, and the rendering of the actual scene (through the camera) follows.

Let's have a look at all the options this shader gives us.

At the top of the shader's panel we have the Bake Entire Object option. Checking this option will bake all the surfaces of that entire object instead of only the surface to which it is applied.

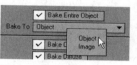

Figure 5-58

This is particularly useful when baking the effect directly to a vertex map assigned to the entire model (using the Bake To Object option, discussed next), since it saves time.

Next, we have the Bake To option, which gives us two choices from a drop-down list: Image and Object.

Figure 5-59

The Bake To Object option bakes all the texture information to a vertex color map that you enter or select from the VMap Name field.

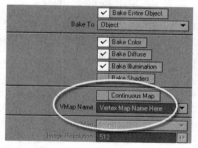

Figure 5-60

Checking the Continuous Map option above the VMap Name field turns on polygon smoothing so that the map is smoothly interpolated between vertices (basically it is the same as the Smoothing option found in the Surface Editor, discussed in Chapter 3). Deselecting the option will result in sharp changes at the vertices, which is the effect you would probably want if you were baking the textures of objects like walls or a sharply edged object that you wouldn't want to have smoothing applied to.

Once you have created the baked vertex map you can apply it to the surface by going to the Advanced panel in the Surface Editor and selecting it from the Vertex Color Map drop-down list.

Figure 5-61

The Bake To Image option lets you choose a UV map (previously created in Modeler) to which the textures will be baked. When baking to an image, you have options to select which UV map you wish to bake to, what image resolution you want the baked texture to be, and what type of image (format) you'd like LightWave to save the image as.

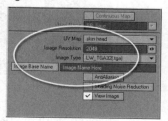

Figure 5-62

> **NOTE:** When saving the resulting baked image as a 32-bit texture, please take note that the wireframe of the UV map is included in the alpha channel of the image. Many people get a bit confused when they apply the baked image as a texture to their model, only to find upon rendering that the image looks really bizarre. If you find this happening, simply open the Image Editor and disable the alpha channel.

Select the UV map from the UV Map drop-down, which lists all UV maps that are currently created for that model. Enter an appropriate image resolution for the baked image. This determines the actual pixel dimensions (width and height) of the image. Remember that larger images are better quality, especially for close-up shots. Choose the format you wish to save the image as from the Image Type list, and enter a name for that image in the Image Base Name field. Clicking on the Image Base Name button allows you to browse for a destination to which LightWave saves the image upon rendering.

When baking textures, you have four basic options for what you actually want to bake into the baked image or vertex color map: Color, Diffuse, Illumination, and Shaders.

Figure 5-63

You can select any or all of these options when setting up the shader. Selecting Bake Color bakes all textures assigned to the Color Texture Editor in the Surface Editor.

Figure 5-64 shows a painted texture combined with some procedural textures that have now been baked into a single image.

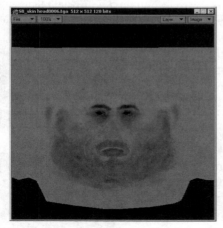

Figure 5-64

The Bake Color option includes any images or procedural textures, as well as any gradients except view-based Incidence Angle (camera angle) gradients. This is because it is pointless to bake details that are dependent on viewing angles into a flat image. You can, however, bake Light Incidence gradients into an image.

The Bake Diffuse option bakes any diffuse shading (textures applied to the Diffuse channel) from the surface into the image. Selecting this option alone creates a plain texture, but when using this together with the Bake Color option you'll notice a considerable difference.

Figure 5-65 shows the color textures from the previous example now combined with Bake Diffuse. A procedural texture that was assigned to the surface's Diffuse channel is now included in the image. Notice that the image is now somewhat darker from the inclusion of the diffuse shading.

Bake Illumination bakes all lighting and shadows from the scene into the textures. This option is great for situations like game environments, where you can simulate all the lighting effects in your tex-

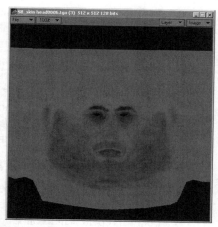

Figure 5-65

tures without having to use real-time lighting in the game engine for this purpose. This option will include all kinds of shadows, radiosity, and caustics from the scene in the image. Only use this option if you want shadows and highlights in your textures. Ordinarily, we wouldn't use this option for visual effects or animation, as it will create lighting discrepancies, especially if the character or object starts moving around.

Figure 5-66 shows the same textures from before with the lighting from the scene included by using the Bake Illumination option.

Lastly we have the Bake Shaders option. As its name suggests, this option simply includes any applicable information from shaders assigned to the surface into the baked image. Of course, once again, incidence-based shaders like the Fresnel shaders cannot be baked since their effect is dependent on viewing angles that make them useless in a flat image.

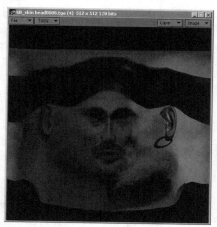

Figure 5-66

At the bottom of the Surface Baker panel we find two options for refining the quality of the baked image — AntiAliasing and Shading Noise Reduction — as well as the View Image option.

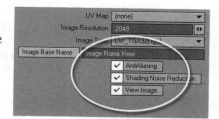

Figure 5-67

AntiAliasing smoothes the image (exactly like using antialiasing on your camera when rendering). While it does add to your rendering time, it produces a much better quality image. Shading Noise Reduction applies a low-level blur to the final image to reduce any grain that might appear within the image. This is particularly applicable when baking illumination, especially radiosity. It is exactly the same as the setting of the same name found in your Global Illumination panel in Layout.

Check the View Image option to have the image open in the Image Viewer once it has been rendered.

## Fast Fresnel and Real Fresnel

The Fresnel effect is discussed a number of times in this book, but to save you the hassle of paging through all the chapters trying to find an explanation, I'll repeat it here once again.

Named after the French physicist Augustin Jean Fresnel, the Fresnel effect is the phenomenon that we observe in the real world whereby the amount of reflection that we see on a surface differs according to the angle at which it is viewed.

Look at the sea as an example. When we are standing in the ocean looking straight down into it, we can see all the way to the bottom. However, as we move away from the sea, and view it from a distance, it appears to be very reflective, as the angle that you are looking at it has decreased. When the sea is on the horizon, far away in the distance, it appears to be almost mirror-like, so that if you never saw it up close, you would never think that the water was actually almost completely transparent.

A common example of this effect can be observed in any glass object. Take a look at a glass, and you will notice that the edges of the object appear far more transparent as they slope away from your direct angle of vision.

We have two shaders in LightWave to create this effect. Let's look at Fast Fresnel first. Figure 5-68 shows the Fast Fresnel shader's control panel.

While the Fresnel effect in reality is concerned with reflections and refractions of light, we can use the Fast Fresnel shader to apply incidence-based effects to any of the surface properties listed, namely Reflectivity, Luminosity, Diffuse, Specular, Transparency, and Translucency.

Above the properties we have a field labeled Minimum Glancing Angle. This value determines the beginning value from which the effect will be measured. Generally, this value would be 0° since that is the angle at which we

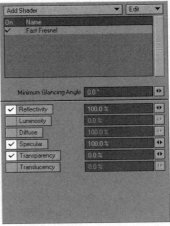

Figure 5-68

view a surface straight on, and having the effect measured from 0° also gives us the widest spread of the effect (which is measured up to a maximum of 90°).

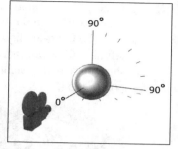

Figure 5-69

The maximum value for this effect is 89° (since this is the area of the surface that slopes out of our vision), so entering a value of 90° in this field would nullify the effect.

Next to each of the surface parameters are fields where you can enter values from 0% to 100%. This basically controls the intensity of the effect for that particular surface property when it reaches the higher glancing angles (90°).

For example, if we leave the reflectivity value at 100% (default), then the reflectivity of the surface will increase from whatever value is assigned to the Reflection channel (in the Surface Editor) to a maximum of 100% at the edges of the surface where it slopes away from our vision.

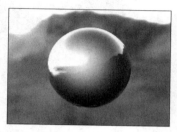

Figure 5-70

So basically this value determines the strength of the effect in that channel on the edges of the surface. While this particular shader has no option for affecting the Glossiness, Color, or Refraction channels, we can fake the effect using gradients. This is discussed in depth in Chapter 9.

> **NOTE:**  It is worth mentioning that when using the Fast Fresnel shader, LightWave's renderer treats your surface as a transparent surface, even if there is no degree of transparency applied to it. This means that the surface takes slightly longer to render than usual.

Moving on to the Real Fresnel shader, we find a much simpler-looking shader interface, as shown in Figure 5-71.

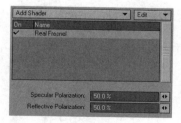

Figure 5-71

This shader has fewer settings because it is based on realistic physics, as opposed to the Fast Fresnel shader that is basically a quick-and-dirty Fresnel solution.

This shader automatically makes your surface transparent when you add it to the shader list and calculates the transparency falloff using the Fresnel algorithm.

The Reflective Polarization and Specular Polarization settings determine the values for those two particular surface attributes when the camera is perpendicular to the surface (90°). This means that the higher these values, the stronger the effect (in much the same way as the glancing angle values worked in the Fast Fresnel shader).

The following figure shows the effect of this shader. The sphere on the left has 100% specular polarization and 100% reflective polarization, while the sphere on the right has 0% specular polarization and 50% reflective polarization.

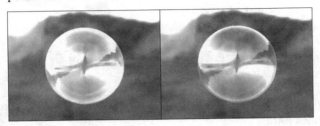

Figure 5-72

## Halftone

The Halftone shader simulates the look of half-tone screens used in printing, which create the illusion of continuous shades of color with patterns of dots. The shader adds selectable patterns in black to the surface color specified in the Surface Editor.

You have a number of different options for determining the look of the effect on the surface.

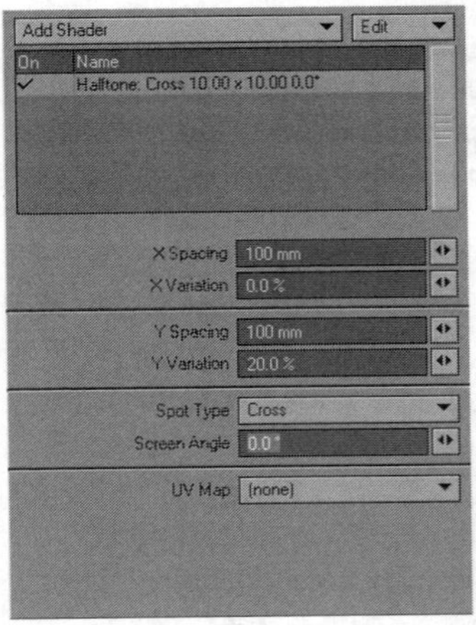

Figure 5-73

The Spacing and Variation values determine the spacing between the patterns and the variations within them along the x- and y-axes. Higher values of variation create a more random patterned effect.

Figure 5-75 demonstrates the effect of increasing these values. The cube on the left has 200% for both X and Y Spacing and 0% for X and Y Variation. The cube on the right has 400% for both X and Y Spacing and 25% for X and Y Variation.

Figure 5-74

Figure 5-75

The Spot Type drop-down list gives you eight different patterns to choose from: Dot, Soft Dot, Block, Cross, Scale, Chex, Line, and CrossHatch.

**Figure 5-76**

The Screen Angle field allows you to change the angle (horizontal angle) of the dot pattern. In the following image, the cube on the left has a Screen Angle value of 0° while the cube on the right has a value of 45°.

**Figure 5-77**

The final option is for using a selectable UV map to determine the direction for the cross-hatch or line pattern types. When you are not using a UV map for this, the patterns are applied to the surface in a cubic projection.

## Interference

This shader simulates the weird rainbow effect that we see on oil slicks, where light is reflected between two substances (water and oil) that are of different thicknesses. The shader creates a spectrum of colors in a banding fashion to the surface, using incidence angles to vary the visibility of the different colors.

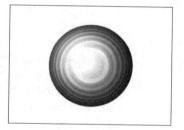

**Figure 5-78**

Controlling the shader is relatively simple, since it has only a few parameters that determine the nature of its effect.

**Figure 5-79**

The Spectrum Scale and Angle Range settings control the colors and position of the effect. The percentage entered into the Spectrum Scale field determines how much of the visible color spectrum will appear on the surface. The entire visible color spectrum consists of red, orange, yellow, green, blue, indigo, and violet. Selecting 100% will show all seven colors. A lower value will display fewer colors.

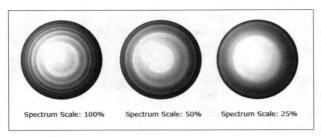

Figure 5-80

The Angle Range values (Min and Max) specify the position of the spectral effect by determining the minimum and maximum incidence angles between which the entire spectrum specified by the Spectrum Scale percentage will travel.

For example, if you leave the shader on its default settings (42° and 50°) with a 100% Spectrum Scale value, then all seven of the spectral colors (red, orange, yellow, green, blue, indigo, and violet) will appear between 42° and 50° on the surface (and will repeat themselves to the edge of your view of the surface as well).

However, if you were to change the minimum and maximum values to 0° and 90° (respectively), then the spectrum will appear only once, and will begin at 0° and end at 90°.

This is shown in Figure 5-81, where the sphere on the left has the default settings and the sphere on the right has the settings just described.

Selecting the Single Band option displays the spectral colors within a single band between the angles specified in the Min and Max fields only, instead of repeating themselves over the entire surface.

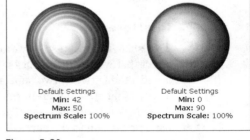

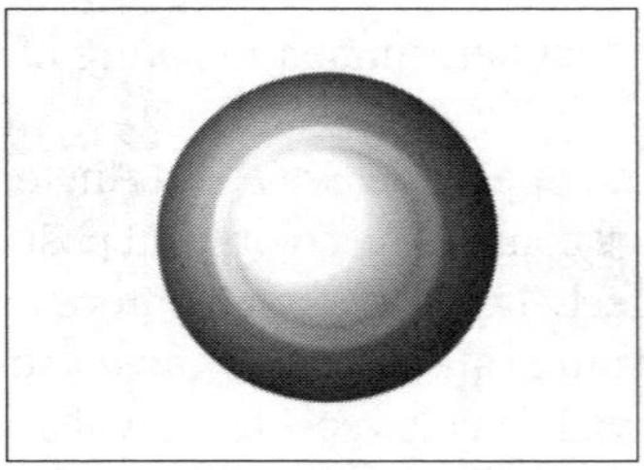

Figure 5-81

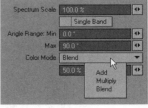

Figure 5-82

The Color Mode option gives you three ways of blending the actual effect with the colors of the underlying surface (created in the Surface Editor). You can choose from Add, Multiply, and Blend.

The Add and Multiply options are much the same as the Additive and Multiply blending modes we find in the Texture Editor (discussed in depth in Chapter 13).

Figure 5-83

Using the Add option, the RGB values of the colors are literally added to the underlying colors.

The Multiply option multiplies the RGB values by a value from 1 to 0, depending on what value each pixel has. For example, any pixels with an RGB value of 255 (white) are multiplied by 1, while pixels with an RGB value of 0 (black) are multiplied by 0. All values in between are multiplied by a corresponding value determined by an even sliding scale between 0 and 1.

The third option, Blend, uses the percentage value in the field below to determine an even blend between the colors of the shader and the colors of the underlying surface. A blend of 100% makes the colors of the shader totally opaque, while lesser values blend them more with the surface itself.

## Super Cel Shader

Cel shading is a method of rendering your surfaces to look like they are flat and 2D, just like a cartoon. *Cel* is the term given to the individual frames of hand-drawn animation. Television shows like *Futurama* use cel shading to great effect for integrating parts that are actually done in 3D into the 2D animation of the show itself.

This particular shader simply alters the renderer's shading algorithm so that the surface no longer has smooth transitions between colors, turning them instead into flat bands of color.

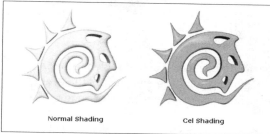

Normal Shading          Cel Shading

Figure 5-84

For best results, any objects being used with this shader should also be used with the Silhouette Edges, Unshared Edges, Sharp Creases, and Surface Borders options selected from the Edges tab of your Object Properties panel in Layout.

The overall effect of the shader is determined by defining the appearance of color zones that create the differences in shading on the surface. Basically, these define the zones where the shading will appear to change so that you can have variations on the surface that give the impression of form and shape.

A maximum of four zones can be defined on the surface from the shader's panel, each with its own brightness settings. (See Figure 5-86.)

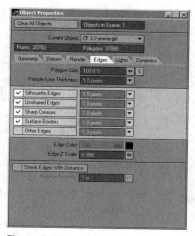

Figure 5-85

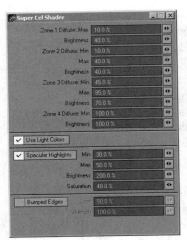

Figure 5-86

The Min and Max settings essentially define the different color zones on the surface, while the Brightness value for each zone is the amount by which the underlying pixel values of the surface are multiplied to create a flat, shaded color. Zone 1 represents the darkest zone (since it represents the areas that are in shadow), while Zone 4 is the lightest, so the brightness values should get progressively higher from Zone 1 through Zone 4.

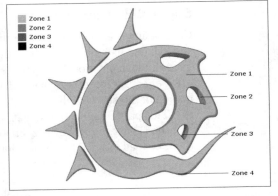

Figure 5-87

The way in which the Min and Max settings actually define the color zones is that their values determine the brightness values between which that zone will appear. While the actual Brightness value determines the color shade (diffuseness) of that region (zone), the Min and Max values set the beginning point and end point of the overall brightness shading of the *entire* surface between which that zone will be active.

So if we think of the entire surface consisting of shades that fall between 0% and 100% brightness (influenced by the lighting in the scene), then the Min and Max values determine where color zones will start and end within that range.

Naturally this means that each progressive zone should begin (its Min value) shortly after the end of the previous zone (previous zone's Max value). Keeping a difference of a few percent (5% to 10%) between the progressive Max and Min values of each zone softens the transition between each zone slightly.

Figure 5-88 shows the difference between keeping a 10% difference between zones (the logo on the left), as opposed to having no difference from the Max of one zone to the Min of the next.

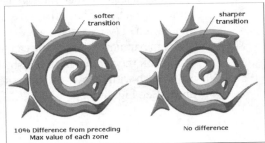

Figure 5-88

As you can see, the difference between the two is quite slight but still noticeable (hopefully!).

It's interesting to note that essentially we could create exactly the same effect using a Light Incidence gradient in the color Texture Editor of your surface by specifying zones within the gradient ramp that change according to their relative position to the light.

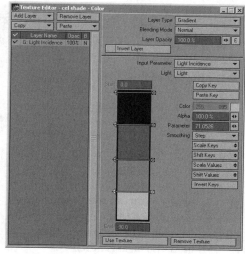

Figure 5-89

Using a gradient would actually allow you to specify even more zones, as well as choose any colors you want, but the shader is generally more convenient.

NOTE:    See Chapter 9 for more information on gradients.

Once we have defined the color zones on the surface, the shader offers a few more options for the overall shading effect.

The Use Light Colors option allows you to use the scene lighting to tint the surface. Usually the color would come directly from the surface's color as specified in the Surface Editor or from any texture applied to it.

Using the Specular Highlights option creates cartoon-like highlights on the surface, over and above the defined color zones.

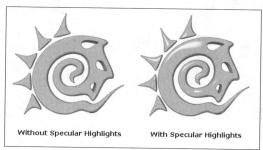

Without Specular Highlights    With Specular Highlights

Figure 5-90

Use the Min and Max values to determine the appearance of the highlights by specifying which part of the specular highlight to show. A value of 0% represents the darkest part of the specularity, while 100% represents its brightest. However, using such a broad range tends to make the highlights difficult to see. Using a tighter range creates stronger, more noticeable highlights on the surface. The smaller the difference between the Min and Max settings, the harder the edge of the highlight becomes, so using the same values for both creates a very hard-edged highlight while having a large difference between the two creates very soft-edged ones, as shown in Figure 5-91.

Using higher Min values creates smaller highlights, while lower values create broader ones.

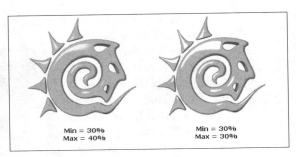

Min = 30%
Max = 40%

Min = 30%
Max = 30%

**Figure 5-91**

Use the Brightness value to determine the overall brightness of the highlight itself, and the Saturation value to add the surface's color to the highlight (similar to Color Highlights in the Surface Editor).

The final option, Bumped Edges, allows you to soften the appearance of

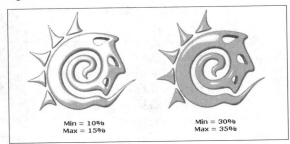

Min = 10%
Max = 15%

Min = 30%
Max = 35%

**Figure 5-92**

the cel shaded object's edges to avoid the very harsh look that they sometimes have. This option is an incidence-based effect that makes the edges appear slightly fuzzy and soft.

Since it is an incidence-based (viewing angle) effect, the Limit value defines the minimum angle that a surface normal has to be facing in order to be affected, where 100% represents areas facing directly at the camera and 0% represents the areas that are sloping away from it (the visible edges).

As the Limit value increases, the effect "creeps" inward from the edges of the surface, as shown in Figure 5-93.

The Strength value determines how strong the effect is at the edges. Higher values have the effect encroaching a lot more on the edges. This

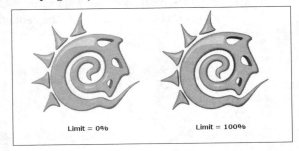

Limit = 0%

Limit = 100%

**Figure 5-93**

value can go higher than 100%, but doing so tends to make the surface look less 2D. (See Figure 5-94.)

Strength = 20%        Strength = 100%

Figure 5-94

## Thin Film

The Thin Film shader is very similar in effect to the Interference shader in that it also creates a spectrum of colors on the surface that change according to the camera's angle in relation to the surface and can be used for effects like a film of oil on water.

Figure 5-95

The interface of the shader has some similar options to those found in the Interference shader, as well as some new ones for determining the actual colors and their position.

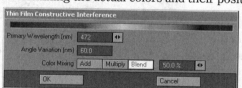

Figure 5-96

The Primary Wavelength value specifies the color in the spectrum that the shader uses as its base color. You can type a value into the field or simply click on a position on the actual color spectrum on the shader panel.

Use the Angle Variation value to determine the (incidence) angle at which the colors begin to shift. Higher values will begin the shift at the areas of the surface that are closer to perpendicular angles to the camera, while lower values have the shift occurring nearer the edges (the angles that slope away from the camera).

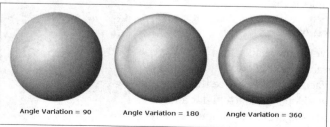

Angle Variation = 90      Angle Variation = 180      Angle Variation = 360

Figure 5-97

**103**

The Color Mixing options work in exactly the same way as the Color Mode options in the Interference shader.

Using the Add option, the RGB values of the colors are literally added to the underlying colors. The Multiply option multiplies the RGB values by a value from 1 to 0, depending on each pixel's value. For example, any pixels with an RGB value of 255 (white) are multiplied by 1, while pixels with an RGB value of 0 (black) are multiplied by 0. All values in between are multiplied by a corresponding value determined by an even sliding scale from 0 to 1.

The third option, Blend, uses the percentage value to determine an even blend between the colors of the shader and the colors of the underlying surface. A value of 100% makes the colors of the shader totally opaque, while lesser values blend them more with the surface itself.

### Z Shader

Probably one of the simplest shaders to use, the Z Shader allows you to change surface attributes based on their distance from the camera (much like the Distance to Camera gradients discussed in Chapter 9).

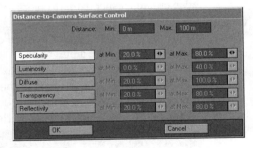

Figure 5-98

Use the Distance Min and Max settings at the top of the panel to specify the actual physical distance range (in units of measurement) from the camera that the shader will use as its input.

Once you have defined these two values, simply assign desired values to the minimum and maximum settings of the Specularity, Luminosity, Diffuse, Transparency, and Reflectivity attributes.

For example, if you have your Distance Min and Max settings at 0m to 100m, and you set your Specularity Min and Max settings to 5% and 100%, then at 0m from the camera, your surface will have 5% specularity, and at 100m from the camera, the surface will be 100% specular. All values between are interpolated.

Simple as that.

### Surface Mixer

A relatively new shader for LightWave, the Surface Mixer allows you to blend two surfaces together. Since this effect can be enveloped, it is useful for animating changes in surfaces without actually morphing objects.

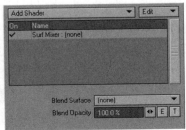

Figure 5-99

Simply select the surface that you want to mix the current surface with from the Blend Surface drop-down list (note that you can only blend with surfaces of other objects that are currently in your scene) and specify the Blend Opacity, which essentially determines how much the surface blends with the selected one. This value can be enveloped (click on the little "E" button to open the Graph Editor), as well as opacity mapped with a texture by clicking on the Texture Editor button (the little "T").

## gMIL Occlusion

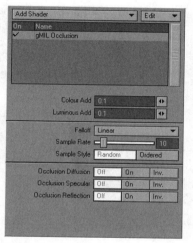

The gMIL Occlusion shader was created by Eric Soulvie. Very little information about this shader is available aside from what is found in the LightWave manual.

Essentially, occlusion is a global illumination solution for determining how much ambient lighting is affecting any part of a surface. It figures out how "accessible" a surface is to ambient lighting in the scene and affects the surface accordingly.

Using this shader is similar to using the Backdrop Only radiosity mode in LightWave, although since you apply the effect using the shader, you can limit the effect to certain surfaces only, which can save time when rendering if you do not

**Figure 5-100**

require global radiosity in your scene. Using gMIL is also faster than using radiosity because it is essentially a simulation effect and not a true radiosity calculation as such (in fact, occlusion is not actually radiosity at all, but rather an alternative, advanced lighting solution).

Looking at the settings in the shader's panel, the first two options are Colour Add and Luminous Add. Essentially, these determine the overall strength of the shader effect by adding color and luminosity values from the scene (and backdrop) to the surface. Setting these values to 0.0 cancels the effect entirely.

Luminous Add obviously gives a certain degree of luminous quality to the surface, while Colour Add creates a stronger reflection of colors of the backdrop to the surface.

Take a look at Figure 5-101. The logo on the left has values of 0.1 for both Colour Add and Luminous Add, while the logo on the right has values of 0.5 for each.

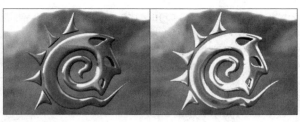

Figure 5-101

Below these options we have some settings for controlling the falloff and samples of the shader. You have two options to choose from to determine the way in which the occlusion falloff is calculated: Linear and $y=x^2$. Falloff is the manner in which the light shades the surface when it hits it, as it darkens the surface while traveling farther from the source of light. Linear gives a totally linear (smooth) shading effect, while $y=x^2$ darkens the shadows slightly by squaring the effect. The difference between the two options can be almost totally imperceptible, though.

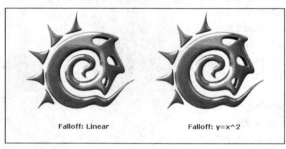

Figure 5-102

Next up we have options for controlling the effect of the sampling. The Sample Rate value determines the quality of the shading, although this does mean that higher values increase render times.

The Sample Style option lets you choose between Random and Ordered. Random (the default) gives you slightly rough, dithered shading, while Ordered creates a softer effect. Again, the differences between these two options can be almost imperceptible, depending on lighting conditions.

At the bottom of the panel are the actual occlusion options for diffuse, specularity, and reflection. You can activate (or deactivate) occlusion shading for each of these surface properties, as well as invert (the Inv. option) the effect for each. Inverting the effect is basically like inverting the falloff, so the entire surface becomes dark.

The following image shows the logo on the left with all three activated, while the logo on the right has the effect inverted on each.

Figure 5-103

## Stress Map

Another great shader that will help you in the texturing process is the Stress Map. This shader will help you show strain or resistance on your polygon objects based on the amount of distortion applied to them via scaling, bone deformations, morph maps, and dynamics.

You can use it to show wrinkles in the area being squeezed when bending the object with bones, or by having the wrinkles slowly vanish as the mesh is stretched, for example. You can also apply color to the stressed area and therefore mimic the discoloration of a plastic pipe when it is bent or a rubber band getting really stretched. (Think Wile E. Coyote trying to propel himself with a giant slingshot!)

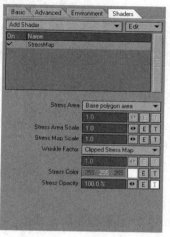

Figure 5-104: Stress Map options panel

The Stress Area setting determines the presumed local skin area if you are using wrinkles. If you set it to Custom you can use a texture, gradient, etc., to drive the size of the area. If you keep it at its default, Base polygon area, it will be equal to the undistorted mesh unless you scale it using the Stress Area Scale option. If you notice that your wrinkles are a little too subtle, you can increase its strength by increasing the Stress Map Scale value. This value will also scale the Stress Color if you are using that feature, so if you notice that the color has increased you may have to fine-tune the texture or gradient that drives the Stress Color to bring it back to what you previously had.

When creating wrinkles, the Wrinkle Factor is set by default to Stress Map, which controls how much bumps will show on the skin area. Sometimes it is more visible than it really should be, giving the impression that the skin is stretched beyond the breaking point. To correct this, set the Wrinkle Factor to Clipped Stressed Map, which will correctly display the bumps in the local stressed area only.

As I mentioned earlier, you can select a color or you can use textures for the stressed area using the Stress Color options. Stress Opacity will control where and how much of the color is visible in the stressed area. Figure 5-105 shows a plastic pipe being bent by the invisible man, with no stress, Stress Map Wrinkle Factor, and Clipped Stress Map Wrinkle Factor. This scene is on the companion CD for you to play with (Tutorials\Scenes\ 5.1-stress map.lws).

**Figure 5-105**

And that basically sums up LightWave's native shaders.

## Third-Party Shaders

There are a number of commercial and free third-party shaders available for LightWave as well. Many of the free ones are developed by prominent members of the LightWave community, and can be found by looking through LightWave community sites like Flay.com or NewTek's forums. Some of the most popular commercial shaders are developed by Worley Labs and Evasion|3D, and can be investigated and ordered from their web sites.

## The Difference between Shading and Texturing

We now know what shaders in LightWave are, and we have had a good look at each of the surface attributes that we deal with when creating surfaces, but before we delve into the world of creating textures, I thought it important to add a note about the differences between shading and texturing.

Put simply, the art of creating surfaces involves three distinct stages: mapping, shading, and texturing.

### Mapping

Mapping, as we discuss later on, is the process whereby we set up coordinates on the surface so that we can correctly apply texture images (and procedural textures sometimes as well) to the model.

This is obviously a good place to start the surfacing process since it essentially creates a template upon which we will create our textures. When I am working on a project, I generally do all my UV mapping and sorting out of projections before I even consider taking the model into Layout for any test rendering.

Of course this is really a choice of habit, but I find it very efficient and it helps to keep me focused, as in my experience I've often found that people who are constantly rendering during the modeling and mapping process tend to waste a lot of time. What is the point in rendering an unfinished model?

Once I am satisfied with the creation and editing of any UV maps for the model, I am ready to take the model into Layout for shading.

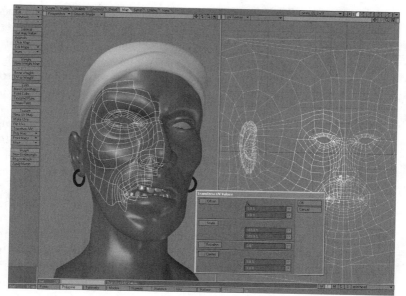

Figure 5-106

## Shading

Shading is the crucial stage of the process whereby we begin to set up our lighting and start assigning basic values to each of the model's surface parameters (its color, diffuse, specular, reflection, etc., parameters) so that it reacts to light correctly.

Figure 5-107

At this stage, there really should be no textures added to the model yet. Naturally, it is important to do one's shading and lighting at the same time, since surfaces can be very sensitive to their lighting, and often require shading changes if the lighting changes in any way. Essentially, shading should define the way in which the surface looks and interacts with its environment and lighting, with the exception that at this stage, the surface has no details on it.

Shading is generally the trickiest part of the process. Determining the correct values for each of your surface's attributes can be a painful process of tiny tweaks and waiting for renders. No two texturing situations are ever the same, so there is no foolproof "recipe" that will always work for any particular type of surface. Of course, as you become more experienced, you do begin to develop a good sense of how to start off the shading process speedily, but even so you'll still find that this stage can be a challenge.

Of course at this stage you might find it necessary to employ some of LightWave's shaders or even some of the gradients found in the Texture Editor (see Chapter 9) on your surfaces, as these can help to create the right effect for your model, as we have already seen in the previous section on shaders.

Once you have set up your lighting and your model's shading, you should have a basic scene that actually looks more or less the way the surface should in real life.

Essentially, we could sum up the shading process as being the stage where we determine the manner in which the surface reacts to lighting and its environment. Is the object matte or dull, is it shiny, translucent, transparent, or reflective? These are all the things that we determine by shading the model correctly. When recreating a real-world substance, we'll study references of that substance and ensure that our CG model has the same *quality and type of surface* as its real-world counterpart.

## Texturing

Now we move onto the final stage of the surfacing process, texturing. This is the process where we actually create the individual textures for our surfaces (whether using images or procedural textures), which should ideally only be there for the purposes of *adding detail to the surface*. The level of additional detail required depends on the surface at hand.

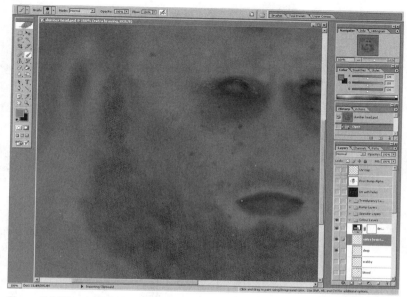

Figure 5-108

　　While the shading made the surface react correctly to light, the textures
we create simply use those same shading values as a base from which to add
details to the surface to make them more realistic.

　　To ensure that your textures do not change the overall shading values
that you have assigned to the surface, and instead add only details and variations to them, you need to start them off by using the same values as a
beginning.

　　This is actually quite simple. For example, let's say you are shading a
face and you have assigned a value of 32% Specularity to the surface. Of
course as we know, skin has a lot of variation in its specularity, so ideally
we'd paint a texture for this particular surface attribute so that we can add in
variations and details where we want them. We know that overall we want a
value of 32% Specularity with variations here and there. The best way to
ensure that your painted texture does not alter this overall value is simply
to start off your specular texture image using a gray value of 32% Brightness. This ensures that when the texture is applied to the model, the basic
overall 32% Specularity value will remain unchanged, and the variations that
you add to the texture image will be correct.

　　To do this, simply open your Color Picker in Photoshop (or whichever
paint program you are using), and select a gray tone from the color palette
on the left side of the window. Now look to the right side of the window and
take note of the hue, saturation, and brightness (HSB) values. The brightness value is the one we need to fine-tune. For this example, we would
simply enter a value of 32% as shown in Figure 5-109.

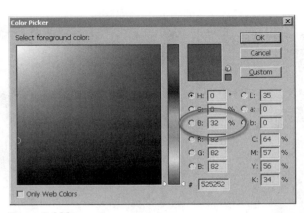

Figure 5-109

So as you can see, ensuring accuracy from LightWave shading values to Photoshop painting is really simple! All we need to do now is begin to make our specular texture with a flat value of this particular shade of gray and we won't alter the overall shading value. The same concept applies to any of the surface attributes that are best created using shades of gray (which are basically all the surface properties with the exception of color).

Once we have created our texture maps, we then simply apply them to our surfaces, and render. If you have been meticulous in ensuring that everything will work correctly, you should get no surprises with the final result.

Figure 5-110

# PART 3

# Creating Textures

# CHAPTER 6

# The Preset Shelf

## Creating and Using LightWave Surface Presets

LightWave ships with a number of predefined surfaces that you can use on your models, contained in a library that you can access by pressing "s" when the Surface Editor is open or by pressing the Presets button (found under Window>Presets Panel). This opens the Preset Shelf, a sizeable window that contains all of these presets, as well as presets that you have created and saved in the Preset Shelf's libraries.

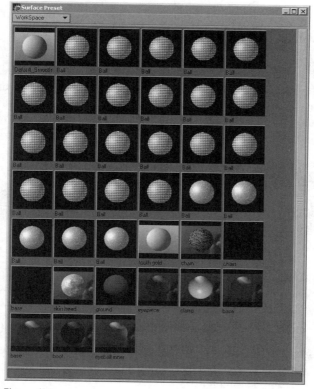

Figure 6-1

> **NOTE:** The Presets button is context sensitive, in that it will open up the appropriate Preset Shelf for whatever you are working on. If the Surface Editor is open, the Surface Preset shelf will open, whereas, for example, if you are working on HyperVoxels, the HyperVoxel Preset Shelf will open.

The Preset Shelf contains all of its settings within different libraries. Libraries are simply groups of presets. You can select the library that you wish to access by choosing it from the drop-down menu at the top-left corner.

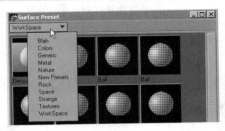

Figure 6-2

The Preset Shelf is not contained simply within your scene or object. It survives as an entity on its own, so that no matter what scene or model you are working on, all the libraries that you create will always be there, regardless of what scene or model you were working on when you made them.

## Adding to the Surface Presets

To add surfaces to the Surface libraries, simply select the library that you wish to add the surface to, and then double-click on the preview window for that surface in the Surface Editor. This will add the surface to the Surface Preset library that you currently have open. Alternatively, you can also right-click on the surface sample window and select Save Surface Preset from the contextual menu.

## Assigning Surface Presets

The quickest way to apply a preset to a currently selected surface in the Surface Editor is to simply double-click on the desired preset. You are prompted to confirm that this is what you wish to do.

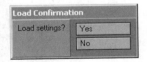

Figure 6-3

Clicking Yes will apply all the settings from the preset onto the surface you have currently selected in the Surface Editor. Selecting No will cancel the operation. You can also load presets by right-clicking on them and selecting Open.

If you wish to only apply certain parts of the preset to the currently selected surface (when using presets that are more complex than just attribute values), you can do so by right-clicking on the preset preview and selecting Open with Parameters.

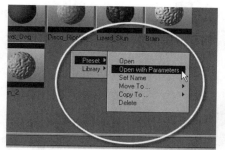

Figure 6-4

This option allows you to choose which parts of the preset you would like to load by letting you select them in a new window.

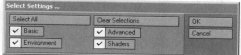

Figure 6-5

The different options obviously correspond to the different tabs in the Surface Editor and the settings that each contain. So if, for example, you don't wish to load the environment settings assigned to the preset (such as a reflection map or reflection blurring), simply deselect the Environment option.

## Organizing and Maintaining Your Presets

When right-clicking on the different preset previews, you also have a few options for organizing your presets and libraries.

You can change the name of a preset by right-clicking on it and choosing Set Name. This presents you with a window in which to enter a new name for the preset.

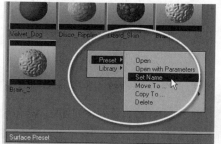

Figure 6-6

Figure 6-7

Entering text into the Description field results in the description being displayed at the bottom of the shelf window when your cursor goes over the preset's preview.

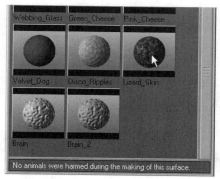

Figure 6-8

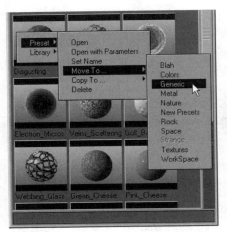

Figure 6-9

If you want to move the preset to another library within the Preset Shelf, you can choose the Move To option and select the destination from the list. This will remove the preset from the current library and move it into the selected one.

If you wish to move the preset to another library without removing it from the current library, you can use the Copy To option, and select the other library from the list.

If you wish to totally remove the preset from the Preset Shelf, select the Delete option. You will be prompted to confirm that you wish to do this with a new window.

Select Yes to confirm the deletion or No to cancel.

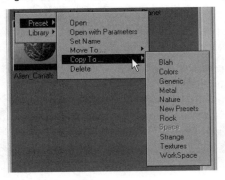

Figure 6-10

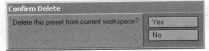

Figure 6-11

## Creating New Preset Libraries

Of course you will feel the need at some stage to create your own libraries within the Preset Shelf. You can do this easily by right-clicking inside the shelf window and selecting Create Library.

A new window will appear for you to enter in a name for the new library.

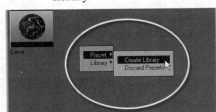

Figure 6-12

Figure 6-13

If you wish to remove all the presets from the current library, right-click in the window and select Discard Presets. This totally removes all the presets inside the current library, though, so use it with caution.

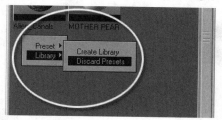

Oddly enough, there is no way within Layout or Modeler to remove libraries or edit their names. To do this, you have to access the folders directly within your OS Explorer.

Figure 6-14

> **CAUTION:**  Make sure that you do so only when Modeler and Layout are not open. Changing the names of the folders or deleting them while the programs are running will cause them to crash.

To edit the library names or to remove them from the Preset Shelf, find the Surface Preset folder inside the Presets folder, located within the Programs folder of your LightWave installation.

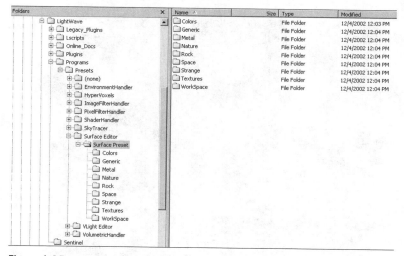

Figure 6-15

Here you will find all the libraries that currently exist in your Preset Shelf, and you can edit them or remove them as you wish. You can even create new libraries simply by creating new folders here.

# CHAPTER 7

# Vertex Color Maps

## What Are Vertex Color Maps?

Vertex color maps are a way that you can add color to the points (vertices) in your model's mesh. You can use them to add simple colors to your models without having to actually texture them or to add colors to an existing texture in your Surface Editor (vertex coloring is multiplied to the surface's base color and textures applied).

The following image shows William Vaughan's pug model with vertex coloring. There is a tutorial on NewTek's web site detailing the creating of the vertex coloring for this model.

Figure 7-1

As you can see, the colors of a vertex color map are visible in your shaded viewports.

How exactly is this useful? Well, when working in games, you can use these maps to create illumination maps for geometry, because of the way in which the vertex colors are added. As mentioned, they are multiplied (in other words, the RGB values of each color are literally multiplied with the surface's RGB values to produce new colors) to the surface, which means that they behave in the same way as a layer in the Texture Editor that uses Multiply as its Blending Mode. You can therefore create (or bake, using the Surface Baker) lighting to geometry. However, you can of course simply use it to create colors on a model for the purposes of coloring alone.

## Creating Vertex Color Maps

To create a new vertex color map, go to the Map tab in Modeler, and click on the New Color Map button under the Color heading.

A new window titled Create Vertex Color Map pops up, allowing you to enter the initial settings and name for the map.

Figure 7-2

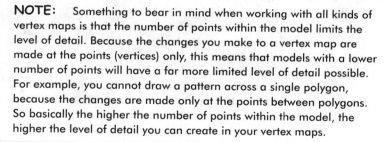

Enter an appropriate name for the map in the Name field. The Use Alpha option can be switched on or off, and the surface to which you wish to apply the vertex

Figure 7-3

color map is selected from the Apply to Surface drop-down menu.

The Use Alpha option allows you to assign an alpha value for each vertex. This allows for more control over the way in which the vertex color map blends with the surface, because as we know alpha values are transparency values. We generally leave the Use Alpha option on since most vertex color maps will utilize alpha values to some degree, simply because they allow that greater level of blending control and flexibility.

> **NOTE:** Something to bear in mind when working with all kinds of vertex maps is that the number of points within the model limits the level of detail. Because the changes you make to a vertex map are made at the points (vertices) only, this means that models with a lower number of points will have a far more limited level of detail possible. For example, you cannot draw a pattern across a single polygon, because the changes are made only at the points between polygons. So basically the higher the number of points within the model, the higher the level of detail you can create in your vertex maps.

When working with vertex color maps, we have a couple of tools at our disposal, which are discussed in the following sections.

## The Airbrush Tool

The first tool that we can use to paint our vertex colors is the Airbrush, found under the General heading in Modeler. If you have ever worked with weights before in Modeler, you will already be familiar with the Weights tool, which works in a similar fashion to the Airbrush tool.

Select the Airbrush tool and hit "n" to open its numeric control panel. Here you find all the options for controlling the effect that the Airbrush has on the vertex map.

First, ensure that you have the vertex color map you wish to affect selected from the Vertex Map menu. The rest of the options simply control the effect that the tool has. The Radius setting controls the size of the actual Airbrush when painting; alternatively you can use the right mouse button when working within your viewport to interactively change the radius size.

Figure 7-4

The Strength setting determines the intensity that the color you are painting with will have on the map, almost like setting the Opacity of the brush itself (not to be confused with the Alpha setting though). Figure 7-5 shows the difference between a low Strength setting (on the left) and a high Strength setting (on the right). The model is by William Vaughan.

Figure 7-5

The Color swatch allows you to mix and select a color for the Airbrush to paint with using RGB values. You can click on the individual values and drag with your cursor to adjust them or you can click on the little swatch to open the Color window where you can mix a new color.

The Alpha percentage determines the alpha value that will be applied to the points of the vertex map when using the Airbrush. As discussed earlier, the alpha values allow for flexible blending of the vertex color map with the surface and textures applied to it. Because the Airbrush tool works with individual points, this means that each point on the model can have its own alpha value as well as a color value in the vertex map. A value of 100% allows the color in the map to remain opaque, while lower values cause the color to blend with that of the surface and any textures applied to it.

To paint with the Airbrush, simply set it up as you would like it, and then click on the model (be sure to click on the points themselves) and drag the cursor left or right to actually affect and adjust the color of the points.

## Vertex Paint

The other tool that you can use for interactively painting your vertex color maps (as well as weight maps) in Modeler is the Vertex Paint plug-in. This plug-in opens a little window with a bunch of controls and options, as well as a window showing your model within which you can paint directly onto your surface.

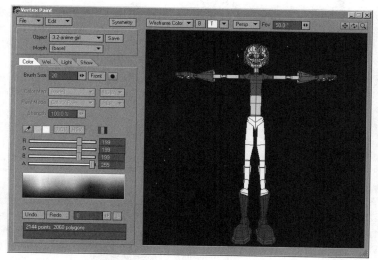

Figure 7-6

You can rotate and navigate within the window just as you do within Modeler's viewports, using the same shortcut keys for rotating, panning, etc., inside.

All the tools for painting color maps are found under the Color tab on the left-hand side, where you can mix colors, set your brush size and shape, and obviously also select which color map you would like to work on, as well as create new maps.

**123**

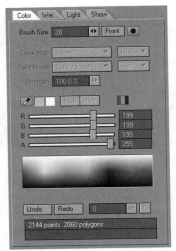

Figure 7-7

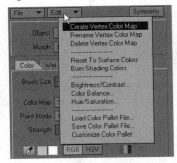

Figure 7-8

Figure 7-9

Figure 7-10

Let's look at each of these tools and options.

At the top of the panel we have our Brush Size option. Simply type a value into the field or use the spinner (little button with the arrows) to adjust the size of the brush.

When painting onto the model, all faces that lie in the direction in which you are painting are affected by the brush. However, clicking on the Front button will cause only the front polygons to receive color from the brush.

Click on the little button with a black circle on it to change the shape of the brush to a square.

Select the color map you wish to edit from the drop-down menu labeled Color Map. Alternatively, you can create a new vertex color map by going to the Edit menu at the top and selecting Create Vertex Color Map.

You can choose to have an alpha channel for blending the vertex map by selecting RGBA (the default) or no alpha channel by selecting RGB, next to the Color Map selection.

There are three Paint Modes to choose from — Color/Point (the default), Color/Index, and Color/Polygon.

Painting with the Color/Point mode applies the brush effect to points only. The effect of the brush is spread out from the point onto all adjacent polygons.

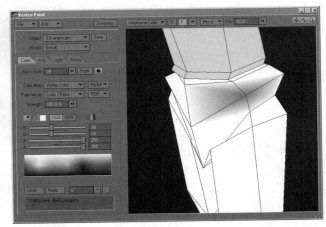

Figure 7-11: Color/Point mode

Color/Index affects only the nearest point index of a polygon. A point index is a unique reference given to the points of each polygon. When using this mode, clicking anywhere on a polygon will apply the color to the nearest point, and the effect will affect only that particular polygon. The Face and Brush Size options are ignored when using this option.

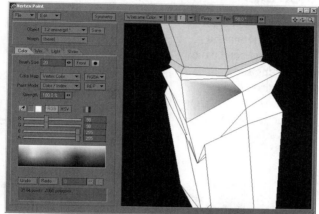

Figure 7-12: Color/Index mode

Lastly, the Color/Polygon option applies the color to the entire polygon that is clicked on. As with the Color/Index option, the Face and Brush Size options are ignored.

To the right of the Paint Mode selection menu we find a few options that determine the manner in which the color is added to the current vertex color. We have four options — Add, Subtract, Replace (the default), and Erase. Their overall effect is controlled by the Strength percentage value as shown in Figure 7-14.

Add basically adds the color to the underlying vertex color, the blending of which is obviously determined by the Strength value. Subtract is the opposite of Add. It subtracts the value of the paint color (the RGB

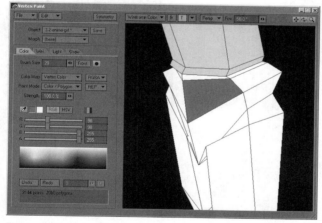

Figure 7-13: Color/Polygon mode

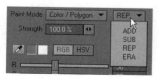

Figure 7-14

value) from the existing vertex color. Replace simply replaces the current vertex color with the new color, while Erase sets the value of the existing color back to 0.

Below these options we have sliders for mixing the actual colors. You can use the sliders to individually select values for each color channel (RGB or HSV), or you can click anywhere within the colored box to select a color from the range.

These are your basic options for creating and editing vertex color maps. For more in-depth information on using Vertex Paint, refer to your LightWave manual, where it is covered in extensive detail.

## Applying Vertex Color Maps

Once you have created your vertex color maps, you can blend them with your surface simply by going to the Advanced panel in the Surface Editor, selecting the map from the Vertex Color Map drop-down selection list, and using the Vertex Coloring value to blend it with the actual surface.

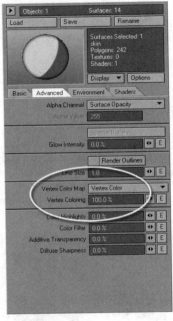

Figure 7-15

# CHAPTER 8

# Procedural Textures

## Using Procedural Textures

Procedural textures are patterns constructed using mathematical algorithms. You use them in the same way that you use any other kind of texture; you simply make a new layer in your Texture Editor or a node in the Node Editor and start from there.

Using procedural textures is not as straightforward as using images as your textures because they have a number of adjustable settings that create different effects. They also require some extra work in terms of applying them to your model in such a way as to prevent the surface from looking overly procedural, and consequently very computer generated and fake. Placing one procedural texture straight onto a surface without making careful tweaks generally does not look particularly nice. A little more cunning is involved. Most of the images in this chapter show the procedurals with their default settings, and trust me, to the trained eye they are instantly recognizable as procedurals!

However, the really great thing about procedurals is that, unlike texture maps, most of them do not require projection coordinates or UV mapping to place them onto your surface, as they are generated by algorithms that place them correctly. In other words, they are generated in 3D space. Only a few of LightWave's procedural textures require any kind of projection settings, and even then, they are very simple. Procedural textures are also, by their nature, completely seamless, so you never have to worry about continuity of the texture on your surface.

To create a procedural texture, simply open the Texture Editor or the Node Editor for whatever surface attribute you want to apply the texture to, and create a new layer with a procedural texture as the layer type or a new 2D or 3D texture node if you are working with the Node Editor.

I recommend that you dive into the Node Editor right away even if you are new to LightWave. The sooner you get comfortable making nodal networks, the better off you will be. The Node Editor is far superior, more powerful, and more flexible than the "classic" layer system. We will discuss the powerful Node Editor in Chapter 14.

NOTE: It is important to know that even though you might be working with the Node Editor you can still use the "classic" layer system in conjunction with nodes. Any "classic" attributes used in the Node Editor will be superseded and will be unavailable to be edited with the layer system.

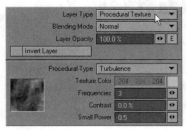

Figure 8-1

You can create as many procedural texture nodes or layers as you wish in any of the surface attributes, but do be aware that procedural textures can add significantly to render times, as they are calculated during the render process. Sometimes, if you have created a number of different procedural layers and are happy with the look but suffer with slow render times, it can be a good idea to bake them to an image, as discussed in the section on the Surface Baker shader in Chapter 5. This basically creates an image from all the procedurals that you can then apply to the surface as a single texture layer, thereby reducing your rendering times. Another cool thing about using the Surface Baker is that you can then take that baked image into a paint program and add even more details to it, which can help make the texture look less procedural.

## Seeing Procedural Textures in Your Viewports

Since LightWave 8.5 we are able to see our procedural texture work in the OpenGL viewports thanks to GLSL shaders. This shading system requires the OpenGL 2.0 standard in order for you to see procedurals in your display. You can switch this off and on in the OpenGL tab in the Preferences panel in Layout ("o"). Use this with caution though; it is quite slow when you have lots of objects loaded and you'll need a high-performance graphics card to really enjoy this feature. The greatest thing about being able to see your procedural textures in your viewport is the ability to eliminate guesswork and immediately see your changes and tweaks without having to do test renders.

If you don't have an OpenGL 2.0-compliant graphics card, you will not be able to take advantage of GLSL; however, there is a clever little workaround that enables you to see the procedural that you are working on in your viewports using Textured Filter, which you can load in your Image Editor. To use this filter to enable us to see a procedural texture in OpenGL, we do the following:

1. Load an image into the Image Editor. This can be any image, as it will be completely covered by the filter, but for the sake of simplicity in this example, let's just load a blank, white image.

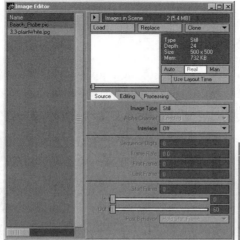

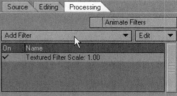

Figure 8-2                                              Figure 8-3

2.  Go to the Processing tab in the Image Editor and add the Textured Filter from the filter list.

3.  Double-click on the filter to open its options panel, and click on the button labeled Texture.

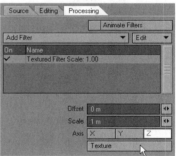

This opens a Texture Editor window, just as we find when working on our surfaces in the Surface Editor. Notice that a layer has been created by default, as per usual.

4.  Change this layer to Procedural Texture from the Layer Type list, and select

Figure 8-4

Value from the Proce-dural Type list. You can change this color to any-thing you want, as it will form the underlying color for the texture.

Of course, the color you select for this proce-dural texture will depend on whether this texture will be used for a color texture or for a texture for any of the other sur-face attributes. If the

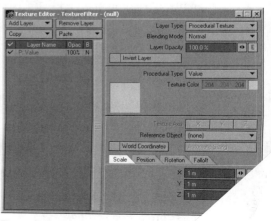

Figure 8-5

texture is to be used for a specularity or bump or reflection texture, or for any of the other surface attributes that use gray values, then you will naturally choose a base shade of gray.

5. On top of this base layer, you can now add whatever procedural textures you wish to use on your surface, and set them up as you want. If your Image Editor is still open, notice how the preview window shows the procedural textures that you have applied to this image.

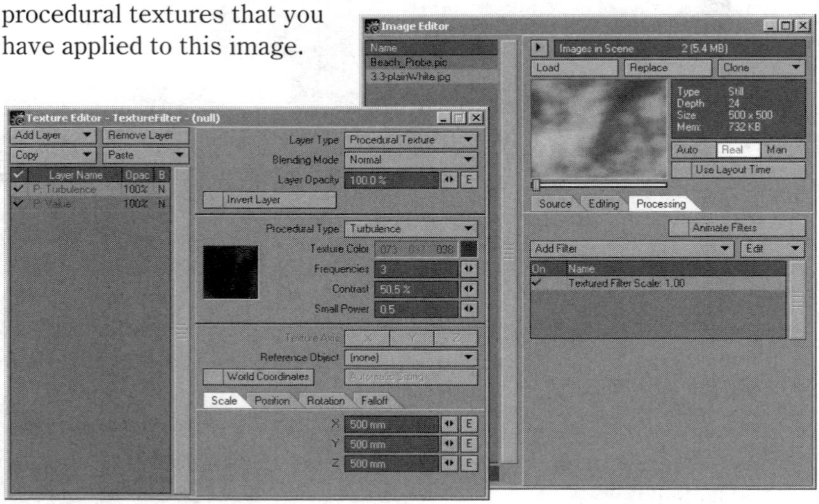

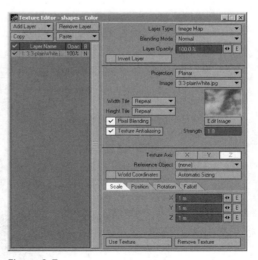

Figure 8-6

6. Go to the Surface Editor of the object to which you wish to apply this surface. If we wish to apply it to the color attribute of a surface, for example, we would open up the color Texture Editor for that surface. Create a layer with Image Map as its Layer Type, and load the image that we just applied Textured Filter to from the Image list.

Of course, something to bear in mind when using this method is that the procedural texture is now acting as an image and consequently requires projection settings.

Figure 8-7

Because of this, your procedural texture will not be calculated as it would be if it were simply applied as a procedural texture in the Texture Editor.

However, this can be useful for checking how the different settings of the texture will more or less look in terms of size and behavior in relation to your surface. So you could use this method simply to check that, and then copy the procedural straight into your Texture Editor as a procedural texture layer.

## Texture Color and Texture Value

When creating procedural textures, notice that the first option in each of their panels is the Texture Color or Texture Value option. Note that this option is always labeled Texture Value unless the texture is applied to the color attribute of a surface, in which case it is labeled Texture Color.

**Figure 8-8**

This value determines the intensity of the texture at its strongest point. For example, if you apply a procedural with a value of 80% as its Texture Value to your specularity attribute, then that value determines the brightest point of specularity in the texture. Because procedural textures have a number of variations of tones within them, the brightest point that you determine with the Texture Value option is simply the most intense of a wide range of values that are then calculated. So in this case you would get a range of values that would not exceed 80%.

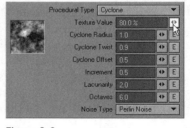

To assign a Texture Value to a procedural, simply type an amount into the field, or drag the spinner left or right with your mouse to decrease or increase the value respectively.

**Figure 8-9**

## Texture Scale

When working with procedurals, as with images, we can alter the scale, position, rotation, and falloff of the textures. Because of the way in which procedurals are calculated, it is not generally necessary to change the Position and Rotation settings, unless you are animating them or holding them in world space using world coordinates.

> **NOTE:** See Chapter 13 for more information about the Scale, Position, Rotation, and Falloff options in the Texture Editor.

However, the Scale value is quite important when working procedurally, as this can have a very drastic effect on the look of the procedural texture when it is applied to a surface, since this value determines the size of the fractal patterns within the texture.

Figure 8-10 demonstrates the difference between two different scales using the same procedural texture.

Procedural Scale = 1m x 1m x 1m    Procedural Scale = 0.1m x 0.1m x 0.1m

Figure 8-10

In most instances, you use values that are smaller than the actual dimensions of the surface when using procedural textures; otherwise, they not only tend to look a little strange, but they also begin to look far too much like procedural textures. In other words, they begin to look a little fake. Once you have been doing 3D for a while, you tend to develop a good eye for spotting procedural textures, so this is why we have to be careful that our textures look natural and not mathematically created.

Unlike using Scale with images, where we usually set the size ratio to more or less the same as that of the image itself, using different values for each of the Scale axes can produce some interesting results. As we know, stretching an image disproportionately along one of its axes will look terrible; however, stretching a procedural differently along its axis is absolutely fine, and you can use this to create the right look for your texture pretty easily. For example, if you wanted to use a procedural texture to create some streaky damage from rain or water that has dripped down the length of a surface, you could scale the y-axis of that texture much larger than the other two axes, so that it would appear to be stretched lengthwise, as shown in Figure 8-11.

Figure 8-11: Image shows the y-axis scaled much larger than the other two axes.

## Using Procedural Textures Creatively

As mentioned before, procedural textures need to be used very carefully so as not to produce an overly computer-generated look on your surfaces.

Remember though, that just as with gradients and images, procedural textures are used not only to actually form solid texture layers on their own, but also to blend different texture layers together, or to enhance other layers by using different blending modes.

> **NOTE:** Refer to Chapter 13 for more information on using different blending modes in the Texture Editor.

Something you also need to bear in mind when using them is that due to their apparently random nature, placing them in the right areas of your surfaces can be quite tricky. As opposed to an image map, where you would simply paint the different details where you want them to be, placing procedural textures can be a little more complicated.

Because procedurals are calculated evenly across the expanse of a surface, you need to develop ways in which you can place certain procedural details onto specific areas of the surface. This can be done easily using weight maps in conjunction with gradients that can then act as alpha layers for the procedural texture or by creating actual images that you then use as alpha layers to limit the visibility of the procedural texture to certain areas only. Using methods like this is really quite important, as having procedural textures applied evenly across an entire surface usually looks pretty fake, because as we already know, surfaces in real life tend to develop details in fairly precise ways, not completely random ones.

> **NOTE:** Refer to Chapter 10 for more information and a tutorial on creating weight maps for the placement of procedural textures.

Above all, probably the most important thing to be aware of when it comes to procedural textures is that very rarely do they work very well on their own. Generally, for the most photorealistic and believable-looking surfaces, a combination of gradients, procedurals, and image maps may be required. Of course, there certainly are instances where a very cunning and complex procedural setup can suffice on its own, but this is not very common. In the end, it really comes down to your own discretion, because invariably you use whatever methods get the results that you are after. It is nevertheless important to note that you are not always likely to produce a totally satisfactory result using procedurals and nothing else.

# Using LightWave's Built-in Procedural Textures

LightWave ships with a number of different procedural textures that you can use in your surfaces. There are a number of third-party procedural collections available for purchase as well, but for the purposes of this book we shall only examine the ones native to LightWave.

Please note that in all of the following examples, the procedural texture is demonstrated using the Color attribute in the Surface Editor, unless otherwise stated.

## Brick

The first procedural texture in the list is the Brick texture. As its name suggests, this texture makes...bricks. So it isn't really one of the most versatile of textures. However, should you need a brick texture on the fly, then this is pretty handy.

When applied to a surface, this procedural texture creates an array of symmetrically spaced bricks with thin mortar between them.

Figure 8-12: Brick texture

The Texture Color for the Brick procedural determines the color of the mortar, not the bricks. The color of the bricks is determined rather by the base color of the surface if the procedural is applied as the bottom or only texture layer in the Texture Editor, or by the color of any underlying layers.

Figure 8-13

The Mortar Thickness value sets the thickness of the mortar between the bricks. Lower values obviously create thinner mortar, while higher values produce thicker layers. If your mortar value gets too high, the mortar will completely cover the bricks.

Figure 8-14: Low and high Mortar Thickness values

Use the Fuzzy Edge Width option to determine how soft the edges of the mortar appear to be. A low Fuzzy Edge Width value has very defined edges, while a higher value results in very soft, blurred edges.

The Brick procedural is one of the few LightWave procedurals that requires projection coordinates. You set this using the

Figure 8-15

Texture Axis buttons in the Texture Editor, choosing to project the texture along the x-, y-, or z-axis.

Obviously, the axis that you choose to project the texture along will depend on the orientation of the surface to which you are applying it. This can sometimes pose some minor annoyances, especially if you are applying the texture to an entire building, as invariably this means that one of the sides of the building is not going to look correct, as demonstrated in Figure 8-16.

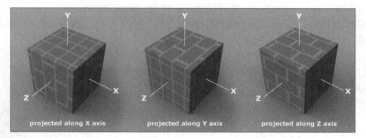

Figure 8-16: Brick Texture Axis options

To counteract this, we generally tend to require at least two layers of this procedural, or multiple surfaces applied to the same object, to ensure that all the walls of the building look correct.

Another funny little thing to keep an eye out for when using the Brick procedural is the possibility that you might apply it to an object and end up with an entire side of the object being covered in plain mortar. This is purely due to the positioning of the texture, as it may end up with a layer of mortar occurring on the edge of an object. To fix this, simply adjust the position of the texture along whichever axis the problem is occurring.

## Bump Array

Second in our list of procedurals is the Bump Array texture. If you ever need to make a golf ball texture, this one is a good bet, as it creates an array of dimples on your surface.

Because this texture is most useful for bump texturing, this example uses the texture in its Bump channel.

Okay, so it doesn't create a perfect golf ball pattern. But it is close enough. Setting this texture up is really simple; all you need to do is specify the radius of the little bumps themselves and the spacing between them.

Figure 8-17: Bump Array texture

Figure 8-18

Obviously, the higher the Radius value, the larger the little indentations, and the higher the Spacing value, the larger the spaces between the indentations. When setting the overall Scale value for this texture, the larger the value, the larger the actual array pattern. So you generally find a good balance using the texture's actual settings, as well as the Scale value in the Texture Editor.

Playing around with the Radius and Spacing values can create some really interesting-looking surfaces. Experiment with this by giving them rather extreme values and see what happens.

You can also get some cool-looking and useful textures by inverting this procedural, which naturally creates little bumps all over the surface instead of indentations.

This can be useful for making textures like bubble wrap, beadwork, or extremely warty, organic surfaces.

The only slightly tricky thing about using this procedural for organic surfaces is that it has a very defined pattern that does not look natu-

Figure 8-19: Inverted Bump Array texture

ral. You might want to try experimenting with the Crust procedural, discussed in a moment, if you wish to create organic bumps more easily, or try using another texture as a displacement below it to break the pattern up a bit. See the "Layer Opacity and Blending Modes" section in Chapter 13 for more information on using displacement layers in the Texture Editor.

> **NOTE:** This procedural texture doesn't have a direct equivalent in the Node Editor.

## Checkerboard

In all honesty, the Checkerboard procedural is a fairly unexciting and mostly not very useful texture that creates a bunch of colored squares all over your surface, just like a checkerboard.

Setting this procedural up is extremely simple. The only setting you have is the Texture Color value, which — you guessed it — determines the color of the blocks in the pattern.

Remember that this effect is a two-tone effect, and therefore the colors that we see on the surface when rendered are the Texture Color that we set within the

Figure 8-20: Checkerboard texture

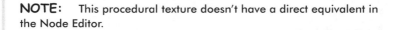

Figure 8-21

procedural's settings along with the color of the actual surface itself. So if the surface color is orange, and you set the procedural's Texture Color to blue, then you will end up with an orange and blue checkerboard pattern. It's almost too easy.

To set the size of the actual blocks within the pattern, simply adjust your Scale values in the Texture Editor. These values determine the dimensions of each square.

Figure 8-22

For example, using a setting of 500mm, 500mm, 500mm for your Scale axes, as shown in Figure 8-22, you would get a pattern with squares that are each 500mm in dimension.

When applied to a box that is approximately 2m by 2m in size, this texture would look like what is shown in Figure 8-23.

Figure 8-23

# Crumple

Crumple is definitely one of the procedural textures that I use the most. It is one of the best procedurals, in my opinion, for use on organic surfaces to create a grain, especially for any type of skin.

This procedural is an extremely detailed texture that looks like something that has been crumpled (crushed and squashed) under pressure, with sharp ridges and scalloped or beaten indentations within the texture. This is really useful for surfaces such as old dried paper that has been crumpled and then unfolded, beaten metal (especially for armor or any metal items that have been handmade), even ground, ice, snow, or anything else that has had some kind of hammering or crumpling. Figure 8-24 shows the Crumple texture applied as a bump map.

Figure 8-24: Crumple texture

When inverted, it creates a great cellular type grain that is excellent for skin and leather.

It is most useful for using as a bump map, although, of course, there is absolutely no reason why you cannot use it for other surface attributes too.

The Crumple procedural has a couple of different settings to control its effect.

The Texture Value, as with all procedurals, controls the overall strength that the texture has on the surface attribute to

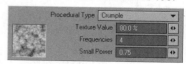

Figure 8-25

which it is applied. The Frequencies value determines the complexity of the actual crumple pattern by varying the number of scales of detail included in the procedural pattern. A value of 0 produces a completely flat pattern. Figure 8-26 demonstrates the effect of increasing this value.

Figure 8-26: Frequencies value for Crumple

As you can see, the ridges stay the same, but the complexity of the detail within the indentations between the ridges increases as this value increases.

While Frequencies determines the complexity of the pattern as a whole, the Small Power value affects the actual details within the procedural themselves by affecting the intensity with which the details are shaded. Higher values of Small Power (1.0 or higher) create an even intensity of shading with both the small and large dents and details in the surface, which results in a very detailed, busy surface with lots of small details while the larger details lose some of their distinction. Lower values (0.50 and lower) have less distinction between the large and small details that results in a smoother-looking surface between the larger ridge areas.

The default value of 0.75 is a nice in-between setting that has distinctly small and large details in the surface.

Figure 8-27: Small Power values for Crumple

As mentioned before, inverting the Crumple procedural is really great for organic surfaces, especially for skin or leather. By inverting the texture, scaling it down to really small sizes, and setting it to a fairly low Texture Value, you can create an excellent base bump map for surfaces like these.

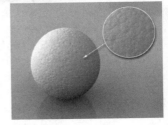

Figure 8-28: Inverted Crumple texture

## Crust

Like the Crumple procedural that we just looked at, the Crust texture is another procedural that is really useful for bump maps. Figure 8-29 shows the texture applied to both the Bump channel and the Color channel of the surface.

Figure 8-29: Crust texture

As you can see, this texture creates raised circular shapes on a surface, great for making warts or spots. When inverted, you can use it to create craters, as shown in Figure 8-30.

Setting up and controlling this procedural is really straightforward, as there are only a few very simple values that you need to define.

Figure 8-31

Figure 8-30: Inverted Crust texture

The Coverage value determines how much of the surface is covered by the splotches. Low values have lots of little splotches, while higher values almost completely cover the surface.

Figure 8-32: Coverage values for Crust

The other two values for the procedural, Ledge Level and Ledge Width, control the appearance of the actual little splotches themselves.

The Ledge Level value affects the edges of the splotches by controlling how far they are spread from the center of each splotch. It is similar in many ways to the effect that the Coverage setting has on the texture; however, changing this value has an extremely strong effect when applied as a bump map, so the value should be altered in very small increments of about 0.1 to get the desired effect. Figure 8-33 shows the difference between the default value, a low value, and a high value of Ledge Level.

Figure 8-33: Ledge Level values for Crust

The Ledge Width value controls the angle of the "slope" at the edges of the splotches. High values produce a soft slope that creates soft, bubbly looking patterns; low values produce a very sharp falloff along the edges of the splotches, creating neat, button-like patterns.

Figure 8-34: Ledge Width values for Crust

## Dots

This procedural is similar to the Bump Array that we looked at previously, except that in this case, the pattern is arranged in vertical and horizontal lines as opposed to diagonal arrays. It basically makes a polka-dot pattern.

This procedural is extraordinarily simple, having only two very straightforward settings in addition to the usual Texture Color setting.

The Dot Diameter value determines the size of the dots themselves. Small values create small dots, while larger values make big ones. A value of 1.0 creates really large dots that have edges almost touching each other.

Figure 8-35: Dots texture

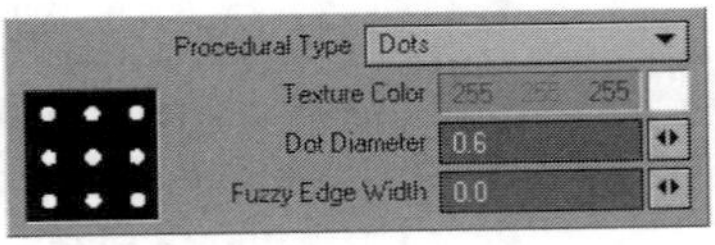

Figure 8-36

Figure 8-37: Dot Diameter values for Dots

The Fuzzy Edge Width value determines how sharp or soft the edges of the dots are. The default value of 0 creates dots that have solid edges. By increasing this value, the edges become blurred and soft.

Figure 8-38: Fuzzy Edge Width values for Dots

## Fractal Noise

This procedural must be the most commonly found procedural across all software packages. It is really just a random fractal pattern with no special features or details, but rather just creates a cloudy pattern that is really versatile due to its lack of specific detail.

Because of its versatility, we find the Fractal Noise texture useful everywhere, from metals to organic surfaces to ground textures, especially as a bump map.

Figure 8-39: Fractal Noise texture

The procedural has three different settings in addition to the Texture Value setting.

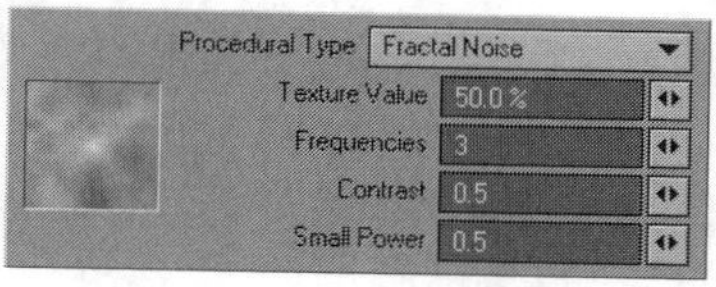

The Frequencies value controls the level of detail within the patterns. The default value is 3.0, which creates a fairly detailed, wispy pattern. It is not advisable to increase this value beyond 5.0 or 6.0, since the pattern becomes rather indiscernible and not really all that useful, and rendering times increase unnecessarily. Once you go over 3.0, the changes in the details become extremely subtle anyway.

Figure 8-40

Figure 8-41: Frequencies values for Fractal Noise

Adjusting the Contrast value of the procedural increases the contrast in intensity between the lighter and darker parts of the fractal pattern. Low Contrast values create subdued, wispy patterns, while higher values create bolder, more starkly defined patterns with slightly wispy edges.

Figure 8-42: Contrast values for Fractal Noise

Similar to the option with the same name found in the Crumple procedural, Small Power determines the amount of intensity with which the small and large details in the pattern are shaded. Low values create fairly even patterns with a subdued mixture of small and large details that have little distinction between them, while higher values have greater contrast between the details, resulting in busier, mottled patterns. The default value is 0.5.

Figure 8-43: Small Power values for Fractal Noise

By scaling this procedural down, setting it to fairly high Contrast and Frequencies values, and increasing its Small Power, you can quickly create a versatile grain that can be used as a bump map for adding a slight roughness to just about anything.

Figure 8-44 shows the texture scaled down to 5mm by 5mm by 5mm, a Texture Value of 100%, Frequencies and Contrast both set to 5.0, and Small Power set to 1.0.

**Figure 8-44**

> **NOTE:** Fractal Noise doesn't have a direct equivalent in the Node Editor; however, you can use a number of different textures as substitute. Turbulence, Turbulent Noise, and FBM Noise are good alternatives.

## Grid

This texture creates a grid pattern on your surface that is three-dimensional.

Another very simple procedural to set up, the control panel for the Grid texture is easy to understand and apply values to.

**Figure 8-45:** Grid texture

**Figure 8-46**

The Line Thickness value determines the thickness of the actual lines that make up the grid. Obviously, lower values produce thin lines, while high values produce thick ones. The maximum thickness that you can set this value to is 0.5, which produces a solid grid.

**Figure 8-47:** Line Thickness values for Grid

Fuzzy Edge Width determines how soft the edges of the lines in the grid are. The default value of 0.0 produces normal, sharp-edged lines; higher values soften and blur the edges of the lines.

**143**

Figure 8-48: Fuzzy Edge Width values for Grid

## Honeycomb

This procedural is very similar to the Grid texture, except that in this case the pattern forms hexagonal shapes instead of a standard grid. However, unlike the Grid procedural, Honeycomb is not a three-dimensional texture, and is therefore another of the few procedural textures that requires a projection axis, like the Brick procedural that we looked at earlier. You select the projection axis by selecting the appropriate Texture Axis option.

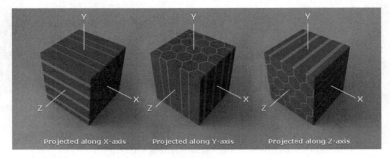

Figure 8-49: Honeycomb Texture Axis options

Because of this, you may find that you require multiple layers of this procedural using different projections or multiple surfaces applied to your model in order to get the correct look when using this texture.

The controls for this procedural are basically identical to the settings for the Grid texture. You simply control the width and the softness of the lines within the texture.

Figure 8-50

Line Thickness controls the thickness of the lines within the pattern, while the Fuzzy Edge Width value determines how soft and blurred the edges of the lines are.

## Marble

The Marble procedural creates fractal patterns similar to the veins found within — you guessed it — marble. This procedural also requires a projection axis that you select with the Texture Axis setting, and wraps the veins around the chosen axis.

Figure 8-51: Marble Texture Axis options

The procedural's panel offers us a number of settings to play around with.

Just as we have seen in a number of other procedurals, the first setting for the Marble texture is the Frequencies value, and just as with those other procedurals, this value determines the level of detail

Figure 8-52

within the texture. Low values here will create very simple, fairly straight, plain veins, whereas higher values produce more jagged veins. It is not advisable to set this value higher than 6.0, as the changes in the complexity become practically indiscernible and render times become unnecessarily long.

Figure 8-53: Frequencies values for Marble

The Turbulence value determines how close the veins may come to one another in the pattern by squashing or expanding the pattern as a whole, thereby pulling the veins closer together or pushing them farther apart.

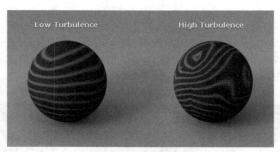

Figure 8-54: Turbulence values for Marble

The Turbulence setting works closely with the Vein Spacing setting. Vein Spacing controls the spacing between veins *within* the pattern itself.

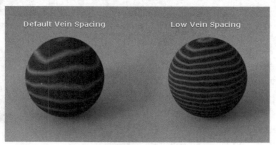

Figure 8-55: Vein Spacing values for Marble

Ideally, the Turbulence value should be a fraction of the Vein Spacing value for the best-looking results. By default, the Turbulence value is half of the Vein Spacing value. When the Turbulence value exceeds the Vein Spacing value, the pattern no longer looks like a marble pattern, and instead becomes a rather strange-looking affair that is not altogether useful since it resembles nothing in particular.

Figure 8-56: Marble Turbulence value that exceeds Vein Spacing value

Use the Vein Sharpness value to determine how soft the edges of the veins are, like the Fuzzy Edge Width value found in other procedurals. The default is 4.0, which creates fairly strong veins with slightly wispy edges. Lower values make the veins very feathery, while higher values create very distinct, contrasted veins.

Figure 8-57: Vein Sharpness values for Marble

When using the Marble procedural, it is ideal to set up the Vein Spacing and the Texture Axis settings first to establish the overall look that you are going for, and then set up the Turbulence, Frequencies, and Scale settings to perfect the effect.

## Ripples and Ripples 2

The Ripples procedurals create ripples such as you would find on the surface of water, and are particularly useful as bump maps, as shown in Figure 8-58.

Ripples and Ripples 2 are only slightly different from one another in that Ripples 2 creates ripples with sharper, more defined crests. The following image demonstrates the difference between the two, where both have been applied using exactly the same settings.

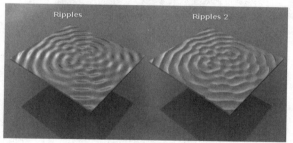

Figure 8-58: Ripples textures

Despite the fact that the two textures are slightly different, both are controlled by the same values.

The Wave Sources value sets the number of ripple sources within the pattern. Low values have few ripples, while higher values create lots of them. So if, for example, you wanted to create a fairly turbulent surface, you would set the value rather high, whereas if you were merely creating the aftereffect of a small stone being dropped into

Figure 8-59

**147**

water, you would probably only use a value of 1.0. Using values higher than 16 is not really recommended, as your rendering times increase and the surface becomes unnecessarily turbulent and unsightly.

Figure 8-60: Wave Sources values for Ripples

Wavelength determines the size of the spaces between the ripples. Bring the ripples closer together by decreasing the value or spread them farther apart by increasing it.

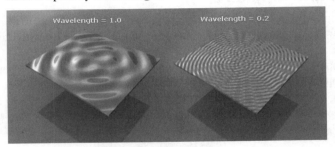

Figure 8-61: Wavelength values for Ripples

The Wave Speed value determines the speed at which the ripples move outward from the center of the pattern. Use this value when animating the ripples.

To ensure that your ripples loop correctly throughout the length of an animation, use the following equation to determine the correct Wave Speed value: Wavelength value/number of frames the ripples need to loop over.

## Smoky1, Smoky2, and Smoky3

The three Smoky procedurals are basically just variations of the Fractal Noise texture, with the addition of a Turbulence value that allows you to control the level of disturbance within the pattern.

Figure 8-62: Smoky textures

As you can see, the patterns within the three different textures are actually very similar; they just vary in terms of the shading of the different levels contained within the pattern itself.

All three procedurals are controlled by the same settings found in each of their panels.

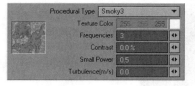

Figure 8-63

Just as with the Fractal Noise procedural, the Frequencies value determines the level of detail within the pattern. Low values yield a simpler pattern, while higher values create a more complex one. Values should not exceed 6.0, as the changes are minute and create unnecessarily long render times.

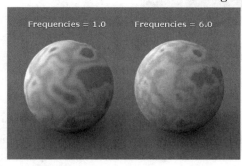

Figure 8-64: Frequencies values for Smoky

The Contrast value of the procedural increases or decreases the contrast in intensity between the lighter and darker parts of the fractal pattern. A low Contrast value creates large, subdued, wispy patterns, while higher values create bolder, tighter patterns with stark edges. This value can be less than 0.

Just as we have seen before in other procedurals, the Small Power value determines the amount of intensity with which the small details and the large details in the pattern are shaded. Low values create fairly even patterns with a subdued mixture of small and

Figure 8-65: Contrast values for Smoky

large details that have little distinction between them, while higher values have greater contrast between the details, resulting in busier, more mottled patterns.

Figure 8-66:
Small Power
values for Smoky

The Turbulence value adjusts the amount of disturbance within the pattern for animation purposes. The changes are fairly subtle, so the value should be changed rather radically for very noticeable results.

Figure 8-67:
Turbulence values
for Smoky

> **NOTE:** These procedural textures are not available in the Node Editor. You can use one of the many multifractal textures as a replacement.

## Turbulence

This texture combines layers of fractal noise with different frequencies to create complex patterns that are similar to the Fractal Noise procedural, but a little more detailed and interesting.

The controls for the Turbulence texture are the same as those found in the Fractal Noise procedural. However, due to the nature of the Turbulence texture, the settings have a higher range of effect in terms of altering the details.

Figure 8-68

The Small Power value in this texture gives you a much wider range of control over the pattern than it does in the Fractal Noise procedural, enabling you to create very wispy patterns as well as extremely coarse, intricate ones, especially if you increase Contrast when increasing Small Power.

The Contrast value here gives you a much starker, and in many ways more effective, contrast than found in the Fractal Noise procedural as well.

Figure 8-69: Turbulence texture

## Underwater

This procedural mimics the caustic patterns caused by refracted light that are found along the bottoms of swimming pools, the sea, or any other body of water that has turbulence on its surface.

The controls for the texture are similar to the controls found in the Ripples and Ripples 2 procedurals, with the addition of an extra option, Band Sharpness.

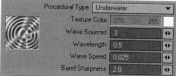

Figure 8-70

As with the Ripples procedurals, the Wave Sources value determines the number of ripples within the texture. The default is 3.0, and produces a fairly detailed pattern. Once again, values higher than 16 are not recommended, as the pattern becomes overly busy and causes unnecessarily long render times.

Wavelength, once again, determines the distance between the ripples within the pattern. Decrease this value to bring them closer together or increase them to spread them farther apart.

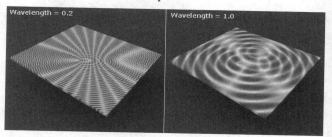

Figure 8-72: Wavelength values for Underwater

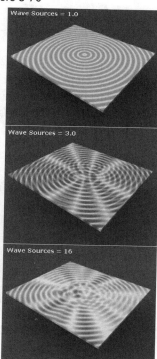

Figure 8-71: Wave Sources values for Underwater

Just as we saw with the Ripples procedurals, Wave Speed controls the speed at which the ripples move outward from the center of the pattern. Use this value when animating the ripples.

Ensuring that the ripples loop correctly for the duration of your animation simply requires the following equation to determine the correct Wave Speed value: Wavelength value/number of frames that the ripples need to loop over.

Band Sharpness acts as a contrast control for the look of the ripples. Decrease this value for soft-looking ripples, or increase it for sharp, distinct ones. Values exceeding 4.0 tend to lose their realism and look more stylized.

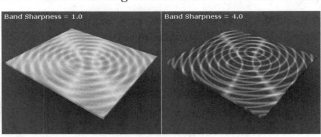

Figure 8-73: Band Sharpness values for Underwater

## Value

The most straightforward and simple of all the procedurals, Value is not actually a texture, but instead creates a solid layer of a single color or value.

Select the color or value by simply clicking on the Texture Color swatch.

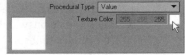

Figure 8-74

## Veins

The Veins procedural produces an intricate web of veins across the surface like a jagged and distorted version of the Grid procedural. This texture is best applied as a bump map, whereby it creates a network of raised veins. Inverting this texture is also very useful for creating textures for cracked mud or old stone walls. Figure 8-75 shows the texture applied to both the Bump and Color channels.

Figure 8-75: Veins texture

The controls for this procedural are identical to those of the Crust texture, with very similar effects.

The Coverage setting only really affects the texture when it is used in the color of a surface. The value determines

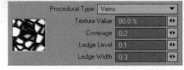

Figure 8-76

how thick the color part of the veins becomes. Values that are less than or equal to the bump texture (assuming all the other values are equal) result in the veins being of a solid color or the color becoming thin atop the bumps. Higher values cause the color to spill out over the edges of the veins and onto the surrounding surface.

Figure 8-77: Coverage values for Veins

The other two values for the procedural, Ledge Level and Ledge Width, control the actual veins within the pattern.

The Ledge Level value affects the edges of the veins by controlling how far apart they are spread from the middle of each vein out into the rest of the surface. This value has a much stronger effect when used on a bump texture than it does on a color texture.

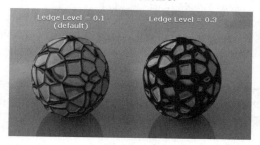

Figure 8-78: Ledge Level values for Veins

The Ledge Width value controls the angle of the "slope" at the edges of the veins. High values produce a soft slope that creates large, almost puffy veins with shallow spaces between them, whereas low values produce a very straight falloff along the edges, creating sharp-edged veins with wider gaps between them.

Figure 8-79: Ledge Width values for Veins

**153**

# Wood

The Wood texture is similar in some ways to the Marble texture, except that its patterns resemble the intricate grain patterns found in wood. This is another one of LightWave's procedural textures that requires a projection axis that you select by choosing one of the Texture Axis options.

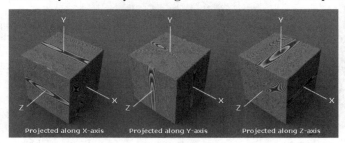

Figure 8-80:
Wood Texture
Axis options

Projected along X-axis    Projected along Y-axis    Projected along Z-axis

The controls for it are essentially the same as those found in the Marble procedural as well, with the vein controls being replaced by ring controls.

Figure 8-81

Frequencies determines the level of detail within the texture. Low values here will create simpler wooden patterns, whereas higher values produce more complex ones. It is not advisable to set this value higher than 6.0, as the changes in the complexity become practically indiscernible and render times become unnecessarily long.

The Turbulence value determines how close the wood rings may come to one another in the pattern by squashing or expanding the pattern as a whole, thereby pulling the rings closer together or pushing them farther apart.

The Turbulence setting works closely with the Ring Spacing setting. Ring Spacing controls the spacing between rings *within* the pattern itself.

Ideally, the Turbulence value should be a fraction of the Ring Spacing value for the best-looking results. By default, the Turbulence value is half of the Ring Spacing value. When the Turbulence value exceeds the Ring Spacing value, the texture no longer looks even vaguely wood-like.

Ring Sharpness determines how soft the edges of the rings are, like the Fuzzy Edge Width value found in other procedurals.

The problem with the wood procedural is that it is very difficult to control and has an unreal look that makes it a bit useless for close-up shots. It does not scale well at all, and quite frankly, I have never had much success with it.

# Additional LightWave Procedural Textures

The following textures are slightly different from the ones that we have so far examined, and are all based on noise and fractal routines.

> **NOTE:** These routines were originally presented in a book called *Texturing and Modeling: A Procedural Approach* by David Ebert, F. Kenton Musgrave, Darwyn Peachey, Ken Perlin, and Steve Worley, published by Morgan Kaufmann Publishers (ISBN 0122287304).

Most of them have settings that you adjust as desired.

The Increment value controls the fractal dimension of the texture pattern. Low values result in tiny repetitious patterns that resemble static or white noise, whereas higher values become smoother, softer, and larger. It is basically like a scale control for details in the patterns.

The following image, which uses the FBM Noise procedural, demonstrates the difference between high and low values of Increment.

Figure 8-82:
Increment values
for FBM Noise

The Lacunarity setting determines the amount of change that occurs in the frequency of noise between each successive iteration of fractals within the pattern. As the value increases, so do the size of the gaps between the scaled fractal clusters. Values lower than 2.0 usually end up losing a lot of detail, while high values create extremely soft, feathery patterns.

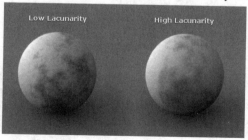

Figure 8-83:
Lacunarity values
for FBM Noise

The Octaves value controls the number of times that the texture is scaled down to a smaller pattern and then added back to the larger pattern. In other words, it determines the amount of small details that are added to the texture. Increasing this value increases rendering times, but also increases the amount of smaller detail within the texture. Low values result in very little detail within the texture at all, leaving only large, smooth shapes in the pattern.

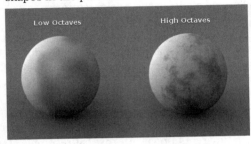

Figure 8-84:
Octaves values for
FBM Noise

The Offset control is available in all of the multifractal textures. Multifractal textures are created with many variations of the fractal dimension within the texture. This means that the surface is more inconsistent and varied across a surface. Low Offset values result in more variation across the surface, creating roughness, whereas high values result in a smoother, more consistent pattern. Change this value in tiny increments of about 0.1 or less, as the effect is extremely sensitive.

Figure 8-85:
Offset values for
FBM Noise

Threshold controls the range of the combined values of Increment, Lacunarity, and Octaves. If the Threshold value exceeds that of the combined value of these settings, the texture will have no effect at all. In other words, it controls how much of the texture pattern is visible.

All of these procedurals can use a selectable Noise Type from the drop-down list at the bottom of the panel.

The default is Perlin Noise, which is the fastest noise option available for these types of procedurals. You can also choose from Value Noise, Gradient Noise, Value-Gradient Noise, Lattice Convolution Noise, and Sparse Convolution Noise.

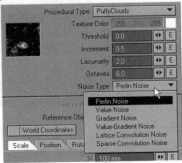

Figure 8-86

The following image demonstrates each of these noise types using the Puffy Clouds procedural texture.

Figure 8-87: Noise Type options

Although some of the other noise types may produce more pleasing results than the default Perlin, be aware that they do take longer to render.

## Coriolis

This procedural simulates the atmospheric flow around Earth that is caused by the planet spinning slower at the poles, but faster around the equatorial regions. If you're standing at the equator, you travel about 25,000 miles for a single rotation — roughly 1,000 miles per hour. If you're standing 1 meter from the North Pole, you only travel about 3.14 meters for a rotation — about 1/8 meter per hour. In terms of the actual Coriolis procedural, this results in larger, smoother turbulence in the middle of the texture with more violent turbulence at the poles. This is another procedural that requires an axis that you select from the Texture Axis options. Essentially, the axis that you select determines where the "poles" in the texture are found. This texture is really useful for creating atmospheric textures for planets.

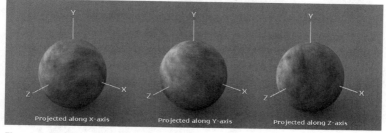

Figure 8-88: Coriolis Texture Axis options

**157**

Apart from the Increment, Lacunarity, Octaves, and Noise Type controls that we have already looked at, we also find a few extra values to play with for controlling this texture.

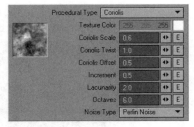

Figure 8-89

The Coriolis Scale value scales the actual coriolis value. Increasing this creates greater contrast between the cloudy areas in the texture and the empty areas that show the underlying surface. Decreasing this value softens the texture.

Figure 8-90:
Coriolis Scale
values

Coriolis Twist controls how much the pattern twists (rotates) between the poles and the equator regions of the pattern. The default is 1.0. Increasing this value creates a more turbulent, faster-looking effect, almost as if the clouds are being stirred rapidly along the axis.

Figure 8-91:
Coriolis Twist
values

Coriolis Offset essentially controls the density of the clouds in the texture by adding its value to the overall value of the texture. Lower values create thinner, wispier clouds while higher values create denser ones.

Figure 8-92:
Coriolis
Offset values

> **NOTE:** This procedural texture doesn't have a direct equivalent in the Node Editor.

## Cyclone

Yet another atmospheric type effect, this procedural simulates the strong swirling effect of a hurricane or cyclone. This is useful for creating tropical storms or vortexes for planetary atmospheric textures. This texture also requires a projection axis to be selected from the Texture Axis options. The axis that you select determines the top and bottom of the storm itself.

Figure 8-93: Cyclone Texture Axis options

Projected along X-axis   Projected along Y-axis   Projected along Z-axis

The controls for this texture are almost exactly the same as those found in the Coriolis texture, along with the Increment, Lacunarity, Octaves, and Noise Type values discussed earlier.

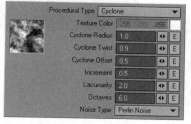

Figure 8-94

Cyclone Radius controls the size of the storm itself by determining the maximum size of the vortex. Clouds outside the perimeter of the radius will not get caught up in the swirling vortex in the middle. The higher the value, the larger the swirl.

Figure 8-95: Cyclone Radius values

The Cyclone Twist value, like the Coriolis Twist value in the Coriolis texture, determines the number of times that the clouds twist (rotate) between the top and bottom of the storm. Higher values produce the effect of a faster-moving storm.

Figure 8-96:
Cyclone Twist
values

Cyclone Offset controls the density of the clouds in the storm by adding its value to the overall value of the procedural. Increase this value for denser clouds or decrease it for lighter, thinner clouds.

Figure 8-97:
Cyclone Offset
values

**NOTE:** This procedural texture doesn't have a direct equivalent in the Node Editor.

## Dented

As its name suggests, this texture creates turbulent noise that emulates a crumpled, dented surface, especially when inverted. It is most useful as a bump texture, as Figure 8-98 demonstrates.

Aside from controls for Octaves and Noise Type, the panel for the Dented procedural offers us options for altering the Scale, Power, and Frequency of the texture.

The Scale value determines the magnitude (size) of the dents in the texture. Increase the value to create rougher, more prominent dents or decrease it to create a surface pitted with smaller, shallower dents. This setting requires quite large adjustments to make noticeable differences (increments of 5.0 to 10 or even higher).

Figure 8-98: Dented texture

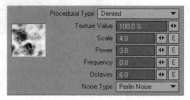

Figure 8-99

Figure 8-100:
Scale values for
Dented

Power adjusts the fractal dimension of the texture. Low values create larger, wider dents, akin to a crumpled surface or a mildly rocky terrain, whereas high values create smoother surfaces pitted with small, isolated dents.

Figure 8-101:
Power values for
Dented

Frequency controls the detail within the dents. Adjust this value in very small increments (0.1 or less), as its effect is very strong.

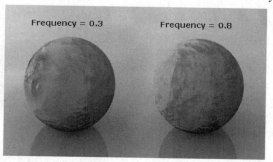

Figure 8-102:
Frequency values
for Dented

NOTE: This procedural texture doesn't have a direct equivalent in the Node Editor.

## FBM and FBM Noise

Based on Fractional Brownian Motion, the FBM procedurals produce a consistent noise pattern across the expanse of the surface. These textures are especially useful as bump maps. Due to their lack of distinguishing, specific

details, they are particularly useful for creating a
general unevenness that
can be used to add a
slight topographical variation to lots of different
types of surfaces, espe-
cially when scaled down.

Most of their con-
trols have already been
discussed, although the

Figure 8-103: FBM and FBM Noise textures

FBM texture includes a control for Small Power that affects the number of
small details within the texture.

## Hetero Terrain

Another multifractal texture, the Hetero Terrain procedural is also particularly useful for
bump maps, as it produces a roughness that
increases as the texture elevation increases.
This is useful for creating actual landscape
roughness (especially for planets), as it simulates the way in which land tends to be flatter
and smoother in low-lying areas, and rough
and uneven at increased altitudes.

Figure 8-104: Hetero Terrain
texture

A cool way of making a quick planetary
terrain would be to shrink the Hetero Terrain
texture to an appropriate scale for an orbit
distance, and then use a bump-based gradient
in your Color channel with different colors for
the different elevations. Figure 8-105 shows a
gradient with blue at the lowest level (for
water), followed by green (for grass), then
brown (for rock), and lastly white for snow at
the tops of the mountains.

Figure 8-105

## Hybrid Multi-Fractal

This texture is very similar to the Hetero
Terrain texture, except that it keeps the
entire terrain smoother, even at the higher
elevations. So it basically produces a
smoother version of the texture. This is a
useful texture for adding a slight unevenness

Figure 8-106: Hybrid Multi-
Fractal texture

to lots of different kinds of surfaces as it is rather homogenous and non-specific.

## Multi-Fractal

This procedural is a plain multifractal pattern, useful as a bump map for adding a general coarseness to surfaces such as paint, sand, nutshells, granite, even rough human skin, especially when you decrease the texture's Scale and Increment values.

Figure 8-107: Multi-Fractal texture

## Puffy Clouds

This texture is, as its name suggests, useful for atmospheric textures as it creates soft cloud patterns using FBM noise controlled with a Threshold value.

> **NOTE:** This procedural texture doesn't have a direct equivalent in the Node Editor.

Figure 8-108: Puffy Clouds texture

## Ridged Multi-Fractal

This hybrid multifractal texture is another texture that is great for creating terrain effects when used as a bump map. Use the Threshold value to create ridges in the terrain.

Using the gradient idea that we saw in the Hetero Terrain example, we can also use this texture in conjunction with such a gradient to produce very mountainous planetary landscapes.

Figure 8-109: Ridged Multi-Fractal texture

## Turbulent Noise

The final procedural, Turbulent Noise, is another FBM-based texture, with the addition of turbulence. This texture is yet another one that is really useful for giving generic roughness to a variety of surfaces. By scaling down the texture and its Increment value, Turbulent Noise creates an excellent non-specific and constant roughness to surfaces.

Figure 8-110: Turbulent Noise texture

**163**

# CHAPTER 9

# Gradients

## Introduction to Using Gradients

Gradients are extraordinary things! If the thought of gradients conjures up images of colors fading into one another such as those that are found in most vector and bitmap editing programs, leaving you to wonder what purpose they may serve for texturing purposes, then banish that concept from your mind! Gradients in LightWave are a rather different affair.

Gradients allow you to set values for any of the basic surface attributes (Color, Diffuse, Luminosity, etc.) based on definable input parameters. In essence, they are actually just a less intimidating, more pictorial method of constructing graphs. Although they are essentially rather complex by nature, constructing gradients is actually very simple once you understand how they work.

The gradient is controlled by the *gradient ramp*, which is the colored bar that you see when you create a gradient layer in the Texture Editor.

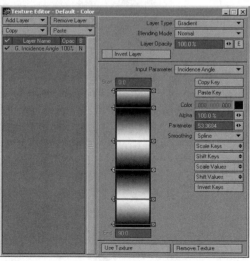

Figure 9-1

You create *keys* within the ramp that correspond to various attribute values, defined by the input parameters that are discussed in more depth in the next section. These keys act like points on a graph that control its spline. See Figure 9-2.

Gradients have many uses. You can use them to add extra details to your textures and extra effects to the overall look of your objects. With a little cunning and creativity, you can use gradients to create a variety of cool effects and to simulate certain looks, which we explore in the tutorials in this chapter.

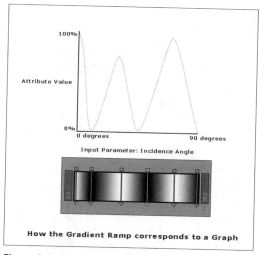

How the Gradient Ramp corresponds to a Graph

Figure 9-2

The power of gradients really lies, I believe, in using them in a very creative sense, since they can fake many different effects and enhance your surfaces in subtle, yet effective ways.

## Input Parameters

The input parameter that you set defines the information contained within another aspect of your model, or the actual LightWave scene, upon which the gradient will be dependent. You select an option from the Input Parameter drop-down list in the gradient panel. We are going to cover the input parameters available in the Texture Editor, but keep in mind that these options change, depending on what you are working on at the moment. There are different input parameter options unique for HyperVoxels where you can create a gradient to drive surface attributes like color and opacity according to the particle age. Adaptive Pixel Subdivision (APS) also has unique input parameters to help you control the subdivision of the mesh at render time. For more information on HyperVoxels and APS, consult your user manual.

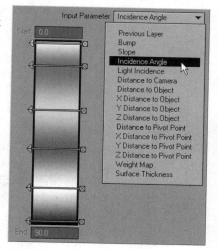

Figure 9-3

## Previous Layer

The first type of input parameter is Previous Layer. This option is simply looking for a "previous" layer. Previous Layer bases the gradient on the brightness levels of the previous (underlying) layer in the Texture Editor layer stack.

This can be useful for varying colors based on a procedural texture in the previous layer, such as a Turbulence or Fractal Noise pattern, where you could assign colors to the various shades of gray within the procedural. You can also use it to assign opacity values to different values within the underlying layer, when used as an alpha layer type.

## Bump

This option uses the settings from the surface's bump map as the input. This can be especially handy for changing settings like color or specularity or diffuse value based on the depth of the bump map, since these attributes often change according to scratches and dents in a surface.

For example, if you were texturing a red car with chipped paint, you could set the gradient up so that the body would be red, but where there are dents that create gaps in the paint, the gray metal could be showing through.

Figure 9-4: Bump gradient

Another example would be using this option to change specularity according to the bump map. For instance, a scratch in a shiny surface would often be less shiny, so you can use the gradient in your Specular channel to create this effect.

## Slope

This input parameter uses the slope angle of the surface to define it. The slope angle changes according to the angle (in degrees) relative to the ground upon which the surface lies (flat on the y-axis).

The gradient ramp for Slope gives you a range from 0 to 1, representing the slope angle, measured as illustrated in Figure 9-6.

Figure 9-5: Slope gradient

As you can see, the top of the gradient ramp corresponds to the areas
that lie parallel to the ground, while
the bottom of the ramp corresponds to
those areas that lie along the other
angles in relation to the ground.

In this example, a white color is
used for all the areas that are parallel
to the ground plane, while the darker
tones are used for those areas that lie

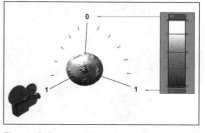

Figure 9-6

at other angles. This sort of effect can be very useful for creating snow on a
mountainous surface, as the white areas, which could represent snow, will
all lie on the areas facing up from the ground, as would happen in real life,
since these are the areas that would receive the snow.

## Incidence Angle

This input parameter is probably one of the most useful gradient types.
Used to create a variety of effects, including the Fresnel effect (discussed

later) and rim lighting, Incidence
Angle allows you to change the
appearance of the surface according to
the angle (in degrees) at which it is
viewed by the camera. The parts of
the surface that are facing directly
toward the camera are therefore lying
at an angle of 90°, while the areas
sloping away are measured at increas-
ingly lower angles.

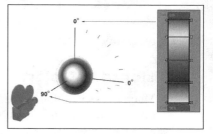

Figure 9-7

In the illustration, we can see the effect of changing the surface color
according to the incidence angle, from white at 90° to black at 0°.

## Light Incidence

Similar to the Incidence Angle, Light Incidence
uses a selected light to set the initial parameter
instead of the camera, so the angle measured is
relative to the position of the light, which you
select from a drop-down list.

Figure 9-8

This particular gradient can be useful for a number of creative effects,
since it essentially allows you to let your lights determine the appearance of
the surface.

Figure 9-9 shows the previously used Incidence Angle gradient
switched to use the Light Incidence gradient instead.

**167**

**Figure 9-9: Light Incidence gradient**

As you can see, the colors that were previously at a 90° angle to the camera when using the Incidence Angle gradient are now instead facing the light at 90°.

Using light incidences can be extremely useful for organic textures, especially when dealing with skin, since they can simulate effects like skin's translucency without having to actually use translucency, which is tricky when texturing thick, solid models like human body parts. (See Part 7 of this book for a tutorial on skin texturing.)

## Distance to Camera

This is rather self-explanatory. The Distance to Camera input parameter simply changes the gradient according to the distance that the surface to which it is applied is from the camera.

You set the distance by entering in the amount at the bottom of the gradient ramp, where it says End.

## Distance to Object

Much the same thing as the Distance to Camera option, this parameter uses another object in the scene as the starting point. You select the object from a drop-down list, and enter the distances in the same fashion as Distance to Camera.

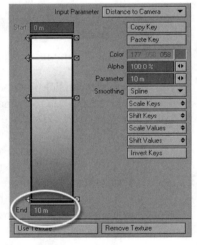

**Figure 9-10**

## X Distance to Object, Y Distance to Object, and Z Distance to Object

Once again, these input parameters use a selected object as the starting point for the gradient, except in these instances the parameters are constrained to the distance along the particular axis that you have chosen to use.

## Distance to Pivot Point

This parameter sets the gradient to take its input from the surface's distance to the pivot point of the object to which the surface is applied.

## X Distance to Pivot Point, Y Distance to Pivot Point, and Z Distance to Pivot Point

This is the same as the previous parameter, only it uses selected axis distance like the axis-dependent Distance to Object parameters.

## Weight Map

This extremely useful gradient type works in conjunction with weight maps, which you create within Modeler. Since this technique is rather more involved than the others discussed here, refer to Chapter 10 for a full demonstration and tutorial.

## Surface Thickness

This gradient allows you to use the object's thickness to apply changes to the appearance of the surface. This can be useful for translucency effects in particular.

In order to have the gradient effects render correctly, you need to have the Double Sided option selected in the Surface Editor, and Ray Trace Transparency needs to be selected in your Render Settings, even if your surface has no degree of transparency.

# Working with Keys

## Creating and Editing Keys

Working with keys is relatively easy. Creating them is simply a matter of clicking anywhere in the ramp, while you can make fine adjustments to their positions and values by entering the desired amounts in the appropriate fields. You can also simply adjust them by manually sliding them into place with the ramp itself. Should you wish to lock the key in place, you can right-click on the little arrow on the left side of the key. Doing this flips the little arrow to face toward the ramp, locking the key in place.

Figure 9-11

Notice that doing this not only locks the key in place, it also locks all the key's parameters, excluding it from any changes you make to the ramp as a whole, such as Shift Keys or Scale Values, discussed in a moment.

To delete a key, you simply click on the little cross on the right side of the key.

You can also copy and paste key values on the ramp using the Copy Key and Paste Key options. So if you want to apply the settings of one key to another, simply click on the key that you wish to copy and click Copy Key, then select the key to which you wish to

Figure 9-12

apply the settings and click Paste Key. This will apply all the settings from the first key to the second.

### Value

The Value setting determines the percentage value of the keys on a gradient applied to any channel, with the exception of color. When a gradient is applied to the Color channel, the Value amount sets the color of the key.

You can manually enter the value percentage or adjust the slider marked with the two arrows accordingly. In the case of a gradient applied to a color channel, the usual text field is replaced instead with RGB values and a color swatch, which you can click on to change to a desired amount. You can also simply drag your cursor on the RGB values themselves to change them.

### Alpha

As you may have noticed when creating keys, there is a field for entering in an alpha amount for each key. This amount controls the opacity of the key within the ramp. This can be useful for blending the gradient nicely with underlying layers with the Texture Editor. As with the Value property, you can adjust the Alpha setting by manually typing in a desired amount or by dragging the arrow button next to the text field backward or forward.

A gray and white checked pattern shows through the keys to indicate a degree of transparency is applied.

### Parameter

The Parameter field allows you to place the position of your keys within the gradient ramp with absolute precision.

As with the Alpha setting, you can adjust the Parameter setting by using the little arrow button next to the text field.

Figure 9-13

### Smoothing

The smoothing of the key determines the way in which the different keys flow into one another, in exactly the same way as the curves in Layout's Graph Editor work. You select the Smoothing type from the drop-down list.

The default smoothing mode is Spline, which is a blend from one amount to the next that eases in

Figure 9-14

and out from one point to the next, much like the splines that you find in LightWave's Graph Editor.

The Linear smoothing mode is similar in effect to Spline, except that it is a straight blend from one key to the next, without any easing in or out.

Figure 9-15: Spline smoothing

Figure 9-16: Linear smoothing

Figure 9-17: Step smoothing

The Step smoothing mode removes any smoothing in the transition between keys, and instead just makes each key totally flat, in a manner of speaking. The value/color of each key basically holds right up until the next key. This smoothing mode is great for achieving a cel-shaded look.

Using combinations of these different smoothing modes can create some very interesting and unusual effects.

## Scale and Shift Keys

Below the Smoothing option are the Scale Keys and Shift Keys buttons.

You use these to scale and shift the positions of all keys on the gradient ramp.

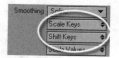
Figure 9-18

Scaling keys up brings the keys on the gradient ramp closer together, while scaling them down spreads them farther apart.

Shifting keys simply shifts the positions of the keys up and down the gradient ramp itself.

This is useful for making mass changes that would otherwise be tedious to do key by key. Note, however, that if any keys have been locked (as discussed earlier), they will be unaffected by these changes.

## Scale and Shift Values

Next are the Scale Values and Shift Values buttons.

Similar to the aforementioned buttons, these do exactly the same thing, except in this case they apply to the values of the keys, as opposed to their positions.

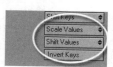
Figure 9-19

Scaling the values up increases the individual numeric percentage values of each of the keys, while scaling them down decreases them.

Shifting values simply shifts the overall base percentage value of all the keys from high to low.

### Invert Keys

Selecting the Invert Keys option switches all the keys on a gradient ramp around. It basically flips them.

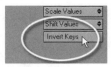

Figure 9-20

## Gradient Tutorials

### Tutorial 1: Making a Velvet Surface for an Old Hat

In this tutorial, we will use a combination of a few different kinds of gradients, as well as some procedural textures, to create a velvet surface. This technique can be varied and applied to any type of surface that requires a soft look, such as fabric or skin.

1.  Open Layout and load the 3.4.4-Tutorial_01.lws scene from the Tutorials\ Scenes folder on the companion CD-ROM. A scene loads, consisting of a hat object on a ground surface, lit by area lighting. Feel free to adjust the lighting or rendering settings to suit yourself.

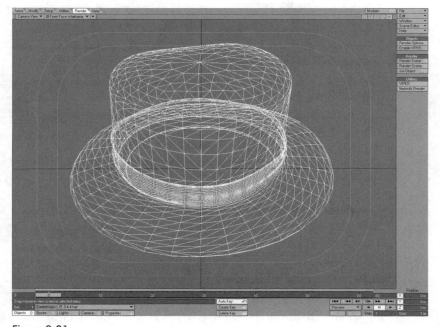

Figure 9-21

2. Open the Surface Editor. Notice the hat has two different surfaces applied to it, one for the hat itself and one for the satin band wrapped around it.

Let's set up the satin surface first.

Assign the following values to the surface attributes:

Color: 13, 14, 28
Luminosity: 0%
Diffuse: 90%
Specularity: 30%
Glossiness: 20%
Reflection: 0%
Transparency: 0%
Translucency: 0%
Smoothing: on

3. Click on the "T" button next to the color values in the Color channel.

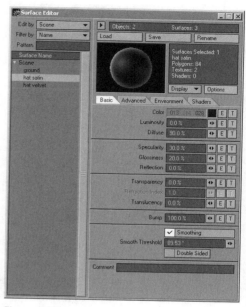

Figure 9-22

**Figure 9-23**

This opens the Texture Editor for the Color channel. What we want to do now is set up some gradients to simulate the falloff effect of lighting on fabrics. This is indeed a faking of the effect, but since it works, we will do it!

4. Make a new gradient layer by clicking on the Add Layer button and specifying Gradient.

We now have a gradient layer. Change the Input Parameter of the gradient to Incidence Angle. We will set up this gradient to mimic the light falling and creating that soft glow that we see along folds of fabric.

**Figure 9-24**

5. Create a new key near the middle of the gradient ramp. In the Parameter field, type in a value of 30; the key will now move to that position on the ramp. Set the color of this key to 243, 243, 243 and set its Alpha value to 60%, as shown in Figure 9-25.

6.  Create another key at the very bottom of the gradient ramp. Make sure that its Parameter value is 90. Change its color to black and set the Alpha to 0%.

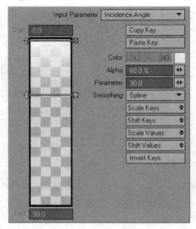

Figure 9-25

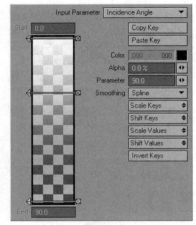

Figure 9-26

7.  Create another key, this time a bit above the bottom key. Set its Parameter to 75, its color to black, and its Alpha to 0%.

    Take a look at the preview window in the Surface Editor, and notice how this gradient affects the surface. It has created a nice "lit" edge to the surface. Now, if we were to render this as it is, it would appear very strange, because all the edges would appear to be lit, when in fact the only areas that would appear this way in reality would be the ones receiving direct light from the lighting source in the scene.

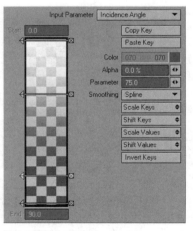

Figure 9-27

    So, what do we do to rectify this?

The answer is rather simple — we use another gradient, this time a Light Incidence gradient.

8.  Create a new gradient layer on top of the first one. This layer will act as a mask for the underlying layer so that the effect will appear to be caused by the lighting.

    Set the Input Parameter for this gradient as Light Incidence, and select Area Light from the Light drop-down list.

9. Create a key at the very top of the gradient, and another key at the very bottom. Select the top one and set its color to white (255, 255, 255) and its Alpha to 100%. Select the bottom one and set its color to black (0, 0, 0) and its Alpha to 100% as well.

   Now create a third key in between the other two. Set its Parameter to 50, and leave its color as it is.

10. Because we want this gradient to act as a mask, we need to set up the layer so that it does exactly that. We do this by changing the Blending Mode of the layer to Alpha. This uses the data in the layer as an alpha channel for the underlying layer. By doing this, the gradient will now essentially mask the effect of the first gradient, so that it appears as if the "lit edges" look we created is actually created by the area light. Pretty clever!

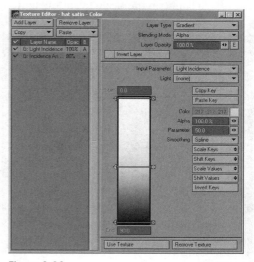

Figure 9-28

11. However, this overall effect is perhaps just a little too strong. Go to the first gradient and set the Blending Mode of that layer to Additive. Change Layer Opacity to 80%. This softens the effect somewhat.

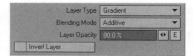

Figure 9-29

   Look in the preview window in the Surface Editor; your surface should now look something like Figure 9-30.

Figure 9-30

12. This is just a little too smooth though, so we need to add a slight bump to it, just to give it a little more texture. Click on the little "T" button next to Bump in the Surface Editor to open up the Bump attribute's Texture Editor.

13. Create a new layer and choose Procedural as the Layer Type. This creates a Procedural Texture layer. For the Procedural Type, choose Turbulence. (See Figure 9-31.)

Set the Turbulence up as follows:

Texture Value: 10%
Frequencies: 15
Contrast: 20%
Small Power: 2.0

Then, on the Scale tab at the bottom of the panel, enter 100mm for each axis, as shown in Figure 9-32.

Figure 9-31

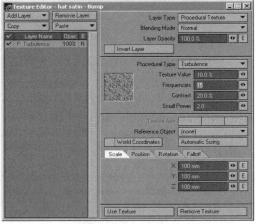

Figure 9-32

That adds a slight texture to the satin material, which gives it a little more substance.

We now move on to the velvet surface.

14. Go to the "hat velvet" surface in the Surface Editor, and enter the following values for each attribute:

Color: 64, 9, 9
Luminosity: 0%
Diffuse: 80%
Specularity: 10%
Glossiness: 0%
Reflection: 0%
Transparency: 0%
Translucency: 0%

Ensure that Smoothing is on.

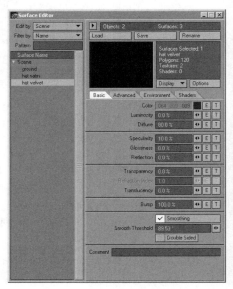

Figure 9-33

15. Open the Texture Editor for the Color attribute by clicking the little "T" button next to it and create a new gradient layer.

16. This process is, for the most part, almost exactly the same as for the satin surface.

   Because of this, we can actually copy the gradients that we previously made into this surface. To do this, go back to the "hat satin" surface and open the color Texture Editor. Select the first gradient that we made (the Incidence Angle one) and click on the Copy button above the layer list. Select Selected Layer(s). This copies the surface into memory.

Figure 9-34

   Go back to the Texture Editor for color in your velvet surface. Select the layer that you made there and press the Paste button above the layer list. Select Replace Selected Layer(s). This pastes all the settings from the gradient you copied into this one.

Figure 9-35

17. We do not want these settings to remain exactly the same in this particular surface, as it is a different type of material. Keep all the keys in their current positions; they are fine the way they are. Select the first gradient, the Light Incidence one, and change its Layer Opacity to 40%. This lessens the effect of the gradient, making it a little softer and more velvet-like.

18. We need to set up the bump map so that the velvet appears nice and fuzzy. Click on the "T" button next to the Bump channel to open the Bump Texture Editor.

   Create a new Procedural Texture layer by selecting Procedural from the Add Layer list.

   From the Procedural Type menu, select Turbulence, and set it up as follows:

Texture Value: 80%
Frequencies: 15
Contrast: 20%
Small Power: 2.0

On the Scale tab at the bottom of the panel, enter 100mm for each axis.

   This creates a perfect fuzzy texture for the velvet.

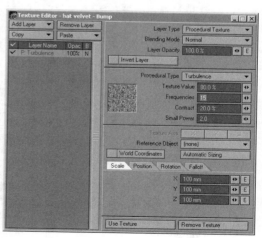

Figure 9-36

19. Close the Texture Editor, and go to the Advanced tab in the Surface Editor. Change the Color Highlights setting to 50% and the Diffuse Sharpness to 40%. This just creates a softer, more appropriate light hotspot falloff for the velvet surface.

Figure 9-37

20. Render the image. You now have a velvet hat!

## Tutorial 2: Snowy Mountain

Okay, let's make some snow on a big mountain. For this tutorial we'll be using the Slope gradient to place snow on the more horizontal areas of the mountain so that the steep slopes remain rocky, as well as the Y Distance to Pivot Point gradient in conjunction with some procedurals to create some greenery around the foothills.

1. Open Layout and load the 3.4.4-Tutorial_02.lws scene from the Tutorials\ Scenes folder on the companion CD-ROM. You see a scene with a volcano object (3.4.4-volcano.lwo in the Tutorials\Objects folder) sitting on a plain ground plane object.

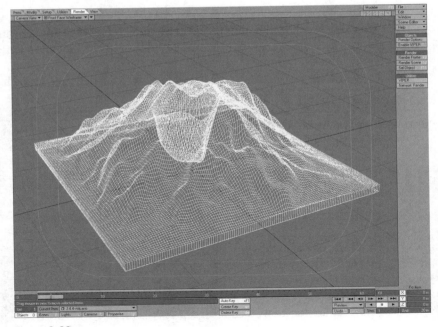

Figure 9-38

2. Open up the Surface Editor and select the "volcano rock and snow" surface. Set up the basic surface attributes as follows:

Color: 65, 40, 35 (a dark reddish brown)
Diffuse: 70%
Specularity: 5%
Glossiness: 20%
Bump: 100%

Leave all the other surface values at 0%. This sets up a plain brown surface
that has a very slight shine to it. This will be the basic dull rock-like surface
of the mountain.

3. Let's start off by creating the bump mapping for the rocks. Click on the
"T" button next to Bump to open the Texture Editor for the surface's
bump attribute. Create a procedural texture on the default layer, using
the Crumple Procedural Type.

Set up the texture settings as follows:

Texture Value: 100%
Frequencies: 4
Small Power: 0.75

Set the Scale parameters to
1m for X, 6m for Y, and 1m
for Z in the Scale tab.

On top of this proce-
dural texture, create a new
Procedural Texture layer by
clicking on Add Layer>
Procedural. Select Hetero
Terrain as the Procedural
Type and set the texture
settings as follows:

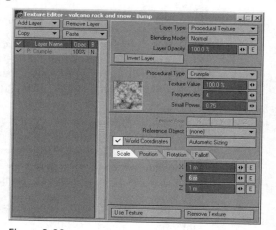

Figure 9-39

Texture Value: 30%
Increment: 0.5
Lacunarity: 2.0
Octaves: 6.0
Offset: 0.35
Noise Type: Perlin Noise

Set each of the Scale parameters to 20m in the Scale tab.
We have now created a fairly generic, bumpy rockiness for the surface.
Now let's make some snow.

4. Go back to the Surface Editor and click on the "T" button next to Color
to open the Texture Editor for the surface's color attribute. Change the
default layer that is created to a gradient layer by clicking on the Layer
Type button at the top right and selecting Gradient.

**179**

Change the Input Parameter to Slope. When you create this gradient, a key is automatically created for you at the top of the gradient ramp. We can leave this key exactly as it is. Click a little way below this top key to create another key. Change its Alpha value to 90% and the Parameter value to 0.2. We are now creating snow that lies on the horizontal and slightly sloping areas of the mountain object.

Click again just below the second key to create a third one. Make sure that its Parameter value is 0.3, and change its Alpha value to 0%.

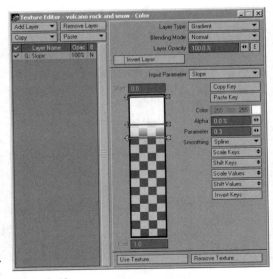

Figure 9-40

This now makes the snow completely disappear as the object slopes downward. If you render your object now, you should get something that looks like Figure 9-41.

> **NOTE:** I have set the lighting up in the scene to use pure radiosity to light it. If you find that the render is too slow for your machine, simply go to your Global Illumination panel and switch the Radiosity option off, then set the Global Intensity value back to 100%.

Figure 9-41

Okay, so we have a mountain that now has some decent snowfall on it. How about adding a touch of greenery along the bottom of the slopes to show some forest areas or just some grassy knolls? This will help to break up the monotony of the brown color on the slopes.

5. Create a new procedural layer (below the Slope gradient layer), and select Turbulence (my most favorite procedural for doing practically anything). Set its color to a nice medium green with the following RGB values: 35, 80, 25. Set up the actual texture as follows:

Frequencies: 5
Contrast: 90%
Small Power: 1.0

Set the Scale values on the Scale tab to 500mm for each axis, as shown in Figure 9-42.

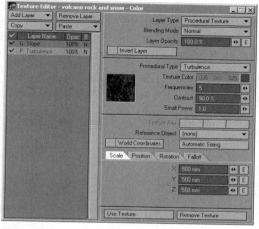

The problem with this procedural is that right now it covers the entire surface. We only really want it along the foothills of the mountain, so we need to have it only growing up to a certain height. This is where the Y Distance to Pivot Point gradient comes in handy.

**Figure 9-42**

6.  Create a new gradient layer by clicking on the New Layer button and choosing Gradient. Place this gradient above the procedural layer, so that it sits between the procedural and the Slope gradient layers.

Change the Input Parameter of this gradient to Y Distance to Pivot Point. Now, if you select the mountain object in Layout, you'll notice that its pivot is exactly at the bottom of the object, on the ground.

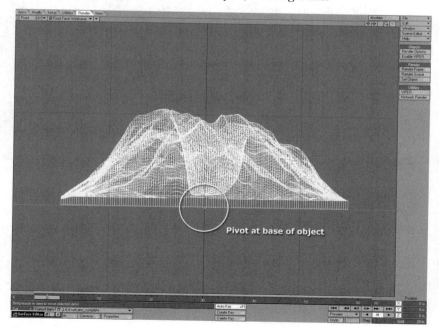

Pivot at base of object

**Figure 9-43**

So this particular gradient will take its information and allow variations according to the distance along the y-axis from that pivot point.

Let's set up the gradient so that it will mask the procedural, and allow it to show only along the base of the mountain.

7.  Change the Blending Mode of the layer to Alpha. This is because we want this gradient to act as a mask for the underlying procedural texture.

> **NOTE:**   Refer to Chapter 13 for more information on blending layers correctly and effectively.

Right now, the entire gradient is white, so it is not masking anything, as the white areas of an alpha layer are the areas that allow the underlying layer to show through. Since black areas mask the underlying layer, we need to mask the procedural as it climbs higher along the y-axis of the object. To do this, we need to first specify the maximum height that we would like the green areas to grow up to.

8.  Click in the field at the bottom of the gradient ramp where it says End and enter a value of 15m. Now create a key at the bottom of the ramp (ensure that the Parameter value is set at 15m), and set its color to black (RGB 0, 0, 0).

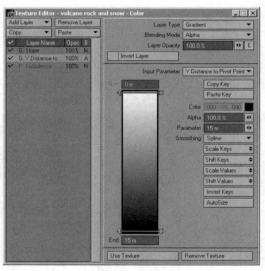

This allows the green procedural texture to be visible only up until it reaches a distance of 15m above the pivot point at the base of the object.

And that pretty much does the trick! Rendering your scene out now, you should get something that looks like Figure 9-45.

Figure 9-44

Figure 9-45

Mmmm ... reminds me of mint chocolate for some reason. And there you have it! A snowy mountain peak. Simple, yet effective for those long-distance shots that call for far-away snowy peaks.

# Tutorial 3: Simulating the Fresnel Effect in Glass

Although LightWave does include two different Fresnel shaders (discussed in the
Shaders section of Chapter 5) to create this
effect, we can also create it very simply using
gradients. This tutorial demonstrates setting
up a glass surface using gradients to simulate
this effect on the LightWave logo.

The Fresnel effect is the phenomenon
that we observe in the real world whereby
the amount of reflection that we see on a sur-

**Figure 9-46**

face differs according to the angle at which we view it.

This effect is not just found in transparent substances, but in anything
that is reflective to any degree.

Now let's get down to business and make it ourselves!

1. Open up the 3.4.4-Tutorial_03.lws scene file from the Tutorials\Scenes
folder on the companion CD-ROM. The scene should load with a
LightWave logo (3.4.4-LW_logo.lwo) placed in the center of the camera
view.

**Figure 9-47**

Because we are working with a glass surface, we need to give the
object an environment to reflect. Check that the Beach_Probe HDRI image

(located in the Tutorials\Images folder) is loaded in the scene and has been added to the Image World in your Backdrop options (Ctrl+F5).

2. Okay, now that we know that the scene is all ready to be worked with, let's go to the Surface Editor. If you have ever tried making glass surfaces before, you may know that they can be pretty darn tricky sometimes. Select the surface "logo glass" in the Surface Editor, and enter the following amounts for each of the basic attributes:

Color: 0, 0, 0 (pure black)
Luminosity: 0%
Diffuse: 0%
Specularity: 30%
Glossiness: 20%
Reflection: 0%
Transparency: 0%
Refraction Index: 1.5
Translucency: 0%

Ensure that Smoothing and Double Sided are on.

You are probably wondering why we have entered in values of 0% for the Reflection and Transparency channels when we are making reflective glass! The reason for this is that when we create the gradients in each channel, we do not need to enter in an overall amount, as LightWave will take all its input for each channel from the gradient itself.

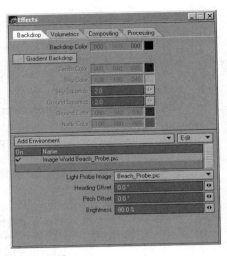

Figure 9-48

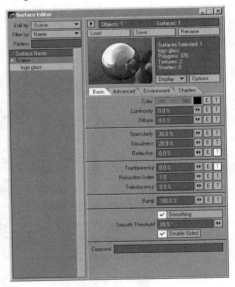

Figure 9-49

3. Now that we have determined all the basic attributes, we need to create the gradients. Go to the Transparency channel and open its Texture Editor by clicking on the "T" button. Create a new gradient layer in the Texture Editor, and set the Input Parameter of the gradient to Incidence Angle.

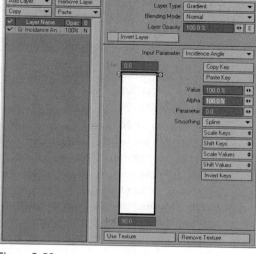

Figure 9-50

4. Now, create a new key at the bottom of the gradient. Make sure that the Parameter value for this key is 90.0. Leave its Alpha at 100%. See Figure 9-51.

This key represents any part of the surface that is facing us at 90°, in other words, the part of the logo that faces us straight on. Having this value set to 100% means that these parts of the surface will appear to be 100% transparent when we look at the logo.

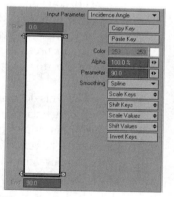

Figure 9-51

5. Go back to the top key at Parameter 0, and change its Value setting to 0%. This should make the color of this key in the gradient go to black. See Figure 9-52.

This key represents the parts of the surface that face us at an angle of 0°. These are the areas that are sloping away from our direct vision, and we have entered in a value of 0, which means that these areas will not appear to be transparent.

6. However, to make the effect a little easier to observe, let's add another key to the gradient to allow for a little more transparency, so that the transparency will appear stronger for a further few degrees.

Figure 9-52

**185**

Create a key a little above the bottom key, and then ensure that its Parameter value is 70 and its Value is 100% as well, as in Figure 9-53.

This means that the effect of the transparency will remain at 100% for a bit more than it would have without this extra key. This is really just for effect, and is not entirely necessary ordinarily.

7. Okay, now we have set up the Transparency channel as we want it. According to the way in which the Fresnel effect works, we understand that the reflection should basically be the exact opposite of the transparency, because the reflection increases as the transparency decreases.

Figure 9-53

So all we need to do now to set up the reflection properties is to copy this gradient and paste it into the Reflection channel. Once you have done this, simply press the Invert Keys button to invert the gradient.

What this does now is give you the exact counterpart of the Transparency channel's gradient. The reflection and transparency values of this surface should now be creating the Fresnel effect perfectly, as the gradients are now creating the effect of decreasing trans-

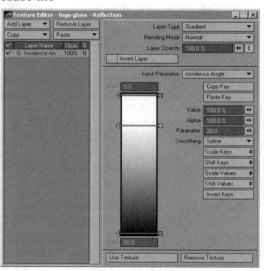

Figure 9-54

parency toward the edges of the object, while the reflection gradient is increasing the reflection value at the edges.

8. We need to adjust one more setting to this surface before it is ready to be rendered. Go to the Advanced tab in the Surface Editor. You see the setting called Color Highlights? Change its value to 50%. This is handy for preventing an overblown look on the glass when it is rendered, which is a common problem when making glass.

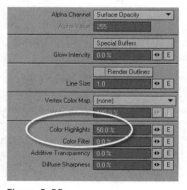

Figure 9-55

9. Now we are ready to render! Ensure that you have activated all your necessary ray-tracing options (Shadows, Reflection, Refraction) in your Render Options panel to ensure that it renders correctly. You can set the Ray Recursion Limit to 8 to save on rendering time.

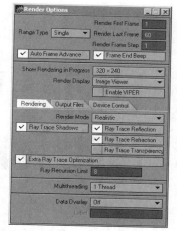

**Figure 9-56**

10. Hit the render button (F9)! To improve the chunkiness of the logo when it renders and give it a smoother glass look, you can change the Render SubPatch Level in the Object Properties dialog to a higher value to increase its smoothness when rendered.

When you render, your logo should look like Figure 9-58.

Notice how the Fresnel effect can be observed in the glass. The reflection becomes much stronger as the surface slopes away from your direct vision.

If we had not used the gradients to create the Fresnel effect on the surface, the glass would have looked like it does in Figure 9-59.

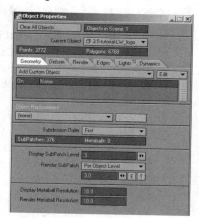

**Figure 9-57**

**Figure 9-58**

As you can see, it is a rather big difference! Render the logo from a few different angles and see how the effect works. As I am sure you will agree, this effect is great for added believability in reflective objects, as its behavior is much more realistic. Remember to incorporate this effect into all your reflective objects!

**Figure 9-59**

# CHAPTER 10

# Using Weight Maps for Texturing

## Using Weight Maps to Control the Input and Placement of Gradients and Textures

Did you know that weight maps have another use apart from their role in preparing models for rigging? Indeed they do! You can use weight maps in conjunction with gradients to easily control the visibility and placement of colors and textures on your model, which, needless to say, is extraordinarily useful!

This can be especially handy when working with procedural textures, since they can otherwise be pretty darn tricky to control.

All you need to do is create a weight map, a really simple process, and then use it as an input parameter for a gradient layer in your surface. You then set this layer up as an alpha layer to control the texture layers that you need to. Easy stuff.

In the Node Editor, weight maps have their own node. You can connect the weight map node output directly to the opacity inputs of other nodes in the network. Even though you don't really need a gradient in order to use weight maps in the Node Editor, you can achieve further control using weight maps along with a gradient. To get the same result as you would in the layer system, just connect the weight map output to a gradient's input.

You can learn more about weight maps and gradients in the Node Editor in Chapter 14, "The Node Editor."

Take a look at this guy (you may recognize him from a texturing contest that NewTek ran in 2003).

All the details that you see on this guy's face and head were created using a combination of

Model by William Vaughan

Figure 10-1

**188**

procedural textures and gradients that are using weight maps. Some of the gradients are used solely to create differences in color, such as to create the subtle changes in skin tone and that little white streak on his forehead, while some of the gradients are used to control the visibility of procedural textures, such as seen on the hair bits.

For this example, I created a number of different weight maps for each of the different details. Figure 10-2 shows the weight map that I created for placing the hair procedurals.

This weight map, used as an input parameter for a gradient, was then used as an alpha layer over the procedural layer that I used to create the hair look.

So how do weight maps work? Well, you simply paint values onto your model, the orangey areas being strong positive values and the blue areas being negative values. The entire range of positive and negative values influences the gradient that they are set up with. Figure 10-3 shows the gradient set up with the previously shown and mentioned painted weight map.

Figure 10-2 (See the color image on the companion CD for a better view of the weight details.)

As you can see, this gradient is acting as an alpha layer (note the Blending Mode setting) for the procedural texture below it, which creates the hair texture. This particular model had quite a few different

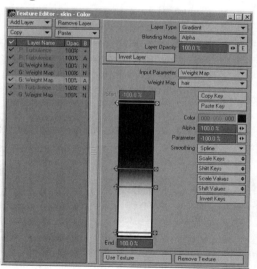

Figure 10-3

weight maps made for it for placing all the procedurals that you see in this image, as well as for placing simple colors. Figure 10-4 shows the weight map and gradient used to create the white markings on the character's face. As you can see, this gradient simply creates color at certain weight values.

**189**

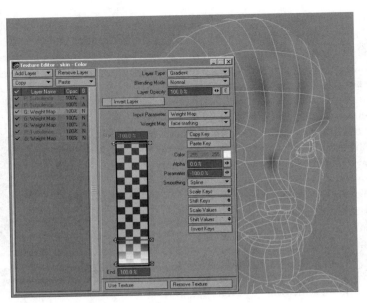

Figure 10-4

So we can use weight maps to control both the placement and visibility of procedural textures when used as alpha layers, as well as use them to pinpoint the positions of different colors by using them in conjunction with gradients that act as solid texture layers.

## Creating Weight Maps and Weight Map Gradients

The process of creating the actual weight maps is really easy. You simply go to the Map tab in Modeler, and select the New Weight Map option under the Weight heading. You then enter a name for the weight map, and you can enter an Initial Value.

Figure 10-5

The Initial Value sets an overall value for the new weight map. Generally, since we would ideally want to make use of the entire range of values available in weight maps (from –100% to 100%), it is usually most practical to enter an Initial Value of 0%.

This creates a weight map that is colored green, basically the weight map equivalent of a blank canvas. You can then paint areas that increase the value, and these areas become a reddish-orange. Decreasing the value results in blue areas.

Use the Airbrush tool under the General
heading on your Map tab to interactively paint
your weight map. You can open its options panel
(by clicking the "n" button) and set up the way
that you want it to affect the weight map.

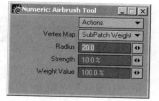

Once you have set this up, you can simply
paint the cursor across your surface, just like an
airbrush. Be aware that this tool can slow down

Figure 10-6

Modeler slightly. Remember that just like UV maps, weight maps are calculated at vertices, so it is only on the points in your model that the values can
be increased or decreased. In other words, you cannot paint an entire pattern onto a single polygon. Because of this, weight maps (just like UV maps)
can work more precisely with models that have higher polygon counts. Your
polygon count need not be extraordinarily high, but just high enough to
ensure you can create enough detail. The more detail you want, the higher
your polygon count will need to be.

My favorite method of creating weight maps is to simply select the
points that I wish to adjust, and then use the Weights tool to adjust their
values.

All you do is select the points that you want to affect while in Points
selection mode (Ctrl+g) and then select the Weights tool. Your cursor
becomes a little crosshair-type cursor.

You then drag the
crosshair over the
selected points to
adjust their weight.
Dragging the cursor
right increases their
values, while drag-
ging them left
decreases them. The
Weight tool also has a
Falloff option, which allows
you to create a smooth
weight gradient to the
selected points.

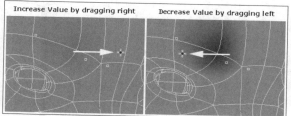

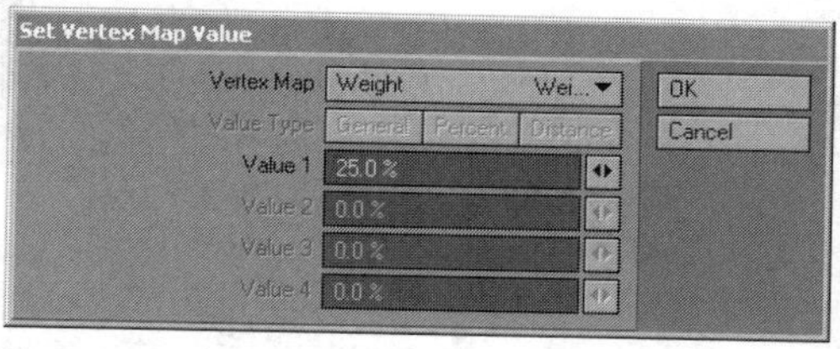

Figure 10-7

Alternatively, you can
use the Set Map Value command at the top of the Map

Figure 10-8

tab panel to numerically change weight values at points. Select the points
that you wish to adjust, and then open the Set Vertex Map Value panel.

You can then enter in a desired value for the selected points and click
OK. This allows you to specify exact values, which gives you a little more
control. You can also, of course, use this to fine-tune an already made weight

**191**

map. Remember that when it comes to setting up your gradient, you often want to have precise values in certain areas, as it makes placing the keys within the gradient a little easier because you know the precise values at which you need to create them.

Now that we have created a weight map, we need to create the gradient that works with it.

When used with a gradient, the green areas in the weight map are in the middle at 0%, the blue areas correspond with the top of the gradient (which begins at –100%), and the orange areas with the bottom, as shown in Figure 10-9.

As you can see, the positive values can exceed 100% if you wish, but generally using values in the range of –100% to 100% suffices. If you create a weight map that contains values exceeding 100%, simply enter in the new highest value at the bottom of the gradient where it says End. Values in a weight map that exceed 100% appear bright purple and pink. Values that go below –100% are dark blue, although you cannot use those in a gradient.

Figure 10-9

So now that we know how the weight map values correlate, in terms of position, to the gradient in the Surface Editor, setting the gradient up to work as a texture layer or alpha layer is straightforward. To link a certain color or value to a particular value in the weight map, we simply create a key on the gradient at that value and set up the color or value as we wish. If, for example, I wanted all the areas of the weight map that are at 100% to have the color white, I would simply create a key at 100% in the gradient, and set its color to white, as shown in Figure 10-10.

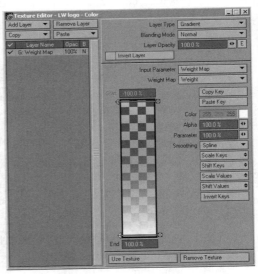

Figure 10-10

And if I then wanted to make all the areas that have weight values of 25% blue, then I would just create another key at 25% and set its color to blue.

If I were using this gradient as an alpha layer for a procedural texture, I would create the procedural texture and set it up as I wish, and then create the gradient layer over it, with a key at the weight map value where I want the procedural to be visible. I would then set that key to be white, and set the other values on the gradient to black. This would ensure that only the white areas of the gradient will allow the procedural to be visible, which means that the procedural will appear in the areas that we painted that weight value.

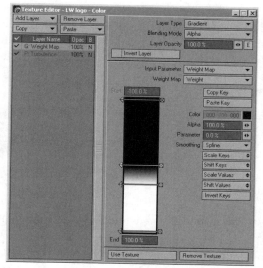

**Figure 10-11**

Figure 10-11 shows a weight map being used to control the visibility of a Turbulence procedural texture. As you can see, the areas of the weight map that have values between 30% (the selected key) and 100% will show the procedural texture.

If I were to create another key at –50% and set it to white as well, as shown in Figure 10-12, the procedural would also be visible in areas of the weight map that have the value of –50%.

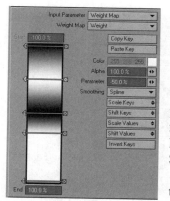

**Figure 10-12**

**Figure 10-13**

As you can see, the falloff of the values between keys is totally linear, and in this instance you can see that the values surrounding the areas that have keys created will also show the procedural slightly. You can fine-tune this by adding more keys or by changing the Smoothing value of the key. This tightens the falloff of the gradient so that the edges of the procedural (in this case) are sharper and more distinct, as opposed to gradually fading into the surrounding areas of the surface.

As you can see, this process of using weight maps and gradients is really simple! And you can create as many procedural textures with weight maps as their alphas as you like in the Surface Editor.

## Weight Map Tutorial: The LightWave Logo

This tutorial briefly covers the process of creating weight maps and using them to create color variations and to control the visibility of procedural textures on a surface.

1. Load the 3.5-tutorial-LW_logo.lwo object from the Tutorials\Objects folder on the companion CD-ROM into Modeler. Set up one of your viewports (preferably the Perspective viewport) to display Weight Shade. This ensures that we will be able to see what we are doing correctly.

2. Go to the Map tab and under the Weight heading, select New Weight Map to create a new weight map. Name the weight map "colors" and set its Initial Value to 0.0%. Press OK.

Figure 10-14

We will use this weight map to assign different colors to different parts of the model.

3. In Points selection mode (Ctrl+g), select all the points of the spikes that surround the main squiggle of the logo. Click on Set Map Value and enter a value of –100%.

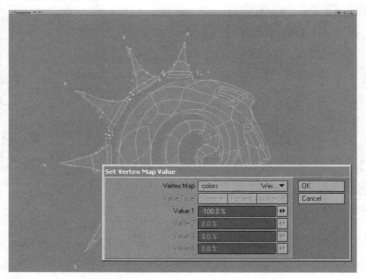

Figure 10-15

You should now have something that looks like Figure 10-16.

Figure 10-16

4. Now select the points on the inner part of the logo spiral. Click on Set Map Value and enter a value of 100%. Your weight map should now look like Figure 10-17.

Figure 10-17

5. Create another weight map. Call it "procedural" and set its Initial Value to 0.0%.

Figure 10-18

We will use this weight map as an alpha layer to control the visibility of a procedural texture.

6. Select the entire tail part of the spiral, and click on Set Map Value. Set the value to 100%. This will be the area where the procedural will be visible.

Figure 10-19

7. Save the model, close Modeler, and go into Layout. Load the model and open up the Surface Editor. Open up the Texture Editor for the color channel by clicking on the "T" in the Surface Editor.

Figure 10-20

8. A layer is automatically created in the Texture Editor when you open it. Change the Layer Type to Gradient and select Weight Map as the Input Parameter. Select the "colors" weight map from the Weight Map list.

9. Create a key at 100% and another key at 0% on the gradient. You should now have three keys on the gradient.

Select the key at –100% (at the top of the gradient) and set its color up as 240, 255, 15. This creates a yellow color.

Now select the key at 0% (in the middle of the gradient) and set it up as 230, 50, 25. Your gradient should now be a yellow fading into a red at 0%.

Select the key at 100% (at the bottom of the gradient) and set up its color as 70, 50, 160.

Your gradient should now look like Figure 10-22.

10. Click on Add Layer and select to create a procedural layer on top of the gradient layer. Set the Procedural Type to Veins and set it up as follows:

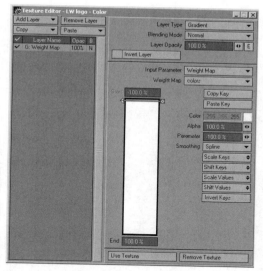

**Figure 10-21**

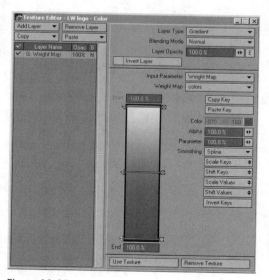

**Figure 10-22**

Set the Color to 255, 255, 255. Set Coverage to 0.02 and leave the Ledge Level and Ledge Width as they are. Go to the Scale tab and set the size to 10mm, 10mm, 10mm. (See Figure 10-23.)

11. The procedural that we have just created is, by default, assigned to the entire surface. However, since we wish to control its visibility using the "procedural" weight map that we created, we create a new gradient layer on top of it. So click on Add Layer, add a new gradient layer with its Input Parameter set to Weight Map, and select the "procedural" weight map from the Weight Map list.

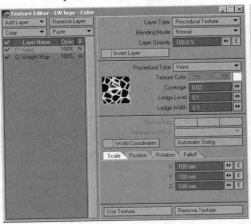

Figure 10-23

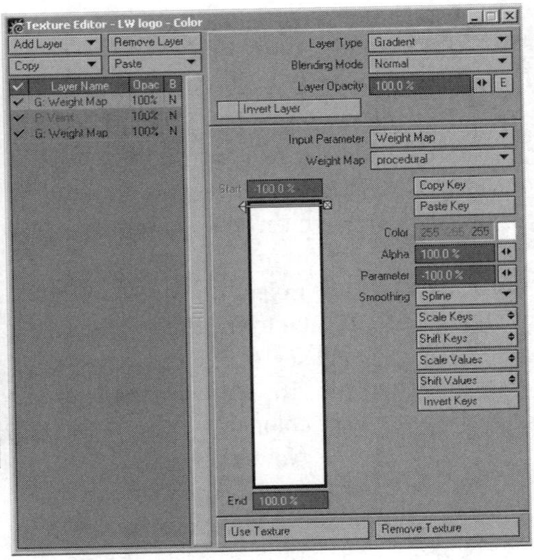

Figure 10-24

12. Remember that when we created this weight map, we selected the tail part of the spiral and assigned it a value of 100%. We will now use that value as the value that "reveals" the procedural. So we create a key at 100% on the gradient and leave its color as white (the default). Create another key at 0% (middle of the gradient) and set its color to black. Select the key at the top of the gradient (–100%) and set its color to black as well.

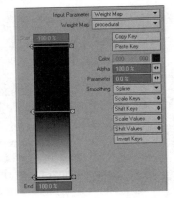

Figure 10-25

We set it up like this because we want to use this gradient as an alpha layer for the procedural layer beneath it. As we know, alpha layers work with black and white, where black hides the preceding layer and white reveals it. Change the layer Blending Mode to Alpha. This gradient will now show the Veins procedural only on the tail part of the spiral to which we assigned a weight value of 100%.

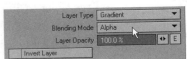

Figure 10-26

Render the image. Your render should look like Figure 10-27.

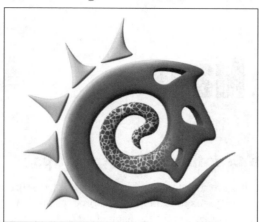

**Figure 10-27**

Of course, this tutorial demonstrates a very simple example of this process. You can create far more complex weight maps and thereby create much more interesting and realistic textures for your models. Remember that you have an entire range of values to create weight maps from, and you can utilize this entire range to place colors and procedurals on your surface.

I have included the model shown at the beginning of this chapter on the companion CD-ROM so that you can have a look at how all those different procedurals were set up on that character. Look in the Models folder and find the Newtek Texturing Character.lwo model, made by William Vaughan.

# CHAPTER 11

# Image Maps

## Conventions for the Creation of Image Maps

Images used for texturing are usually called image maps or texture maps.

The art of creating image maps is an involved process and a very exciting one! But before we start exploring this fascinating task, we need to discuss some of the conventions and options that you must take into consideration before you start painting.

> **NOTE:** This entire chapter requires that the reader have access to and a working knowledge of a 2D painting application such as Adobe Photoshop.

## Deciding on Image Resolution and Size

Deciding on an appropriate size for your image maps is very important for a number of reasons, and the size you select in the end will be decided upon according to your needs as well as your computer resources.

The first thing that you need to consider is the size at which the final frames will be output. This will depend on the intended output format: video for television, film, CD-ROM, or larger formats like IMAX.

Some common broadcast and film resolution sizes are as follows:

**Broadcast resolutions:**

| | |
|---|---|
| D1 NTSC | 720 × 480 |
| D1 PAL | 720 × 576 |
| HDTV | 1280 × 720 |
| HDTV | 1920 × 1080 |

**Film resolutions:**

| | |
|---|---|
| Cineon Half | 1828 × 1332 |
| Film (2K) | 2048 × 1536 |
| Cineon Full | 3656 × 2664 |

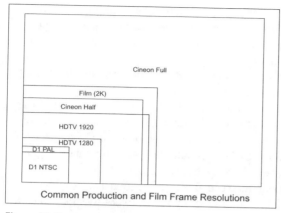

Common Production and Film Frame Resolutions

**Figure 11-1**

Now that you know your final output size, you need to ensure that your textures are going to look great when viewed at this size.

Since image maps are raster images (images made out of pixels, as opposed to vector graphics), they are prone to losing detail and tend to appear jagged (pixelated) when viewed up close. Pixellation is basically when your image becomes ruined due to the pixels within it being stretched beyond their original size or being overly compressed. This results in the image being pretty horrible to look at since it loses all its clarity. Since you want to ensure that your textures will always look good, no matter how big they appear on-screen, you need to make sure that your image maps are large enough to be viewed at such sizes without any loss of clarity.

The best way to do this is to roughly work out the largest size at which any portion of the texture will appear on-screen. If, for instance, you are texturing a face that is seen full-screen at any point in time, then you want to make sure that your texture maps that are used on the face will look good if they fill the screen. If the camera zooms in on the face, and there is a close-up shot of, for example, the character's mouth, you are going to have to ensure that the image maps for the face are so large that they will look good even when only that small portion of them is viewed full-screen.

If this latter shot were to be broadcast on television at a resolution of 720 × 576 pixels, then you would have to consider that the image maps used on the face are going to have to be large enough to ensure that the textures around the mouth will look fine even though they will fill the entire screen. This means that your texture maps for the entire face are going to have to be pretty big, to be sure that just the section around the mouth does not look jagged or blurry.

Once you have roughly ascertained the largest size at which any portion of the image map will appear on the screen, you can work out an appropriate size by then multiplying that size by two, and working out the size of the entire map like that.

To illustrate that a little more simply, let's assume that you are texturing a human face, and that the largest the face appears in the final cut is in a shot where the face fills the screen. This means that the entire image map for the face will appear at a size of 720 × 576 pixels at this point. The safest way to calculate an appropriate size for the image maps for the face would then be to multiply 720 pixels by two, to get a total of 1440 pixels. If you were to texture this face with UV maps, which are always square-shaped, you would then ensure that you make all your UV-mapped images a minimum size of 1440 × 1440 pixels.

Obviously, as illustrated previously, this calculation can be a little trickier if there are any major close-ups involved.

Let's return now to the previous example of the mouth close-up. Let's assume that in the close-up shot of the mouth, approximately one-third of the face will appear on the screen. This means that one-third of the face will be appearing at a size of 720 × 576 pixels, and therefore the image map for that area of the face has to be at least twice that size, for that area alone. In order to ensure that the image map remains crisp at such a close-up view, you will first need to multiply that number by three, to get the total size (at a one-to-one ratio) for the image maps for the entire face, and then double it to get a safe size, to ensure that the quality remains acceptable. This means that your safest bet for the size of your image maps for that face would therefore be 4320 × 4320 pixels.

Although using this double image size is highly recommended for the best clarity possible for your textures, you may find that your computer may not always be able to handle such large images, especially if you are going to be rendering for film, in which case your image sizes are going to be huge.

Large images use a lot more system memory, both during the actual creation process and during rendering. If you are working on a computer that is slightly older or not particularly powerful, it is advisable to take your system's resources into consideration. An image's size in megabytes will use approximately 10 times that amount of system memory when used within LightWave. In your Image Editor (see Chapter 12) you can monitor the total amount of memory being used by the images in your scene.

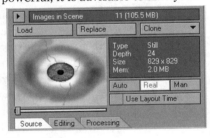

**Figure 11-2**

Naturally, if you are using a computer that has low resources, this can significantly slow things down.

This means that sometimes you may be forced to use smaller images in order to increase the speed of your workflow and rendering. If this is the case, it is still important to try to keep your images as large as you possibly can; however, should you be in a situation where you cannot even match a one-to-one size with the image maps, as compared to the final frame size, then perhaps it is time for a system upgrade!

If you have a super fast and powerful workstation, then by all means go wild with your image sizes, since the larger they are, the crisper and clearer your textures are going to appear, and the more delicate details you can include in them.

## Using Grayscale Images to Control Attribute Values

As discussed in the upcoming sections detailing the creation of image maps, the only image maps that we use color for when making textures are the color maps. All the maps for the other attributes, from Luminosity to Bump maps, are best done in shades of gray.

This is simply because it is easier to predict the manner in which the gray values will be translated into attribute values within LightWave itself, and because grayscale images work best to describe these attributes.

Basically what happens is that gray values within an image are translated as equivalent percentage values for the attribute to which you are assigning the image map. As a general rule of thumb, pure white is 100% and pure black is 0%, while all shades of gray in between range from 1% to 99%.

So if, for example, you load a gray map into your specular channel that contains pixels that have gray values of 24%, those pixels will have a specular value of 24% when the object is rendered.

> **NOTE:** You can check the gray value of a pixel in Adobe Photoshop by selecting the pixel with the Eyedropper tool, opening the Color Picker dialog, and checking the percentage value in the box labeled "B" just below the swatch preview. Be sure that the gray is pure gray — the RGB values should all be equal.

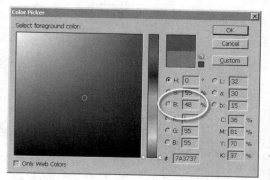

Figure 11-3: Checking the gray value of a pixel in Photoshop.

These values can be dependent, however, on the overall settings assigned within the Surface and Texture Editors themselves. If your overall setting for Specularity in the Surface Editor is 0%, and the opacity of the layer itself in the Texture Editor is set to 100%, then loading images will work exactly as I described above. However, when you start adjusting these settings, bear in mind that this slightly alters the way in which the gray images are treated.

If you were to set your overall Specular setting in the Surface Editor to 10%, and you added a gray image that contains black pixels, these black pixels will not be 0% as per normal, but rather 10%. This overall value basically sets the lowest value at which the range of grays in your texture maps will be interpreted.

However, when mapping with images, it is usually simplest to leave this overall value at 0% and instead control the channel with the images.

This overall value will take on a more meaningful role when we start using procedural textures.

# Creating Image Maps for Individual Surface Attributes

## Overview of Creating and Using Image Maps

Now that we have explored the use of gradients and procedural textures for creating details within your surfaces, let's move on to how we go about creating images to use as textures.

The really cool thing about using images for texturing is that you can create any detail you want on your surfaces simply by painting them. Easy. The tricky thing about using images is that they require projection parameters, discussed in greater detail in Part 4 of this book. Once we have gotten over the initial phase of mapping your model, or of planning your different texture projections, we move to the texture creation phase, which is definitely my favorite part of the entire texturing process.

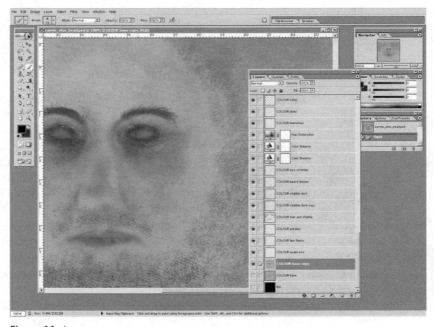

Figure 11-4

You can use any paint software to paint textures, from 2D painting programs like Adobe Photoshop or Corel PHOTO-PAINT (among many others) to 3D painting packages such as Right Hemisphere's Deep Paint 3D, Maxon's BodyPaint 3D, Pixologic's ZBrush (a full 3D package that includes a 3D painting toolset), or Alias's StudioPaint (a slightly older package that is no longer developed but is still used in some studios). You may think that 3D painting programs do not work with images, but that is essentially what they actually do. Even though you are painting directly onto the model when using them, they are outputting those brush strokes to an image that is then applied to the model. The following image shows the workspace of Deep Paint 3D.

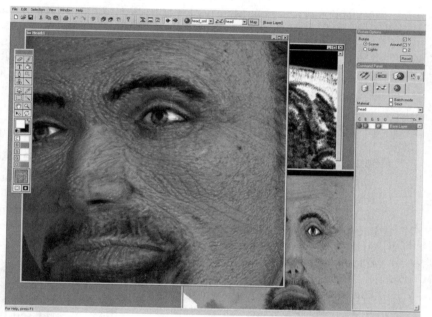

Figure 11-5

Painting textures does not necessarily require an enormous amount of artistic talent, but it does require a good eye for detail and an excellent knowledge of your painting package. Of course, artistic talent can certainly aid you in creating interesting and detailed textures, but the process of painting textures can also be a purely straightforward and logical one. Paint what you see and paint what you need. The reason that I say a good knowledge of your painting program is essential is because there are so many ways to go about creating textures that involve a lot more than merely painting strokes onto a canvas. Good work habits within your paint program are also important, such as managing your image layers efficiently and knowing the right tool for the right job.

**205**

Textures can be created in so many ways, from painting everything totally from scratch to using photographs or textures baked directly from LightWave (using the Surface Baker shader, described in Chapter 5, as a starting point) or using a combination of all of these. The methods you use can depend entirely on the project at hand, the type of texture you need to create, and the amount of time that you have at your disposal to complete the work.

Some people are texturing purists who like to paint everything by hand without using anything besides their own brush strokes, and while this does indeed allow the artist to create absolutely everything in precisely the way that he or she wants it, this method is not always the most practical. You shouldn't feel bad about using photographs as a starting point or blending them with other photos or painted textures to create different effects. Sometimes you may find that a photograph of a dirty piece of metal makes a really great grunge map for a piece of wood, or a photograph of noodles makes a good image of a hook and loop type fastener. You just never know! Textures like skin, wood, and metal are often tricky to create entirely from scratch, while using a lot of photographic reference and even parts of the photos within the texture can actually work really well.

## Preparing and Using Photographs for Image Maps

When you are working with photographs that will be incorporated into your textures, the most important thing that you need to attend to is the lighting that is in the image. Unless they are taken in extremely controlled environments that are designed to avoid noticeable lighting information appearing in the photo, all photographs have highlights, shadows, and other lighting information in them.

Take a look at Figure 11-6. You can clearly see highlights and shadows within this photograph, which would make it unsuitable, as it is, for use within a texture.

You often notice beginners using photographs such as this one as textures. The problem with using images like this is that you end up with discrepancies in your renders because the shadows and lighting in the

Figure 11-6

photograph do not match the lighting rig in your 3D scene. Because of this, it is important to remove all traces of lighting from photographs that you use in your texturing.

The method you use to remove the lighting can differ according to what kind of texture you actually want to use the photograph for. For example, removing the lighting because you want to use the photo as a color map will involve different steps than removing lighting from a photo that you wish to use as a bump map. Although in my personal experience photos are generally fine as color maps, once prepared, they are generally grossly misused as bump maps, specular maps, etc., since they are usually too generic in detail and totally inaccurate, especially in the case of bump maps. A photo of a brick wall can be prepared to make a great color map, but all too often people simply desaturate it and then use it as a bump map. Why won't this work? It should be obvious. Take a look at Figure 11-7.

Figure 11-7

While we can obviously quickly remove the shadows appearing in certain areas using tools like cloning or even straight painting to create a color map, this image would not necessarily be suitable as a bump map. The problem is that many artists think nothing of simply desaturating the image to gray, so that they end up with the image in Figure 11-8 that they then apply to their model as a bump map.

Figure 11-8

If you are looking at this image now and thinking "Ummm, why can't I use that as a bump map?" then give yourself a slap and listen up. Take a close look at the color version of that photo (see the color image on the companion CD) and then at the gray version. As we know, the different gray levels in an image will create different levels of amplitude when applied as a bump map. In the color photograph, we can clearly see that all of the bricks are more or less protruding the same distance from the wall, with the exception of a few of the bricks that have slightly rough edges that protrude a little farther.

Look now at the gray version. Because some of the bricks have much lighter colors than some of the other bricks, we have light gray bricks as well as dark gray bricks in the image. This means that if we apply this as a bump map, we are going to get very uneven looking bricks that are going to look very little like the original photo. And when you are creating this brick wall as part of an architectural model, believe me, the clients are not going to be too impressed that you have created sloppy, uneven brick work on the model they are paying you to make.

Ideally, the gray version would have to be edited to look something like Figure 11-9,

Figure 11-9

**207**

where all the bricks are more or less the same lighter shade of gray while the mortar in between is darker so that it works correctly when applied as a bump map. I have also darkened all the mortar to the same shade.

All too often I see people using this dreaded "Oh, just convert your color map to gray and use that as your bump map" philosophy when it really doesn't make sense if you are aiming for accuracy.

So, how do we quickly and efficiently remove lighting from images? One of the most popular methods of doing this is to use the Lab color model found in programs like Adobe Photoshop.

The Lab color model includes a channel for lightness. The cool thing about this is that you can then go into the Lightness channel and edit it so that you can even out the lighting.

Let's look at a practical example. See Figure 11-10.

The middle part of the manhole has a highlight on it. Leaving this highlight in the image and then applying it as a texture could cause problems if the lighting you create in your LightWave scene does not match it. So we need to remove it. Basically, we need to equalize the highlighted area so that it no longer appears to have the highlight on it.

Figure 11-10

If I open the image in Adobe Photoshop and go to Image>Mode>Lab Color, the image is converted into a Lab image. Going to my Channels palette, I now find the Lightness channel.

If I select the Lightness channel, I get the following channel appearing in my canvas.

Figure 11-11

Figure 11-12

Yes, it looks very much as the image would look if you were to convert it to gray. The cool thing, however, is that by editing this channel, we can even out the lighting in the color channels.

I now go in with my Rubber Stamp (clone) tool, and carefully clone the darker areas onto the lighter areas in the middle of the manhole and use my Burn tool to clean areas up (the Burn tool makes things darker), until it looks like Figure 11-13.

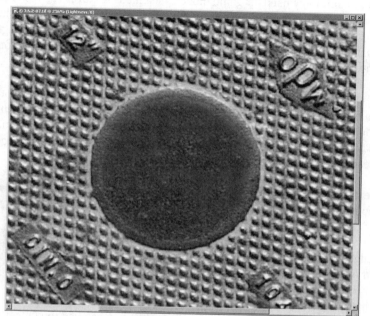

Figure 11-13: Zoomed-in view of image after highlight is removed.

Switching back to the color channels of my image, you can see that the highlight is now gone from that area!

This method isn't 100% foolproof, as most images will invariably need some careful attention to areas with other tools, sometimes even directly onto the color channels, but this is a quick way to remove lighting initially, leaving the small tweaking until later for the areas that need it. Sometimes I even find myself manually painting or cloning areas directly in the color channel to remove shadows and highlights. It really depends on the image.

Figure 11-14

But as you can see, removing lighting from images is very important for ensuring accuracy and consistency when placing it into a digitally lit environment. So no more laziness! Get that lighting out of your images.

## Creating Seamless Textures

Very commonly used for game models, seamless textures can also be useful
for tiling onto areas in the background when you simply don't have the time
to create intricate detailed textures for arbitrary things like walls or ground
that you are not going to see in great detail in a moving shot (thus not giving
the viewer time to register that the background textures repeat
themselves).

Of course, in order to tile an image repeatedly onto a surface, you need
to ensure that all its edges meet without visible seams. Luckily when dealing with non-UV textures (where seams are dealt with differently since they
have a shaped template to work with), the process of making an image
seamless at its edges is really quick and extremely simple.

Figure 11-15 shows a block that has a
texture tiled a number of times onto it. Of
course you'll obviously notice that the edges
of the texture are quite conspicuous.

I need to edit the image so that the
edges meet up seamlessly. I open the image
in Adobe Photoshop.

I need to first shift the edges around so
that I can see why it is that they are not

**Figure 11-15**

meeting up properly. To do this in Photoshop you can use the Offset filter,
found under Filter>Other>Offset. You can use this filter to shift your image
so that the edges move inward. If I shift the image 500 pixels to the right
and 500 pixels down, using the Wrap Around option, the edges shift to the
side and down as shown in Figure 11-16.

**Figure 11-16**

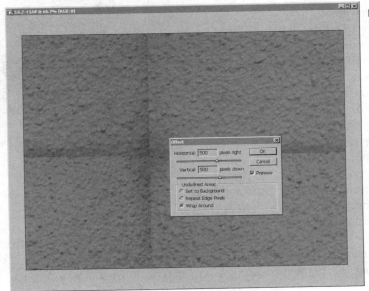

I can now apply the filter and use the clone tool to remove the darker areas. The image ends up looking like Figure 11-17.

Figure 11-17

When I apply this image now to my model, the seams are now no longer visible! In fact, it's not even that noticeable that the texture is tiled.

Figure 11-18

## Creating and Using Images with Alpha Channels

Alpha channels, as discussed in numerous other parts of this book, are additional channels contained within an image that define areas of transparency. Only 32-bit images, such as TGA or TIFF files (saved in 32-bit format), can contain alpha channels.

When creating alpha channels in images, the white areas of the channel will allow those areas of the actual image to remain opaque, while the black areas will be transparent.

Take a look at Figure 11-19. The color channels of the image are shown on the left, and the image's alpha channel is shown on the right.

Figure 11-19

When we apply this image as a texture to the wall we saw in the previous example (the image is applied as a new texture layer above the brown wall texture in the Texture Editor for the color attribute in LightWave), we can see that the areas not included in the alpha channel are ignored by LightWave.

Figure 11-20

Remember to make sure that the Alpha Channel option is enabled in the Image Editor in LightWave in order for it to work properly.

This is a simple example showing a simple alpha channel, but remember that you can make far more complex alpha channels using shades of gray to vary the transparency in areas. Using more complex alpha channels can be useful for blending multiple textures using multiple projections in LightWave. Techniques for blending textures are discussed in Part 4, which deals with projections.

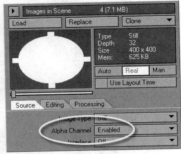

Figure 11-21

## Only Use RGB and Grayscale Images!

Although you may, by personal preference, work in different color models such as CMYK or Lab color while creating your color textures, it is very important to make sure that when you save your images as color textures to use in LightWave, you save them in the RGB color mode. This is because LightWave cannot correctly work with images using other color models, and you'll find yourself staring at the preview pane in the Image Editor asking yourself, "What on earth happened to my image?!" as it will show up as a weird distorted mess, as demonstrated in Figure 11-22 (bear in mind that the image itself is a lovely deep red brick wall).

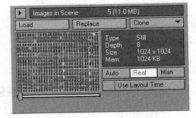

Figure 11-22

When saving images that use shades of gray only, such as your Bump, Specularity, Reflection, etc., maps, you can convert the images to grayscale color mode. This saves on RAM usage while rendering since they are smaller files that use less memory.

# Practical Examples for Painting Image Maps

As discussed in the previous section, painting textures requires, probably most of all, an attention to detail. And a healthy dose of common sense. Don't just paint a few strokes and call it a texture. You need to put thought and effort into it so that it is believable and interesting to look at. Of course I cannot demonstrate how to paint every type of texture you'll ever need to make, but the principles of painting textures apply across the board.

It's a mindset and an eye for detail that you need to develop. Once you understand what it is that makes a good texture, you'll no longer need tutorials. You'll be able to paint your own without having to ask questions or refer to tutorials. As I have said time and time again, texturing is simply a process of painting what you see and what you need. If you need to paint a face, look at a photo of a face, look at the details, and paint the same thing. No two ways about it really. You even have a face of your own. So look in the mirror if you're in doubt. Don't stop halfway through and ask someone, "How do I paint the wrinkles around the eyes?" because when you do that you just aren't using your brain. And you'll just end up annoying the person you are asking. You know what wrinkles look like, you know how to paint a line, so paint the wrinkles — because a wrinkle is really just a line.

Eventually you'll get to the point when you don't even need to look at references all the time as you develop a sense for instinctively knowing what sorts of details you need.

Let's look at the process of painting textures for each of the surface attributes that we can map in LightWave. These are just examples demonstrating the process I have gone through to create certain textures, and not actual step-by-step tutorials. For step-by-step tutorials, refer to Part 7 of this book.

The purpose of these examples is to demonstrate my thought process while texturing, and the steps I take to create the details that I need in my textures.

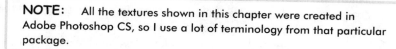

NOTE:    All the textures shown in this chapter were created in Adobe Photoshop CS, so I use a lot of terminology from that particular package.

There are those who believe that people simply don't learn anything from step-by-step tutorials because they show you a bunch of steps to take without you actually understanding why those steps are necessary. Consequently, you don't actually learn anything since all you are doing is observing and copying a single way of doing something. It basically doesn't teach you to think, and thinking is the only way to learn.

Of course, for absolute beginners, they are useful since they show what tools can be found and how to use them, but once you have progressed past the beginner stage, you should do yourself a favor and give your brain more to feed on.

However, since a book generally requires tutorials, I have included some in Part 7 for those beginners who need some pointers regarding tools and quick techniques for introducing them to the art of texturing. I recommend that all beginners try the step-by-step tutorials and then immediately dive into some major experimentation. Trust me, you'll have loads of fun, and then if you get stuck on any areas, have a look through this section and see how I tackle things. By observing the examples of others, we encourage ourselves to adapt those concepts into our thought process, and consequently develop our own techniques of using those concepts.

So for those of you who love to engage your brain, I have written this section for you.

## Making a Color Map

There is no rule that dictates that your texturing should always begin with color (or any other surface attribute for that matter), but I personally am a creature of habit and tend to create my color maps first, most of the time. There is no real reason for this, apart from the fact I just prefer to do it that way. If you want to start off your texturing process by creating your bump maps, or your specular maps, or any other maps, by all means please go ahead.

It is important to make a mention here before we get started of the tendency that people often have to paint shadows and highlights into their textures. I should hope that by now (providing you have read all the preceding chapters of this book) you understand how the different attributes of a surface work, and that shadows and highlights are created by the lights in your scene, and are therefore *not* needed (or wanted!) in your textures. So if you feel that weird urge to go and paint shadows in your character's nostrils or a shiny highlight on the hilt of a dagger, then STOP!!! Unless you are painting textures for a game engine (where these are often needed), then stop yourself right now, slap your hand for doing such a thing, and think properly. No shadows or highlights are welcome here.

Okay, let's get back to painting color maps, and have a look at the color textures for a human head, as a human head has lots of cool color variations that make it a good example for demonstrating color maps.

A good way to begin a color map is simply to create a general wash of color for the entire thing. Figure 11-23 shows the initial color layer I have made for the skin for the character's face, which will eventually be a very fair-skinned, unshaven male character. I've left the UV map visible so that you can see where the facial features will be.

> **NOTE:** Color images of the figures are on the companion CD.

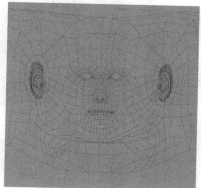

Figure 11-23

As you can see, this is simply a flat layer of a suitably fleshy color. I don't have to worry too much about the overall tone of the layer, as it can always be changed at a later stage with an adjustment layer (in Adobe Photoshop) or even by altering the actual tone of the layer itself. The current RGB values are 171, 158, 124.

In fact, I decide to make the color a little more pink right now. So I simply create an adjustment layer (Color Balance) and adjust it so that the red tones become stronger and the overall tone of the layer becomes less yellow.

Now, a very lazy person would leave this layer as it is. However, this will not look great if it is supposed to look realistic (and that lazy person will never make a good texturing artist). If you look in the mirror, you'll see that your skin has loads of different little details and color variations in it. So we need to make some of those here. Remember, paint what you see!

Figure 11-24 is a photo of part of a face. As you can see, there are subtle color variations everywhere, as well as freckles and spots.

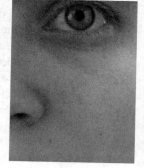

Figure 11-24

I'm going to need some details like that.

My personal method of quickly adding variations and little details to textures is to use the Dodge and Burn tools in Photoshop. However, you can use any method you want for this, including painting them with a paintbrush. Find tools that you are comfortable using. It's the final look that counts, not the method you use. What I do is make a very small brush with a very low intensity setting, and make lots of tiny, almost imperceptible little brownish dots on the flesh. Yes, this does take some time. Basically they are like faint freckles. I then make the brush slightly bigger and create beauty spots (small moles). Once I am happy with my spots and moles, I make the brush size of the Dodge and Burn tools even larger, and simply create larger spots of color variations all over the place. I always keep these tools on very low intensity, as they can really wreck an image if used too strong.

My base color layer now looks like Figure 11-25. The variations are very subtle, but far better than a plain flat color, don't you think?

If you are interested in what colors these spots are, the RGB values are 167, 132, 94.

The overall skin tones now have many variations. Some of them are 198, 167, 138, which is a fairly light fleshy color, and others are 181, 146, 116, which is a slightly darker fleshy color.

Figure 11-25

Next up are the eyebrows. Eyebrows are really simple. What are eyebrows made of in reality? Hairs. And what are hairs? Lines. Lines are the simplest things in the universe to paint, so I just make a new layer, select some brown tones, and paint strokes on a medium level opacity, constantly varying the color. I build up the strokes until they eventually form solid eyebrows. If you need references for eyebrows, simply look in a mirror. Paint what you see. This texture is for a male, so I make fairly thick eyebrows in the texture.

Figure 11-26

I painted them first using a layer of brown with the RGB values of 88, 65, 46, a rather dark, chocolatey brown. I then created slightly lighter brown strokes, using the values 113, 84, 61.

Simple so far, isn't it? Well, this is the part where it now gets a little more arty. I know I said before that there isn't always a great deal of artistic talent needed for textures, but having a sense of color and a delicate yet steady approach to painting can definitely help here, especially since the color variations we need to add to the face now require a great deal of subtlety and delicacy.

When we look at Caucasian human faces, we see a lot of reds and blues in the skin. These colors actually come from beneath the surface (more specifically, from the blood beneath the surface), and are not actually directly on the surface itself. However, when painting skin textures we need to add them in, because we have to cheat a lot in the world of CG.

Figure 11-27 is a photo of a person who seems delighted by the dancing hamster he is holding.

Figure 11-27

If we look closely, particularly at the area immediately surrounding the eyes, we see some subtle blue tones, and farther downward toward his cheeks and also on his nose, we see stronger pink and red tones. These redder tones are rather more apparent than they would be ordinarily because this person is in a state of insobriety, but images that show extremes generally make the best practical examples. And interestingly enough, I often find that making textures that show slightly more exaggerated tones work best. Especially since it is better to initially create something where the tones are too strong, since they can always be lessened by changing opacity levels at a later stage. Making tones that are too subtle stronger at a later stage generally proves to be slightly more difficult.

So let's get back to painting. I now make a whole bunch of new layers, so that I can vary their opacity levels to obtain the right blending once I have had fun with my paintbrush, painting red and blue tones where I want them, each area of tones on its own layer, for that extra control.

Once again, I use my brush on a medium level opacity, and build up my tones gradually and intuitively.

> **NOTE:** It is for this kind of work that I can highly recommend using a digital stylus (such as a Wacom) to paint the details, since it allows pressure sensitivity and provides a far more intuitive approach to digital painting. It is not impossible to paint with a mouse, but I find painting with my Wacom far more comfortable and efficient.

I pay particular attention to the nose and the area directly beneath the eyes. This is because these are the areas where the blue and red tonal changes on a real person's skin are the most apparent. Again, this is a very intuitive process. You can look at a human face, see where these tones are, and simply paint what you see and what you know needs to be there.

My texture now looks like Figure 11-28. I've made some nice, relatively subtle red and blue tones, and even darker purple tones to build up the effect of the blood beneath the surface of the skin.

Just as a reminder as to where these details are actually situated, Figure 11-29 is a shot of the texture with the UV map showing over it.

Figure 11-28

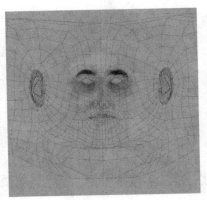

Figure 11-29

Next on the agenda is some stubble. When I create stubble, I generally do so with the aid of a few little custom brushes. Making brushes in your paint program (if you have the option) can greatly speed up the process of creating often-needed details. Stubble is something I often have to paint, so I have a few stubble brushes that I always use.

To make a stubble brush (or any kind of brush for that matter) in Adobe Photoshop, you need to start off with a new layer. I generally just create a new document, and start from there. I then take a small fine brush (usually one or two pixels in diameter) and paint a little stubbly pattern in black ink, as shown in Figure 11-30. Make sure that you have created the little dots on a totally new layer with transparency.

Figure 11-30

Once you have a pattern that you are happy with, select the layer by holding down the Ctrl key and clicking on the layer name in the Layers palette. Once the little dots are selected, go to Edit and select Define Brush Preset. A new window pops up with a preview of the brush and a field into which you can type a name for the brush.

Figure 11-31

This creates a new brush that you can use in your textures. Create a few different variations and constantly switch between them when painting your stubble to avoid creating regular repeating patterns.

With my current character, I start off by first defining some fairly coarse stubble on the upper lip, the chin, and the sideburn areas.

I now want to make a softer stubbly layer, not only for the beard but also for the actual hair on the head. Even if you are going to use something like Sasquatch for

Figure 11-32

the hair, I still recommend painting some semblance of hair on the head to create a slightly thicker-looking head of hair.

For this latter example I actually paint some solid color with a soft-edged airbrush on a medium opacity. I then take the Eraser tool and, using the stubble brush I made previously, I erase areas from this new stubble layer. This creates a slightly more solid, yet patchy-in-places layer of almost dirty-looking stubble.

Now, I could leave the stubble the way it is and get away with it, but I won't. I am going to go that extra mile and add some shaving rash. These are the kinds of details that separate okay-looking textures from cool-looking ones. Anyone can paint stubble, but will everyone paint shaving rash too?? I think not. Well, perhaps (hopefully) after reading this, you will.

**Figure 11-33**

A rash is easy to paint. Simply take a soft-edged brush and paint some pinkish dabs in a few places. Easy.

My texture is coming along quite nicely now. And this has taken very little time too — about half an hour.

What next? Ah yes, I want to make the ears a little red. You know how people's ears glow when they are lit from behind? I'll let you in on a little secret of mine, and that is that I often add a tinge of pink to the ears in my color map to help enhance that effect. At this point I also add some spots to the face (just a sprinkling of little light brown spots as blemishes helps to enhance realism) as well as some very faint veins.

**Figure 11-34**

One more detail remains — the lips. I want this guy to have quite dark, fleshy lips, so I paint a rather bold shade of red for

**Figure 11-35**

them. While I am going wild with the red tones again, I add some darker reds to the cheek areas and also to the eyelid areas. I also add some more dark reds to the ears. Once I have painted a basic dark red base for the lips, I use the Burn tool to add some variations to them so that he doesn't end up looking like he's wearing lipstick.

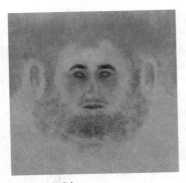

Figure 11-36

Figure 11-37

Figure 11-38

I'm almost happy with the texture now. I just realize that perhaps the overall color needs a bit of adjusting. The best (and safest) way to do this is to use our trusty adjustment layers. The reason I say this is the safest way to do it is because the adjustment layer does not actually directly change the color of the pixels in your texture layers; it simply alters the color of the layers below it. If I then decide I don't like the change, I simply kill the adjustment layer or change its setting. This way the original layers I painted are never actually changed directly.

I use a Color Balance adjustment layer to shift the overall tone of all the layers to a more saturated red and yellow tone that I feel will suit the character more.

I am now satisfied with the way that the color texture looks for my model. I quickly whip up my remaining textures, slap them on the model, and voilà! I am happy with the way my character looks.

If you are hungering for more, please refer to Part 7 of this book for a more in-depth tutorial on creating human skin textures.

Let's now look at another color texture example — wood. More specifically, the wood of a guitar. Wood is something that a lot of people struggle with (as well as metal). This is where photographs come in handy. You should never feel ashamed of creating textures using photographs, as long as you use the photos correctly. If you have not read the section "Preparing and Using Photographs for Image Maps," then you should do so now.

Now back to the subject at hand, the guitar. I have taken a screen shot of the front of the model to use as a template for painting the texture. So I take this into Adobe Photoshop. I then scrounge through my rather vast texture library, and locate two nice wood images from my RansomActive texture collection. I like the look of the maple for the body, but I also want a knot in the wood, which the rosewood image has.

Figure 11-39

Honey Maple

Rosewood

I now drag the maple image into my guitar texture template. I size the image down somewhat and copy it over so that it covers the entire space that the guitar body occupies within the image. See Figure 11-40.

Then I take the Rubber Stamp (clone) tool and remove the darker streaks from the middle of the image, and also make some random changes to certain areas of the image so that it is no longer obvious that the maple image is repeated.

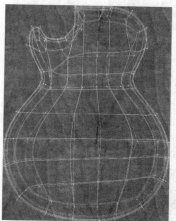

Figure 11-40

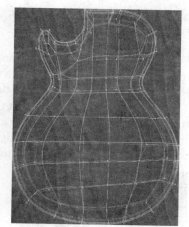

Figure 11-41

Now it's time to add the wood knot to the body. I copy the entire rosewood image into my guitar file, and then take a soft-edged eraser and erase all around the image so that I am only left with the knot detail. I then desaturate the layer to gray and use the Hue/Adjustment tool (found under Image>Adjustments) to match the color of the knot to the color of the maple. See Figure 11-42.

Developing an eye for matching colors may not come immediately to you, but trust me, with time you'll find it becomes a lot easier.

So far I have a decent-looking wood for the body of the guitar. I am happy with the way that the wood grain and knot look, so it's time to add the paint detailing to the bodywork. I simply take a large, very soft-edged air-brush with a very dark maroon color, and carefully detail the edges of the guitar to create what is known as a sunburst pattern on a guitar. I do this painting on a new layer so that if I make a mistake, it is easy to erase.

Figure 11-42

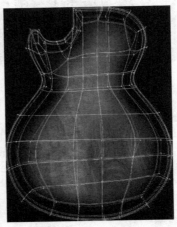

Figure 11-43

Luckily, the contours of the actual model in the screen shot I used help me to position the painting details with perfection. Figure 11-44 is a shot of the texture so far without the model showing.

I am happy with the way that the wood is looking, but it is just a little too light for my taste. So I create a new Hue/Saturation adjustment layer on top of everything and adjust the lightness and the saturation so that the wood is now a darker shade of brown, as shown in Figure 11-45.

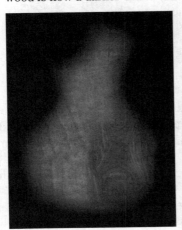

Figure 11-44

Figure 11-45

This looks perfect for my needs. I go back into LightWave and slap the texture onto my model, give it some specularity, glossiness, and a touch of reflection, and I have a great-looking guitar!

Figure 11-46

## Making a Luminosity Map

Luminosity maps are the easiest things in the world to create. If you want something to be luminous, make it really bright in the texture and leave the areas that you don't want luminous plain old black. Simple.

Of course you can always take a more creative route when the chance arises. For instance, say you were working on a scene that takes place at night, and in the scene is a window with frosted glass that is lit from the inside. Frosted glass is generally opaque, so it would probably work best if you were to paint a luminosity map for the window instead of trying to make it appear solid and shine a light through it and all that. Well, I have actually created a scene just like this for this example. How nice of me.

Take a look at Figure 11-47. Sure, the glass does work in that it appears to be lit from within, but it looks really boring. The surrounding walls are pretty grimy and skanky, so I would imagine that these windows probably don't get washed all that often either.

So I decide to make a nice grungy luminosity map. I start off by taking a screen shot of my glass panes in Modeler, and then going into (you guessed it) Adobe Photoshop and initially making both panes totally white.

Figure 11-47

If I were to apply this texture now as it is, it would give me exactly the same effect as we saw in the previous render, where I had simply taken the Luminosity value of the window surface up to 100%.

Figure 11-48

First, I want to create some old drips on the window. My absolute favorite method of creating drippy details is to use the Wet Edges option on my brushes (I am sure that most paint applications have something similar), and then set the brush to a medium to low level of opacity with a soft edge. Painting with this type of brush is fantastic for things like thin layers of actual paint, water damage, streaks, etc. I paint a few drippy bits on the window, and also build up some layers of darker shades at the bottom and corners of the window panes.

Figure 11-49

Obviously, these darker areas will lessen the luminous effect of the surface. We need more though, as these are simply watery marks that are not actually solid grit or dirt. One of the quickest ways to make dirt is to use a technique commonly known as grunge mapping. This technique involves taking detailed photographs, especially of things that have gritty details in them, making them high contrast, and then using them to make selections or blending them with layers to get the desired effect.

I look through my texture library and find a suitable image as shown in Figure 11-50. I then take this image, desaturate it, and pump up the contrast until it looks like Figure 11-51.

Figure 11-50

Figure 11-51

I then drag this image into my luminous texture file, change the blending mode to Multiply (so that the white areas become transparent), and use a soft-edged eraser to erase the details from the middle of the pane, so that the grit lies only along the sides, top, and bottom of the window pane.

Figure 11-52

I want more drippy details, so I look for another image to use as a grunge map to create them. I choose the image shown in Figure 11-53.

I then desaturate and increase the contrast of this image as well, and drag it into my luminous texture file. I switch the blending mode of the layer again to Multiply, and adjust the opacity so that the streaks are gray in the image. I then take my eraser to the layer and erase the parts I don't want, until I am left with something like Figure 11-54.

Figure 11-53

Figure 11-54

Of course this grime is only on the left-hand pane, and I want some more grime on the right-hand side as well. I find yet another image that will make a suitable grunge map.

Figure 11-55

Once again I increase the contrast of this image until it becomes very high contrast, and add it to the layers of my texture. I take the Eraser tool and erase the parts of the texture that I don't want, until I have a nice layer of grime on the window on the right.

Figure 11-56

Looking at this image now, we have a great sense of grime build-up in all the appropriate areas for a dirty, unkempt window. Applying this now to the window and rendering it gives the effect shown in Figure 11-57.

Far more interesting and suitable than just a plain luminous piece of window, wouldn't you say?

Figure 11-57

## Making a Diffuse Map

A diffuse map is one of those things that is usually not all that necessary, since simply adjusting the overall Diffuse amount is generally sufficient for preventing the surface from becoming oversaturated. However, in some cases you can use diffuse maps to darken areas, such as if a character's clothes have liquid spilled on them, which changes the diffuse property of the surface. You can also use a diffuse map as a dirt map for adding grime to a surface without actually adding it to the color map.

Another use for diffuse maps is to prevent reflections from textures from becoming too milky; using a diffuse map can help to deepen reflections. For this purpose I often find that simply inverting my reflection map and placing it in the Diffuse slot works perfectly.

### Creating Procedural Diffuse Textures

Let's have a look at making a diffuse map for the purposes of grunging up a surface. I know this section is about painting textures, but for this particular example I will simply create a procedural texture in my Diffuse slot to dirty up the surface a bit.

So I have this crate model (incidentally, you'll find a tutorial on creating the textures for it in Part 7), and it has some nice flaky paint on it.

Figure 11-58

Since I am going to map the diffuse values entirely with a texture, I change my Diffuse value in the Surface Editor to 0.0% and open the Texture Editor for Diffuse.

I change the default layer that is created to a Procedural Texture layer, and change the Procedural Type to FBMNoise. I invert the procedural because I want the actual darker diffuse areas to be small, while the majority of the surface remains normal (by default, this particular procedural covers most of the surface, so inverting it creates the opposite effect of the majority of the surface remaining unchanged while small areas acquire little details). I set the Texture Value to 80%. This means that the majority of the surface will have a value of 80% Diffuse, while the darker areas of the procedural patterns will create lower values of diffuse.

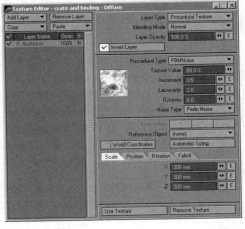

Figure 11-59

I set the scale to 300mm on all three axes.

Rendering the crate, I now have the image shown in Figure 11-60. The procedural texture has created a very quick and easy and decent-looking dirt to the crate that almost looks like burn damage or wood damp rot from being in storage.

Figure 11-60

And the really cool thing about this is that since I have a UV map created for this object already, I can simply bake this diffuse texture out to my UV map now, so that if I so wished, I could take it into Photoshop and edit it a bit.

Another very nifty use of this method is if you have a number of cloned items of the same object in a scene, you could apply a procedural diffuse to the surface that will then randomize the clones from each other somewhat, as demonstrated in Figure 11-61.

Figure 11-61

Very useful indeed, eh?

## Making a Specular Map

We know that specularity in CG is a fake reflection, so why bother mapping it? Well, it's useful because it provides a very quick way of giving a surface some shine without using reflections, and creating shininess on a surface helps to convey a lot of information to the viewer about what a surface feels like to the touch.

Specularity (and reflection) is something that is never consistent across a surface, which is why it is one of the more important surface attributes to create textures for. Creating variations in your specularity helps to convey a sense of imperfection on a surface without adding dirt. Sure, adding dirt is fun, but you don't always want everything to look like it's just been pulled out of a swamp.

Let's look at specularity in human skin.

We all know, without even looking, that on a human face the skin is shinier in some areas than others. Generally, on a "normal" human face in "normal" conditions (in other words, the person does not suffer from a bizarre skin disorder and is not sweaty or suffering from dry, flaky skin), areas like the bridge and tip of the nose, the area directly beneath the eyes, the middle of the forehead, and the lips are shinier than the cheeks and the chin. The cheeks and chin are generally fleshier and softer looking (although they do have a certain amount of shine — they are not dry looking). Generally, the driest-looking area of a person's face is the little patch where the nostril meets the cheek — the skin in this area is often slightly rougher and drier.

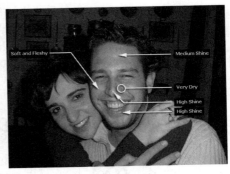

Figure 11-62

Of course, these are generalizations and there are always exceptions, but these are good general guidelines for the average face.

So when painting a specular map for a face, we need to take these guidelines into account. We can see that some areas are very shiny, some areas are relatively shiny, and other areas are soft and fleshy with a broader falloff of light on them.

So I start off my specular map for the face by roughly defining these areas, as shown in Figure 11-63. I start off the entire map with a relatively dark shade of gray — the RGB values are 25, 25, 25 — the equivalent of a specular shading value of 10% assigned to the Surface Editor in LightWave. This is a relatively natural fleshy value for specularity, as it is not too plastic looking.

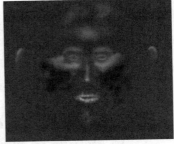

Figure 11-63

> **NOTE:** I have brightened all the shots of my specular maps by 35% so that the details will be more clearly visible in print. Ordinarily such light grays would be a little too high for human skin.

As you can see, I've simply used the Dodge and Burn tools to intuitively lighten and darken certain areas, respectively. As with all organic textures, a delicate approach is essential. Simply going in with an airbrush and painting large splotches of white and black (yes, I have actually seen people doing exactly that) is going to look awful. Of course I don't mean that you can't use the Airbrush or Paintbrush tools at all, because by all means you must use the tools that you are comfortable with. It's your technique that makes the difference. The key lies in slowly building up the different tones using subtlety and delicacy, using low intensity settings on the tools (whether you are using a brush tool or a touch-up tool like dodge or burn), and gradually working the areas to be lighter or darker where necessary, and always with a soft edge. It is essential that you adopt careful painting habits for textures, especially with organic textures, where variations on surfaces are generally not harsh, but rather gradually changing between different areas, which is why using soft-edged brushes is usually the safest route.

You'll notice that I also have the eyebrows included in the specular map. This is because on this particular model, I have the eyebrows in the texture instead of creating them with Sasquatch. And of course hair has a different specularity than skin, and since it is often quite shiny, I copied the painted eyebrow hairs from the color map where I already made them, desaturated them, and lightened them in the specular map so that the hair will appear nice (and different from the surrounding skin) and shiny when rendered. It is important to remember that where there is a different substance or a change of surface quality on a single surface, you always need to reflect this in your textures.

Next up I need to add some details to the eye rims, because these areas are generally wet from the liquid around your eyeballs. So I create a new layer and paint some light values around the edges of the eye, building up the lighter tones until they are really quite bright.

Figure 11-64

This particular character (which some of you may have seen before in *Keyframe* magazine) has a scar running down his cheek, and since scar tissue is generally quite shiny, I need to make that area have a higher level of specularity. Since I have already painted my color textures for the face, I have the scar already painted on its own layer, so I simply copy that layer into my specular map layers, desaturate it, and adjust its brightness. When I feel that I have the right level of brightness, I have a specular texture like the one shown in Figure 11-65.

Figure 11-65

I am relatively happy with the actual overall look of the map, but it is a little too plain for my liking. Sure, I have all the necessary variations in the appropriate areas, but I would prefer for the map to have a little more detail to it. When I created the bump maps for the character, I gave him a lot of wrinkles and blemishes in his skin, and I would like for those areas to have a variation in the specular map as well. So I copy those layers from my bump map (the wrinkles and blemishes), and blend them with my specular layers. I have chosen to have the wrinkles less shiny, so that they will break up the overall levels of specularity across the face, providing a nice irregular and rough specular appearance to the face as a whole.

When applied to the model, the specularity of the skin works as it should, with the nose, forehead, lips, the areas directly beneath his eyes, and the scar on his cheek being shinier than the rest of the face.

Figure 11-66

Figure 11-67

Without the specular map applied to it, the skin would look like dull cardboard, since the specularity really helps to create a sense of fleshiness to the surface.

## Making a Glossiness Map

Glossiness, like diffuse, does not always require a texture map. This is because in most cases, simply adjusting the overall value of it suffices, since it is essentially an extra control for specularity, as opposed to an entirely new surface parameter.

The only time I have ever actually painted a texture map for glossiness is when I had already created the specular map for something, and then wanted certain areas of that specular map to look slightly wet, while the other areas would simply have "normal" specularity, the falloff of which was already controlled by the value assigned to Glossiness in the Surface Editor in LightWave. So basically I allowed the overall gloss value to determine the falloff of the specularity created by the specular map (as is the function of the Glossiness value), and then used the gloss map to allow just some of those areas to have a higher degree of glossiness so that they appeared to be moist.

One such character that I used a gloss map on was a *Lord of the Rings*-style orc that I made some time ago, and actually don't particularly like, but I thought it would make a good example of what glossiness mapping can do. For this particular character, I used the gloss map to make him look very sweaty on parts of his face, to make the areas around his

Figure 11-68

piercings look as if they were seeping liquid, to make his eyelids appear wet, to make a cut in his forehead appear to be oozing fresh blood, and to coat his lips with spittle issued forth from his war lust.

The reason you can't create wet areas with a specular map and an overall Glossiness value in the Surface Editor alone is because in order to make things look wet, you need to have similar values (usually with approximately 10% to 5% difference) of the two surface attributes, generally at rather high percentages, such as 80% Glossiness and 100% Specularity. However, once the gloss values begin to exceed the specular values, even when the specularity is from a texture, the entire surface begins to look wet. So if I were to apply my specular map and then simply push the Glossiness value up, the entire surface would begin to look wet. Instead, I create a gloss map with very light areas in the areas that I want to appear wet, while leaving the rest of the map on a suitable overall value for the rest of the surface. Make sense?

Remember, the function of Glossiness is essentially to "tighten" the specular highlights. High values of both Specularity and Glossiness produce a plastic look with small, tight highlights, while lower levels of Glossiness produce broader, softer highlights. So the function of the glossiness map is simply to tighten *certain* areas of shininess created by the specular map, instead of tightening the highlights of the entire surface equally.

So let's first take a look at the specular map for the orc's head. As you can see in Figure 11-69, there are many variations on this particular map, especially since not only is he sweating, but he also has some war paint on his face that has a different specular quality than the skin. I also used the same guidelines I would use for painting a specular map for a human head, making areas like the forehead, nose, and the area directly beneath his eyes shinier than the other parts of his face.

Note that I have made the areas that I want to have wet looking very bright in the specular map, since it requires a high value of both specularity and glossiness to create an ideal wet look.

Figure 11-69                          Figure 11-70

Now let's take a look at the glossiness map as shown in Figure 11-70. I basically copied all the layers from the specular map into my glossiness layer set and played around with all their values, deleting some of the layers that I didn't need.

Notice how I've increased the gloss values on all the areas where I want tighter highlights. The forehead has higher values so that it will appear slightly sweaty. Notice the lines running down the forehead to create rivulets of sweat. Also note how areas like the cut and his lips have very high values to create that very wet look. You'll also see that the area of war paint has a very low level of glossiness because I wanted the paint to remain fairly dry looking. I have also created very bright spots at all the "exit" points of his facial piercings to create that icky, seeping liquid look around them. The bright areas beneath his nose create a look on his skin as if his nose has been dripping down onto his upper lip.

Figure 11-71 shows how the head would look if this map was not applied to it, and a simple Glossiness value was assigned to it in the Surface Editor. Not very nice at all.

This very clearly demonstrates how the glossiness map "tightened" up the specularity of the surface, because without it the shiny areas created by the specular map simply become blown out and white.

Figure 11-71

## Making a Reflection Map

Reflection maps are one of my favorite types of maps to paint. Using them carefully can actually help to create far more realistic highlights on your surface when placed in nice environments (especially HDR image-based environments that project a lot of color onto your models, particularly when used in conjunction with radiosity) with good lighting rather than using regular specular maps.

When creating reflection maps for things like skin or wood, I often find that a really quick way of making them is simply to take your specular maps and darken them a lot, and use those as reflection textures. This is because substances like these are not mirror-like by any stretch of the imagination, so they require very low levels of reflection.

But for the purposes of this example we are looking at something that is very reflective: metal. The key to making realistic metal lies in creating good reflection maps for it and placing the objects into environments that give the metal a lot to reflect in its surface. The trick is to avoid overdoing it — when we all started learning 3D, we loved making perfectly reflective chrome objects, didn't we? Objects that have too much reflection are one of the telltale signs of a beginner artist. We need to learn to control those urges to make everything chromey, and begin to concentrate on more realistic looks for our metal.

Of course, there are some occasions when you can get away with really over-the-top chrome-looking metal, especially for fantasy swords and armor or really slick cars. Figure 11-72 shows a piece of armor that I created for an elf character.

**Figure 11-72**

Okay, so I made it really chrome-like and probably far too reflective to be realistic, but hey that's fantasy for you (well, that's the excuse I use).

But what happens when this metal begins to rust or it has been exposed to extreme weather conditions for a few years? This is when a good reflective map becomes very important, since unrusted metal has very different reflective properties than rusted metal, which is very dull and generally very dry looking.

So I start off my reflection map with a fairly light shade of gray, and add some noise to it simply so that the reflections in the reflection bits will have some noise in them. I use Photoshop's noise filter for this, since it's the easiest and quickest way of adding noise.

I then create a new layer on top of this layer, and with a low opacity brush I paint darker, scratchy areas where the armor has been damaged.

**Figure 11-73**                     **Figure 11-74**

Now I add a new layer with additional darker areas in it for where the little leather straps that hold the rings in place are (the little rings that connect each piece of armor). I figure that all the rubbing from that leather over the years would probably wear those areas quite a lot. This area is also likely to build up some dirt from the leather, which would also lessen the reflectivity in those areas.

Figure 11-75

Figure 11-76

The next layer is one that I often make when creating metal textures — a brushed detail. Many metals have brush marks in them from machining, resulting in what is usually called a brushed steel look. Of course I am using artistic license here, because a piece of ancient armor would not have been machined, so for this particular piece of armor I will put the brushed layer on a very low opacity.

Creating the brushed look is simple. All you do is create a new gray layer, then add some monochrome noise with a fairly high contrast. Once you have a contrasted black and white noise, simply add some horizontal motion blur to it using a fairly long distance. Easy! You'll get something that looks like Figure 11-76.

So I make a layer like this, and then take the layer's opacity down a lot. Why do I bother doing it when it's barely visible in the texture? Because it makes me feel better and it does actually make a bit of a difference.

Now it's time to add the rust to the reflection map. Obviously, rust is matte and powdery, so we don't want it to reflect at all in the render. I have already created my color textures for this particular model, and because I am very careful always to keep everything on its own layer, I have all the different rust details on their own layers. So all I have to do is copy these layers into my reflection layer set, desaturate them, and darken them to black.

Figure 11-77

Figure 11-78

Everything seems to be as it should. I apply the texture to my model as a reflection map, and render it in a scene with an HDR image in Image World to create an environment for it to reflect. I now have the image shown in Figure 11-79.

The rusty areas look nice and dry and powdery, while the non-rusty areas remain relatively shiny and reflective. Perfect!

Figure 11-79

## Making a Transparency Map

First of all, I think it is worth mentioning that transparency maps are *not* for making objects vanish out of your scene. Transparency is not the same as invisibility. Are glass objects in the real world invisible? No, they aren't. They are transparent. So there is no point in using transparency maps if you are trying to fade objects in and out of your scene or anything like that. If you need to do that, use a Clip Map in your Object Properties panel in Layout.

Transparency is for transparent surfaces, of course, such as glass, plastic, and liquids. As we have seen previously in this book, setting up transparency usually requires the use of gradients or Fresnel shaders for realism, so why map it with a texture? You would use a transparency texture when you are making a glass or plastic object dirty or adding a decal to a transparent object (without actually modeling that decal and applying a separate surface to it, of course).

> **NOTE:** Liquids wouldn't ordinarily require that textures be applied to them since they move around, which makes image-based textures a little tricky and cumbersome. If you need to add murkiness or any other kind of transparency variation to liquid, try using procedural textures instead.

Remember the dirty window from the luminosity texture example? Let's go back to that and have a look at making some transparency textures for the glass.

Making the transparency map for the glass will be very easy because I already created those nice textures for it in the luminosity section. All I need to do is alter them a little for the transparency texture. Figure 11-80 shows the color map for the glass,

Figure 11-80

**235**

which is simply a copy of the luminosity texture that I then saturated with color.

This is pretty much the same kind of thing that I need to create the transparency map, because the streaks will have lower transparency than the clean glass, which needs to be 100% transparent.

So all I do is take the dirty, streaky layers and simply alter their blending so that I have some nice variations of gray. This is because I don't want the glass to just be 100% transparent where it is clean and 0% transparent (opaque) where there is dirt. I want variations so that there are different levels of transparency because it is more interesting to have variations.

Figure 11-81

Looking at this texture we can see that the clean areas will be perfectly transparent, while the streaky bits and the grime along the bottom of the panes will create different levels of transparency.

When I apply this to the model and render, I get the image in Figure 11-82.

You'll notice that I don't have refraction on in these renders. Sorry about that, but it was simply taking far too long to render them with refraction!

Figure 11-82

And that's it for transparency maps.

## Making a Translucency Map

Moving on to translucency now, we find yet another of those surface properties that doesn't always necessarily require mapping. Generally, you only really need to create translucency maps for organic surfaces, as substances like fabric or translucent liquids can get away with a simple shading value of the attribute.

For this example we are looking at a heart model. I want to make a translucency texture with veins in it, so that when I place a light inside the heart and switch off all other lighting in the scene, I get a cool-looking effect with all the veins showing.

I create a square texture in Photoshop, and apply a base layer of light gray. This will provide a fairly high initial translucency value for the flesh of the heart model.

On top of this I create a new layer and draw some fairly bold, thick veins in dark gray.

These darker veins now decrease the translucency of the model, so that light will not pass through them as much as it passes through the light areas. However, simply having thick bold veins on a plain gray base is boring, so I take my Dodge tool and, with a soft edge, I build up nice light patches around the veins. These brighter areas will now appear even more translucent when applied to the model.

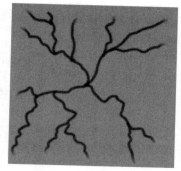

Figure 11-83

Now to add some more veins. Obviously, I want a nice variety of veins for my heart, so I create another layer and paint a bunch of medium thickness veins in a slightly lighter gray than the thick veins I created previously.

And now for the final bunch of veins — nice little thin ones running along the surface. I create two different layers, each containing small veins of different thickness. The really thin ones I make a rather light shade of gray, so that they will be a lot more translucent than the thicker veins.

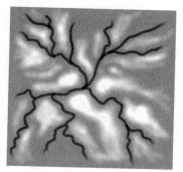

Figure 11-84

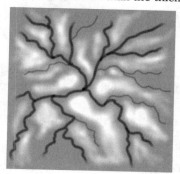

Figure 11-85

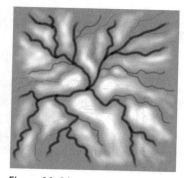

Figure 11-86

Now it's time to apply the texture to the model. I go into Layout, load the model, and apply the texture to the heart. I then create a point light inside the model so that we get the translucent effect correctly.

Next, I select the default light in the scene and open its Properties panel. I switch off Affect Diffuse but leave the Affect Specular option on. This is so that this light will not actually affect the surface in the normal way of affecting its diffuse properties, but will allow specularity to show on the surface. So basically it won't actually light the surface as such, but instead will create some specular highlights on the surface.

Figure 11-87 shows the rendered heart. Note that the only textures applied to this model are the translucency map and the bump map. There is no color map applied at all — all the vein details come purely from the translucency map, where the light is able to pass through the lighter areas and the darker veins block it to varying degrees.

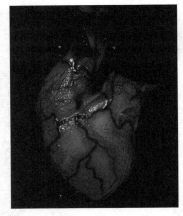

Figure 11-87

Pretty cool, huh? I've used this same technique on things like dinosaur and dragon wings in the past, so that when they fly in front of the sun (or any other light source for that matter), you can see all the veins.

Creating a translucency map for a character's head where the ears are a light shade of gray is another popular use of translucency mapping, because it creates that glowing ear look when your character is lit from behind, as seen in Figure 11-88.

Figure 11-88

## Making a Bump Map

Finally we get to bump maps. Bump maps are probably one of the first types of textures that most people make when they begin to experiment with texturing their models, and a lot of people actually like to start off their entire texturing process by creating them.

Oddly enough, though, many people struggle with them. The first law of bump mapping (as mentioned at the end of Chapter 4) is that a bump map should never be used to compensate for a lack of geometry. It should only be used for minor topographical details such as scratches, small dents, minor irregularities, cellular grain, machining, light wrinkles, blemishes (on skin), and anything else that can be successfully cheated as an illusion on the surface.

Let's look at a bump map for a face.

The bump map in Figure 11-89 is that of a character who is middle aged and therefore has a lot of lines in his face.

Let's look at each of the elements in this bump map, beginning with the basic facial features — the mouth and eyes. I start off by taking the base color layer that I created (the same way that I created that initial color base layer in the color map example at the beginning of this chapter).

Figure 11-89

Desaturating that layer gives me a base for the bump map that has some minor details in it, so it is not a plain gray layer. You can even add a little bit of noise into it to make it slightly rough.

Now on to the mouth. Take a look at your lips and you'll notice that they are pretty bumpy and have little sharp lines in them. Your bump map needs to include these lines. What sometimes works quite well is to take a photo of your lips and use that as a guideline for painting them. You can actually incorporate it into your texture (if you can get the lighting in the photo suitable enough) or simply use it as a guideline to paint over. Not only do your lips have these delicate little grooves, but they also have a larger unevenness to them. So first you would paint the little fine lines, and then paint a slightly blotchy layer to give them a bit of lumpiness.

Figure 11-90

Moving to the eyes now, I paint some basic crow's-feet wrinkles coming out from the outer corners of each eye. Most people over the age of 15 have begun to develop these fine wrinkles.

The trick with bump mapping is making sure that your details are fine enough. This means that bump maps should ideally be created in large files (dimension wise), so that a one-pixel brush creates a very fine line. This is to avoid having big ugly thick wrinkles where there should be fine wrinkles, for example.

The other trick to bump mapping lies in the way that each layer you create blends with the layers beneath it. While you may initially paint your wrinkles as plain thin lines, leaving them like that will create an effect like a cut, such as you would get if you were to etch in wet clay with a fine piece of wire. Figure 11-91 shows some wrinkles that look fine, shape-wise, but will make the skin look hard if applied as they are.

The trick is to go in and gradually work around these wrinkles so that the skin dips into the wrinkles and rises between them to create a fleshier look, as shown in Figure 11-92.

Figure 11-91

Figure 11-92

As always, it is absolutely essential that you use soft-edged brushes so that the effect isn't blotchy. It also helps to keep the brush on a relatively low intensity so that you can gradually build up these tonal changes. As I have said before, it is about subtlety and delicacy. Approaching your painting in this manner is crucial to intuitively building up lovely textures.

As you can see in Figure 11-93, I did the forehead wrinkles in this manner so that they would appear softer on the skin.

Next up I continue working wrinkles into the face. These wrinkles are really roughly painted initially — I create rough crisscrossing lines and then go into the area and work the area around the wrinkles as I showed above.

The veins are next. I create these with a low opacity white brush, and then once I have painted the actual shapes, I use a soft-edged eraser and erase the starting and ending points of the veins so they gradually fade in and out of the rest of the map.

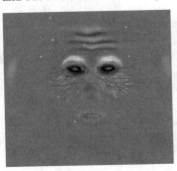

Figure 11-93

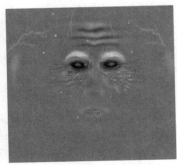

Figure 11-94

Bump maps are very intuitive to create because they are easy to visualize. Unlike specular or reflection maps, you can look at a bump map and instantly visualize exactly what effect it is going to have on the surface. With textures for specularity, reflection, translucency, etc., you often find that once you apply it, it was brighter than you thought it would be and has created an effect that is too strong, or even the opposite, that the effect is too weak. So you have to lighten or darken or increase the contrast of those textures to tweak them. However, with bump mapping, it is much more intuitive since you are interactively raising or lowering the terrain of your model's surface with a touch of a brush. Looking at a bump map you can instantly get a feel for how it will affect the model, with all the lighter areas raised and all the darker areas indented into the surface.

You'll notice that I have also added bright spots onto the bump map — these are for facial blemishes that were in the color map, which I created first. Remember, it is very important to ensure that your different surface textures match each other and share details that affect each surface property independently, and in different ways. It is no good creating abrasions or other details in your bump map that are not going to show up in the color map in any way. For this reason, a lot of people like to take their bump map details and blend them with their color maps on low opacity. Of course, I work the other way around generally, like in this example, so I simply copy the blemish layer from my color map into my bump map and desaturate and blend it accordingly.

I now do the same with the layer of stubble I created for this character. I simply copy the layer into my bump map, and increase its brightness until it is white. This will create a nice roughness on the beard area of his skin when rendered.

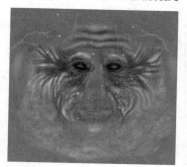

Finally (and this is the most fun part), I simply go mad with my Dodge and Burn tools.

As you can see, I have painted even more wrinkles into the skin, very bold this time. I've taken my Dodge tool and worked in between the grooves and wrinkles to soften it and give it a fleshier look.

Figure 11-95

Figure 11-96 shows this without all the other layers, so that you can more clearly see what I have done.

It looks oddly like Albert Einstein. This process of building up all the wrinkles and grooves in the skin is just great fun, and only took a few minutes. Because I was using the Dodge and Burn tools, I was working directly on the initial base layer that I created. But whenever I do that, I always copy the layer so that if I make a

Figure 11-96

**241**

mistake or mess it up really badly, I can always delete it and I'll still have a copy of the original unedited one to start with again.

Always play it safe like this. Texturing often involves a lot of trial and error, so be sure to keep your important layers safe because, believe me, you will make a massive mess of your textures at some stage.

## Good File Habits

This section is about files. More specifically, the Photoshop files (or whatever paint program you are using) and the files that you save your textures to.

There have been many occasions in the past few years when I have had to fix the texturing on other people's models and have found myself wanting to pull my hair out because their files were so disorganized. It is extremely important, especially when working in a studio environment where a lot of artists are assigned to work on various aspects of the same models, to adopt a logical file naming structure and a clear way of organizing your texture files.

First, let me show you how I arrange my Photoshop files. Whenever I start working on a new texture, I create layer sets. Layer sets in Photoshop are folders of layers contained within an image. As I have mentioned many times before, it is really important to keep your different details within your textures on separate layers. This is not only to keep things safe (because carefully erasing a bunch of wrinkles painted directly onto your base skin layer that didn't turn out too well is going to take a lot longer than simply trashing the wrinkle layer and creating a new one), but also because you can then easily copy those different layers into each of your new texture layers for the other surface attributes.

This means that you generally end up with a lot of layers in your file, and this can make navigating the file a bit cumbersome. So I arrange my layers into layer sets. When I start my new Photoshop file, I create all the layer sets I am going to need, for example, color layers, bump layers, reflection layers, etc. I create input layers, such as the imported UV map and any matte layers, on top of the layer sets.

The useful thing about layer sets is that you can switch off all the layers within each by simply clicking on the eye icon next to the layer set's name, instead of having to switch off the visibility of each layer, which is a pain.

**Figure 11-97**

The other important thing with your main texture creation files is naming your layers appropriately. The tiny preview next to each layer name is useless if the details painted on that layer are so small or faint that you cannot see them in the preview. So naming your layer appropriately, such as "wrinkles" or "pimples" or "dragon scales" not only helps to improve your own efficiency when navigating between layers, but it also helps anyone else who may have to use your files.

Once you have created all your different textures, save them using logical names. It is really frustrating when you are working in a studio and there are hundreds of models in the project, and someone is using stupid names like "color head" when there are 13 characters in the scene. Whose head is the texture for? It would be more appropriate to name it "Franky head color" so that anyone looking in the directory would instantly know which model the texture was for. I tend to shorten the texture terms to simple things like "col," "spec," "ref," etc. For example, the color texture for a Tyrannosaurus rex I am working on is saved as "T-Rex_head_col" and its specular map is saved as "T-Rex_head_spec." This makes things simpler for everyone, and also makes your workflow more efficient since it saves you (and everyone else) the time of having to constantly search for items that you have forgotten the names of because you gave them stupid, non-specific names.

## 3D Paint Solutions

Of course paint applications like Adobe Photoshop and Corel PHOTO-PAINT are not the only available tools for painting your textures. There are several other 3D painting applications available on the market these days, including Deep Paint 3D (by Right Hemisphere), BodyPaint 3D (by Maxon, the makers of Cinema 4D), and ZBrush 2 (by Pixologic). These programs allow you to paint directly onto your model in a real-time 3D viewport. For people who struggle with the sometimes frustrating concept of UV maps (especially when you have quite a few of them applied to your model, making it rather complex to match up different maps to each other), and also simply for the sheer comfort of it, these 3D painting solutions can make great additions to your working toolset.

I personally use a combination of 2D and 3D paint programs when creating textures, although I still do the majority of it in 2D (simply because I am so used to it). But as the quality of 3D painting applications has really improved over the last few years, I'll probably be using these 3D programs a lot more in my workflow.

So I thought it worth mentioning these particular applications, all of which have working demos available for download from the developers' sites.

Deep Paint and BodyPaint support LightWave natively; ZBrush does not. This makes it very simple to take your models into them for painting since you don't need to export them to another format, which can sometimes be a bit of an inconvenience as well as an annoying interruption of your workflow.

To give proper coverage and examples of these programs would require an entire book on its own, so for the purposes of this book we'll just take a quick look at each program, and you can make up your own mind as to whether or not you would like to check them out further.

Exactly the same texturing theory principles apply to creating textures in 2D and 3D environments. It is just the workflow that differs. Many people find it more intuitive to paint in 3D simply because it feels more natural than painting on a flat image that will then wrap around the model.

In the case of ZBrush, it goes a bit further from just texture painting on 3D models; you also have the ability to subdivide and sculpt your meshes. So read on, then download the demos and see which one fits your style and workflow the best.

## Right Hemisphere's Deep Paint 3D

Deep Paint 3D is a program developed by Right Hemisphere for painting directly onto your models in real-time 3D. Basically, you just load your LightWave models into it, and paint directly on them using a variety of brushes.

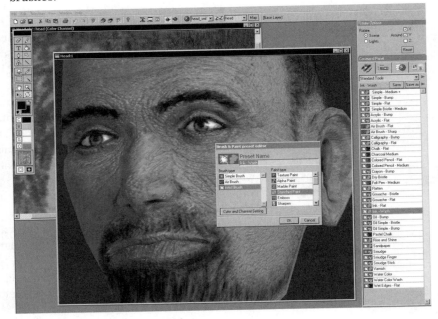

Figure 11-98: Deep Paint 3D interface

The really cool thing about Deep Paint 3D is that it lets you paint onto your different surface channels independently (color, bump, shine, glow, opacity), or together, allowing you to set up the appropriate values for each beforehand. Because of the nature of this painting process, you do not need to worry too much about seams, because not only are you painting directly onto all your applied UV maps, you also have a brilliant tool called Projection Paint that specifically lets you paint directly onto the seams.

The program is intuitive and relatively easy to use, giving you a variety of textures or natural media that can be brushed directly or projected onto 3D models and scenes loaded into the program.

## Program Overview

The environment supports an integrated workflow with 3ds max, Maya, Softimage, and, of course, LightWave, and comes complete with a bidirectional interface to Photoshop and supports Wacom tablets. (Many Deep Paint 3D tools respond to changes in pen pressure, angle, direction, or speed of movement. Extra features are provided for Wacom tablets and the Intuos Airbrush and 4D-Mouse.)

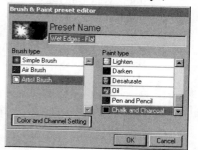

Figure 11-99

The program can be used standalone or in conjunction with Deep UV, an application also developed and released by Right Hemisphere for creating and editing UV maps.

Brush cursors display the true brush shape in 2D and 3D modes, while the brush stroke preview window in the Presets panel displays an example stroke of the current preset.

Deep Paint 3D works with layers, similar to those found in paint programs like Adobe Photoshop. Layers are stacked on top of one another, and can be reordered and arranged as desired.

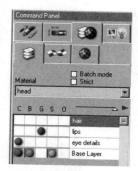
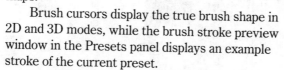

Figure 11-100

Each layer has its own Opacity slider for controlling its visibility, as well as a number of different blending modes for blending it with underlying layers.

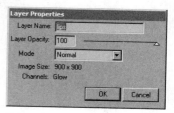

Figure 11-101

Presets are combinations of brush and paint settings that can be quickly changed, created, or edited, and saved for later use.

Texture Paint, a preset category, lets you paint with images as brush tips, much like using custom brushes in Adobe Photoshop.

One of the drawbacks to Deep Paint 3D is that it does not support LightWave's subdivision surfaces, so the model appears in the viewport as it does when your object is in Polygon mode within Modeler.

For more information about Deep Paint 3D, visit Right Hemisphere's site at www.righthemisphere.com.

## Maxon's BodyPaint 3D

A slightly newer addition to the 3D painting market, Maxon's BodyPaint 3D feels very much like a 3D version of Photoshop, since its toolset is very similar. For artists who are familiar with Photoshop, learning BodyPaint will be a relatively easy task.

BodyPaint also has built-in UV tools, which can help to extend your UV mapping toolset as it offers some tools that LightWave does not, such as a Relax function.

Another handy thing about it is that unlike Deep Paint 3D, it supports subdivision surfaces, so your model appears smooth in the BodyPaint viewport.

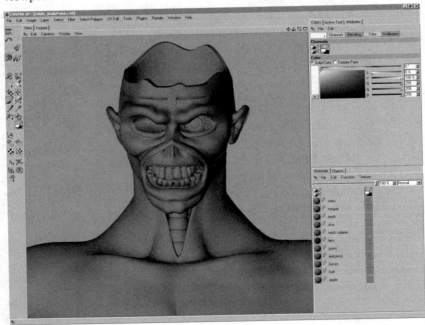

Figure 11-102: BodyPaint 3D interface

In terms of its features, it offers a very similar package of tools to that which Deep Paint 3D offers. Let's take a brief look at these features.

## Program Overview

BodyPaint is powered by a technology called RayBrush, a very powerful real-time rendering engine that gives you a superb ray-trace quality view of your model while painting. This means that you can see your specularity, transparency, and reflection maps in real time, which is really convenient since you don't have to keep going back and forth between LightWave and BodyPaint to see how these surface attributes look.

The Multibrush function allows you to paint directly onto a maximum of 10 textures simultaneously. Like Deep Paint 3D, BodyPaint also has a Projection Paint feature for covering up seams between UV maps and painting distortion-free textures.

The program also supports third-party Adobe Photoshop filters for those of you who like to use them.

One of my favorite things about BodyPaint, as mentioned before, is its similarity to Photoshop. The layers work in the same way, and it even has Dodge, Burn, and Sponge tools like Photoshop. Additionally, if you have been working on your textures in Photoshop beforehand, you can import your entire PSD file into BodyPaint, with all the layers and blending modes intact, and continue working on that file while it is applied to your model in real time.

The brush tools are intuitive to set up (see Figure 11-103) with lots of controls for defining their appearance and effect, and the program itself is very fast and handles large images well without slowing down too much.

And if you want to switch to 2D painting mode, all you have to do is go to the Texture tab at the top of the viewport to switch to a 2D image painting mode.

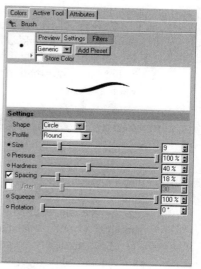

Figure 11-103

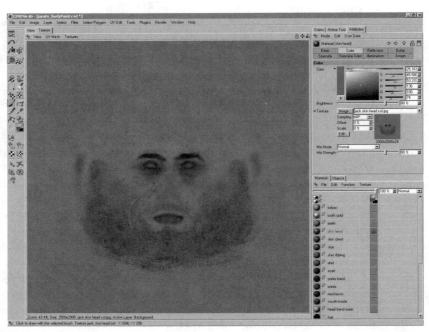

Figure 11-104

The program's interface is also totally customizable, with docking windows that you can rearrange as you wish.

Of course there are loads of other features, but going into them now will make me sound like an ad for Maxon! I highly recommend checking this program out, especially if you are comfortable with Photoshop's workflow.

For more information about BodyPaint 3D, visit Maxon's site at www.maxon.net.

## Pixologic's ZBrush 2

ZBrush is one of my favorite tools to complement LightWave. It has become extremely popular in the last few years with individual artists as well as production studios in general, mostly due to its ability to add incredible detail to your objects and then export this to a displacement map or normal map that can then be applied in your 3D program of choice. LightWave v9 has native support for both displacement and normal maps from ZBrush. Its odd-looking interface might appear somewhat intimidating at first, but after a session or two you will be navigating through it with ease. Those of you who dread UV mapping will find that ZBrush basically automates this process for you so you can avoid the technicalities of UV mapping and concentrate on doing what you like to do best — be creative!

The ZBrush canvas is quite unique as well, as it operates with a technology called "pixols" where the pixels hold depth and material information. Keep in mind that when an object is dropped on the canvas and the Edit button is no longer active, your mesh will be converted to this 2.5D environment and you will no longer be able to edit your mesh with the intention of using it in an external package.

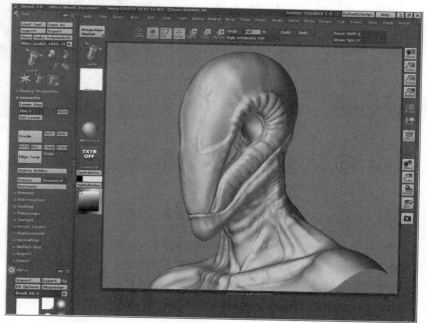

Figure 11-105: ZBrush interface

## Program Overview

ZBrush has a very complete toolset for the creation of displacement maps, normal maps, and texture maps, but the most important asset of ZBrush is probably its speed. You can add detail to your objects and reshape the general forms of the mesh with hardly any slowdowns. In order to achieve the fine details, you subdivide your mesh in increments, so at high levels of subdivision you add the finer details and at low levels you change the general shape. Since this subdivision is hierarchical, changes made in a particular level get propagated up or down the hierarchy. In addition to the great modeling tools, you have access to several brushes to aid you in the texturing process. I personally use the Blur, Highlighter, and Colorize brushes quite often. Pressing the Alt key lets you switch the brush between the Sharpen, Burn, and Saturation tools.

Another great feature is Projection Master, which lets you use alphas (black and white images) to add detail to your objects by projecting the alphas onto your mesh and thus deforming it. With Projection Master you can also bring in texture maps, apply an alpha, and texture your object so you can paint textures, deformations, or both at the same time.

Painting textures in ZBrush is a lot of fun as well, especially painting bump maps. If you apply the Bump Viewer Material to your object, you can paint bumps as they would actually look in LightWave when rendered!

These are just a few of the features available in ZBrush 2. For more information, see Chapter 25, "Light-Wave ZBrush Workflow," where I'll show you the workflow between LightWave and ZBrush by guiding you

Figure 11-106: Projection Master

throught the creation process of an alien head, including covering modeling details, creating displacement, normal, and texture maps, and combining them in LightWave for final rendering.

# CHAPTER 12

# The Image Editor

## Introduction to the Image Editor

### Loading Images

The first and foremost use of the Image Editor, in both Modeler and Layout, is to load images that you wish to use on your model and within your scene.

To load the Image Editor, press Ctrl+F4 or click on the Image Editor button, which is found a little way down from your File menu (the top corner of your toolbar).

Figure 12-1

NOTE: You can also quickly access the Image Editor by pressing the Edit Image button displayed below the image thumbnail in the Texture Editor when working on surfaces.

To load an image, simply press the Load button, which will open the Load Images... window where you locate and select the images that you wish to load.

LightWave can load a variety of different image and animation formats, including the most popular

**Figure 12-2**

formats such as JPEG, TGA, TIFF, AVI, MOV, etc. See Appendix B for a complete list and description of all formats supported by LightWave.

There are some image formats, such as PIC (a format used for some radiance files), that you will not see automatically in the Load Images... window. To make sure that you can see all the images located in a folder, be sure that you select All Files in the Files of type box. This will ensure that all files of any type will show up in the window.

**Figure 12-3**

Once an image is loaded into the Image Editor, a little bit of information about the image and a preview of it are displayed at the top right of the window.

The Type specifies whether the file is a still image, part of a sequence, or an ani-

**Figure 12-4**

mation file. Depth indicates the bit depth of the image. Most images that we use are 16- or 24-bit, while images that contain alpha channels are 32-bit. Size simply specifies the actual dimensions of the image in pixels, while Mem shows the amount of physical memory that the image uses when it is loaded. The amount of memory that your images use in your scene is quite important, so keep an eye on it. Remember that the more memory they use, the longer your render times will be, so make sure that you do not use up too much memory on images that may be unnecessarily large or even totally unnecessary.

Below the preview window is a slider that you can use to preview the file if it is an animation or an image sequence.

Once you have loaded your images into your scene or into Modeler, you can select them from drop-down lists within the Texture Editor and from any other dialog that has a drop-down list for selecting images, such as your Compositing and Backdrop options in Layout.

> **NOTE:** To delete an image from the scene or from Modeler, simply select the image and press Delete. You can also right-click on the image and select Delete. Keep in mind that if an image is no longer used within a scene or on a model, it will no longer load the next time you open the scene or model.

## Replacing Images

Once you have images loaded into your scene or on your object, you occasionally need to replace them. Why would you need to replace them? Well, when I am working, I am often making changes to the textures at the same time as I am working on a scene in Layout. If I make a change to a texture (in Photoshop) and that texture is currently being used in my scene, then I need to reload it into my scene because LightWave does not automatically detect that the original image file has been edited when I save the new version in Photoshop. This is an example of when I would use the Replace Image option.

You can replace your current image with an entirely new one, which will then take the place of the previous one, wherever it was used, or you can use the command to update your current image with a new version of it. You replace images by selecting them from the list in the Image Editor and then clicking the Replace button, which opens the Replace

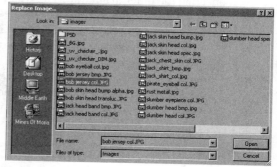

Figure 12-5

Image... window in which you can choose the image you want.

To replace your image with an entirely different image, simply select your image from the list on the left-hand side in the Image Editor, press Replace, and then select a new image to replace the current one.

If you wish to simply update your image to a newer version of it (assuming you have saved the newer version by simply overwriting the original), you can simply press Replace and then press Open in the Replace Image... window, since the image should automatically be selected here.

# Cloning Images

Should you wish to make copies of an image sequence within your scene without actually loading a separate version of the sequence, you can make a copy of it.

You do this with the Clone option. When you press the Clone button, you are presented with two choices: Instance and Duplicate.

Choosing the Instance option creates a copy of the image that will reflect any changes you make to the original of the image in the scene.

**Figure 12-6**

For example, if you make an instance of an image and you then make any adjustments to that original image, such as a Hue adjustment or a Brightness adjustment in the Editing tab, those adjustments will also affect the instance. However, you can make adjustments to the instance itself without affecting the original. You can make as many instances of an image as you like within your scene.

A duplicate is a copy that is entirely independent of the original. You can make any changes you wish to both the original and the duplicate without affecting the other in any way. The Duplicate option, however, is only available for image sequences, not still images or animation files. You can make as many duplicates of a sequence as you like within your scene.

The great thing about cloning images and sequences is that it saves on memory, since you are not loading in entire extra files.

> **CAUTION:**  Deleting an image, animation, or sequence from the Image Editor will remove any clones of it from the scene as well.

# Preview Display Options

The preview window of the Image Editor has a few different options that you can choose from.

The Auto, Real, and Man buttons determine how the preview window is updated.

**Figure 12-7**

The default is Real, short for Realtime. Using this option ensures that the preview window will update while you make any changes to the image within the editor. This means that while you are making any adjustments using sliders, you will see this preview update as you make the adjustment, without having to actually release your mouse button.

Auto (Automatic) makes the preview update only when you release the mouse button after making any adjustments to the image.

When set to Man (Manual), you will have to click on the preview window itself to see any changes you have made. This can save on memory if you are using a slower computer, in which case you sometimes have to wait a while for the image to update, especially when working with very complex scenes that have lots of images. And since it isn't always absolutely necessary to see changes you have made to the image, you can use your memory more efficiently by setting the display to Manual.

The Use Layout Time check box can be activated to use the time slider in Layout to preview an image sequence or animation file as it is used in the scene, instead of the slider below the preview window itself.

This can be useful for checking when an animation starts to play within the scene, and how and when it loops.

## The Source Tab

The Source tab is the first tab we encounter on the Image Editor. It contains information about the image, as well as settings you can adjust for animation files and image sequences.

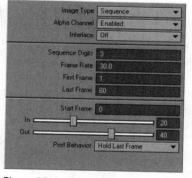

Figure 12-8: The Source tab

## Image Type

The first thing that is displayed in the Source tab is the information regarding the type of image that you have loaded and selected.

This can be a still image, an image sequence, an animation file, or a reference.

### Still

A still image, as discussed before, is simply any image file, such as a texture map or an image for the background, that you wish to use in a scene.

### Sequence

An image sequence is a sequence of image files that form a clip, usually a numbered sequence rendered from a program such as LightWave or any other program that can render out animations or images. Ideally, you should use sequences that are numbered correctly, using digits from 001 to whatever the final frame is. Having a correctly numbered sequence will ensure that the clip will play back without any hitches.

To load an image sequence, simply load an image as you ordinarily would by clicking on Load and selecting an image within the sequence. You can select any image from the sequence that you wish; it doesn't necessarily have to be the first image in the sequence. This will load the image into the Image Editor as if it were a still. To ensure that the entire sequence is loaded, select the image from the list on the left, go to the Image Type drop-down list, and select Sequence.

Figure 12-9

This will automatically load up the other images that LightWave can detect are in the sequence.

> **NOTE:** To ensure that your image sequences load without too many hassles, it is a good practice to keep sequences in their own folders. Also ensure that your sequences are named and numbered correctly, ideally with a filename followed directly by a digit, such as "character_animated.0001.tga."

If there are any gaps in the sequence, then the previous image in the sequence holds until the next one is encountered. For example, if there are frames numbered from 0001 to 0004 and then there are some frames missing until 0007, then the frame numbered 0004 will hold until frame number 0007 loads.

### Animation

To load an animation file into the Image Editor, simply click Load and select the file you want. Common animation file formats include AVI (Windows Media files) and MOV (QuickTime) files. LightWave does not support MPEG animation files.

### Reference

If you make an instance of an image or sequence as discussed earlier, then the Image Type of that file when selected will be Reference. You cannot change this setting.

## Alpha Channel

If the image or image sequence consists of 32-bit images with an alpha channel, you can choose to enable or disable that channel by selecting the appropriate option from the Alpha Channel drop-down list. By default, alpha channels are enabled. Using the Alpha Only option discards all the color information from the image, and instead treats the image as a black and white mask from the alpha channel. This is useful if you wish to use the image as a mask in the Texture Editor.

Figure 12-10

Notice that the Alpha Channel options are only available in images that contain alpha information. With any other image, this option is grayed out.

Working with alpha channels can be a bit confusing though, so be careful when using them. When you load images into the Image Editor, always be sure to check whether there is an alpha channel or not, if you are not accustomed to using them.

Because OpenGL does not take alpha channels into account, it can sometimes cause a lot of confusion. If an image you are using as a texture has an alpha channel, which then masks out part of the texture when you render it, you may wonder why on earth parts of the texture are not showing when they were there in your viewport while you were working!

So if you load up an image and you notice that it has an unneeded alpha channel, just disable it by selecting Disabled from the Alpha Channel drop-down list.

## Interlace

Select your interlacing options from this list. Interlacing is only found in digitized video that uses fields. If you are using any other kind of file, this should be set to Off. If the video is using fields, select either Even First or Odd First, depending on which applies to the clip.

**Figure 12-11**

This ensures that the clip is interlaced correctly, and will therefore play back correctly.

> **NOTE:** Refer to the LightWave manual for more information on fields and field rendering.

## Sequence Digits

You use this setting to specify the number of digits used in the numbering sequence when using image sequences.

**Figure 12-12**

Although LightWave does attempt to discern this information when loading image sequences into the Image Editor, it can occasionally have trouble, especially if there are any peculiarities in the numbering system used. If this is the case, you can manually enter the number of digits that LightWave should be looking for in the filename to ensure that the sequence loads correctly.

When loading an image sequence, LightWave examines the filenames used and attempts to discern which part of the filename is the number of the frame. For instance, if the files in a sequence are named animationsequence.0001 through animationsequence.0100, LightWave will know that "animationsequence" is the base filename, while the remaining numbers are the actual sequential digits. In this case, Sequence Digits would be set to 4, since there are four digits in the numbers.

## Frame Rate

The Frame Rate setting applies only to animation files or image sequences. You can enter in the desired frame rate at which you wish the files to be played back within LightWave.

## First Frame and Last Frame

The number entered for First Frame determines the frame number at which an image sequence or animation file begins.

Figure 12-13

If you load an image sequence in which the first number is, for example, 0003, then the First Frame number will be 3. The first frame for an animation file is 0 by default.

Likewise, the Last Frame number is the last digit that is used in the sequence. So if your sequence ends on frame number 0567, then this number will be 567.

Due to the nature of number sequences, which can be infinite, you may find that you sometimes will have to manually adjust these numbers according to the sequence that you have loaded.

> **NOTE:** Do not use these numbers to try to trim a clip. In other words, if you have a sequence that goes from frame 0000 to 0500, but only wish to use frames 0100 to 0200, do not use the First Frame and Last Frame settings to try to set this, as it can cause some annoying problems. Instead, use the In and Out sliders, discussed below.

## Start Frame

The number entered in this field determines the frame in Layout's timeline at which the clip will begin to play.

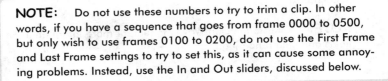

Figure 12-14

For example, if you want the clip or sequence to begin playing at frame 25 in Layout, you will enter 25.

## In and Out

Use the In and Out sliders to determine the starting and ending points of the actual sequence or animation file.

Figure 12-15

For example, if you have a sequence of 60 frames going from frame 001 to 060, and you only want to play frames 020 to 040, then you would adjust the sliders to do this, as shown in Figure 12-16.

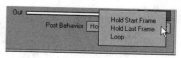

Figure 12-16

You can use these sliders for animation files and image sequences.

## Post Behavior

This setting determines what the animation or sequence does once it has finished playing. There are three options: Hold Start Frame, Hold Last Frame, and Loop.

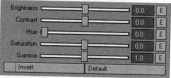

Figure 12-17

The default is Hold Last Frame, which continues to display the last frame in the sequence or animation once it has finished playing.

Likewise, Hold Start Frame will hold on the first frame upon completion, while Loop will repeat the animation or sequence indefinitely.

# The Editing Tab

The Editing tab is where you can make tonal adjustments to your images in the Image Editor, using controls for Brightness, Contrast, Hue, Saturation, and Gamma. All of these controls work on the image master settings, as opposed to separate channels, so the effects of each are very strong.

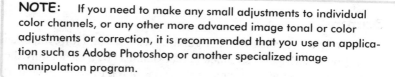

Figure 12-18

Each of these sliders can be animated by clicking on its Envelope button.

> NOTE: If you need to make any small adjustments to individual color channels, or any other more advanced image tonal or color adjustments or correction, it is recommended that you use an application such as Adobe Photoshop or another specialized image manipulation program.

## Brightness

A pretty basic and common adjustment setting, the Brightness slider simply allows you to make the image brighter or darker by adjusting the values of the tonal range within the image.

Dragging the slider all the way to the right will make the image pure white, while dragging it all the way to the left will make the image totally black.

## Contrast

You adjust the contrast within your image by using this slider. Contrast increases or decreases the values between the darker tones and the lighter tones in the image. This is useful for adding some spark to slightly dulled images. Too much contrast, however, can make an image seem very oversaturated, as well as make any details in the image difficult to discern, especially when there are a lot of darker tones in it. Too little contrast can make images washed out and extremely dull.

## Hue

Hue adjusts the overall color master for the image. As you move the slider, the colors cycle through the colors of the spectrum, tinting the image. Notice that when you pull the slider all the way to the right, it returns to its normal state, since you have cycled through all the colors.

## Saturation

The saturation amount determines the amount of color contained within an image. Bringing the slider all the way to the left removes all color from the image, leaving it in grayscale (desaturated/unsaturated). Increasing the saturation amount increases the saturation of each color pixel, bringing each to a purer value of that color. In other words, red tones will become redder, yellow tones will become more yellow, and blue tones will become more blue.

Be careful of your use of saturation, as oversaturated images are really nasty to look at, since they become garish and can become distracting and unsightly in a scene.

The Saturation slider is very useful for making adjustments to images used in surfaces that need to be diffused, as discussed in Chapter 4.

## Gamma

Gamma controls the overall brightness of an image. However, this is different from the Brightness slider, in that Gamma changes not only the brightness of an image, but also the ratios of red to green to blue; in other words, it affects the hue of the image as well. Gamma correction is important in ensuring that an image will display well on different monitors or other display media.

Gamma and gamma correction are pretty complex subjects though, and would require a lot more than just this paragraph to explain, so let me make this as brief as possible.

All images contain a point called the gamma point, which is the level of the tonal range within the image that is 50% gray. In terms of luminosity within an image, it is the point at which half the pixels are darker and half of them are lighter. Adjusting gamma does not affect the darkest and lightest points (the black and white points) within an image, only those values in between.

The effect of gamma is also non-linear, as when you make adjustments to it, you affect the pixels closer to the gamma point more than those that are farther away. When you adjust the gamma up, you basically make more light pixels in the image, causing the image to become lighter. When you decrease the gamma, you make more dark pixels in the image, causing it to become darker.

As I mentioned before, this is important for ensuring that the image displays correctly when viewed on different displays, as all monitors and TV screens have gamma points of their own as well. However, this is an entirely separate topic that I will not deal with here.

## Invert

This button inverts the image in the same way that Adobe Photoshop inverts images. Invert is useful mostly for black and white images, as the result of using this on color images is usually quite bizarre.

## Default

If you decide you don't want any of the changes you have made with the sliders, clicking on the Default button restores all the sliders to their default positions.

# The Processing Tab

The Processing tab is where you add and animate filters that you wish to use on the images and sequence files that you have loaded into the Image Editor.

Many of these filters are more concerned with rendering effects and not really texturing or surfaces as such, and a handful of the filters can also be used to directly enhance our surfaces for an extra touch of realism.

Refer to Chapter 19 for information on using image filters to add effects to your actual surfaces during post-processing.

**Figure 12-19**

Of course since this is the Image Editor, these filters are actually applied to the images themselves as opposed to render buffers, as we find when using filters in the Effects panel in Layout.

You can use any of the non-post-processing filters from this list on images. These include: Anaglyph Stereo: Compose, Anaglyph Stereo:

**261**

Simulate, Bloom, Corona, Full Precision Blur, Full Precision Gamma, HDR Exposure, Textured Filter, Video Legalize, Virtual Darkroom, and Watermark.

For more information on each of these filters, consult your LightWave manual. Bloom and Corona are covered in depth in Chapter 19.

# CHAPTER 13

# The Texture Editor

## Layer Opacity and Blending Modes

As discussed earlier, the Texture Editor is where you create your textures to apply to each individual surface property. You open the Texture Editor by clicking on the little "T" next to a surface channel's name.

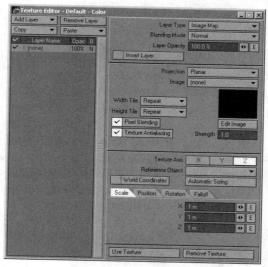

Figure 13-1

Since the subject of creating actual textures is covered in various other chapters of this book, this chapter deals solely with the functions that you use within the Texture Editor to manipulate the texture layers that you create.

To create a new texture layer, click on Add Layer. You can choose to create a new layer for an image map, a procedural texture, or a gradient.

Once you have a number of layers in the Texture Editor, you start blending them to get the right effect that you need for the surface,

Figure 13-2

**263**

since stacking layers on top of one another without any form of blending is not going to do anything other than leave the top layer the only visible one.

## Using Layer Opacity

The simplest way to blend one layer with another is by changing its opacity. The opacity of a layer simply controls the visibility of that layer. The higher the opacity of the layer, the more *solid* it appears, whereas a lower value makes it more transparent, blending it more with any underlying layers.

Look at Figure 13-3. The sphere on the left has a grid texture of 100% Opacity, whereas the sphere on the right has a grid texture of 20% Opacity. Notice how it blends with the Turbulence procedural below it.

Figure 13-3

To change a layer's opacity, you can use the spinner or you can type in a new opacity amount yourself.

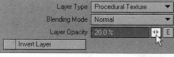

Figure 13-4

Notice that the opacity value for each layer is also listed next to the layer's name in the layer list in the Texture Editor, under the column heading abbreviated "Opac."

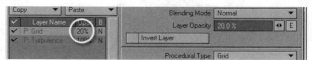

Figure 13-5

The problem with using only opacity to blend layers together is that it doesn't really take color or intensity of the layer into account, which often results in a very washed-out effect, as opposed to a nice, rich blending of two layers. This can work fine for things like specularity or bump textures, but not for color. Changing the opacity of a color layer takes away the richness and saturation of that color, since the effect of opacity is so linear.

To counteract this effect, we use different blending modes in conjunction with opacity changes to determine the way in which the layers blend with one another, in order to create richer textures.

# Understanding and Using Blending Modes

To anyone who has a good working knowledge of any image editing program such as Adobe Photoshop, the concept of blending modes, with regard to image layering, is simple to understand and to use. The blending options found in LightWave are fairly similar to those found within Photoshop's layer blending modes, and recently several of these Photoshop blending modes were incorporated into LightWave. Keep in mind that even though some blending mode names are similar, the math under the hood is different and therefore produces different effects.

The blending mode of a layer defines the manner in which it blends with the other layers within the Texture Editor.

Blending is different from opacity in that it considers certain factors when blending with surrounding layers, depending on what mode you use. This is great for achieving interesting effects that you can use to enhance or control other layers using the one you are blending with.

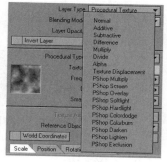

Figure 13-6

To change the blending mode of a layer, click on the Blending Mode button and choose a mode from the list. There are 18 different modes from which to choose, including the Photoshop blending mode equivalents.

Notice that the different blending modes applied to layers are indicated in the layers list, under the column labeled "B" (for Blending mode), by different symbols or letters.

Figure 13-7

The letter N represents Normal.

The + symbol represents Additive.

The – symbol represents Subtractive.

The +– symbol represents Difference.

The * symbol represents Multiply.

The / symbol represents Divide.

The letter A represents Alpha.

The letter D represents Texture Displacement.

The letter P represents Photoshop Blending Mode.

If you are familiar with using a computer-based calculator, then you will be familiar with some of these symbols, such as the +, –, *, and / symbols being used for adding, subtracting, multiplying, and dividing, respectively.

## Normal

This is the default blending mode that is applied to layers that you create. A layer that is set to Normal will result in the layer being totally solid and not blending in any way with any underlying layers unless you change its opacity.

**265**

If you are creating a texture that has only one texture layer, this is usually the best option.

If you wish to create a perfectly even blend between a number of different layers, you can do so using this mode and setting up the Opacity amounts according to a simple equation. You divide the number of each layer (as it appears in order from the bottom up) into 100 and use the resulting values to determine the Opacity values for each layer.

For example, if you had five layers, you would do the following:

The bottom layer (in other words, layer 1) would have an opacity value of 100%, since 100 divided by 1 equals 100. The second layer (the one above the bottom layer) would have an opacity value of 50%, because 100 divided by 2 equals 50. The third layer would have an opacity value of 33%, because 100 divided by 3 equals 33. The fourth layer would have an opacity value of 25%, because 100 divided by 4 equals 25. And the fifth layer, being the topmost layer, would have an opacity value of 20%, since 100 divided by 5 is equal to 20.

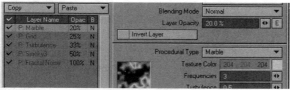

Figure 13-8

Using this method ensures that all the layers will blend evenly when using the Normal blending mode.

## Additive

Using Additive blending will *add* the layer times its opacity to the underlying layers. So if, for example, the layer's opacity is 35%, the layer will be multiplied 35 times to the layers underneath it.

This effect is slightly similar to the Dodge blending mode found in older versions of Adobe Photoshop.

This is a quite strong effect, and can be extremely useful for enhancing parts of layers.

Look at Figure 13-9. The texture layers on the sphere on the left are all set to Normal, whereas the sphere on the right has the same layers, but with two of them set to Additive. Notice how the additive blending makes parts of the texture much more enhanced.

Figure 13-9

When used with gradients, you can create some really nice effects as well. In the following image, the sphere on the left has an Incidence Angle gradient applied with normal blending, while the sphere on the right has the gradient set to Additive. Notice how much more intense the effect of the gradient is when set to Additive.

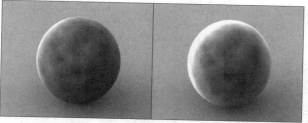

Figure 13-10

To see another example of where the Additive blending mode is used to create a cool effect, take a look at the tutorial in Chapter 9 on making a velvet hat. This mode is used with a gradient to create the effect of light falloff on the material.

## Subtractive

Subtractive mode subtracts the layer from underlying layers, usually resulting in a darkening of underlying layers. It is basically the opposite of Additive. It subtracts the value of the layer, multiplied by the layer's opacity, from the layers below it.

This effect is slightly similar to the Burn blending mode found in Adobe Photoshop.

Figure 13-11 shows a procedural texture using Subtractive blending with increasing opacity values.

Figure 13-11

Notice that the lighter tones in the underlying layer in this example still appear lighter until the Subtractive layer is at 100% opacity. This is because the pixels in the Subtractive layer are subtracting themselves based on a multiplied value of the overall opacity of the layer, which means that lighter pixels in the underlying layer will be less affected than darker pixels, since the darker pixels will be multiplied to black sooner than the lighter ones.

**267**

## Difference

The Difference blending mode is similar to Subtractive, except that instead of multiplying the effect according to the layer's opacity, Difference uses the absolute value of the difference between the pixels in the layer and the underlying layers.

Take a look at Figure 13-12.

**Figure 13-12**

Both spheres use the same texture with the same opacity value, the difference being that the left sphere uses Subtractive blending while the right sphere uses Difference.

Notice that in this case, the effect of Difference is quite subtle, since the gray value that the texture uses is quite light.

This means that the value of this gray is subtracted from the underlying layers, and since it is a medium shade of gray and the layer's opacity is only at 50%, it does not have a dramatic effect when subtracted from the underlying layers.

If you make the color of the texture lighter and increase the layer's opacity, the effect becomes much stronger, as in Figure 13-13.

Since the tonal value of the pixels has increased, as well as the opacity, a higher value is being subtracted from the layers below, resulting in a stronger effect.

**Figure 13-13**

## Multiply

This mode multiplies the value of the layer according to the values of the underlying layers. Values that are lighter in layers below this one will result in parts of this layer brightening, and darker tones in the underlying layers will make this layer darker.

In Figure 13-14, the sphere on the left has a very light underlying layer, while the sphere on the right has a rather dark layer underneath it.

Figure 13-14

## Divide

Divide multiplies the underlying layers by the inverse of the values within the layer to which it is applied. The following image demonstrates the effect of using lighter tones in the layer (on the right) and using darker tones (on the left).

Figure 13-15

This effect is basically the opposite of the Multiply blending mode.

## Alpha

One of the most useful options in the entire Surface Editor, in my opinion, is the Alpha blending mode option for layers. This allows you to control the visibility of underlying layers by using layers on top of them that act as alpha channels (mattes).

When using this mode, remember that the black areas of a layer will allow the underlying layer to show through, while the white parts block out the underlying layer, and the gray areas show varying amounts, depending on the value of the gray.

> NOTE: The Alpha blending mode only affects the layer directly beneath it, not all the underlying layers.

Figure 13-16 shows a procedurally textured sphere, an alpha map, and the same sphere with the image applied using the Alpha blending mode on top of the procedural texture.

Figure 13-16

> **NOTE:** When using images that actually have their own alpha
> channels (such as 32-bit TGA files), you do not need to use this option
> in order to use the alpha channel. You simply have to ensure that the
> alpha channel is enabled in the Image Editor (see the section on the
> Source tab in Chapter 12).

You can use any type of layer as an alpha layer, whether it is an image, a procedural texture, or a gradient.

Using gradients with alpha blending can create some cool effects. For example, if you want to create a surface where there are details on the surface that can only be seen from certain angles, you could use an Incidence Angle gradient set to Alpha blending to control the visibility of those details, as in Figure 13-17, which reveals the underlying layer along the edges of the sphere.

Figure 13-17

In a similar fashion, you could also use a Distance to Camera gradient with Alpha blending to create the effect of an underlying layer becoming more visible as the object moves closer to the camera.

If you wanted to use a light in the scene to reveal details on a surface or to control the visibility of a layer, you could place a Light Incidence gradient over that layer, and set it to Alpha. This technique is used in the "Making a Velvet Surface for an Old Hat" tutorial in Chapter 9 to control an Incidence Angle gradient in order to create the illusion that the Incidence Angle gradient appears only where the lighting is hitting the object.

Figure 13-18

Another great use for this is to use gradients with weight maps to blend different textures together. This can be particularly useful for covering up seams between different UV maps in a single surface, a problem that many artists struggle to deal with.

Similarly, you can also use gradients with weight maps to place procedural textures onto your object.

The model in Figure 13-19 is textured using only procedurals, which are placed using a number of weight map gradients set to Alpha blending.

In fact, one of the greatest strengths of gradients is in being able to use them as alphas for other layers by using the Alpha blending mode. The possibilities are endless!

Model by William Vaughan

Figure 13-19

## Texture Displacement

This blending mode affects all the layers above the layer it is applied to and causes the layer to displace all those layers. Displacing is similar to bump mapping in that it creates the illusion of distortion. However, this blending mode can be applied to any surface property, not just the bump map.

Displacement can be particularly useful for giving variation to otherwise very uniform patterns, such as the Grid and Veins procedural textures. You control the amount of displacement using the opacity of the layer, as well as the texture value and the individual texture settings when using procedural textures.

The following example shows the results of using a Turbulence procedural to displace a Veins procedural, in varying strengths.

Figure 13-20

## PShop Multiply

All of the Photoshop blending modes in LightWave work exactly the same as their Photoshop counterparts. Multiply evaluates the color information of the layer and multiplies the base color or underlying layer with the blending color. Multiply always results in the darkening of color. White has absolutely no effect on the color blending; if the blend color is black, the Multiply mode will result in black.

Figure 13-21

## PShop Screen

Screen is the exact opposite of Multiply. Screen evaluates the color information of the layer and multiplies the inverse of the blending color and base color or underlying layer. Screen always results in the lightening of color. Black has absolutely no effect on the color blending; if the blend color is white, the screen mode will result in white.

Figure 13-22

## PShop Overlay

This mode is a mix of PShop Multiply and PShop Screen; it will multiply or screen the colors depending on the base color while leaving shadows and highlights of the base intact. This mode produces rich, saturated colors.

Figure 13-23

## PShop Softlight

Softlight is like a soft mix of dodge and burn. If your color grayscale value is lighter than 50%, then the color is softly lightened like a soft dodge. On the other hand, if the color grayscale value is over 50%, the color is softly darkened like a soft burn. Black or white will result in the darkening or lightening of color respectively, but will not result in pure black or white.

Figure 13-24

## PShop Hardlight

This blending mode is like a mix of PShop Multiply and PShop Screen. If your color grayscale value is lighter than 50%, then the color is lightened like a Screen. On the other hand, if the color grayscale value is over 50%, the color is darkened like a Multiply. Black or white will result in pure black or white.

Figure 13-25

## PShop Colordodge

With Colordodge the blending color is evaluated and the base color is brightened to show the blend color by reducing the contrast. Black produces no effect at all.

Figure 13-26

## PShop Colorburn

With Colorburn the blending color is evaluated and the base color is darkened to show the blend color by increasing the contrast. White produces no effect at all.

Figure 13-27

**273**

### PShop Darken

With Darken the blending color and the base color are evaluated and the darker of the two will be used. The areas lighter than the blend color are replaced, while areas darker than the blend color remain the same.

Figure 13-28

### PShop Lighten

This is exactly the opposite of PShop Darken. The blending color and the base color are evaluated and the lighter of the two will be used. The areas darker than the blend color are replaced, while areas lighter than the blend color remain the same.

Figure 13-29

### PShop Exclusion

Exclusion subtracts the color depending on which one is the brighter of the two, the base or the blending color. If you use white you will notice that the base color is inverted.

Figure 13-30

## Other Options in the Texture Editor

Apart from providing methods of controlling the visibility of layers, the Texture Editor also has a number of options for controlling the placement of layers and some extra options for image layers, falloff options, and a few others.

## Invert Layer

The Invert Layer option totally inverts
the current layer. To invert a layer,
click on the Invert Layer check box.

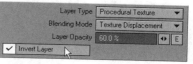

**Figure 13-31**

This is particularly useful if you
have accidentally inverted an alpha
map and don't wish to go all the way back to your image creation program to
change it. Another use for Invert Layer is if you need to use the image in
both ways, in which case it saves on RAM to simply invert the single image.

**Figure 13-32**

This function is also great when texturing with procedural textures, as
inverting them can create very different effects.

Figure 13-33 illustrates the vast difference between the Crumple procedural when it is not inverted (on the left) and when it is (on the right).

**Figure 13-33**

When the texture is not inverted, it is useful for effects like crumpled
paper or beaten metal, whereas when it is inverted, it appears far more
organic, which is great for surfaces such as leather or even skin.

Here is another example of how radically different a procedural can be
when inverted. In Figure 13-34 we see a Ridged Multi-Fractal procedural as
it usually is (on the left) and inverted (on the right).

**Figure 13-34**

Of course you can also use this for any kind of image map layer, as well as gradient layers. However, using them on colored image maps can produce rather odd results, apart from the fact that there would be few instances, if any, where you would need to do that anyway.

## Texture Axis

The Texture Axis option is available for images used in layers, except when using UV maps. It is also available for certain procedurals that require an axis projection, namely the Brick, Honeycomb, Marble, STClouds, Wood, Coriolis, and Cyclone procedurals. Most procedurals do not require an axis along which to project since they are mathematically calculated in 3D space and cover an object entirely along its normals.

Choosing the correct axis along which to project your texture is very important, and differs according to your model and how you wish to place your texture onto it.

The options are pretty self-explana-tory. You can choose either X, Y, or Z as your texture axis.

Depending on what direction you wish to project your texture, you choose

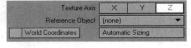

**Figure 13-35**

an appropriate axis. Remember that x is from side to side, y is from above and below, and z is from front to back.

## Reference Object

This option is useful for controlling textures using another object, usually a null object. This reference object can be used to control the position, size, and rotation of textures within a surface. To use an object in this manner, click on the Reference Object button and select the object you wish to use as a reference from the drop-down list.

**Figure 13-36**

Both image layers and procedural layers can use this option. Using a reference object can make the process of animating the position, size, and rotation of textures a lot simpler than using envelopes, as you do not need to use anything complex like graphs. You simply keyframe the changes on the reference object and the texture will react accordingly.

For example, you could use a reference object to make the textured irises of eyeballs follow a null object, which would be a lot simpler than try-ing to use the Graph Editor to do this. All you would have to do is move the null object to the point where you want the eyes to be looking and they would follow it.

## World Coordinates

Usually when texturing we want the textures to stick to the object, so that when the object moves around, the textures move with it.

However, sometimes you may need to have the textures held in place, so that when you move the object, the texture remains static and the object appears to move through the texture. Selecting World Coordinates locks textures on your object to LightWave's origin instead of to the object.

**Figure 13-37**

For example, if you wanted to create the effect of a submarine passing through light beams filtering down from the surface, you could create an underwater ripples texture in the color and luminosity channels for the submarine vehicle. You could then set the ripples texture to World Coordinates, so that as the submarine moves forward, it appears to move through the ripples that are seemingly filtering down from the surface of the water.

## Automatic Sizing

Use the Automatic Sizing option to size a texture image or procedural texture to the model that you are applying it to.

The size of the object is calculated by an imaginary box completely surrounding the section that the surface is currently applied to. This value is then determined and is used as the size for the texture you are applying when you use this option.

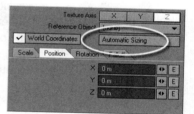

**Figure 13-38**

For example, if you have a plane that is 4m × 8m, and you have created a texture of the same ratio, you could quickly fit it perfectly to the plane by using Automatic Sizing.

Automatic Sizing is also a useful starting point when texturing with procedurals, as it can give you an immediate indication of the size of the procedural in relation to the size of the object.

> **NOTE:** Automatic Sizing is not available when using UV maps because UV maps have their own sizing.

## Scale

You use the fields or the spinners in the scale options to manually set the size that you want your texture to be on the surface. You can set your own scale amounts for the x, y, and z axes individually by typing the desired amounts into the respective fields or by dragging the spinners accordingly.

Figure 13-39

This is very important, particularly when working with procedural textures. You have no other way of setting the size of a procedural since it has no set boundaries and is not visible in OpenGL. When working with procedurals, it is usually better to set the scale of the texture to a value smaller than the surface itself, to allow for more detail. However, this can really vary from object to object, depending on what sort of surface you are creating.

> **NOTE:** As with Automatic Sizing, you cannot change the Scale amounts for a texture when it is UV mapped. Gradient layers also have no Scale options, since scale has no bearing whatsoever on the effect of a gradient.

## Position

The position spinners and fields allow you to set the position of your texture in 3D space.

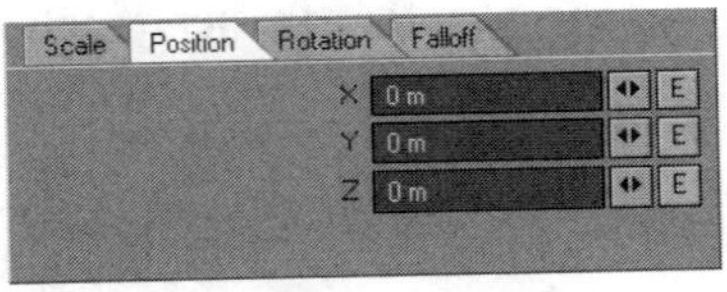

These amounts basically set the center point for the placement of the texture. By default, the position of any texture applied is 0.

Notice that when Automatic Sizing is used, LightWave automatically calculates the position for the texture. The position value is calculated at the center of the imaginary box surrounding the surface.

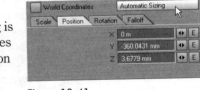

Figure 13-40

Figure 13-41

When applying an image map to a texture, you sometimes find that the image will tile, depending on the Scale and Position settings. As we discussed earlier, using Automatic Sizing stretches the image to adjust exactly to the surface, thus eliminating tiling. However, if the position of this image is adjusted, the image will begin to tile again, depending on which way you adjust the setting.

Take a look at Figure 13-42.

Figure 13-42

The sphere on the left has the image applied in a planar fashion along the z-axis, with Automatic Sizing applied. Notice how the image stretched to fit this projection perfectly. The image on the right is still using Automatic Sizing; however, the position has been altered along the x-axis, causing the image to move sideways, and consequently tile. There are a number of tiling options, which are discussed a little later.

## Rotation

Use the spinners and fields in the Rotation panel to rotate textures applied to your surface. Manually enter your own values or drag the spinners to adjust the rotation as you wish.

The default rotation settings are

**Figure 13-43**

always 0. Rotation in 3D space is done along the x, y, and z axes, which are referred to as heading, pitch, and bank, respectively.

Figure 13-44 demonstrates the differences between the three axes and how they are used.

**Figure 13-44**

Heading            Pitch            Bank

## Falloff

Essentially, falloff is used to fade textures along a selectable axis. For example, if you are using a procedural texture, but you want to fade it away at some point on your model, one way of doing that would be to use falloff.

Admittedly, I do feel that falloff is a bit of a throwback to an older LightWave world, before we had things like gradients, since in many cases where a falloff type effect is needed, a gradient, or even an image used as an alpha layer, would actually give you far greater control.

To use falloff, you select the type of falloff that you want, and enter in an appropriate value where you want the falloff to happen. You can do this by typing in an amount or by dragging the spinners. You can use positive and negative amounts of falloff to create the desired effect.

**Figure 13-45**

When deciding on what values to enter, you need to know what unit of measurement LightWave is currently set to, because the falloff is calculated as units of distance from the center point of the texture, which, as we discussed before, is set with the Position value. If, for example, your default unit in LightWave is set to meters, then this is what the distance will be measured in.

> **TIP:** To check your current default unit setting, go to the General Options tab in your Preferences panel in Layout. In Modeler, you can check your unit settings in the Display Options window.

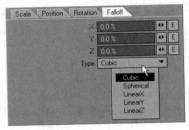

To choose the type of falloff that you want, select an appropriate option from the list labeled Type.

There are five different types of falloff, and each essentially defines the shape of the falloff.

The first type, Cubic, is the default falloff type. Cubic basically creates falloff that occurs evenly along the edges of the object, in a cubic shape.

Figure 13-46

Be aware that Cubic works simultaneously in both negative and positive values, despite what you type into the fields. Unlike the Linear types that occur in only one direction (depending on whether you enter a positive or negative value), Cubic falloff occurs in both directions of each axis.

The second type, Spherical, works the same way as Cubic, except that it has a (you guessed it) spherical shape.

Figure 13-47: Cubic falloff

Figure 13-48: Spherical falloff

The third type, LinearX, works solely on the x-axis. Depending on whether you enter a positive or negative value for this type, you will have the falloff occur on either the right or the left side of the center position of the surface.

The fourth type, LinearY, works the same as LinearX, except that its effect occurs along the y-axis. A positive value will cause the falloff to occur above the center of the surface, while a negative value will cause falloff below.

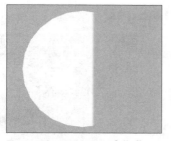

Figure 13-49: LinearX falloff          Figure 13-50: LinearY falloff

The last type is LinearZ, which is the same as LinearX and LinearY, except that it works along the z-axis.

> **TIP:** If you want to create a linear type falloff, but with the falloff occurring on both sides of the object (above and below, left and right, or front and back), then you could use the Cubic or Spherical types. Simply limit them to only one axis by entering an appropriate value and leaving the other two axes at 0.

A handy use of falloff is for limiting the distance that a texture travels through a surface. If, for example, you were texturing a small box, and you placed an image of a logo onto the front of the box, by default that image would continue all the way to the back of the box if the same surface was applied to the entire model. You could prevent this from happening by applying a falloff to the image along the appropriate axis so that the image no longer shows up on the other side.

Falloff can also be quite useful for creating fake volumetric effects such as flames, gaseous balls, or even fake volumetric light beams.

Take a look at Figure 13-51. The model is a simple disc, and the textures are just procedurals. The textures have Spherical falloff on them, so that it creates the effect of the disc being a gaseous element that has no solid edges.

Do be aware, however, that despite what this image may look like, the falloff does not affect the alpha channel of the render, which stays completely solid, regardless of your fall-off settings, unless you also set up the falloff in exactly the same manner in the transparency channel as well.

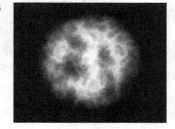

Figure 13-51

As I mentioned before though, do remember that the effect of falloff can often be better created using gradients, especially with weight maps, or by using images as alpha layers, as those methods give you far greater control and variation.

## Extra Options When Using Images

The Texture Editor has a few extra options that are available only in layers that contain images.

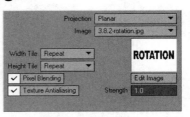

Figure 13-52

### Width and Height Tile

When using images that are not UV mapped, you can tile them as many times as you like across the surface of your object. Tiling images is used often in the gaming industry to use less memory for real-time graphics. The drop-down lists under Width Tile and Height Tile contain a number of options for tiling your textures.

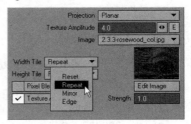

Figure 13-53

The first option on the list is Reset. Using this for your tiling setting creates no tiling for the image. The image will simply appear by itself on the surface, with all its edges clearly visible, provided the image is smaller than the surface itself.

The second option, which is the default when applying images, is Repeat. This simply repeats the image all over the object.

Figure 13-54: Reset option

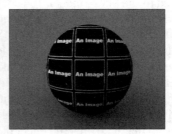

Figure 13-55: Repeat option

The third option is Mirror. Mirror is similar to Repeat, except that it flips the images around so that each repeat of the image mirrors the ones alongside it.

Something to be aware of when using the Repeat and Mirror options is that ideally your images should be totally seamless. Seamless images, as we discussed in Chapter 11, are images that have identical details around the edges, so that when they lie alongside each other, you cannot see any breaks in the texture; all the repeated images flow into one another.

The fourth and final tiling option is Edge. When using Edge, the colors along the edge of the image continue to the edges of the surface.

Figure 13-56: Mirror option

Figure 13-57: Edge option

However, if the image contains an alpha channel that extends to the edges of the image, then this particular setting will not show the pixels at the edge of the image, and will therefore not extend the edges of the image to the edge of the surface.

> **NOTE:** The Width and Height tiling options for an image do not necessarily have to be the same.

## Pixel Blending

Activating Pixel Blending for an image helps to smooth out the pixellation that can occur when textures are viewed up close. As we discussed earlier in Chapter 11, it is always better to use high-resolution textures, especially for television or film broadcast work; however, when in extreme close-ups, some textures can still show some slight pixellation. Figure 13-58 shows a texture applied without Pixel Blending (on the left) and with Pixel Blending (on the right). As you can see, the one with Pixel Blending is smoother.

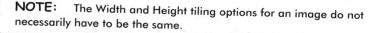

Figure 13-58

By default, Pixel Blending is on. To deactivate it, simply click on the check box.

Figure 13-59

**283**

## Texture Antialiasing

This option is used to avoid annoying rendering artifacts that often appear on objects, especially when they are in the distance and have detailed textures on them.

A common problem that appears in renders is *scintillation*, those unsightly lines that appear on textures with fine line details in them when the objects are viewed at an angle that causes those detailed lines to converge in the render. To prevent this from happening, simply use Texture Antialiasing.

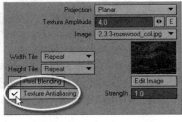

Figure 13-60

It is generally good practice to use this on objects that are distant in your scene, as these are the ones that usually cause problems that are particularly noticeable when there is a lot of movement in the scene.

> **NOTE:** Texture Antialiasing is not the same as the antialiasing settings that you choose in your Camera Properties panel. Texture Antialiasing affects only the texture maps, not the actual antialiasing of the objects themselves when rendering.

## Strength

When you select Texture Antialiasing, you should notice that a new field, Strength, which was previously grayed out below the image thumbnail on the panel, becomes active.

This value controls the amount of strength of the antialiasing applied to the image. The default setting is 1, and this value should work for most cases. Using higher values can cause the image to become blurred.

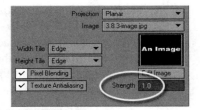

Figure 13-61

## Texture Amplitude

Texture Amplitude is available with bump maps only. When using an image in your Bump channel's Texture Editor, notice that there is a field labeled Texture Amplitude on your panel.

This setting determines how strong an effect the bump map will have on the surface. The default setting is 1. Be careful when using this setting, as having it

Figure 13-62

too high can look pretty nasty. Remember that bump maps should only be used for slight abrasions or irregularities in the surface, not to compensate for any lack of geometry, so lower values for this setting usually suffice. Values from 1 to 3 are usually adequate for most bump maps.

# CHAPTER 14

# The Node Editor

The Node Editor is a new and extremely powerful tool for texturing and shading in LightWave. Node-based texturing systems have been the standard in the industry for a while and are far superior to layer-based systems like the "classic" Texture Editor, which is restrictive and can be difficult to edit content with. A node is basically a data holder if you will. This data holder can be linked to other data holders forming a network of nodes passing data to each other. This network of nodes is represented on the computer as a flow chart very similar to the schematic view in Layout.

Even though this might seem very technical and a departure from layers in LightWave and Photoshop, you will see that it is extremely powerful and easy to learn. The Node Editor is easy enough for beginners to get great-looking surfaces, and powerful enough for the advanced user using heavy math to make some incredible shaders previously impossible to achieve in LightWave. With the new LightWave Node Editor you do not lose the capability of using layers either; on the contrary, it is enhanced, since it has "Layer" nodes specifically made for this purpose. You can also work with both environments simultaneously, so if you have color layers already built in your surface using the "classic" layer system but you wish to change the Diffuse shader and add subsurface scattering (SSS) to your surface with nodes, you have the power to combine the two texturing systems so the color layers don't have to be rebuilt.

Before we begin looking at all the different nodes available to us (of which there are quite a few), let's study the Node Editor interface and some basic usage concepts that you need to be familiar with to make understanding this incredible system a snap.

## Getting to Know the Node Editor

### The Destination Node

The Node Editor in LightWave v9 is located in three different places, each of which is dedicated to a specific task: surfacing, displacements, and volumetric lights. The greatest difference between these is what is called the destination node. We are going to be concentrating on surfacing, but the same concepts apply to displacements and volumetric lights. The destination node is simply the master or root node of the surface network; it contains all the surface property inputs that make that particular surface, such as Color, Diffuse, Specular, etc.

Figure 14-1: Surface destination node

> **NOTE:** Even though we are going to be focusing on surfacing, you can see examples of displacements using the Node Editor in Part 7, "Tutorials."

### The Node Editor Interface

Let's take a quick look at the Node Editor interface, which is actually very simple to navigate and use.

Open the Surface Editor and click on the Edit Nodes button to launch the editor. On the far left you will see a drop-down menu called Add Node. In this menu you select the nodes you would like to add to the workspace. This menu can also be accessed by pressing and holding Ctrl+Right Mouse Button anywhere on the workspace area. Next to the Add Node menu is the Edit drop-down menu. This menu contains functions such as Rename, which allows you to rename the node, as well as Copy and Paste, Select All, and Invert Selection. Other options that you will find useful are Export Nodes and Import Nodes. With Export Nodes you can select a group of nodes and save them for future use. All the connections of those nodes and their relative locations will be saved as well; however, the destination node will not get exported nor the connections made from the saved node network to the destination node. Import Nodes opens a file requester where you can select the .node file to be imported to the current Node Editor, so you can interchangeably use saved node networks between surfaces, displacements, and volumetric lights.

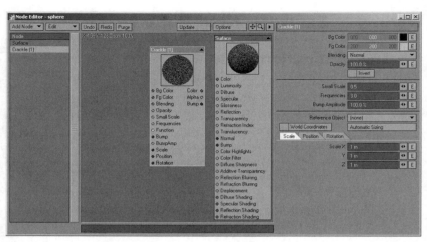

Figure 14-2: The Node Editor interface

The Edit menu also has a Preview submenu, from which you can select what you would like to see in the Surface ball of the node if one is available. Some of the preview options are: Color, Alpha, and Bump. Other options may be available, depending on the type of node you have selected. The Edit menu can also be accessed with a shortcut; select the node on the workspace and right-click on it to get to the whole Edit drop-down menu right on the workspace. To the right of the drop-down menus you have the standard Undo and Redo buttons followed by a Purge button. This button gets rid of all of the Undo history in memory.

Figure 14-3: Drop-down menus and buttons on the left side of the screen

At the top right of the screen there is a button called Update. This button forces the Node Editor to refresh all of the Preview balls of the nodes in the workspace. The Options button, which is the same as the options in the Surface Editor, lets you change the size of the Preview Surface ball, the background, and the refresh method (Auto or Manual). Next, you see widgets for panning and zooming, and another one to collapse or embed the Node Edit panel. If you decide to collapse it, the Node Edit panel will display a floating panel. This is how I personally use it since I like to have more real estate open for the workspace.

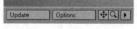

Figure 14-4: Buttons on the right side of the screen

Below the buttons are two large areas. On the left is a Node list column, where you can see all the nodes you have available on the workspace. On the right you have the workspace, where you make all your node connections. Below the workspace is a Comment area, where you can type in comments to describe something or to give directions.

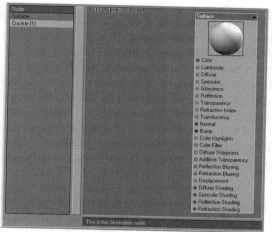

Right on the work-
space you will see a node
already there waiting for
you. This is the destina-
tion node that I talked
about earlier. This is
where you connect nodes
in order to create the
final look of that particular surface.

Figure 14-5: Node list, workspace, and Comment area

# Connection Types

Now this might be a bit boring, but it is absolutely essential for you to know
just what all these connection types are all about. After all, how on earth are
you supposed to create beautiful shaders if you have no idea what the connections are actually doing? So let's look at the destination node, where you
can see all the attribute slots that make the surface. Notice that these inputs
are color-coded; these colors give you a visual cue of the type of connection
that is recommended for that particular attribute.

There are six different types of connections in the Node Editor: Color
(red), Scalar (green), Vector (blue), Integer (purple), Function (yellow), and
Material (cyan). These connections are described below.

## Color Connections (Red)

Color is probably the easiest connection type to understand since the data
that it outputs is simply red, green, and blue values (RGB). You will most
likely want to plug color attributes to color inputs; however, there might be
times when you will want to plug dissimilar types of connections to color
inputs. In these instances the incoming data will be converted and fed to
each of the RGB channels. If the incoming data is a scalar value, that same
value will be fed to each RGB channel equally. On the other hand, if the
incoming input is a vector (position, rotation, or scale), then the position and
scale X value will be connected into the Red channel, the Y value will be fed
to the Green channel, and Z to the Blue channel. For rotation, the heading
value will be connected to the Red channel, the pitch value will be connected to the Green channel, and the bank value will be input to the Blue
channel.

## Scalar Connections (Green)

A scalar is a floating-point number, so it can be either positive or negative (such as 5, 80.55, or −30.66). A Scalar connection holds one value at a time, as opposed to connections such as Color, which holds three values (RGB), or Vectors, which hold three values as well (XYZ or HPB). Since scalars can only hold one value at a time, if you make dissimilar connections, then the Node Editor makes a conversion and not all the data will get used. In the case of Color connections, the Node Editor will convert the RGB values to Luminance and use that instead. In the case of a Vector connection, only the first value will be used, such as X if it is position or scale and H if the vector is rotation.

## Vector Connections (Blue)

In the most simplistic description, Vector designates direction in the form of position (XYZ), rotation (HPB), or scale (XYZ). Vectors are necessary for bump maps, normal maps, and displacement maps, to name a few. For example, without a vector, the surface won't know in which direction you wish to apply a bump map and thus the results would be unpredictable. You can make dissimilar connections to Vectors, but like Functions, all the data might not get used or it might give unpredictable results. If you connect a Color output to a Vector input, the RGB values will be fed into the XYZ or HPB values, respectively. Remember that when making dissimilar connections, if the connection is Scalar or Integer, the same value will be used in all three channels.

## Integer Connections (Purple)

Integer connections are whole numbers, usually to tell a node to pick an item from a list, such as blending modes. You might be asking yourself, "Why would I need to use a node to select the blending mode of a node?" Well, if you have a simple network you can just open the node and do it manually, but what if you have 10 nodes that use the same blending mode? Then you would use an Integer node to control all 10 blending types of those nodes at once, which is a very efficient way to handle this type of situation. You can also make connections of dissimilar types with Integer connections, but just like Scalars, not all the data is put to use; for example, Color connections will use the Luminance value rounded to the nearest whole number of either 0 (black) or 1 (white). In other words, if the Luminance value is above 50%, the integer will be 1; if the Luminance value is lower than 50%, then the integer will be 0. If the dissimilar connection is a Vector, then just like with Scalars, the only value used is the first one, either X for position and scale or H for rotation; the other values are discarded.

You can reference the following table to find the correct integer for any of the blending modes available along with a brief description.

**Table 14-1: Blending modes**

| Number | Description |
|--------|-------------|
| 0 | Normal. This option doesn't transform the textures at all. This is the default value. |
| 1 | Additive. Adds the values of Bg Color to the values of Fg Color. |
| 2 | Subtractive. Subtract the values of Bg Color from the values of Fg Color. |
| 3 | Multiply. Multiply the values of the Bg Color with Fg Color, thus darkening the texture. |
| 4 | Screen. This is basically the inverse of Multiply. The result is always a lighter color blend of the Bg Color and Fg Color inputs. |
| 5 | Darken. Uses the darkest texture values as the result; lighter values get replaced. |
| 6 | Lighten. Uses the lightest texture values as the result; darker values get replaced. |
| 7 | Difference. This is similar to Subtractive but uses the difference of values instead of their subtraction. |
| 8 | Negative. Has the same effect as Difference. |
| 9 | Color Dodge. The Bg Color is evaluated and the Fg Color brightens in a similar way as Screen, but colors tend to get saturated as well. |
| 10 | Color Burn. This option is similar to Multiply; the Bg Color is evaluated and the Fg Color darkens as a result. Colors tend to get saturated as well. |
| 11 | Red. The red channel from the Fg Color input is used, and the green and blue channels from the Bg Color are used for the color output. |
| 12 | Green. The green channel from the Fg Color input is used, and the red and blue channels from the Bg Color are used for the color output. |
| 13 | Blue. The blue channel from the Fg Color input is used, and the red and green channels from the Bg Color are used for the color output. |

## Function Connections (Yellow)

Functions are graphs that are able to transform a texture or shader value. Always connect Function outputs to Function inputs. Making dissimilar connections with functions is not recommended since results are unpredictable. Functions work as a two-way communication between the connected nodes, so data is sent to the function, it gets transformed, and then it is sent back to the connected node.

## Material Connections (Cyan)

Material nodes help you in the process of simulating physically accurate materials such as metals (conductors) and glass (dielectric), among others. They are color-coded in cyan. I recommend making similar connections when using Material nodes for more predictable results.

## Making Connections

It is recommended for beginners to make connections that belong to the same category; however, the Node Editor is flexible enough to allow dissimilar connections to be made. When this happens, the connection type is automatically converted, but in some cases not all the data is used. For example, connecting any other type of output to a Function input will yield unpredictable results. As your skills develop, you will find instances where making dissimilar connections not only makes perfect sense but sometimes is necessary, so when the time to make dissimilar connections comes, don't be afraid to do so and experiment. There are just a couple of things that you need to remember when making dissimilar connections in your network: You can only plug Vector connections to the Normal and Bump slots of the destination node and only plug Function outputs to Function inputs. For now, let's stick to similar types of connections and get comfortable using and navigating through the Node Editor.

Connecting nodes is actually quite simple; just click on the output and drag the arrowhead to the input you wish to plug to. To disconnect, click and release the arrowhead. Simple, right? When you make a connection of similar types, the connection line between the nodes will be the color of that particular type; for example, for a Color output to a Color input the line will be red, for a Scalar output to a Scalar input the line will be green, and so on. If you make a connection of dissimilar types, the color of the line will change from the color of the output to the color of the input. This is a great way to tell visually that the connection is of dissimilar types.

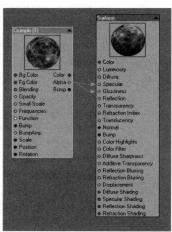

Figure 14-6: Nodes connected

Let's make a couple of connections to get you comfortable with this concept.

1. Load the know_the_node_editor.lws scene file from the Tutorials\Node Editor folder on the companion CD.

2. Activate VIPER (F7) and make a render (F9) to save the buffer for VIPER.

3. Open the Surface Editor (F5) and turn on the Node Editor by clicking on the check box, then select the plane surface and click on the Node Editor button to open it.

We have the destination node there waiting for us to connect some nodes to it. We are going to make a simple dirty floor texture, so click on the

Add Node button and add a Turbulence2D node (Add Node>2D Textures>Turbulence2D). This is going to be the dirt layer of the dirty floor.

4. Click on the node to see the attributes in the Node Edit panel if it is embedded on the Node Editor interface. If you have decided to collapse the embedded panel to gain more real estate, then double-click on the node to open the Node Edit panel as a floating panel. Once opened, change the following attributes (see Figure 14-7):

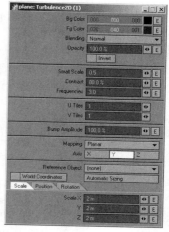

Figure 14-7

Fg Color: 38, 40, 1
Small Scale: 0.5
Contrast: 80%
Frequencies: 3
Mapping: Planar
Axis: Y
Scale X, Y, and Z: 2m

5. Now, grab the Color output of the node and plug the arrowhead to the Color input of the Surface destination node.

VIPER should update, showing large greenish and black tones on the floor. Congratulations! You have made your first node connection.

6. Okay, let's add some detail to this rather boring texture. Add a Planks node (Add Node>2D Textures>Planks2D) and change the following attributes of this node:

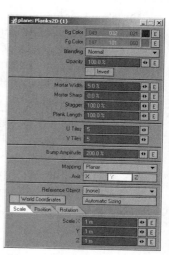

Figure 14-8: Planks2D texture

Bg Color: 49, 32, 21
Fg Color: 147, 101, 60
Mortar Width: 5.0%
U and V Tiles: 5
Bump Amplitude: 200%
Mapping: Planar
Axis: Y

7. Connect the Color output of this node to the Bg Color input of the Turbulence2D node.

Once again, VIPER updates after the connection is made, showing us a planks pattern with disgusting green dirt on top.

8. Change the UV Tiles values of the Planks node to see how this affects the pattern. I ended up leaving it at 5 tiles.

9. Let's add some texture to the planks to make it look more like actual wood (Add Node>3D Textures>Wood) and open the Node Edit panel to change some of its attributes.

Bg Color: 198, 162, 101
Fg Color: 181, 89, 1
Opacity: 80%
Frequencies: 3
Turbulence: 2
Ring Spacing: .0.05
Ring Sharpness: 3
Axis: Z
Scale: X, Y, and Z: 3m

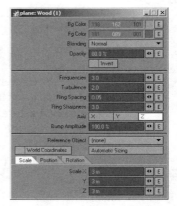

Figure 14-9: Wood texture

10. Connect the Color output of this node to the Fg Color of the Planks2D node. Now you see in VIPER that the planks have a woodgrain pattern.

11. Now I would like to break up the dirt layer. To do this add a Crumple texture to the workspace (Add Node>3D Textures> Crumple), and open the Node Edit panel to change the following:

Small Scale: 1.0
Frequencies: 3

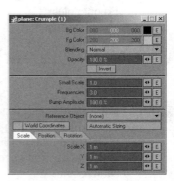

Figure 14-10: Crumple texture

12. Now, right-click on this node, choose Preview, and select Alpha. The sample ball will update to show the alpha output of the node.

13. Connect the Alpha output of the Crumple texture to the Opacity input of the Turbulence2D node. You will see in VIPER that the greenish dirt layer's opacity is now driven by the alpha output of the Crumple texture. Very cool!

14. Change the Diffuse value of this surface since as you already know nothing is 100% diffuse; there is always light absorption, even if it is very little (Add Node>Constant>Scalar). Change the Scalar value to something like 0.85, and connect it to the Diffuse input of the Surface destination node.

15. Now take the Bump output of the Planks2D node and connect it to the Bump input of the Surface destination node. Also take the Alpha output of the Turbulence2D node and connect it to both the Specular and Glossiness inputs of the Surface destination node.

Make a test render to see the results. Your dirty floor is finished. Notice that all the connections are of similar types.

One thing that I really love about surfacing in the Node Editor is the ability to see *every* texture for every attribute of the surface at once. Before, in the "classic" Surface Editor, you would have to open each attribute by clicking the "T" button in order to see what made that particular attribute. You could not have the Color and Bump texture editors open at the same time. Another thing I absolutely love that you will find extremely useful is the ability to connect outputs of nodes to several different inputs at the same time, thus having the control of changing several properties with one single node or output.

Consider this scenario: In the classic Surface Editor you have 50 different color layers, and each layer needs an alpha layer to control the opacity of each color layer. This approach is tedious to edit as you would have 100 layers total (yes, I have done textures this complicated before), not to mention that you also need the same alpha for the diffuse and specular channels. With the Node Editor you can have just one alpha node controlling everything, including the color, diffuse, and specular layers. Just edit one alpha node and everything updates automagically!

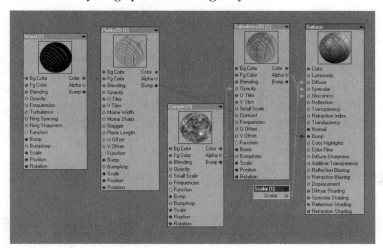

Figure 14-11: Finished node network

By now you should feel pretty comfortable making connections and getting around the Node Editor. Figure 14-12 shows the result of the node network that we just created for the floor. As an exercise, go ahead and texture the sphere that is sitting on the floor on your own and see what you come up with. Start with easy networks and build detail from there; try to replicate what you could do with the "classic" layer system.

Figure 14-12

Next we are going to review the built-in nodes available in the Node Editor.

LightWave v9 comes with a great library of nodes built in for you. The LightWave v9 SDK also allows you to build your own nodes; if you happen to be a coder, that is. Here we are going to go through the nodes included with LightWave, some of which you might be familiar with since they are available in the form of layers in the "classic" Texture Editor. The vast majority, however, are new textures or utilities that you might not have heard of before. Let's review these textures in a linear fashion from top to bottom as they appear on the Add Node pull-down menu. Also, for illustrative purposes, any image of the nodes presented will be applied to the Color input of the surface unless otherwise noted. Keep in mind that the basic concepts of procedural textures as described in Chapter 8 are still applicable.

## 2D Textures

2D Textures are either procedurals or image maps that can be mapped to objects using common projections such as Planar, Spherical, Cylindrical, or UV maps. LightWave will project the textures realistically on objects with basic geometric shapes such as planes, spheres, cubes, etc. Another advantage of using these 2D procedural textures is that they are 100% tileable; just enter the number of tiles you wish the texture to have and LightWave will do the rest. If you happen to find some unexpected errors in your images, such as artifacts or completely blurred textures, try turning Mip Mapping off; this is the usual suspect when render errors like those come up.

## Bricks2D

The first texture in the 2D Textures list is Bricks2D. This texture is pretty much the same as in the classic Texture Editor with the exception that all of the attributes that designate the texture are available as inputs, so these attributes can be driven by other nodes in the network. Let's take Fg Color for example. This attribute can be driven by the color that makes a Crumple texture in order to give color to the bricks. The Bg Color input will color the mortar of the bricks, and also can be driven by other nodes in the network. You can also connect nodes to Mortar Width and Mortar Sharp in order to make the bricks irregular shapes. Remember that if the value of Mortar Width is too high, the mortar will completely cover the bricks. A couple of inputs that are available in this node that its layer cousin lacks are the U and V Offset values. With these inputs you can plug other nodes into the network to offset the texture and provide you with a different look; Figure 14-13 shows the result of plugging a Crumple texture into the U Offset value.

Bricks2D

Bricks2D
With other network connections

Figure 14-13: Bricks2D with nodes driving different attributes

> **NOTE:**  Refer to Chapter 8 for more information on the Brick procedural.

Other inputs that most textures have are the Bump and Bump Amplitude inputs. Bump designates the bump of the surface, while Bump Amplitude designates how strong the bump will be. Try not to connect dissimilar types to these inputs unless you absolutely know what you are doing. By plugging the Bump output of other nodes into the Bump input, you are able to mix bumps together, as shown in Figure 14-14.

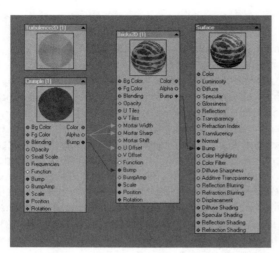

Figure 14-14: Connecting Bump output to Bump input

## CheckerBoard2D

Guess what this node does! All joking aside, this node will be useful if you are making any type of texture that requires a checkerboard pattern. Yes, you can make chessboards with this, but think of other possible uses this node can have, such as stainless steel tiles in a kitchen, wallpaper coverings, fabrics, and more. Think outside the box. This texture will also come in handy if you want to quickly check for texture stretching in your UV maps. This texture, as with most 2D textures, needs a projection axis, whether it is Planar, Spherical, Cubic, UV, etc. Also, as with Bricks2D, you can offset the UV tiles, thus opening the door to more possibilities of what you can do with this texture.

Figure 14-15: CheckerBoard2D texture

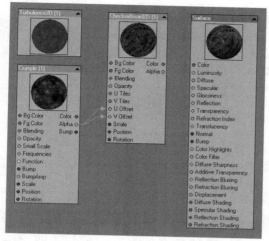

Figure 14-16: The node network

Strangely enough, this texture doesn't have a Bump input or output, therefore limiting its potential uses.

## Grid2D

This texture is very similar to Bricks2D, but the tiles it creates are arranged in perfect vertical and horizontal lines as opposed to a stacked and staggered pattern. This node is very easy to understand. The Bg Color input describes the mortar, and the Fg Color input describes the tiles. Mortar Width determines the thickness of the lines that make the grid, while Mortar Sharp determines the sharpness of the lines. This is a very useful node if you want to make tile for a bathroom, for example.

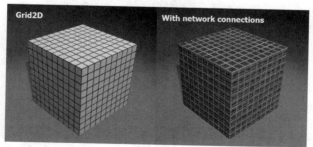

Figure 14-17: Grid2D texture

Also remember that all of these textures can serve as masks. You can make these tiles really large and the lines very thick and plug other textures into the Bg Color and Fg Color inputs to make some interesting textures.

# Image

You will likely use this node quite often. Here you specify an image available in your scene or you can load one from disk using the Node Edit panel. Image is also an axial texture, so it needs to have an axis specified, such as Planar, Spherical, Cylindrical, Cubic, or UVs in the Node Edit panel. Images are extremely powerful in the Node Editor since you can drive the attributes of other nodes using an image.

Make sure you read Chapter 11, "Image Maps," for more information on the creation and usage of image maps. This node also has Bump input/outputs and Bump Amplitude inputs so you can mix different bumps together.

Figure 14-18: Image node

NOTE: See Appendix B for a list of file formats that can be imported and exported from LightWave.

# Normal Map

Normal Map uses a technique similar to bump mapping that adds detail without adding more polygons to your geometry, but unlike a bump, which modifies the existing normals (the direction a polygon is facing) of a model, a normal map will replace these normals entirely. Normal maps are also based on RGB values instead of the one color that a bump map is able to use, and thus saves more information than a regular bump map. In other high-end 3D applications, a network of utilities is needed in order to use normal maps; in LightWave it is as simple as loading your map and connecting its Normal output to the Normal input of the destination node.

If you work with ZBrush, this is the node you will need in order to use the normal maps that were generated with ZBrush from a high-resolution mesh.

Figure 14-19: Normal mapped cube

NOTE: For more on using normal maps generated in ZBrush, refer to Chapter 25, "LightWave/ZBrush Workflow," in Part 7 of this book.

If you open the Node Edit panel of the Normal Map node, you will see three check boxes under the Edit Image button called Invert X, Y, and Z. With these buttons you can invert the normals for that particular axis to give the impression that the detail is coming from a different direction. In Figure 14-20 I inverted the normals of the y-axis and thus made it look like the detail is a relief instead of an emboss.

Figure 14-20: Inverted Y Normal Map

## Parquet2D

Parquet is another simple node to figure out. Parquet is the pattern that you will find most commonly on wood floors. This texture, like Bricks2D, has Mortar Width and Mortar Sharp inputs so you can control the thickness of the virtual grout. One input that you will find useful is Tiles, in which you can specify the number of tiles to put on each block. If you specify one tile, then the result will be like the Grid2D node. Just like any other 2D texture, Parquet2D is also an axial texture, so you need to specify a texture axis for the projection of the texture to the object.

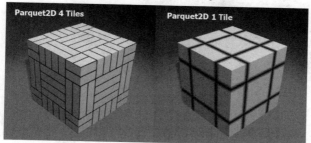

Figure 14-21: Parquet with four tiles (default) and one tile

## Planks2D

You should already be familiar with this node, as we used it for the first exercise in this chapter. Very similar to Parquet2D with the exception of its pattern, this texture is mostly used to create floors, but with a little imagination you can come up with other uses. This node offers inputs to change the Stagger and Length settings of the planks.

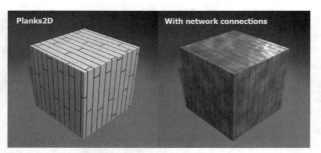

Figure 14-22: Planks2D texture

## Turbulence2D

This node is very similar to its 3D texture cousin. Turbulence2D combines different layers of fractal noise to create complex and interesting patterns. This texture is axial in nature like the other 2D texture nodes. Since this is a 2D texture node, the image is tileable. The higher the number of tiles, the smaller the pattern will get in order to fit within the number of tiles specified. The Frequencies input determines the level of detail within the pattern. Small Scale in the classic Surface Editor is called Small Power here. This value determines the amount of change between the transition of large detail and small detail areas of the pattern.

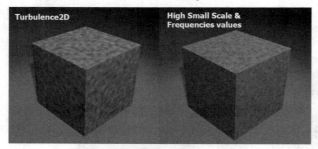

Figure 14-23: Turbulence2D texture

Turbulence2D is one of those textures that has many different uses, from dirt and grime to scratches and rust. The possibilities are limited only by your imagination.

## 3D Textures

If you read Chapter 8, "Procedural Textures," you will know that 3D textures are computer generated, but unlike procedural 2D textures, 3D textures follow the geometry as if it had volume. One great advantage of procedural 3D textures is that you don't have to worry too much about axial projections since for most they are not needed. For those few that do require an axis, it is very simple to set up since it works in a similar fashion to the 2D textures discussed above.

Also remember that these textures are for the most part identical to the procedurals in the classic Texture Editor, with the exception of some attributes available as inputs so they can be driven by other nodes in the network.

## Bricks

This texture produces, well, bricks, and just like any other texture node, the attributes of this texture can be driven by other nodes in the network, thus making it possible to come up with interesting textures other than the average brick pattern. Think outside the box.

By opening the Node Edit panel you will see the attributes that make the texture. The top part of this and every other 3D texture node has to do with the colors, blending method, and opacity. Just like 2D textures, the attributes can be driven by other nodes in the network. In the second section of this panel you will find a couple of options specific to this texture: Thickness, which should really be named Mortar Thickness, controls the thickness of the mortar between the bricks, and Edge Width controls the bevel of the brick edges. Notice that these options can now be animated.

You also have options to control the Scale, Position, Rotation, and Bump Amplitude (Strength). These settings are found across the board for all textures and can also be animated.

Figure 14-24: Bricks texture with a Crumple bump

## Checkerboard

Well, just like the 2D Checkerboard, think of other possible uses this node could have besides chessboards. By connecting other nodes to the different attributes you can come up with some interesting effects previously impossible to achieve. I hope a Fuzzy Edge option is added in the future to make this texture even more useful.

Figure 14-25: Checkerboard texture

# Crackle

This is one of my favorite textures for creating natural and organic looking surfaces due to its cellular pattern. You can create a great variety of surfaces like dried mud, lava, and even small rocks!

The Node Edit panel shows all of this texture's attributes, and like before, the top part has to do with colors, blending mode, and opacity. The blending modes are listed in Table 14-1 near the beginning of the chapter. The middle section of the Node Edit panel has some options to control the look of the Crackle pattern: Small Scale, which determines the amount of change between detail levels of the pattern, and Frequencies, which is the actual amount of detail contained in the pattern. This option is also known as Octaves in the "classic" Texture Editor.

Figure 14-26: Crackle texture

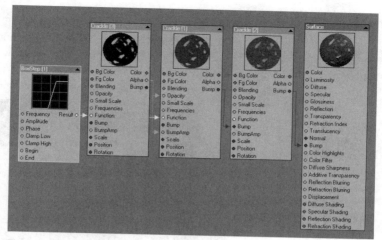

Figure 14-27: Crackle small rocks

# Crumple

This is probably the second most useful procedural, topped only by Turbulence, in my opinion. This texture can be used for water, rocks, ground, skin, leather, and organic objects (such as neurons) at the microscopic level, to name a few. Like the other textures, this node can receive inputs from other nodes in the network. The options are very similar between these 3D textures; you can change the look of the texture by changing Small Scale, Frequencies, and the various transformations such as Position and Scale.

In Figure 14-28 I made some minor changes to the Small Scale and Frequencies settings, and I also inverted the texture and changed the scale to provide the beginnings of a skin texture. Be sure to see the Ocean tutorial in Chapter 24 to see how I put the Crumple texture to work in the creation of water.

Figure 14-28: Crumple texture as bump

## Crust

This texture is really great for bump maps; you can create pimples and warts, and you can even use it for creating speckles on rocks or snow. A couple of attributes unique to this texture are Width and Contrast. Width controls the diameter of the circles, and Contrast controls the fuzziness of the circle's edges, so the higher the contrast, the sharper the circles. Two options that are not available in this node that the layer counterpart has are Ledge Level and Ledge Width; these options are covered in the Crust section of Chapter 8. I really don't know why these two options are not available in the node, but if you absolutely need them you can still use a Layer node and add the Crust layer there.

Figure 14-29: Crust texture

## Dots

This node simply creates a grid of circles. I have used this texture for fabrics, wall coverings, metal grates, and other textures that require an even pattern of circles.

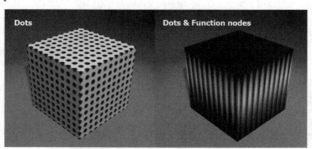

Figure 14-30: Dots texture

## FBM

FBM stands for Fractional Brownian Motion. This texture is great for the creation of natural textures and is also great for bump maps in particular to add a general unevenness to the surface. This texture can receive attributes from other nodes in the network. As with the many other 3D procedurals we have covered, this one also has Small Scale and Frequencies settings, in addition to a Contrast setting. Just by applying the texture using the default settings you can see right away that it has a marble type of look to it, which is useful for several different things.

Figure 14-31: FBM texture

## Grid

This texture creates a procedural grid pattern. This texture is useful for the creation of textures that require a square pattern, such as kitchen and bathroom tiles.

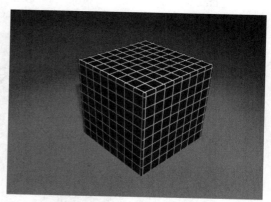

Figure 14-32: Grid texture

## HeteroTerrain

This is a multi-fractal texture that works best in bump maps and displacement maps, since it simulates the naturally occurring pattern of how land tends to be flatter and smoother in valleys and rough and uneven in peaks. There are a couple of texture attributes whose terminology is different compared to other nodes, but they perform the same job. Lacunarity determines the amount of scale of the successive levels of details in the fractal pattern. Octaves set the number of levels of detail used by Lacunarity. Increment sets the strength between the layers of details. The layers are overlaid on top of each other in order to add detail to the texture. Offset determines where the combined results of the previous three options begin. You also have a pull-down menu with different noise types to pick from; some of those noises have a noticeable hit on render times with Sparse Convolution as the most expensive of the pack.

Figure 14-33: Different Offset values

## Honeycomb

This texture requires a projection axis. It is great for metal grilles, fabrics, and sci-fi looking patterns if it is stretched and deformed.

Figure 14-34: Honeycomb texture

## Hybrid-MultiFractal

This texture is very similar to HeteroTerrain since it works best in bump and displacement maps for the creation of terrains. Also like HeteroTerrain, the valleys tend to be smooth while the peaks tend to be rougher, and it also shares the same types of options covered for HeteroTerrain.

Figure 14-35: Hybrid-MultiFractal texture

## Marble

This procedural texture creates fractal patterns to mimic the patterns found in marble. It is also one of the few textures that requires a projection axis to specify which axis to wrap the texture around. The attributes unique to this texture are Vein Spacing, which controls the spacing between veins within the pattern itself, and Distortion and Noise Scale. Noise Scale sets the size of the noise, while Distortion sets the amount of noise that is applied to the veins of the texture. In the "classic" Texture Editor, Marble has an option called Vein Sharpness. In the Node Editor, this option is simply called Contrast, which does exactly the same job by setting how fuzzy or sharp the vein edges are. By connecting functions you can expand the possibilities of this texture.

Figure 14-36: Marble texture

**309**

## MultiFractal

This is yet another multi-fractal texture that is most useful for bump maps to add a general coarse look to surfaces such as rust, sand, rocks, etc. The options in this texture are the same as the other multi-fractal textures already covered.

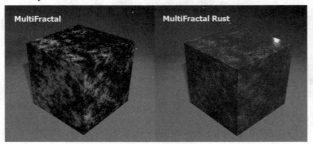

Figure 14-37: MultiFractal rust

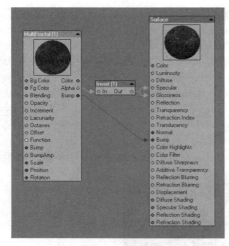

Figure 14-38: The rust node network

## RidgedMultiFractal

This multi-fractal texture is most useful for bump and displacement maps to create terrains. The options in this texture are the same as the other multi-fractal textures already covered with the exception of Threshold. By increasing this value you increase the number of ridges in the texture.

Figure 14-39: RidgedMultiFractal with different scale values

# Ripples

This texture is also particularly useful for bump maps since it simulates the ripple patterns found on the surface of water. Ripples is covered in detail in Chapter 8, but here is an overview of its attributes. The Wave Sources value determines the number of sources that create the ripples; high values create lots of ripples while low values create fewer ripples. Wavelength determines the size of the space between ripples, and Wave Speed controls the speed of the ripples as they travel outward from the center of the source. Notice that all of these options in this node, unlike the layer counterpart, can be animated.

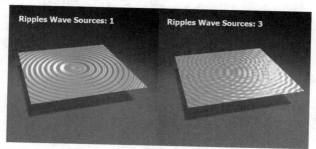

Figure 14-40: Different Wave Sources values

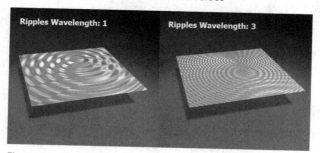

Figure 14-41: Different Wavelength values

## Turbulence

This is probably the texture I use the most as it is extremely versatile and can be used for tons of different kinds of surfaces, from walls and rust to micro bumps and natural surfaces. The attributes that make this texture are the same as in many other 3D textures: Small Scale and Frequencies, with the addition of a Contrast input.

Figure 14-42: Turbulence applied as bump and color

## Turbulent Noise

This is another noise texture that can be used for many different things. The attributes that makes this texture are the same as in many other textures in this category.

Figure 14-43: Turbulent Noise texture

## Underwater

This texture is used to replicate the pattern caused by refracted light through bodies of water, which is called *caustics*. You can see this phenomenon at the bottom of swimming pools for example. The attributes of this texture are similar to those of Ripples with the addition of Band Sharpness, which works like a contrast control, dictating how soft or sharp the bands look. As in Ripples, all of these attributes can be animated.

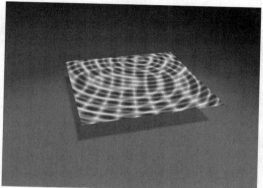

Figure 14-44: Underwater texture

## Veins

This procedural texture creates patterns similar to spider webs; it is useful for creating cracked dried mud or cracked old paint for example. You can control the Width and Contrast of the veins in this texture. Width controls the thickness of the veins while Contrast controls how sharp (or fuzzy) the veins are.

Figure 14-45: Veins texture applied to color and bump

## Wood

As mentioned in Chapter 8, this texture is similar to Marble but the pattern is meant to mimic the concentric rings found in wood. The attributes that makes this texture tick are also covered in Chapter 8 since its layer counterpart is the same; regardless, here is an overview of the attributes.

Frequencies controls the level of detail within the texture. Turbulence determines how close the wood rings are from one another as a whole. Ring Spacing controls the space between rings within the pattern itself, and Ring Sharpness controls how soft the edges of the rings are.

Figure 14-46: Wood texture and Turbulence for bump

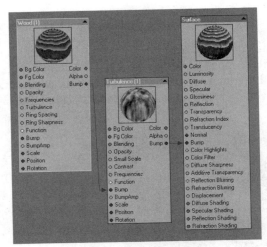

Figure 14-47: The node network for Wood

## Wood2

This procedural also has the ability to mimic wood rings in a similar way to Wood, with the exception that it allows you to phase or move the transition gradient of the rings and thus randomize the look of the rings. Like the other procedurals, you can animate the attributes of this texture so you can come up with some funky animations.

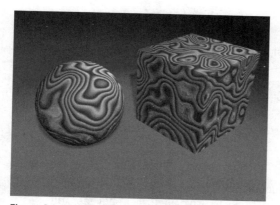

Figure 14-48: Wood2 and a Crumple for bump

## fBm Noise

This node is very similar to FBM with the exception of some options unavailable in FBM. The options for the variation of pattern and detail in this texture are Increment, Lacunarity, and Octaves. The terminology of these options is different from other 3D textures but they really do the same thing. Increment controls the fractal dimension of the texture pattern, Lacunarity is the same as Small Scale, and Octaves is the same thing as Frequencies. This node, in its Node Edit panel, has a pull-down menu from which you can select the type of noise to be used in the texture, so you can create very different looks by just changing the Noise Type setting.

Figure 14-49: fBm Noise texture

## Constant

Constant nodes simply hold a fixed value that can be used to drive and/or control other nodes' attributes in the shading network. A couple of good examples of Constant nodes would be connecting a Scalar constant to the Specular and Glossiness inputs of the destination node, or using the Integer constant to drive the blending mode of several textures at once. These are just a few examples of what you can do with these nodes.

### Angle

This node has no inputs, only an output. You can enter a value in the form of degrees to drive angular properties. You can enter values beyond 360 degrees if you need to. The Angle output of this node can also be animated.

Figure 14-50: Angle node

### Color

This node is known as the Value procedural in the "classic" Surface Editor. This node simply holds color information. You can use the Color output of this node to drive the Color input of other nodes in the network from one spot; if you have created a complex shading network to create a red clay ground shader and then the art director decides to make it gray, instead of going node by node changing color values, just add this node with the new color and plug it into the input color of every node that needs to be changed. To quickly go back to the red clay color, just unplug the node and you are done.

Figure 14-51: Color node

### Direction

With this node you can change the direction vector of different direction inputs, which is especially useful when you need to change the direction (heading, pitch, or bank) of several nodes, in a single place instead of manually changing the values of each node individually.

Figure 14-52: Direction node

### Integer

This node is usually used to select items from a list such as blending modes or several nodes at the same time, as mentioned earlier in this chapter. You can also use this node to change the number of UV tiles in a texture.

Figure 14-53: Integer node

### Pi

The value of Pi is 3.14159. Pi is defined as the ratio of a circumference of a circle to its diameter. I haven't run into a situation where I have had to use this node, but when the time comes, I know where to find it.

Figure 14-54:
Pi node

### Scalar

Here you can type a value, positive or negative, to drive several different inputs of nodes such as Diffuse or Refraction Index.

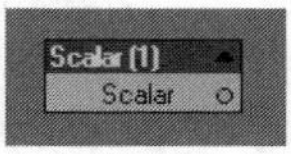

Figure 14-55:
Scalar node

### Vector

This is similar to Direction, which is explained above, but it works with position outputs (X, Y, Z) instead of rotational values.

Figure 14-56:
Vector node

## Functions

Functions have their own connection type; try to connect Function outputs to Function inputs to avoid any problems. Functions are graphs; the node that the function is attached to gets transformed according to this graph. You can drive the different inputs of these nodes with other nodes in the network.

### Bias

This function can control the brightness levels of the node that it is connected to.

For all functions, the Frequency input determines how long it takes for the function to finish one cycle. Amplitude controls the size of the function.

Throughout all function nodes you will see a couple of inputs called Clamp Low and Clamp High. What these mean is that if the graph value exceeds this number, the graph gets clipped so it doesn't go above (Clamp High) or below (Clamp Low) the entered value. The Phase input allows you to shift the graph in time, right or left. If you open the Edit panel for this node, you will find a Mode pull-down menu that contains three options: Constant, Repeat, and Oscillate. These options control the graph after one cycle has been completed, just like the Post Behavior in the Graph Editor. Constant keeps using the value used at the end of the first cycle. Repeat repeats the graph cycle from the beginning, thus making a sawtooth pattern. The Oscillate mode causes the graph to cycle backward to its starting position and start over, sort of like ping-pong for graphs.

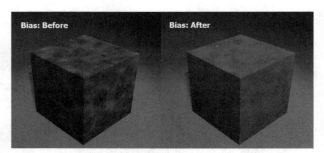

Figure 14-57: Bias before and after

These options are available in every function node in the Node Editor and are also animateable so you can create some really interesting textures.

The Bias input controls the actual bias of the function. This input can have a value from 0 to 1, with 0.5 being "normal" or the default value. Changing this value up or down will output more or less bias, respectively.

## BoxStep

This function creates a box step graph so you end up with flat peaks and valleys between two values. By using this node and tweaking the Clamp Low and Clamp High values, you can control how much detail of a texture you can see and how intense it is.

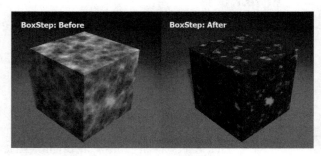

Figure 14-58: Isolating detail using BoxStep

## Gain

Gain is similar to Bias, but Gain controls the contrast of textures instead of the brightness. All of the options are the same with the exception of Gain at the bottom. This option controls the overall contrast of the function. Just like Bias, 0.5 is the default value; increasing or decreasing this number will increase or decrease the amount of contrast.

Figure 14-59: The result of Gain

## Gamma

Gamma is a curve that defines luminous values in images. The Gamma node collectively controls both the Bias and Gain of the texture it is connected to. The Gamma control in the Node Edit panel can go above the value of 1 but not below the value of 0.

Figure 14-60: The Gamma node at work

## Modulate

With Modulate you can combine two different functions together, which opens the door to even more interesting possibilities. The two functions are combined via different modes that are similar to some of the blending modes for color inputs of texture nodes. The blending modes are as follows:

- Add: Adds the input of function 1 to the input of function 2.
- Subtract: Subtracts the input of function 1 from the input of function 2.
- Multiply: Multiplies the inputs of both functions.
- Maximum: The output is the highest value of the two functions.
- Minimum: The output is the lowest value of the two functions.

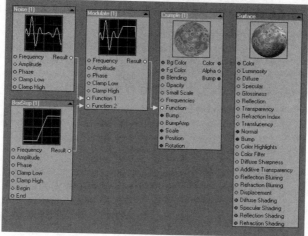

Figure 14-61: Node network using Modulate

Figure 14-62: Modulate in action

## Noise

This is a standard Perlin Noise function used to perturb the pattern of the texture it is connected to. Easy enough, right? This node doesn't have the mode options that most functions have. Since it is based on a Perlin Noise, the end value will be different as you increase the Frequency input or shift it in time using the Phase input. Figure 14-63 shows an FBM texture with a Noise function.

Figure 14-63: FBM texture with a Noise function

## Sine

Sine allows you to regulate the transition of the texture it is connected to based on a wave-like function. The options on the top section of this node's Edit panel are the same as the other function nodes: Frequencies, Amplitude, Phase, and Mode.

## SmoothStep

This node is very similar to BoxStep with the exception that the curve is smoothed. If you find that your transitions are too sharp using BoxStep, use this node instead; it yields better, smoother transitions. Load the Smooth-Step surface from the Surface Presets\LW9 Texturing folder on the companion CD to compare the subtle difference between SmoothStep and BoxStep; just make a render of the two and switch between them to see the difference.

Figure 14-64: SmoothStep on a Crumple texture

## Wrap

This node allows you to modify a Scalar input with a function. This is useful because you are not constrained to the Function input. This node will be very useful to you if you happen to be using math nodes with Scalar outputs in your network.

Figure: 14-65: Wrap node used as a mask with Ripples3d

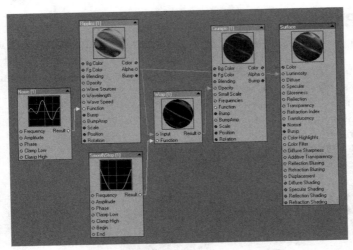

Figure: 14-66: Wrap node network

# Gradients

Ah, the almighty gradients! As discussed in Chapter 9, a gradient is a graphic way to represent a graph so it is easier for us to understand the effect of this graph on the surface. Gradient nodes in the Node Editor are a bit different from the gradient layer in the "classic" Texture Editor due to some new functionality that is not available in its layer counterpart; this is discussed further in the node descriptions below. In addition to the Gradient node, you also have a couple of dedicated tools available to quickly add an effect to your network.

## Tools

### Incidence

This is a dedicated gradient that allows you to change the look of a surface based on the camera viewing angle. The part of the surface that faces the camera directly is at an angle of 90 degrees by default. The advantage of using this node over a gradient with the input parameter set to Incidence Angle is that in the Node Edit panel you have the option to have the angle at 90 or 180 degrees. What if we could change the actual direction of the Incidence effect? This can be done with the Vector input; you can connect the Vector output from other nodes in the network to change the direction of the Incidence effect. For example, you can drive the Incidence Angle with a light. Figure 14-67 shows the 90° and 120° Incidence options; notice the sharp black rim on the 120° image is gone. This is followed by a gradient being driven by the direction of a light in the scene; notice that the intensity of the reflection is controlled by the alpha of the gradient. See Figure 14-68 to see how this was set up.

Figure 14-67: Incidence tool settings

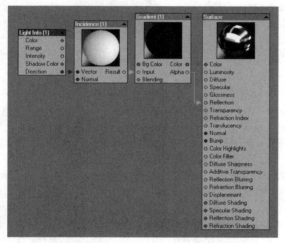

Figure 14-68: Incidence node network with a gradient

## Thickness

The Thickness node evaluates the length of the ray hit point to the back of the object where the ray exits. Since this node uses rays to determine length, it is necessary to have at least one of the ray-tracing options on in the Render Globals panel. There are two inputs in this node: IOR (Index of Refraction) and Normal. The IOR input value determines how much the ray is refracted or bends; the Normal Vector input allows you to change the direction of the rays that are fired back. This node works perfectly with colored glass and water by connecting the Length output to a gradient's input so the color of the glass is based on its thickness while using the gradient's colors, as seen in Figure 14-69. Figure 14-70 shows the node network. Some of these node connections might not make too much sense right now, but it will become clearer as you keep reading.

Figure 14-69: Thickness using the gradient's colors

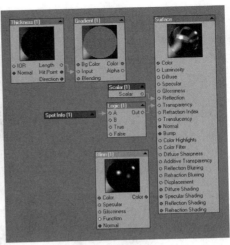

Figure 14-70: Thickness node network

## Gradient

The Gradient in the Node Editor has more functionality than the Gradient layer in the "classic" Texture Editor. One of those new improvements (and a big one too) is that nodal gradients can be animated! The attributes that can be animated are Background Color, Color, Alpha, and Position of the keys. At first glance the node's inputs are similar to those of other color nodes; you have Bg Color where you can connect (preferably) color attributes from other nodes in the network, or you can also enter RGB values manually via the Node Edit panel. There is also an Input slot where you can connect other nodes' attributes to drive the gradient. What exactly does that mean? Well, it means that the gradient itself can be transformed by the connected input. Let's say that you have a Crumple texture and a color gradient. You can connect the alpha of the Crumple to the input of the gradient to perturb the gradient based on the alpha value of the Crumple. (See Figure 14-71.)

Figure 14-71: Crumple driving a gradient

The Blending Integer input is used to select the blending mode that will be used to blend the gradient with the Bg Color input. This list of inputs can grow according to the gradient's keys, which we'll discuss further in a little bit.

Let's study the Gradient's Node Edit panel to see all of the options. At the top of the Gradient Node Edit panel you will find the usual Bg Color input, where you can manually enter an RGB value or connect attributes from other nodes in the network. You also have the same Blending pull-down menu, just like any of the other nodes we have covered. Now to the really cool part, the actual gradient! You create keys on the gradient by clicking on the spot where you would like to drop a key. Then you can change the color, alpha, and position of that particular key. Notice the "E" (envelope) button, which means you can animate the color of that key over time, its alpha, or its position. Just above the Color attribute is a check box labeled Show Output. When activated, this little gem will add Color, Position, and Alpha to the node; you can do that to every key on the gradient if you want. By doing this you are able to change the color of each key with any kind of texture! You can have an earth strata effect in no time with a different texture in each layer. I'll show you how to do just that in the Red Rocks tutorial in Chapter 24. With this technique you can easily blend a number of images together by just connecting their color output to a particular key color input.

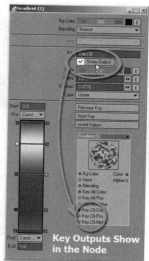

Figure 14-72: Gradient node key outputs

Figure 14-73: Driving key inputs

Deleting gradient keys is just as easy; just click on the little square with the "x." If you wish to lock the key, then right-click on the little colored square on the left side of the key to change the square into an "x" (see Figure 14-74). You will no longer be able to move it; however, you can still make other kind of edits such as changing its color or alpha.

Figure 14-74: A locked gradient key

You also have buttons to navigate through the keys and a button to invert the values of the gradient as a whole. Another cool feature of the nodal gradient is the Pre and Post behaviors. The default is Constant, which means that the color of the first and last key will remain the same along the length of the gradient. If they are set to Repeat, the gradient will repeat along the length with the settings entered in the Start and End boxes. For example, if you have a mountain that is 100 meters tall you can type a value in the End box to make the gradient the same height as the mountain. If you create a gradient with the default values of 0 to 1, and set the End value to Repeat, the gradient from 0 to 1 will repeat 100 times.

Gradients are extremely versatile and you will be using them quite often in your texturing work.

## Item Info

These nodes provide you access to information about the specific item selected in the Node Edit panel. This allows you to create textures based on information provided by the items you have selected. The information changes according to the type of item you intend to use. Cameras and lights have their own dedicated nodes, which provide specific information related to cameras or lights. The Item Info node provides information regarding the selected object from the pull-down menu, such as position and rotation.

### Camera

This node provides you with the settings of the camera selected in the Node Edit panel.

### Item Info

Item Info allows you to select items in the scene, such as objects, lights, cameras, or nulls. It outputs vector information including world position, scaling, rotation, etc.

**Figure 14-75: Camera node**   **Figure 14-76: Item Info node**

### Light Info

This node provides you with the settings of the light selected in the Node Edit panel.

**Figure 14-77: Light Info node**

## Layers

The Layer nodes allow you to integrate the "classic" layered texturing system of LightWave previous to version 9. This is a great way to get both seasoned and beginner LightWave users introduced to the new "nodal" texturing system at the same time. There are also some procedural textures that are not yet available as nodes, such as Dented. Even though you can create similar looks and effects using other texture nodes, functions, and clamps, it would still be nice to have it available as a node. In the meantime we can access them through the Layer nodes. Layer nodes are available as color, scalar, and vector types, so you can make similar connections. By double-clicking on the node you will see the "classic" Texture Editor where you can add layers and mix them together to achieve the look that you are after. For more on the Texture Editor, see Chapter 13, "The Texture Editor."

## Bump Layer

With this node you can build a stack of layers that can be connected to the Bump input of other nodes in the network or directly to the Bump or Normal slots of the destination node. This node provides a Bump input where you can plug the bump of other nodes in the network into the background bump of the Layer node. The output of this node is vector which, as you know, has X, Y, and Z components. The alpha of this Bump Layer node is available as a Scalar output and is acquired by using the intensity of the last layer on the stack.

## Color Layer

The Color layer node is identical to the Bump Layer with the exception that its output type is color (RGB). You can connect dissimilar types but not all of the information will be used.

## Scalar Layer

A Scalar Layer is like the Bump and Color layers with the difference being the output type, which of course is scalar.

Figure 14-78: Bump, Color, and Scalar layer nodes

## Materials

What if you run into a situation where a client hands you a book with some data sheets of the physical properties of aluminum, for example, and asks you to replicate it in the current pre-vis project? No, don't pull your hair out; just use Material nodes. These Material nodes can help you simulate physically accurate materials. This is especially useful when matching live action plates or for artists in the science and medicine fields, where accuracy is extremely important. It is recommended that you make similar type connections to the destination node for more predictable results. Material nodes can be considered a bit advanced, but don't let that stop you — experiment!

## Conductor

This node is used to simulate physically accurate metals. Materials that can transfer electricity, heat, or both are conductors; metals are excellent conductors. This node can receive data from other nodes in the network or by manually inputting values via the node's Edit panel. The Advanced tab of

**327**

the node's Edit panel resembles the Environment tab in the Surface Editor. Here you can select the Reflection mode you wish to use in that particular material, just like in the Surface Editor Environment tab. Remember that the use of Reflection Blur will increase your render times, so use it with caution.

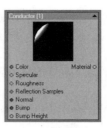

Figure 14-79: Conductor node

## Delta

Delta is an energy conserving material, which simply means that the sum of Specular and Diffuse will always equal 1. For example, if you change the node's Specular value to 40%, then Diffuse will equal 60%. In case of a Specular value of 100%, the Diffuse value will be 0%.

## Dielectric

This node is used most commonly for materials like glass and liquids where the index of refraction (IOR) changes according to the different materials that the rays travel through, such as air to glass to air or air to glass to liquid to air. These are just a couple of possible scenarios where this node might be useful. Dielectric uses Snell's law to calculate refraction angles and Beer's law to calculate absorption. It's important to note that for this node to work properly, Double Sided should be on and Spot Info may be necessary in order to give a different IOR to both sides of the polygons being evaluated.

Figure 14-80: Delta node

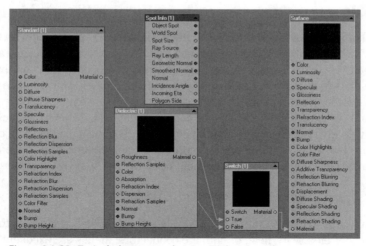

Figure 14-81: Typical glass network using Dielectric node

## Make Material

This node is quite versatile. It allows you to make materials out of the various Shader nodes. You can also input values via the node's Edit panel.

## Material Mixer

Material Mixer is very similar to the Mixer tool, with the exception that it is designed to mix, well, you know… materials. The amount of mixing is controlled by an Alpha input, which can be manually set or controlled by other nodes in the network.

**Figure 14-82: Make Material node**

## Standard

Standard replicates the built-in shading model of LightWave found in the Basic tab of the "classic" Surface Editor. When you open the node's Edit panel you will find an Advanced tab, which mimics the Environment tab of the Surface Editor with added options such as Reflection and Refraction Blurring. This is useful when you need to create layered shaders or when using the Transparency and Refraction Index options to create glass and liquids.

**Figure 14-83: Material Mixer node**

## Switch

You can compare Switch to the Logic node since you can use it to assign different properties to both sides of a polygon. This is very useful for creating glass, liquids, and any other semi-translucent material. Remember that your surface has to be double sided, and the Polygon Side output of the Spot Info node has to be connected to the Switch input inside the Switch node in order to assign different materials to the polygon sides correctly.

**Figure 14-84: Standard node**

**Figure 14-85: Switch node**

# Math

We are artists, not coders. What the heck is this math doing here!? As I said earlier in this chapter, the Node Editor is easy enough for beginners and intermediate users but also powerful enough for the advanced math geniuses out there. I won't delve into math too much; however, there are nodes here that at some point or another you will have to use in order to mix nodes together, and maybe eventually you might want to jump into more advanced things such as trigonometry... gulp!

The Math nodes are divided into three subcategories, making it easier to find the particular operation that you would like to use by its type. The subcategories are:

- Scalar: The input and output of these nodes are always scalar values.
- Trigonometry: Trigonometry, or trig for short, is an area of mathematics that deals with angles and triangles.
- Vector: Vectors involve the concept of direction (XYZ or HPB).

Some nodes are repeated between Scalar and Vector, with the exception being the type of input they receive, which is the same type of output they produce. In other words, Scalar math nodes only input and output scalar values from and/or to other nodes in the network. Trig nodes are all Scalar, but they are separated into their own subcategory for organization purposes.

## Scalar Subcategory

### Abs

Absolute values are always positive or 0, never negative, so this node will convert a negative input value to a positive value. In other words, the absolute value of 350 and –350 is 350.

### Add

This node adds the value of input B to input A. You can enter this value manually or it can come from other nodes in the network. The result of the addition can be connected to other Scalar inputs. This is a very useful node since you can use it for blending textures together.

### BoxStep

This node basically clamps or limits the input according to the Begin and End values using a BoxStep function. Therefore, if the value of the input is smaller than the Begin input, the output will be 0.0. If the value of the In input is higher than the End input value, the output will be 1.0. If the value of the In input is in between Begin and End, the changing values transition proportionally using a box step ramp.

### Ceil

Ceil, short for ceiling, rounds a scalar value to the closest whole number. For instance, if the input value is 1.3, the output would be 2.

### Clamp

Clamp will limit the input according to the Low and High input values, so the output cannot go below or above (respectively) the specified values.

### Divide

The value of B is divided by the input of A.

### Floor

The opposite of Ceil. It will round the input value but will use the lowest integer instead of the highest, like Ceil. For example, if the input value is 5.9, the output will be 5.

### Invert

This node inverts the input value, so 0.0 would become 1.0 and 1.0 would become 0. In other words, the input is subtracted from 1.0. For example, if the input value is 0.9, the output would be 0.1.

### Logic

The Logic node is an IF statement. Conditions can be selected from the pull-down menu; if the condition is met, then the node will use the appropriate output as specified. The node evaluates the input information and then performs an action according to the selected condition. You can select from the following conditions: A equal to B, A not equal to B, A greater than B, A less than B, A greater than or equal to B, A less than or equal to B. In the IF inputs you can enter values or have the values be driven by other nodes in the network. This node can be used alongside the Spot Info node so that you can create double-sided objects with different IOR (Index of Refraction).

### Max

Max will evaluate the inputs and will output the larger of the two.

### Min

Just like Max above, but it will output the smaller of the two inputs.

### Mod

Mod (short for modulus) will evaluate A and B and output the remainder of A divided by B. For example, if the input of A is 5 and the input of B is 3, then the Mod result would be 1.

### Multiply

This node will multiply the value of input A times the value of input B.

### Pow

I'm still trying to find a practical use for this node, but I know that the coders out there are already thinking of ways to use it.

### Sign

Sign converts the incoming value of the input to its opposite sign, so a negative value becomes positive and vice versa. For example, –50.56 becomes 50.56.

### SmoothStep

This is similar to BoxStep, with the exception of having a smooth ramp.

### Subtract

The value of the B input is subtracted from the A input value.

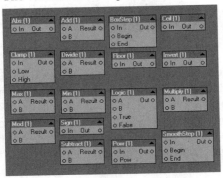

Figure: 14-86:
Scalar math
nodes

# Trigonometry Subcategory

### ArcCos

This node outputs the inverse cosine of the input.

### ArcSin

This node outputs the inverse sine of the input.

### ArcTan

This node outputs the inverse tangent of the input.

### Cos

This node outputs the cosine of the input. Cosine is defined as the ratio of the side next to a given angle to the hypotenuse.

### Sin

This node outputs the sine of the input. Sine is defined as the ratio of the side opposite a given acute angle to the hypotenuse.

### Tan

Here the output is the tangent of the input. In trig, tangent is defined as a function that equals the ratio of the ordinate of the endpoint of the arc to the abscissa of this endpoint. (I bet you wish you hadn't skipped this class in high school now, don't you?)

Figure 14-87: Trig nodes

## Vector Subcategory

### Add

Unlike scalars, vectors have component outputs in the form of XYZ. This node will add the values of input A: XYZ and input B: XYZ respectively, so the Result output would be: AX + BX, AY + BY, and AZ + BZ.

### Add4

This node allows you to add four different vectors. Since vector values are component (XYZ), the Result output of X is the sum of all four X values; the same goes for Y and Z.

### Add Scaled

Similar to Add, with the exception that after the addition is finished the result is multipled by the Scale input value.

### Cross

Cross calculates the Result as the product vector perpendicular to both the A and B inputs.

### Distance

The output of this node is the distance between input A and input B. For example, with this node you can calculate the distance of an object to the camera or light.

### Divide

This node will divide the corresponding individual component input values of A and B respectively, so the Result output would be AX / BX, AY / BY, and AZ / BZ.

### Dot

Dot calculates the cosine of the angle between two vectors.

### Length

This node calculates the length of a vector and outputs the result value as a scalar.

### Multiply

This node will multiply the corresponding individual component input values of A and B respectively, so the Result output would be AX × BX, AY × BY, and AZ × BZ.

### Normalize

This node calculates the length of all three vector components and then divides each vector value by its length.

### Scale

Scale simply multiplies each vector component by the value in the Scale input.

### Subtract

This node will subtract the corresponding individual component input values of A and B respectively, so the Result output would be AX – BX, AY – BY, and AZ – BZ.

### Subtract Scaled

Similar to Subtract, with the exception that after the subtraction is finished the result is multiplied by the Scale input value.

### Transform

This node will allow you to transform the input vector between world and object coordinates and vice versa. The Node Edit panel has a Type pull-down menu that lets you select either Object to World or World to Object.

### Transform2

This node transforms a vector using a 3 × 3 matrix table. The Right input provides the top row of the matrix table, the Up input is the middle row, and Forward is the bottom row of the matrix table.

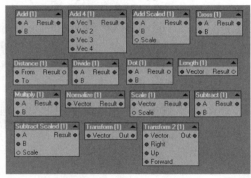

Figure 14-88: Vector math nodes

# Ray Trace

## RayCast

This node allows you to cast or "fire" a ray from any position in the scene. The position is derived from the vector Position input of the node. The ray will travel in the direction taken from the Direction vector input. It will keep traveling through the scene until it hits another surface; if no other surface is hit, the result value will be –1.0. The length of the distance traveled will be the output of the node in the form of a Scalar output.

## RayTrace

RayTrace works like RayCast above, with the exception that when the ray hits another surface, that surface is evaluated as well and the result is kicked back as the Color output. The Position and Direction have to be world coordinate inputs. If no other surface is hit, the resulting Length value will be –1.0.

Figure 14-89: Ray Trace nodes

# Shaders

Shaders allow you to change the default Lambert shading model used in LightWave. By changing this shading model we can change how light interacts with an object's surface and therefore we are able to create more realistic surfaces.

At the bottom of the destination node you will see four color type (red), entries: Diffuse Shading, Specular Shading, Reflection Shading, and Refraction Shading. LightWave includes several shading models for each of these properties. So what's the difference between these and the Diffuse, Specular, Reflection, and Refraction scalar (green) entries at the top of the destination node? This question comes up very often in discussion forums. The difference is that shaders allow you to change the default Lambertian diffuse and Blinn specular models with something else altogether, while the scalar ones simply allow you to add detail using textures. They define which areas of the surface are more diffuse or more specular, for example. Shaders are organized in subcategories to make them easy to find.

## Diffuse Subcategory

### Lambert

This is the default diffuse shading model in LightWave. This model diffuses the reflected light evenly in all directions. This shader is especially good for plastics and high-gloss materials in general.

Figure 14-90: Lambert

### Minnaert

This model was developed to describe nonatmospherical terrain surfaces such as the Moon and so it is also known as a "moon shader." In this Node Edit panel you are able to pick from two implementations of the shading model; Minnaert-A is great for porous surfaces such as moons, dirt, rocks, and stone; Minnaert-B is great for fibrous surfaces such as fabrics. The Canyon tutorial in Chapter 24 uses Minnaert-A as the diffuse shader. In the Edit panel you can also play with an option called Darkening. Increasing this value to high levels will invert the surface shading.

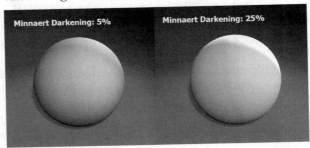

Figure 14-91: Minnaert

## Occlusion

Occlusion or Ambient Occlusion, also known as "dirt map," is a shading model that gives you a way to add realism to your images by taking into account how light is blocked from surfaces. The result is the darkening of such surfaces as objects get closer together (and hence the name dirt map). Ambient Occlusion is not limited to reacting to objects getting closer together; it also affects its own geometry at the same time, which is called "self-shadowing." This is great for creating images with soft shading, similar to the shading in a radiosity render without the huge render times. Of course this only affects shading, so bounce lighting is not calculated. This node can be used in many different and creative ways; the output can be connected to different node attributes in the network in order to achieve several different looks. There are just a few options to control the look of this shader: Samples, Mode, and Maximum (max).

Samples determines the number of directions a surface evaluates in order to calculate the occlusion solution. So the higher the number, the better the quality, and therefore the longer it would take to render. I tend to use 2 × 6 for test renders and 4 × 12 for final renders, although Occlusion tends to need more samples to get a smoother result.

Mode gives you two options: Infinite, which simply means that the rays have no limited range, and Ranged, which means that you can set an amount to limit the length of the evaluation rays.

Max determines the amount to be used by the Ranged mode.

Figure 14-92: No AO, Infinite, and Ranged

Since Occlusion uses rays to determine the occluded areas, Ray Trace Shadows needs to be on in the Render Globals panel for this node to work as expected. In the examples above, I connected the Occlusion node to the Diffuse Shading slot of the destination node.

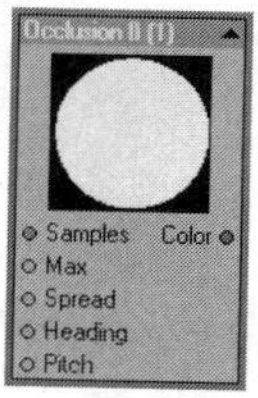

## Occlusion II

Occlusion II is very similar to Occlusion, with the biggest difference being a Color Mapping option in which you can select a spherical map, light probe, or background image from disk. If

Figure 14-93: Occlusion II node

you use a light probe image, the Pitch option can be accessed along with Heading, which is available for every color mapping option.

## OrenNayar

This shading model was designed as an improvement to the Lambertian model. It is especially good for recreating rough, matte surfaces such as clay and fabrics. The Roughness setting simulates the effects of long rows of symmetric cavities, making it a good choice to mimic the effects of velvet in a similar way as Minnaert-B can.

Figure 14-94: OrenNayar

## Theta

This is a more accurate translucency shader. Many of this node's attributes are associated with subsurface scattering; however, it doesn't involve the massive render times commonly found in physically accurate SSS models. This shader uses IOR (Index of Refraction), which allows you to specify how much light is bent as it passes through the surface, and Spread, which is the amount of scattering as light travels through the object. Figure 14-95 shows Theta on a plane; notice the sphere showing through.

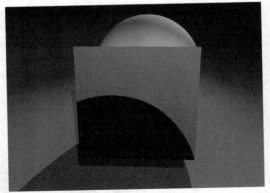

Figure 14-95: Theta

## Translucency

Translucency is the quality of a substance's surface that allows light to diffusely pass through it. As you know, translucency is not the same as transparency. Translucent objects do not reveal the colors or any other attribute of the object that is behind; however, light penetrates the surface and the object behind will show through. The look of translucency is greatly affected by the angle from which the surface is being seen. This node has a Color input where you can connect a texture that will show up in the rendered image at certain angles. The perfect example of this effect is leaves. This shader is almost the same as the Translucency input channel and therefore it works best if it is used alongside another diffuse shader and the

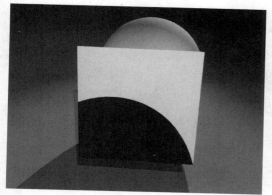

Figure 14-96: Translucency

two are mixed. A feature that sets this node apart from the channel is that it lets you select the maximum range of light diffusion. In the Node Edit panel you will find a pull-down menu that allows you to select between two Range options: 90 and 180 degrees. This shader works best with thin objects such as paper and window treatments (curtains).

## Reflection Subcategory

### Ani-Reflections

Anisotropic reflections are dependent on direction just like anisotropic speculars. Besides being able to connect color attributes to this node, you can also tint the reflection and change the dispersion based on samples. Sampling is the number of directions evaluated in the surface in order to determine its shading value. The more samples, the better the quality, but it comes at a very render-expensive cost. I have found that $3 \times 9$ or $4 \times 12$ suits most of my needs most of the time.

Figure 14-97: Ani-Reflections

### Reflections

This is similar to the Reflection slot in the destination node but with some added features. Besides being able to connect color attributes to this node, you can also blur the reflection and change the dispersion based on samples. Sampling is the number of directions evaluated in the surface in order to determine its shading value. The more samples, the better the quality, but it comes at a very costly render expense. You can tint the reflections as well.

Figure 14-98: Reflections

## Specular Subcategory

### Anisotropic

Anisotropic speculars are dependent on direction. This is a great model to use with materials (usually man-made) that have tiny grooves in them such as brushed metal, stainless steel, and the classic example... CDs. The Anisotropic specular shader will also do a great job with fibrous objects like Christmas ball ornaments and velvet. In the Node Edit panel you will see options that allow you to control the shape and direction of the anisotropic highlight. Anisotropy U and Anisotropy V control the amount of anisotropy, while Axis controls the direction of the highlight. The Mapping pull-down menu gives you three options for the anisotropic shape: Cylindrical, Linear, and UV. You can also offset the position by entering values in the center tab or by connecting a node attribute to the input. Remember that just like every other attribute in the Node Editor, any manually entered values will be overridden once a node attribute is plugged into the input.

Figure 14-99: Anisotropic specular

### Blinn

Blinn is the default specular shading model; it simulates the direct reflection of light by a surface, creating a smooth hot spot called a "specular highlight." Blinn and Phong are almost identical, with the main difference that Phong's highlight spreads out more. Blinn is computationally more expensive than Phong since the specular highlight tends to be more realistic than Phong. Blinn is great for materials such as glass, shiny metals, plastic, and wet, slimy surfaces.

Figure 14-100: Blinn

## CookTorrance

This shader model is the most realistic of the specular shaders and is far more versatile. At high glossiness settings, the highlight will get tight and sharp, making it perfect for glossy, reflective materials such as plastic, glass, and water. At lower glossiness settings, the highlight will spread out and diffuse more, as seen on materials with less reflective properties such as skin.

Figure 14-101: CookTorrance

## Phong

This specular shading model was developed by Phong Bui Tong in the '70s. It is computationally faster than Blinn but not as accurate. As mentioned in the Blinn section, the Phong specular highlight spreads out more to the point of causing rims if the light is directly behind the object. Blinn's specular highlight will remain concentrated and will not spread out like Phong.

Figure 14-102: Phong

## Subsurface Scattering Subcategory

Subsurface scattering (SSS for short) is the phenomenon where light penetrates a semitranslucent surface, scatters inside the volume, and exits at a different angle. SSS is important to accurately represent materials such as milk, wax, and skin, to name a few. LightWave has two shaders to aid you with the creation of such effects: Kappa and Omega. While these are diffuse shaders and can be connected directly to the Diffuse Shading slot in the destination node, you will get better results if you mix the shader with another diffuse shader such as Oren Nayar. SSS is considered by many, including me, to be an advanced technique that requires a bit of experience with the Node Editor and its nodes, as well as good general surfacing skills. That said, I still wanted to cover these shaders here just in case you feel adventurous. The reality of SSS is that there is no right "recipe" to get good effects in your models, but there are some things you can think of when trying it:

- The physical size of the object
- The apparent thickness of the object
- The lighting environment
- The type of material
- The object's internal volume

SSS is found in different type of materials and is different in all of them. Wax and skin are good examples. Wax, while a solid surface, has no internal structures (besides the wick) so light has more room to scatter before it exits. Skin has a more complex structure; we have muscles, veins, organs, bones, etc., and light will interact with all of these elements before it exits and therefore the SSS effect will be different.

## Kappa

Kappa is also known as a "fake SSS" effect. It is not based on an accurate SSS model but its advantage is that it is a lot faster than a physical model like Omega. Like Omega, Kappa works best in a ray-traced environment, so make sure you turn ray tracing on in the Render Globals panel. If you open the Kappa Node Edit panel, you will see the following options:

**Color** — Determines the color of the surface; you can enter an RGB value manually or you can connect attributes from other nodes in the network.

**Range** — Essentially determines how deep inside the volume you would like the samples to reach. This is why you need to have in mind the actual size of your object. A 1m object with a 10mm range will look different from a 0.5m object with a 10mm range. Using the same wax and skin examples, wax will have a greater range than skin.

**Amount** — This is the intensity of the SSS effect, or how strong it is.

**Samples** — Determines the number of directions a surface evaluates in order to calculate the SSS solution, so the higher the number, the better the quality and therefore the longer it will take to render. I tend to use 2 × 6 for test renders and 4 × 12 for final renders. If it is not enough, I'll go to the next option down the list.

**Mode** — Here you select between Forward, which means that the main light source is coming from a similar direction as the viewer, and Backward. Backward means that the light source is away from the viewer, like in backlit environments.

Of course, lighting changes from scene to scene depending on the mood that you are trying to convey, but in most cases you should use a mix of two Kappa nodes, one set to Forward and the other set to Backward. This will give you good results in most lighting situations.

Figure 14-103: Kappa

## Kappa II

In Kappa (described above) you can select either forward or backward scattering, making it necessary to build a two-Kappa node network to create a convincing SSS effect in your surface. Kappa II streamlines this process by providing the ability for you to select forward and backward colors and amounts in a single node. There are no other "extra" options in this node; it simply combines two Kappa nodes into one.

Figure 14-104: Kappa II

## Omega

Omega is NewTek's implementation of a physically correct SSS shading model. We all know what "physically correct" means... long render times! Omega has some options to help reduce render times a bit, though. In order to create a good SSS surface with this shading model, you need to have either an "air" surface, which is a duplicate object with the poly normals flipped so that they face inward, or you can use the Spot Info node along with a Logic node in order to give each side of the polygons a different refraction index. This is the method I use since "air" polys can produce artifacts in the render. If you are new to subsurface scattering, start with Kappa; Omega is more challenging so it's better to start easy and then expand on it once you feel comfortable enough. Let's review the options in this node's Edit panel.

**Surface Color** — Determines the color of the surface; you can enter an RGB value manually or you can connect attributes from other nodes in the network.

**Subsurface Color** — Determines the color of the subsurface; you can enter an RGB value manually or you can connect attributes from other nodes in the network.

**Color Falloff** — Determines at what percentage of penetration the subsurface color is at 100%.

**Falloff Bias** — This is a curve that will favor color falloff over surface color (start) or subsurface color (end).

**Amount** — This is the intensity, or how strong the SSS effect is.

**Spread** — Determines the variation amount of the evaluation ray's distribution over a surface. High values mean wider angles, while smaller values mean tighter angles.

**Index of Refraction** — Determines how much light bends while traveling through the material.

**Penetration** — Determines the distance at which the subsurface color is at 100% falloff. This is affected by both Color Falloff and Falloff Bias.

**Mode** — Here you select the method of evaluation for the surface.

- Single Scattering (No RayTracing) — All of the options that use No RayTracing calculate thickness by firing a "measurement" ray, so other properties in the scene like Ray Trace Reflections are not calculated.

- Single Scattering (Full RayTracing) — Full RayTracing allows other objects and properties in the scene environment to be taken into account during the evaluation, which in turn affects the look of the SSS effect.

- Multiple Scattering (No RayTracing) — This works the same as Single Scattering but the ray bounces inside of the surface multiple times, collecting samples before it exits.

- Multiple Scattering (Full RayTracing) — Try this setting if you feel courageous. It works the same as the option above, but it takes into account ray tracing of the scene environment and objects and is therefore the most computationally expensive option of the bunch.

**Samples** — Determines the number of directions a surface evaluates in order to calculate the SSS solution, so the higher the number, the better the quality and therefore the longer it will take to render. I tend to use $2 \times 6$ for test renders and $4 \times 12$ for final renders. If that is not enough, I'll go to the next option down the list.

**Recursions** — This is the value used by the Multiple Scattering options described above.

By selecting one of the No RayTracing options you can save a lot of render time. It is still slower than Kappa but it is better than using Full RayTracing.

Figure 14-105: Omega

## Transparency Subcategory

The shaders in this section are intended to be connected to the Refraction Shading slot of the surface destination node. These nodes work in direct correlation with the Basic Transparency value of the Surface Editor or the Transparency attribute in the surface destination node. By applying a different set of normals you can achieve the illusion of depth in a layered surface, like carbon fiber, for example.

### Ani-Refractions

This shader allows for anisotropic qualities to the refraction of a transparent surface, like quartz or ice, for example. The top section of the Node Edit panel is very similar to that found in the Refraction Options in Surface Editor's Environment tab, where you can select from a list of refraction mapping modes and an image to refract. In this node you have the option to tint the refractions, and the color can be animated. Another useful option is Dispersion, which is the phenomenon where a wave is divided into components with different Index of Refraction (IOR) levels. The perfect example of this would be a prism.

### Refractions

This is another refraction shader that provides you with more control over the refraction look of the surface. As in Ani-Refractions, you can tint the refraction and you can add dispersion as well. Here you also have the option to blur the refraction; the quality of the blurring is derived from the Samples option that you select. Just keep in mind that with high sampling levels, the render times will take a serious hit. Find a good balance between quality and speed.

Figure 14-106: Tinted Refraction

## Spot

The only node in this category is Spot Info. Spot Info gives you access to data regarding the current spot. Let's translate that into something a little more understandable. A spot is a pinpoint of undetermined size being evaluated on the current surface. Since we are working on the Surface Node Editor, the evaluated data corresponds to an object's surface, such as the length of the incoming ray, its source, and where it is headed relative to the spot being evaluated. There are many uses for this node, ranging from normal and displacement maps to creating double-sided surfaces with different properties on each side of the polygon. Since Spot Info simply evaluates the surface and returns information, there are no inputs available; however, the information is available as outputs that you can connect to other nodes in the network. The Spot Info outputs and their types are as follows:

Figure 14-107:
Spot Info node

**Object Spot (vector)** — This is the current spot being evaluated in Object Coordinates XYZ.

**World Spot (vector)** — This is the current spot being evaluated in World Coordinates XYZ.

**Spot Size (scalar)** — The size of the spot being evaluated.

**Ray Source (vector)** — The XYZ position of the ray source.

**Ray Length (scalar)** — This outputs the length of the ray from the ray source to the spot being evaluated.

**Geometric Normal (vector)** — Determines the normal information of the flat-shaded polygon being evaluated by the current spot.

**Smoothed Normal (vector)** — Determines the normal information of the smooth-shaded polygon being evaluated by the current spot.

**Normal (vector)** — Determines the normal information of the smooth-shaded, bump-mapped polygon being evaluated by the current spot.

**Incidence Angle (scalar)** — This is the incidence angle between the source ray and the normal.

**Incoming Eta (scalar)** — This is the incoming refraction index.

**Polygon Side (integer)** — This determines the sides of a double-sided surface. The back side is 0 and the front side is 1.

# Tools

This category contains tools to help you with different tasks while building nodal networks. They allow you to make "type" conversions and mix nodes together using different modes.

## Color Scalar

This node is used to convert a Color output to a Scalar output. In the Node Edit panel you have a pull-down menu where you can select a method of conversion. They are as follows:

Figure 14-108:
Color Scalar node

**Average** — Outputs the scalar value by averaging the values of the color RGB components. Scalar = (R+G+B)/3.

**Maximum** — The Scalar output takes the largest value of the three RGB values.

**Minimum** — The Scalar output is the smallest value of the three RGB values.

**Red Channel** — Outputs the scalar value by using the Color input's red channel value.

**Green Channel** — Outputs the scalar value by using the Color input's green channel value.

**Blue Channel** — Outputs the scalar value by using the Color input's blue channel value.

**Luma** — The scalar outputs the luminance value from the Color input.

## Color Tool

The Color Tool lets you adjust several color properties in a single node based on the HSV color model. Most likely you have used this in an image editor such as Photoshop before, but here is a quick rundown of the available options.

Figure 14-109:
ColorTool

**Color** — This is the color that will be affected by the other attributes of the node. It can be an incoming color from other nodes in the network, or manually specified.

**Hue (H)** — Measured as degrees from 0 to 360 on the standard color wheel. You can change the hue of the input color by changing the degree value, essentially going around the color wheel.

**Saturation (S)** — Determines how much of the hue you see. The default of 100% means that the input color remains the same, while a value of 0% means that the hue is completely gone, leaving you with a grayscale image. Any values over 100% will accentuate the hue further.

**Brightness (V)** — Determines how light or dark the color is. As with Saturation, this is measured with a percentage value. The default value of 100% means no change in brightness, and a value of 0% means black. A value over 100% will incrementally be changing to white.

**Contrast** — Controls the tonal range of an image. The colors of a low-contrast image will look dull, which makes it hard to differentiate between foreground and background elements. On the other hand, an image with high-contrast values will have richer colors and elements will be easier to see. An image with too much contrast will look almost neon-like and the image will have a posterized look.

## Limiter

Limiter is basically a clamp that works on every channel of the Color input RGB channels at once. The RGB will not go above or below the specified Low and High input values.

## Make Color

This node allows you to create a Color output based on Scalar inputs, either manually entered in the Node Edit panel or by connecting attributes from other nodes in the network.

Figure 14-110: Limiter

## Make Vector

This node allows you to create a Vector output based on Scalar inputs, either manually entered in the Node Edit panel or by connecting attributes from other nodes in the network.

Figure 14-111: Make Color

## Mixer

You will be using this one quite often. It allows you to mix between two color type inputs based on the blending modes that I talked about earlier in this chapter. This is a great node for mixing any color inputs, including shaders!

Figure 14-112: Make Vector

## Vector Scalar

This node is used to convert a Color output to a Scalar output. In the Node Edit panel you have a pull-down menu where you can select a method of conversion. They are as follows:

**Maximum** — The Scalar output takes the largest value of the three vector components (XYZ).

Figure 14-113: Mixer tool

**Minimum** — The Scalar output takes the smallest value of the three vector components (XYZ).

**X Channel** — Outputs the scalar value by using the Vector input X channel value.

Figure 14-114: Vector Scalar node

**Y Channel** — Outputs the scalar value by using the Vector input Y channel value.

**Z Channel** — Outputs the scalar value by using the Vector input Z channel value.

**Length** — Outputs the scalar value by using the Vector input length.

# Vertex Map

These nodes allow you to access the information of vertex maps that were created in Modeler.

## Morph Map

This node gives you access to any morph map that you have created in Modeler. With this node and a little logic we can change the color of an object based on the amount of morph being applied to it.

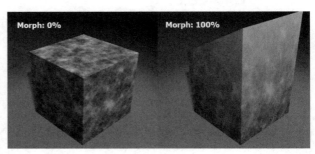

Figure 14-115: Morph map

## Vertex Map

This node gives you access to any vertex color maps available in your object. You have the ability to mix the vertex map with other color nodes in the network. You can then connect the Color output to different nodes' attributes or simply connect it to the Color input of the destination node.

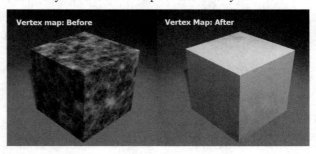

Figure 14-116: Vertex map in action

> **NOTE:** See Chapter 7 for more on the creation of color vertex maps.

## Weight Map

This node gives you access to every weight map available in your object. You select the map in the Node Edit panel's pull-down menu. The Value output can be connected as-is to other node attributes, but to gain more control you can connect the value output to a gradient's input; this way you can control the map using the values of a gradient.

> **NOTE:** Check out the Canyon tutorial in Chapter 24 on to see weight maps in a real-world example.

# Putting Nodes to Work

Now that we have gone through all of the different nodes available in the Node Editor and have a better understanding of the job they perform, it's time to put them to work with some quick exercises. I admit that some of those nodes might not make a heck of a lot of sense right now, but after these exercises, things will begin to "click."

## Blending Images with Gradients

In the "Gradient" section I told you that you can use the key outputs of a gradient to blend images together; here is how to go about doing that.

1. Load up the scene called blending_images.lws from Tutorials\Node Editor on the companion CD. As you can see, it is a simple sphere.

2. Open the Surface Editor (F5) and select the "sphere" surface from the Surface list, then click on the Edit Nodes button to open the Node Editor. To better see what we are doing, open VIPER (F7) and make a render to save the buffers for VIPER.

3. Add a couple of image nodes to the workspace by going to the Add Node pull-down menu or by accessing the contextual menu by pressing Ctrl+ right mouse button, and then choosing Add Node>2D Texture>Image.

4. Now with the image node selected, double-click it to open its Edit panel. If you have the Edit panel embedded to the Node Editor, the panel should show just by clicking on the node. Load the image called newtek_ concrete16.jpg, set MipMap Quality to Off and Mapping to Spherical, and then click on the Automatic Sizing button to fit the texture to the sphere's size. With one image node set up, you can copy (Ctrl+c) and paste (Ctrl+v) the node, so now the only thing you need to change is the actual image to be used. Open the Node Edit panel of this node and load a different image; you can load stone06.jpg.

5. With the image nodes ready, we can now set up the gradient. Add a gradient node to the workspace by choosing Add Node>Gradient> Gradient. Connect the Color output of the gradient node to the Color channel of the surface destination node.

6. Double-click on the node to open the Edit panel. All we need to do now is add an extra key to the gradient and change the key color to white. This is not absolutely necessary to do, but it will give you a better idea of how the blending is being controlled by the gradient.

7. Before we make any connections, change the input of the gradient to Y Coordinate. Now that we are ready to make connections, activate Show Output for both keys in the gradient. Six more connections are added to the list of the node, three for each key on the gradient; they correspond to Color, Position, and Alpha.

8. Connect the Color output of Image 2 to Key (1) color. Once you do this VIPER should update. It'll be a little too grainy, so make a render to better see the result. You should see a white sphere (Key 2 color) and the texture of Image 2, which is a little faint but it is there. At this point you can fine-tune the keys of the gradient to adjust the blending if desired.

Figure 14-117: Gradient with keys adjusted

9. Connect the Color output of Image 1 to Key (2) color; VIPER should update again and now you can clearly see that the color of Key 2 has been replaced with the image. You can fine-tune the gradient's keys to suit. You can also keep adding as many keys and images as you want, memory dependent, of course. Before, in the "classic" Texture Editor, you had to create an alpha gradient layer for each image on the stack, which made it a tedious task to edit them. Now you have just one gradient node doing all the blending for you, which is much easier to edit.

Figure 14-118: Two images blending

I took this a little further; I added a Crumple 3D texture and connected it to the Bg Color of the gradient node. Then I changed the Alpha of Key 2 on the gradient to 50%. The result is that the image is 50% transparent, therefore allowing the Bg Color to show through. I also added an Add vector node and connected the Bump output of both images to the inputs A and B. The result output is then connected to the Bump channel of the surface destination node. I finished this surface off by adding a Divide node and connecting the Image1 Luma output to the A input of the Divide node. The B input is 0.8, which I entered manually in the Node Edit panel. The result output was connected to the Diffuse, Specular, and Glossiness channels of the surface destination node. If you feel that the surface is too bumpy, you can reduce the Bump Amplitude attribute of the image nodes. You can see this network in Figure 14-120; this is also available as a preset named LW9T_imgBlend on the companion CD.

Figure 14-119: The final surface

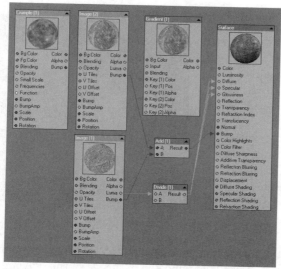

Figure 14-120: The finished node network

## Assigning Different Textures to Double-sided Surfaces

Before LightWave v9 if you wanted to make very thin objects with different textures on each side of the polygons, such as book pages, you would have to make a copy of the polygons, flip them, and offset them a tiny bit so they are no longer on top of each other and to avoid Z sorting problems.

LightWave v9 has a node in the Node Editor that can differentiate one side of the polygon from the other, allowing you to do several different things previously tough or inefficient to do in the "classic" Texture Editor. This node is called Spot Info (Add Node>Spot>Spot Info). This node has an attribute at the bottom of the list called Polygon Side. This attribute's type is integer, outputting 0 (black) for the back side or 1 (white) for the front side.

We can use this information in a number of different ways; for this exercise we are going to assign different textures to each polygon side.

1.  To do this we can use the handy Mixer node (Add Node>Tools>Mixer); change the Bg Color to a very light beige color, which will be the inside of the apple; then change the Fg Color to a green color, which will be the skin of the apple.

2.  Connect the Color output of the Mixer node to the Color channel of the surface destination node. Now make a test render to see what we have so far and to save the buffers for VIPER.

    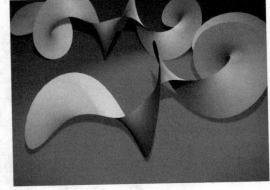

    Figure 14-121

    You will notice that the apple peel object is the same color on both sides (Figure 14-121); that's because we haven't connected the Polygon Side output of the Spot Info node.

3.  Just connect that output to the Opacity input of the Mixer node and make another test render. Now you should see each side of the polygons with the colors we assigned in the Mixer node, as seen in Figure 14-122.

Figure 14-122

All we have left to do is make it look more like an apple peel with some textures.

4. I added a Crumple (Add Node > 3D Textures > Crumple) and an Image (Add Node > 2D Textures > Image) node. For the crumple texture I increased its size quite a bit: Scale X 10m, Y 5m, Z 10m; this makes the crumple texture really large and gives us the hint of the surface on the other side. I also made the background color a light beige color and the foreground color the same apple green as seen on the tiling 2D apple texture found on the companion CD.

5. I loaded this apple tiling texture to the Image node, changed UV Tiling to 2, and Planar mapped on the x-axis of the object.

   Now we have an object with different textures on both sides of a double-sided object without the need of duplicate polygons and two separate sets of surfaces. You can take this further by adding a clip map to add irregularities on the border edges.

Figure 14-123: Apple peels

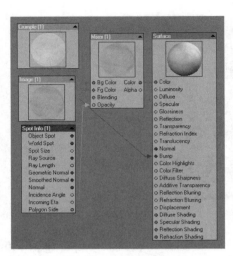

Figure 14-124: The apple peel's node network

Let's take a look at another Polygon Side example.

## Air Polys No More!

Prior to LightWave v9, in order to create realistic glass you needed a duplicate copy of your glass object with the polygon normals flipped, then you had to assign an IOR (Index of Refraction) of 1 and a very high transparency value to correctly duplicate how light rays enter a surface and bend and exit on the other side. This is called an air polygon. This approach has two major drawbacks: One, it increases the poly count of the object and two, you have two different surfaces to deal with.

With the help of the Spot Info and Logic nodes in LightWave v9, we can assign different IORs to both sides of the polygons and thus get rid of duplicate geometry while accurately replicating the effect of air polys.

> **NOTE:**  Refer to the previous sections of this chapter for a description of these nodes.

1.  Load the scene called spot_info_glass.lws from the companion CD if it isn't already loaded. Make sure that Double Sided is on for the sphere surface in the Surface Editor; also make sure Ray Tracing is on in the Render Globals panel.

2.  Open the Node Editor like we have done before, and then add a Spot Info node (Add Node>Spot>Spot Info) and a Logic node (Add Node>Math> Scalar>Logic).

3. Connect the Polygon Side output of the Spot Info node to the A input of the Logic node.

4. Go to the Logic node Edit panel and change the If True attribute to something other than 1 (let's try 1.1 for now).

5. Now, connect the output of this node to the Refraction Index channel in the surface destination node.

We know that the front side of the double-sided poly is identified as 1 and the back side as 0, so basically what the Logic node is saying is, "If A(1) equals B(0), then the statement is True and therefore 1.1 will be the value used for the refraction index. If A(1) doesn't equal B(0), then the value used as the refraction index will be 1.0."

Before making a test render, assign a transparency amount to the sphere surface se we can actually see

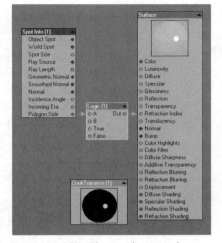

Figure 14-125: Glass node network

the refraction at work. Also go ahead and load the "dirty floor" surface preset for the plane surface so there is something for the sphere to refract; this preset is found on the companion CD. Now make a test render to see your results. Play with the refraction values to see the effect. Cool, right? Adios, air polys!

Figure 14-126: Different IOR for the sphere

## Making Targeted Eyes

At one point or another we probably have all made eyes with a simple gradient, whether they were realistic or cartoony. If not, then these will be your first! As you can probably imagine, eyes can be created easily with a gradient set with multiple colors. That's the easy part. But how do you make the gradient target an item in the scene using the Node Editor? Ah, now things get a bit more complicated. Don't worry, though, it really isn't all that tough.

1. Load the scene called eye_follower.lws. This scene is quite simple; just a sphere, aka the eyeball, a camera, and a couple of lights.

2. Open the Surface Editor and then open the Node Editor by clicking on the Edit Nodes button.

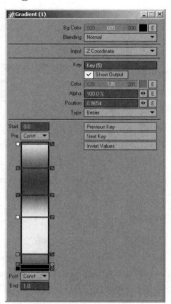

3. Create a Gradient node (Add Node>Gradient>Gradient), then create the color keys for your eye. Figure 14-127 shows the gradient I created. Most likely you used Incidence Angle as the input parameter, but for the eye to properly target the null, use Z Coordinate instead. The gradient will look slightly different as it isn't using the camera viewing angle anymore.

4. Now create a null object and place it in front of the eye.

5. Select the eyeball object and open the Motion Options panel (m). Click on the Target Item pull-down menu and select the eye-ref object.

   That's it! Move the null object around and make test renders to see the eyeball correctly targeting the null.

Figure 14-127: Gradient

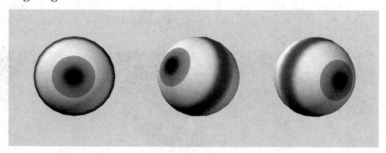

Figure 14-128: Targeted eye

> **NOTE:** VIPER cannot preview this setup properly. To assure it works, you need to make test renders (F9).

## Skin with Subsurface Scattering (SSS)

As technology and computer power have evolved, so have the techniques used to achieve realism in our work. Subsurface scattering is an example of this. SSS has become very popular in the last few years and now we have two built-in shading models to help us with this effect. I consider SSS to be an advanced technique best explored when you have a full understanding of texturing, building node networks, and lighting, but if you feel adventurous, by all means experiment with it. In this exercise we are going to build two nodal networks. The first one is based solely on Kappa, which renders more quickly than Omega. The second network that we are going to create is based on a mix of the SSS models Kappa and Omega, but be warned; since it uses Omega, it is far slower than an exclusive Kappa setup. This technique was developed by fellow artist Werner Ziemerink, who also provided the awesome Scientist model and maps for us to work with.

## Kappa SSS

1. Load up the scene called SSS_Scientist.lws, then open the Surface Editor and select the Head surface from the list.

2. Open the Node Editor and start by adding an Image node (Add Node>2D Textures>Image). Now open its Edit panel and load the image called M_Head_bump.jpg, switch MipMap Quality to Off, and set the projection to UV.

3. Select the OBJ_texture UV map from the pull-down menu and set Bump Amplitude to 32%. Connect the node's Bump output to the Bump input of the surface destination node.

4. Since we have an image node set up, copy and paste it on the workspace. Open its Edit panel and load the image called M_Head_spec.jpg, then add a Blinn node to the workspace (Add Node>Shaders>Specular>Blinn). Connect the spec image node's Luma output to the Specular input of the Blinn node, change the Blinn's Glossiness setting to 40%, then connect the Color output of the Blinn to the Specular Shading slot of the surface destination node.

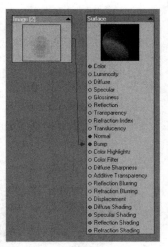

**Figure 14-129: Bump**

5. Add a Kappa node to the workspace (Add Node>Shaders>Subsurface Scattering>Kappa). Also paste the image node again (it should still be stored in the clipboard), open its Edit panel, and load the image called skin2.png. Connect the Color output of the image node to the Color input of the Kappa node. In the Kappa Edit panel, enter 25mm as the Range and set Amount to 100%. I generally use 2 × 6 samples for test renders and 3 × 9 or 4 × 12 for final images; this is up to you, but remember that the higher the sample number, the longer the render times will be as well. Make sure the Kappa mode is set to Backward. In order to have a nice SSS effect for characters using Kappa, we need two

Kappa nodes, one for the back (backscatter) and one for the front (epidermis). NewTek developed another SSS node called Kappa II, which combines this two-Kappa node setup into one single node and therefore streamlines the process. Figure 14-130 shows the network so far.

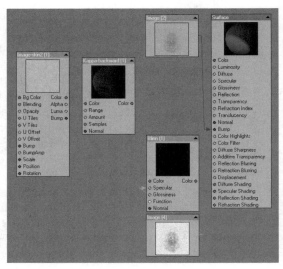

**Figure 14-130**

6. Paste the image node once more, then open its Edit panel and load the image called skin.png, and set Blending Mode to Multiply. Now copy and paste the Kappa node, change Range to 12mm, Amount to 90%, and Mode to Forward. Connect the Color output of the image node to the Color input of the Kappa node we just created. If you right-click on this Kappa node or hit "r" on your keyboard, you can rename it to something a little more descriptive, like "Kappa-forward."

7. I wanted to saturate the image color a little, and there are a few ways to do this. In this case we can just use a color node (Add Node>Constant> Color), make this an orange-reddish color, and connect the Color output to the Color input of the skin image node. This will saturate the image a little since Blending Mode is set to Multiply. Figure 14-131 shows the Kappa network.

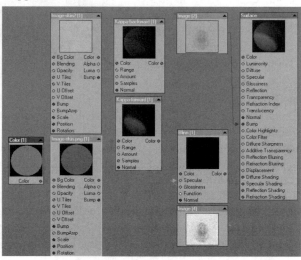

Figure 14-131: The Kappa network

8. In LightWave v9, as you know by now, we can change the Diffuse shading model to something other than the default Lambert. Let's add an OrenNayar node to the workspace (Add Node>Shaders>Diffuse> OrenNayar).

9. Connect the Color output of the skin image node to the Color input of the OrenNayar node. Open its Edit panel, and change the Diffuse value to 60% and Roughness to 35%.

10. All we have left to do is connect all of these diffuse shaders together; to do this we can use our handy Mixer tool (Add Node>Tools>Mixer). First we are going to connect the Kappa nodes together by connecting the Color output of Kappa-backward to the Bg Color input of the Mixer node, and connecting the Kappa-forward Color output to the Fg Color input of the mixer node. Next we want to connect the OrenNayar node to the rest of the network. To do this, copy and paste another Mixer node in the workspace. Connect the Color output of Mixer (1) to the Bg Color of Mixer (2), and the Color output of OrenNayar to the Fg Color of Mixer (2). Finally connect the Color output of Mixer (2) to the Diffuse Shading slot in the surface destination node. Figure 14-132 shows the finished node network.

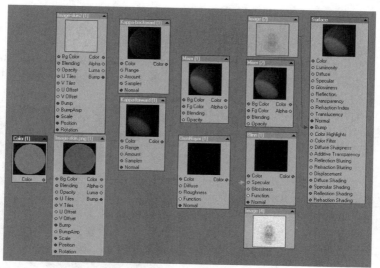

Figure 14-132: Finished node network

11. You can now make test renders since VIPER doesn't gives an accurate representation of the SSS effect. If you feel that it might be too waxy looking, then play with the number of variables in the nodal network. Play with the Kappa amounts and ranges as well as the colors and try the different Diffuse and Specular shading models to see what you come up with. Make a preset of this shader for later use. Figure 14-133 shows the

final result with a bloom layer created in
Photoshop. The bloom layer is simply a
copy of the base layer with the colors saturated using levels and then blurred. This
layer is then screened over the base layer;
play with the opacity to control the amount
of bloom.

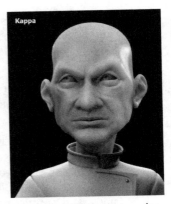

## Omega SSS

Omega yields better results than Kappa, but
the drawback is that it is painfully slow. If you
have the time and render power, then I think
you will be happier with the results of Omega
for skin in particular. The following setup
uses a mix of Omega and Kappa.

Figure 14-133: The test render

1. Load up the scene called SSS_Scientist.lws. Open the Surface Editor and
   select the Head surface from the list. Open the Node editor, and add an
   image node like we did in the Kappa example (Add Node>2D Tex-
   tures>Image).

2. Load the image called M_Head_bump.jpg, change the Mapping to UV,
   and select the OBJ_UVTextureMap from the pull-down list. Copy and
   paste this node a couple of times and load the skin2.png texture to one
   and the M_Head_spec.jpg texture to the other. Remember that you can
   change these node names to something more descriptive. I used Bump,
   Specular, and Color, respectively.

3. Go ahead and connect the Bump
   map to the Bump slot in the surface destination node.

4. Let's add a Blinn specular shader
   to the network (Add Node>
   Shaders>Specular>Blinn).
   Connect the Luma output of the
   Specular texture map to the
   Specular input of the Blinn
   shader, and change the Glossiness setting to 25%. Then
   connect the Color output of the
   Blinn node to the Specular Shading slot of the surface
   destination node.

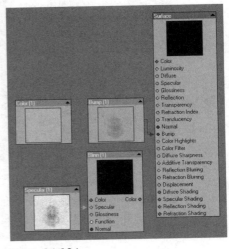

Figure 14-134

   Figure 14-134 shows the
nodal network so far.

5. Let's add the rest of the nodes needed in the network. We need Kappa and Omega nodes (Add Node>Shaders>Diffuse>Kappa and Omega). We also need a Diffuse shader, so use Lambert this time around (Add Node>Shaders>Diffuse>Lambert), and lastly add a Mixer node (Add Node>Tools>Mixer). Change Blending to Additive and Opacity to 100%. Copy and paste this Mixer tool and put it aside for now.

6. Select the Omega node, and change the settings as follows:

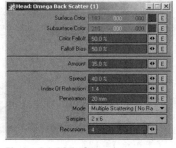

Surface Color: 183, 000, 000
Subsurface Color: 210, 000, 000
Color Falloff: 50%
Falloff Bias: 50%
Amount: 35%
Spread 40%
Index Of Refraction: 1.4
Penetration: 20mm
Mode: Multiple Scattering (No RayTracing)
Samples: 2 × 6 (for testing)
Recursions: 4

Figure 14-135: Omega

7. Select the Kappa node and change the following:

Color: 247, 165, 111
Range: 12mm
Amount: 75%
Samples: 2 × 6 (for testing)
Mode: Backward

Figure 14-136: Kappa

8. With the nodes set up, we can make all of the connections. Connect the Color output of the Omega node to the Bg Color of the first Mixer tool, then connect the Color output of Kappa to the Fg Color of the same Mixer tool. The second Mixer tool is to connect the result of the first Mixer tool and the Lambert shader. Connect the Color output of Lambert to Bg Color of Mixer 2, and the Color output of Mixer 1 to Fg Color of Mixer 2. To finish the setup, connect the Color output of Mixer 2 to the Diffuse Shading slot of the surface destination node. Figure 14-137 shows the finished nodal network, and Figure 14-138 shows the finished image after adding a bloom layer done in Photoshop.

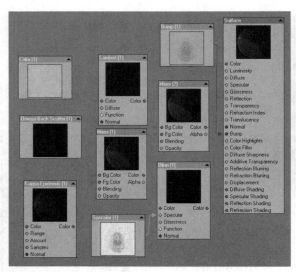

Figure 14-138

Figure 14-137

Remember that these are just a couple of the many different setups and looks that you can create with SSS. You can use SSS for other semi-translucent materials like milk, candles, plastic, ice, etc.

In Part 7, "Tutorials," you will find a couple more node-specific tutorials for you to practice with. In Chapter 24 I guide you through the texturing process of a canyon similar to the Grand Canyon or Bryce Canyon using only procedural textures. I also guide you through the making of an ocean. They are both fun and good exercises for creating node networks in both the Surface Node Editor and the Displacements Maps Node Editor.

# PART 4

# Texture Projections and Mapping

# CHAPTER 15

# Standard Projection Techniques

## Introduction to Standard Projections

When working with images for texturing, we have to define exactly how the image is to be placed (projected) onto the surface of the object, as no program is so intelligent as to know exactly how to place an image onto a surface without some coordinates that tell it where to put the image and in what manner the image should be applied. Even in the adjacent image, we would need to tell LightWave how to project this texture straight onto the surface, even though the placement may seem pretty straightforward and obvious.

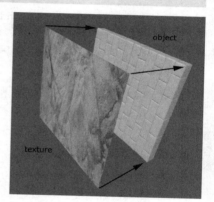

Figure 15-1

Defining these projections involves a process called *mapping*, of which there are a number of different types. Mapping can be roughly divided into two main categories: standard projections and UV mapping. Both offer a few different options for you to use, and are suitable for different situations.

To use a real-life analogy, let's assume that you make a sculpture and then paint all the surface detail for that sculpture onto a piece of cloth. Okay, I know it would be a bit odd to not just paint directly onto the surface, but bear with me here! So you have your sculpture, and you have your cloth, and now you need to figure out a way of wrapping the cloth onto the sculpture so that it looks right. That is basically what mapping is. Do you stick the cloth straight onto the front of the sculpture or do you strategically arrange the cloth onto it?

**367**

> **NOTE:** You only have to specify a projection type for images and for a few procedural textures, as gradients and most procedurals do not require them due to the way that they are created.

What makes mapping really challenging is that in any situation, a number of different approaches could be applicable. The trick is to choose the best one, and deciding on that requires a bit of planning and thought.

To define the manner in which an image will be projected onto a surface, you need to choose an option from the Projection list in the Texture Editor for the channel into which you are placing the image.

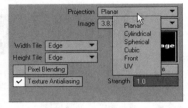

**Figure 15-2**

As you can see, there are quite a few choices.

The first five options in the list — Planar, Cylindrical, Spherical, Cubic, and Front — are standard (basic) projection types. Standard projection types offer perhaps the most straightforward methods of placing textures onto your surface. All you have to do is decide on the most appropriate method for the object upon which you need to apply the texture, as the choice you make will really depend on the shape and orientation of the surface with which you are working.

# Planar Projection

## Using Planar Projections

Planar is probably the simplest method to use of all the standard projection types. It is also possibly the most popular way of placing textures onto surfaces. Its simplicity can be deceiving though, because as straightforward as it is, this option is by no means simplistic or stunted in its actual use. In fact, you could almost say that as a general rule of thumb, if an object cannot be planar mapped, then it cannot be mapped. Sure, for some objects, planar mapping the entire thing would be quite a task, but nevertheless it is totally possible.

Anyway, enough waffling about all that, as you are probably wanting to know exactly what this simple method is!

Planar projection basically takes an image and projects it straight along an axis, through the surface.

## Applying an Image Using Planar Projection

We apply an image by selecting Planar from the Projection list in the Texture Editor, and then deciding which axis to project the image along by clicking on it in the Texture Axis option.

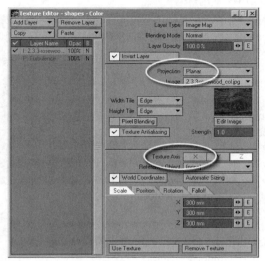

Figure 15-3

This is demonstrated in Figure 15-4. As you can see, we take an image and simply slap it straight onto the object along the same axis that the front of the object is facing.

Figure 15-4

So basically all you do is consider the direction in which the surface is oriented, and then apply the image along that axis. In this case, the surface of the object is facing sideways, so we basically apply the planar image along the x-axis.

**369**

Likewise, if the surface faces upward or downward, we would apply it along the y-axis, whereas if it were facing toward the front or back, we would project along the z-axis.

## Planar Stretching/Dragging

Now if we look closely at the object with the texture applied, we notice a slight problem. Do you see how the texture stretches through the length of the object, leaving those rather unsightly lines? This is an unfortunate problem that we always face when using planar projections.

Figure 15-5

Think of it like this. Say we have a block, and we have a nice little piece of paper with a little design on it that is the size of one of the block's sides. To apply that paper design onto the block, we would simply take the piece of paper and stick it onto one side of the block.

However, because the piece of paper is flat and only the size of one side, we cannot bend it around the edges of the block, so instead it just stays stuck on the side that we have glued it onto. Similarly, a planar projection cannot bend around edges; it simply stays stuck on the face that you have applied it to, along the parts of the face that are oriented in the same direction

Figure 15-6

as the axis that you have projected it along. Planar mapping obviously works like a *plane* (hence the name), and as you probably know from modeling, you cannot bend planes, because in reality that is impossible.

So how does this explain the nasty stretching shown in Figure 15-7? Well, consider this. If the design on this piece of paper that you have stuck on your block has been painted onto the paper, and the paint is still wet, you could try to get the design that is painted onto it onto the other sides of the box by smearing the wet paint along the edges of the paper along the surrounding sides of the box. This would look pretty hideous.

Figure 15-7

Think of the pixels at the edge of an image being like the wet edges of that piece of paper. Now does that make sense? Obviously the best way to get the design onto each side of the box would be to stick a piece of paper with the design on it onto each side of the block, not by smearing the paint.

In LightWave, you could do this by using a combination of a couple of different planar projections along different axes, so that the image could be projected onto each side correctly. The easiest way to do this would be to assign different surfaces to the block according to their orientation and then simply project the images accordingly, as in Figure 15-8.

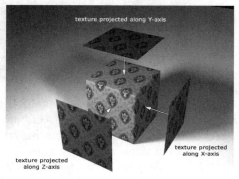

**Figure 15-8**

In this example, I have assigned three different surfaces to the box, one for each projection axis. So basically the top and bottom polygons have one surface assigned to them with the image projected along the y-axis, the side polygons have one surface applied to them with the image projected along the x-axis, and the front and back polygons share a surface with the image projected along the z-axis.

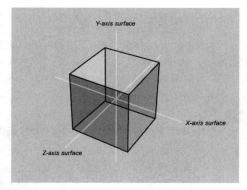

**Figure 15-9**

This, however, is not the only method. Instead of assigning separate surfaces, you could also apply a single surface to the entire box and simply set up three different layers within the Texture Editor, each with its appropriate planar projection. You could then use falloff (covered in Chapter 13) to ensure that none of that nasty planar stretching is visible.

So now we understand how planar mapping works on objects like blocks, but what about uneven surfaces? Well, you can use planar mapping on some irregular surfaces, but surfaces that are very uneven cause problems, because that horrible stretching that happened in the block example becomes visible. In Figure 15-10, I have projected the dirt texture along the y-axis, and as you can see, this works fine with the fairly flat surface, but when applied to the very irregular surface, we get stretching.

Figure 15-10

image applied to slightly uneven surface
no visible stretching

image applied to very uneven surface
visible stretching!

Although you could probably get away with this sort of thing in a distance shot, it will not suffice for objects that are close to the camera.

As you can see, the more the surface slopes away along the projection axis, the worse this problem becomes, as more stretching appears.

This makes planar mapping really mostly ideal for flattish objects such as

Figure 15-11

walls, doors, floors, or any polygonal surface that is predominantly facing toward one axis and does not have too much visible depth where stretching would occur.

## Blending Planar Projections

As I mentioned at the beginning of this chapter, pretty much any object of any type or structure can technically be planar mapped. Sometimes, however, this requires you to use a number of different images projected along different axes that you blend together using falloff in each texture layer that needs a different projection axis, or by using gradients (especially with weight maps) as alpha layers, or even alpha channels in the images themselves. Sounds complex, but it is actually fairly logical and simple to execute.

### Blending with Falloff

The most logical way of blending planar projections would be by using falloff on each layer that needs to be blended, and then carefully positioning each image so that it all works nicely.

> **NOTE:** For more detailed information on using the Falloff options in the Texture Editor, please refer to Chapter 13.

Using the same irregular ground object from the previous example, all I have to do is create two separate layers in the Texture Editor, each with the dirt image in it. One of the layers is projected along the y-axis, as before, while the other is projected along the z-axis. The image that is projected along the y-axis will not have to have any falloff settings applied to it, because in this instance, it will be on the bottom layer, while the other layer will blend with it from above.

But let's do this step by step so that everything is very clear.

So, starting right at the beginning, I create one layer in the Texture Editor. Figure 15-12 shows the surface once again, with the image applied along the y-axis only.

Figure 15-12: Texture applied to y-axis

Take a look at where the stretching occurs, and remember that this stretching is happening along the surfaces that slope downward, along the same axis the image is projected along, which is the y-axis. In order to cover up these areas, we need to apply something along the z-axis so that these areas will no longer be visible.

Now let's add a second layer to the Texture Editor above the bottom layer, this time with the same image projected along the z-axis. This step of the process looks like Figure 15-13.

Yes, I know this looks wrong, but don't worry! Once blended correctly, this image will cover up the stretching along the z-axis.

Figure 15-13: Texture applied to z-axis

So how do we get these two layers to blend together correctly? Well, all I need to do is add some falloff to the top layer (the one that is projected along the z-axis) and reposition it slightly.

So what I do is set up some falloff to the layer as shown in Figure 15-14.

The percent of falloff refers to percent per meter of falloff, which means that 100% falloff creates a linear falloff to 0% at 1 meter.

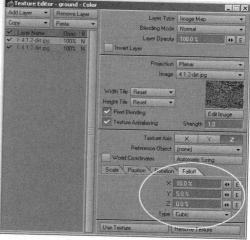

Figure 15-14

The falloff on the y-axis prevents it from stretching along the bottom of the object, while the falloff on the x-axis prevents the stretching from appearing too much along the sides.

I also shift the actual position of the image slightly upward (to make absolutely sure that the image does not drag along the bottom of the object), and remove all tiling options so that the image does not repeat itself at all by selecting the Reset option in my tiling options (see Chapter 13 for more information on tiling images).

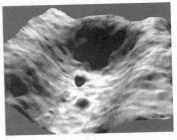

For the sake of this example, I have hidden the bottom layer so that you can see the way in which the falloff and repositioning of this image has faded the image out along the y-axis.

Figure 15-15

As you can see, we have a nice fading that will blend well with the bottom image. Notice that I did not fade it out completely along the side and bottom, as this would basically make the entire image disappear.

When I switch the bottom layer back on and render it, the stretching is covered up by the top layer.

Pretty nifty.

Figure 15-16

## Blending with Gradients

The next blending method we can try out is using gradients in conjunction with weight maps. This method is not always as effective as the falloff method, depending on the model, but is nevertheless worth a mention. Although it requires a little more work, it is, in many ways, easier than the falloff method, which can sometimes be a little confusing.

For this method you simply create weight maps that will act as alphas to place the images where you want them to be, and then create gradient layers over those image layers in the Texture Editor, with the appropriate weight map set up as the alpha for that particular image. Let's examine this process.

Figure 15-17 shows the object and the three images that we wish to apply to the object. For the sake of simplicity I am using a very simple object, a cube, but this principle could be applied to any type of shape. Image 1 will be projected along the x-axis, Image 2 will be projected along the z-axis, and Image 3 will be projected along the y-axis.

First, I need to create a weight map for the object to determine where the different images will be visible. Now remember, once we create the weight map and use it with the gradient, it will act as an alpha layer for the

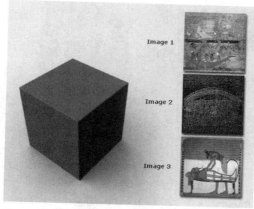

Image 1

Image 2

Image 3

**Figure 15-17**

image that we wish to place onto the model. This means that we must create the weight map with a nice solid area of one particular value to determine the area where the image will be visible. So, I start off by creating a new weight map and calling it "texture image 1," and selecting the areas where I want the image to be visible. I then assign a single value, 100%, to this selection.

This area, which has now been assigned a value of 100% in this weight map, can now be used as an alpha layer with Image 1, and the image will only show through this particular part of the weight map.

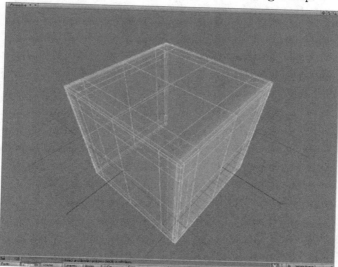

**Figure 15-18**

I now create a second weight map called "texture image 2" that will act as the alpha for the second image. I do exactly the same thing as for the first one, except that for Image 2 I set the weight map's value to 100% on the areas that lie along the y-axis.

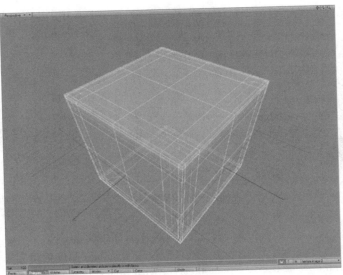

Figure 15-19

And once again, I create yet another weight map, "texture image 3," that has the 100% area located on the areas of the object that lie along the z-axis.

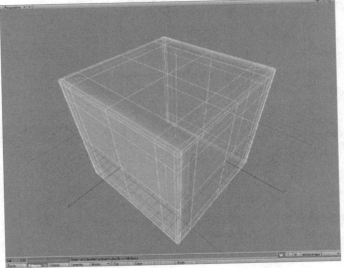

Figure 15-20

I now have three weight maps, each of which will act as an alpha layer for its respective image when applied to the model. I now switch to Layout and begin to set up my surface.

I first apply Image 1 to the color channel of the cube. I set the projection to Planar along the x-axis.

Figure 15-21

As you can see, the projection is working as per normal planar manner. However, since we only want the image to show up on the parts of the cube that lie along the x-axis, I now create a gradient layer above the image to act as an alpha for it. I set the gradient's Input Parameter to Weight Map, and select the "texture image 1" weight map. I then create a key in the gradient at 100%, and set the color of that key to white. I also create keys at 0% and 99%, and set the colors of those keys to black. I set the gradient's Blending Mode to Alpha.

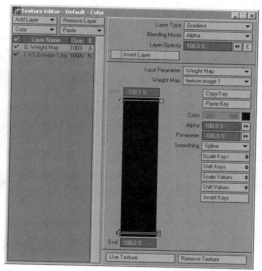

Figure 15-22

This will now allow the image to only show through the areas of the weight map that are 100%, as we can see when the cube is rendered again. See Figure 15-23.

I now repeat these steps for the other two images, creating for each of them a gradient that acts as an alpha layer with its corresponding weight map.

Once all of that is done, I have a cube with all three images placed on their correct sides, as shown in Figure 15-24.

Figure 15-23

Figure 15-24

So, as you can see, this is actually a very easy way of placing images and controlling them, even though it requires a bit of extra work.

**377**

### Blending with Alpha Channels

While the weight map and gradient method provides a nice hands-on and visual solution to creating alpha channels within Modeler for your textures, you can, of course, also just create alpha channels within the images themselves. Certain file formats, such as TGA, can support 32-bit image depth that includes an alpha channel embedded in the image itself.

To do this, all you really need to do is to create a falloff along the edges of the image within the alpha channel, as shown in Figure 15-25.

As you can see, this alpha channel in the image would show only the areas that are within the white part of the alpha, so the edges of the image would be invisible when applied to the object.

Figure 15-25

If we were to take three images and create an alpha channel like this for each one, and could stack them on top of each other in the Texture Editor on the surface of the cube from the previous example, they would automatically blend together without a problem. Figure 15-26 shows three different images, each applied to a separate axis and blended by using their own alpha channels.

The only tricky thing about using this method on an object like this is that the images fade out along the edges of the cube, showing the surface's color beneath it. So just be sure to make the surface's color similar to the overall colors of the images.

Figure 15-26

# Cylindrical Projection

## Using Cylindrical Projections

Well, you will be happy to know that cylindrical projections are really straightforward. You use them for mapping cylindrical objects — it really is as simple as that. Unlike planar projections that can be used for so many different occasions and in so many ways, cylindrical projections are there for when you are texturing tubes, poles, spears, arms, legs, soda cans, and anything else that is, well, cylindrical in shape.

## Applying an Image with Cylindrical Projection

To use a cylindrical projection for a texture, select the Cylindrical option from the Projection list in the Texture Editor.

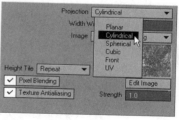

Once you have selected this type, you need to choose an appropriate projection axis from the Texture Axis options. Just like with the planar projections we looked at in the previous section, the axis that you choose for the texture to project along depends on the orientation of the object to which you are applying the texture. Upright cylinders would have the texture applied along the y-axis, whereas cylinders that are lying on their sides would have the texture projected along the x-axis or z-axis, depending on whether they are facing from side to side or front to back respectively.

**Figure 15-27**

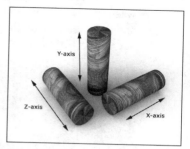

**Figure 15-28**

Think of it as taking a piece of paper and wrapping it around a tube, because that is essentially what cylindrical mapping does, as demonstrated in Figure 15-29.

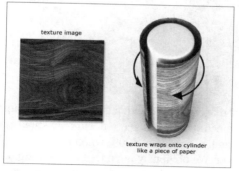

texture image

texture wraps onto cylinder
like a piece of paper

**Figure 15-29**

## "Capping" Cylindrical Objects

As you see, the actual use of this projection type is extremely logical. The only problem that we really face with it, even when using it correctly, is the pinching that happens at either end of the cylinder, on the cylinder "caps." This really cannot be avoided if the ends of the cylinder have the same surface applied.

Of course, we can use a variety of methods to cover it up, such as using falloff or any of the other methods discussed in the previous section, or we could simply assign a separate surface to the end faces.

Figure 15-30 shows a method using weight maps in combination with gradients to control the visibility of the image on the top. This is using a single surface with the gradient (together with the weight map) being used as an alpha layer on top of the image projected in a planar fashion along the y-axis onto the top part.

**Figure 15-30**

As you can see, it works quite nicely, and it was really easy to set up. All I did was create a new weight map on the cylinder that had an initial value of 0%, and then selected all the points along the top and bottom of the cylinder and set them to 100%, as shown in Figure 15-31.

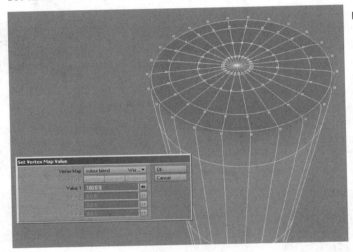

**Figure 15-31**

I then use this weight map, together with a gradient, and set up the gradient so that the image projected onto this section will only show in the areas where the weight map has a value of 100% when the gradient layer is placed above the image layer. We obviously need to use this weight map to avoid the planar stretching that we looked at in the previous section, which would occur from the image on top being projected down the length of the cylinder.

### Ensuring Seamless Mapping

It is important when working with cylindrical projections to bear in mind that somewhere along the object the ends of the texture are going to meet. Because of this, you might want to ensure that the image can *tile* correctly if you do not want any visible seam. Tiling images is placing repeating versions of an image on a surface. Ideally, in order to create a smooth look to the surface, we would not want to be able to see where each copy of the image ends within the pattern, because this would look rather odd. These visible edges are called *seams* and are generally to be avoided at all costs.

Obviously you are not always working with images that have to have all the seams hidden, as some surfaces, like a soda can, might actually have a visible seam on the label. However, when working with other types of surfaces, especially organic surfaces, you have to make sure that the images are going to meet without any noticeable seams.

Figure 15-32 demonstrates what happens when an image's two sides do not match, resulting in a seam, and also shows a correctly made image that tiles the right way.

**Figure 15-32**

As you can see in the example on the left, the image used as a texture has sides that do not match up, resulting in an image that will not be seamless when applied to an object. Notice in the little block below the image itself that when the image is placed alongside itself, you can see the separations at the edge.

In the example on the right, no seams are visible when using this image, as this particular texture is tileable because the edges are matched.

## Using Adobe Photoshop's Offset Filter to Hide Seams

The easiest way to make sure that an image can be tiled is by using the Offset filter in Adobe Photoshop. If you create an image that you wish to tile on a surface, all you have to do is offset it along the top and one of the sides, and then simply cover up the visible overlapping areas using airbrushing or the cloning tool. Let's take a look at Figure 15-33, which shows the image used in the previous example that had unmatched sides.

Now, we go to the Offset filter in Photoshop (Filter>Other>Offset), and offset it from the top and the right, both by 100 pixels. We get the result shown in Figure 15-34.

**381**

Figure 15-33

Figure 15-34

As you can see, we now have a visible seam within the image itself. All we have to do now is hide it. In this example, I just use the Rubber Stamp (clone) tool. See Figure 15-35.

If we try tiling this image now, we will have no visible seams, as shown in Figure 15-36.

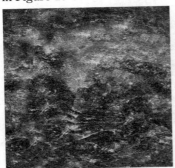

Figure 15-35

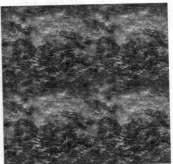

Figure 15-36

And if we were to wrap this around a cylinder, we would have no visible seam either. So that is a nice quick method of ensuring seamless textures!

> **NOTE:** Refer back to Chapter 11 for more information on creating and using seamless textures.

## Using the Width Wrap Amount Option

The most astute of you may have noticed that there is an option when using cylindrical projections in the Texture Editor called Width Wrap Amount.

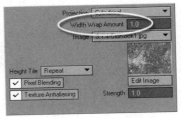

Figure 15-37

The value you enter into this field determines the number of times the texture is wrapped around the object to which it is applied. So if, for example, you wanted to wrap an image around a cylinder five times, you would enter a value of 5 in this field.

Figure 15-38 shows the result of wrapping a texture a total of eight times around the cylinder.

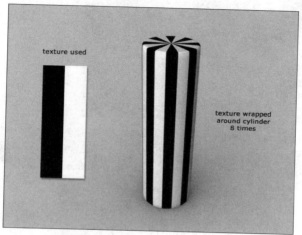

Figure 15-38

texture used

texture wrapped
around cylinder
8 times

Obviously, this is great for adding any repeating details without having to actually make one big image that includes the repeating, especially since smaller images use less memory. In a case like this, it is beneficial to use the simplest, smallest image that you can get away with. Of course this is also a quicker method than creating a long image with the stripes repeated eight times.

Setting your width wrap correctly is also important for preventing an ill-sized image from becoming hideously stretched if it wrapped 360° around an object that the image is technically too small for. Increasing this amount would therefore reduce this stretching by repeating the image more times along those 360°, thereby making each repeat of the image cover less space, and therefore distort less.

## Cylindrical Projection Tutorial: Applying a Label to a Soda Can

This tutorial briefly demonstrates the process of applying a label to a can of soda.

1. Open Modeler and load the 4.1.3-sodacan.lwo object from the companion CD. Notice that the can has two separate surfaces applied to it: one surface for the label and one surface for the metal parts.

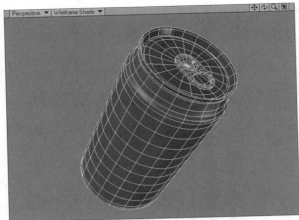

Figure 15-39

2. Open the Surface Editor (Ctrl+F3), and go to the label texture. Click on the "T" button next to the Color channel to open up the Texture Editor.

Figure 15-40

3. Go to the layer list and click where it says "(none)." By default, all new layers created when the Texture Editor is first opened are image layers, so you do not have to specify that this is an image layer. Notice that the default projection type is always Planar. Click on the Projection drop-down button and select Cylindrical. Leave the Width Wrap Amount option that appears at 1.0.

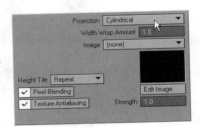

Figure 15-41

4. Click on the Image drop-down button and select Load Image. Find the 4.1.3-sodalabel.jpg image on the companion CD and load it.

    As you can see, the image looks a little strange on the can, but we will fix that in a moment.

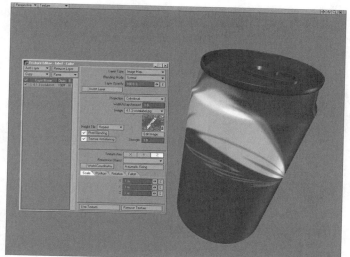

Figure 15-42

5. Go to where it says Texture Axis and select Y by clicking on that button. This now projects the image down the length of the object (its y-axis) in a cylindrical fashion.

6. Now just click on the Automatic Sizing button, and hey, presto! The image fits perfectly onto the soda can as it should. That looks much better.

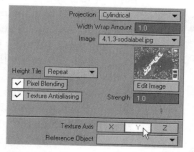

Figure 15-43

Figure 15-44

You now have a cool-looking soda can that you can do with as you wish.

Figure 15-45

# Spherical Projection

## Using Spherical Projections

As its name suggests, this mapping projection type is for objects that are more or less spherically shaped, or even perfect spheres (of course!). So when it comes to mapping planets, balls, and sometimes also certain kinds of heads, this is the projection to use.

The way it basically works is almost identical to the way that cylindrical mapping works, except that it wraps from both poles (the top and bottom points of the model), creating a single seam along the axis of the model. This means that the image you are using will meet up not only along the seam but also at both poles.

The one thing that sometimes makes this projection type a little tricky to work with is the way in which textures applied shrink toward the poles on the objects. Naturally, you can always work around this to compensate for it, but it can be a little annoying at times.

Figure 15-46 demonstrates this shrinking that occurs toward the poles of the object.

Figure 15-46

Image Used

You compensate for this effect by altering the image, stretching the top and bottom parts of the texture to compensate for their shrinkage once applied. Of course this sort of alteration might not always be entirely necessary, as you may find that when working with textures for things like planets, this shrinking may not actually be all that noticeable, as shown in Figure 15-47, which uses a totally unaltered rectangular map of the world as a texture.

Figure 15-47

## Applying an Image with Spherical Projection

To wrap an image spherically around an object, simply select the Spherical option from the Projection list in the Texture Editor.

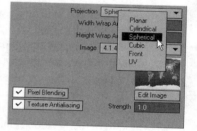

You then select an appropriate axis along which you wish to project the image. Most spherical mapping situations use the y-axis.

Figure 15-48

Figure 15-49

You'll notice that we also have options called Width Wrap Amount and Height Wrap Amount when using spherical projections. Like the Width Wrap Amount for cylindrical projections, here this value simply determines the number of times that the image is repeated as it is wrapped around the width of the model. The Height Wrap Amount value determines the number of times that the image is repeated along the length of the object (as opposed to its breadth). These values basically work as tiling options for this type of projection.

If we change each of these values to 4.0 using our world image, the way in which these values work is clearly illustrated. In Figure 15-50 you can see that the image is repeated four times around the width and four times along the height of the sphere. For most situations, you'll find that the value of 1.0 is most appropriate.

**387**

Figure 15-50

## Ensuring Seamless Mapping

As with the cylindrical projections that we looked at in the previous section, spherical projections also have the risk of visible seams on the axis along which we have projected the image.

This means that generally we should always try to ensure that the edges of the image will meet seamlessly.

Refer back to the previous section on cylindrical mapping and review the technique of using Adobe Photoshop's Offset filter for correcting this.

Figure 15-51

However, when dealing with spherical mapping, not only do we have to watch for seams along one side of the object, we also have to be aware of how the image looks when it meets up at the poles.

## Using Adobe Photoshop's Polar Coordinates Filter to Check Seams

A quick and easy way of checking to see how the image will look when applied spherically is to use Photoshop's Polar Coordinates filter.

This filter is found under the Distort filters in Photoshop. Use it only to *check* your image, as leaving the filter applied to the image will mess up the image, making it no longer useful for our purposes.

Basically what you do is open the filter's panel and ensure that the Rectangular to Polar option is selected. The little preview window will show you a decent representation of how the image will more or less behave when wrapped spherically around your model in LightWave.

You can use this to ensure that the image is seamless at the poles. In Figure 15-52, we can see that the Earth image has

Figure 15-52

no problems as the two poles (the two polar regions) meet up with no visible seams.

On the other hand, if we take a look at an image that has visible seams in it, these seams will show up when looking at the preview pane in the filter's panel.

Figure 15-53

As you can see, the seam is clearly visible. Using this as a guide to check our progress, we can then use the Offset filter technique and lots of Clone Stamping and Healing Brush work to eliminate the seam.

## Spherical Mapping Tutorial: Applying a Texture to a Planet

What better way to demonstrate the use of spherical mapping than to do a tutorial on planet texturing?

1. Load the 4.1.4-planet_tutorial.lws scene from the companion CD. You should see a scene that has a planet object consisting of two layers: planet surface and planet atmosphere. See Figure 15-54 on the following page.

2. Open the Surface Editor (Ctrl+F3), and go to planet surface. Click on the little "T" button to open its Texture Editor, and set up the default texture layer as follows: Load the 4.1.4-planet_color.jpg image from the CD and select Spherical as its projection type. Select Y as the axis, and set its Scale settings to 1.9m for each axis. Leave the Width Wrap Amount and Height Map Amount at 1.0 each. Your Texture Editor window should look like Figure 15-55.

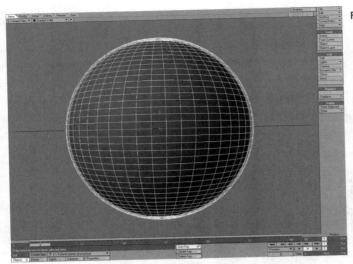

**Figure 15-54**

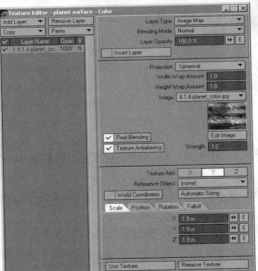

**Figure 15-55**

3. We want to add a little luminosity to the planet just to give its lit side a little more definition. Go back to the Surface Editor and open the planet surface's Luminosity Texture Editor. Set up the default layer that is created as a gradient using Light Incidence as its Input Parameter. Select the light in the scene as the light that will affect the gradient.

4. Now let's create some keys in the gradient so that we get the right look on the planet surface. Select the key that is automatically created at the top of the gradient, and change its Value to 0%. This ensures that areas that are facing away from the light will not appear luminous. Create a key at the very bottom of the gradient (make sure that the key is directly on

90.0 in the Parameter field), and change its Value to 150%. This makes the area of the planet that the light is hitting very luminous. We want the change to only happen on the very edge of the planet though, instead of a smooth transition from the nonluminous area to the luminous one, so let's create a final key to do this. Create a key at 85.0° (check the Parameter field to ensure this) and change its Value setting to 90%. See Figure 15-56.

This gradient has now created a luminous strip along the edge of the planet that faces toward the light in the scene. It basically serves to fake the effect of extreme brightness caused by a sun on a planet as seen in space.

5. Go back to the Surface Editor and change the Diffuse setting to 40% and the Specularity setting to 5%. Leave the other settings as they are.

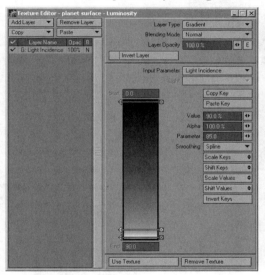

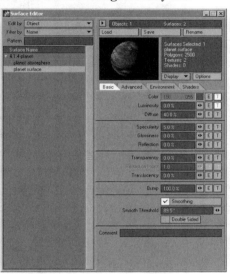

Figure 15-56                                    Figure 15-57

6. Let's set up the planet atmosphere surface. We'll use this part of the object to simulate an active atmosphere for the planet with the help of a few gradients.

Set up the surface's color as 200, 120, 60. This creates a nice orange color.

7. Open the surface's Transparency Texture Editor, change Layer Type to Gradient, and select Incidence Angle as its Input Parameter. This is because we want the atmosphere to appear transparent on top of the actual planet surface, and only have it visible along the edges in space.

8. Leave the key at the top of the gradient as it is, and make a new key at the bottom, at 90.0°. Leave this key's settings as they are as well. Now make a key in the middle of the gradient (make sure the Parameter setting for this key is 45.0) and leave its settings as they are too. Finally, create a key in between the one you just made and the top key. Make sure that its Parameter setting is 20.0 and change its Value to 50%.

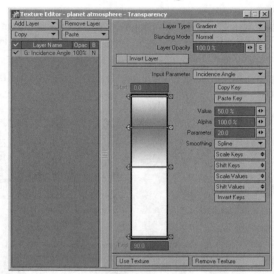

Figure 15-58

We have now created a basic atmosphere that gives the impression of a halo around the planet. To give it a little more life, we'll quickly give it a touch of luminosity to make it a little stronger.

9. Copy the layer you just created in the Transparency Texture Editor by clicking on the Copy button and choosing Selected Layer(s).

Figure 15-59

10. Now go to your Luminosity Texture Editor and replace the default layer with the copied one by clicking on Paste and selecting Replace Selected Layer(s).

11. Essentially, the luminous aspect of the atmosphere now has the same position and falloff as its transparency, so now the entire atmosphere is glowing. The glow is a little too weak though, so invert the keys on the gradient by clicking on Invert Keys at the bottom of your gradient option to switch the effect over. The glow is now a little stronger along the edge of the planet.

Figure 15-60

We don't want the entire rim of the planet glowing, since part of it is unlit by its local sun. Let's make sure that the glow only appears on the illuminated face of the planet by masking this gradient layer we just created in the Luminosity channel.

12. Create a new Gradient layer above the previously made one, select Light Incidence as its Input Parameter, and choose the light in the scene from the Light list. Select the key at the top of the gradient ramp and set its Value to 0%.

13. Now create another key at the bottom of the gradient and change its Value to 100%. Change the Blending Mode of the layer to Alpha.

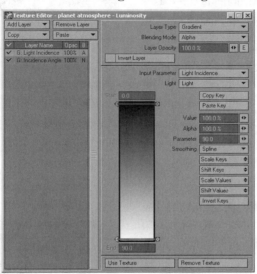

Figure 15-61

This now makes the gradient below this layer visible only where the light is illuminating the planet.

Render your scene; it should look like the following figure.

Figure 15-62

**393**

# Cubic Projection

## Using Cubic Projections

A cubic projection is really simple. It is basically the same as planar projection, except it does not require an axis. Instead, it takes the image map and simultaneously projects it along all three axes.

This means that you end up with the same image projected along all three axes of the model to which the surface is applied, as shown in Figure 15-63.

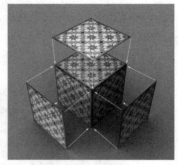

This projection method is particularly useful for tiling images on structures like buildings, especially if you ensure that your images are seamless. Of course, the drawback to using this particular method is that tiled textures can look a little monotonous, and if the repeating texture is very obvious, this can look quite bad.

Figure 15-63

To help break up the monotony somewhat, try using a procedural layer on top of the images with some kind of blending applied to it, so that it adds an element of randomness to the texture.

Figure 15-64 shows a Turbulence procedural applied to the surface on top of the cubic mapped image. The Turbulence adds a nice dirty look to it that breaks up the repeating pattern somewhat, and makes the overall surface more interesting.

Of course, this is a rather extreme example. You wouldn't necessarily have to make it look so dirty! Using different blending modes (discussed in greater depth in Chapter 13), you can create a number of different blending effects.

Figure 15-64

I generally tend to use cubic projection on background elements that are never really seen in any detail and that I just don't have the time or inclination to paint textures for. Basically, it's the quick fix projection type.

# Front Projection

## Using Front Projections

Front projection is an essential part of your compositing work. It will aid you in the process of matching your CG objects to background plates. The concept behind front projection is simple: You essentially replace the selected surface with your background plate image or sequence, which is usually the same one as in the Compositing tab in the Effects panel (Ctrl+F7).

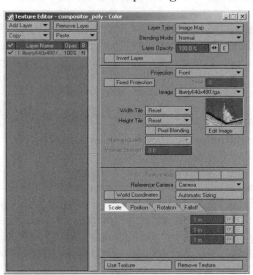

Figure 15-65:
Front Projection
texture

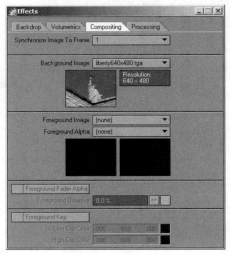

Figure 15-66:
Effects
Compositing tab

Front projection doesn't "stick" the texture to the object unless Fixed Projection is on, but we'll talk more about that in a bit. You can move, rotate, scale, and deform your object, and the texture will always face the selected camera; hence its name. The way this works is by "pin-registering" the surface image to the background, giving the impression that the CG objects in the scene are interacting with the background plate. By matching a piece of geometry to a piece of your background plate, you can create accurate shadows and reflections cast by your CG objects. You can also occlude CG objects with portions of the plate to create, for example, a UFO hovering behind a building.

It is important to note that the texture transformation options (Scale, Position, Rotation, and Falloff) are unavailable with front projection since the texture is tied to the selected camera specified in the Reference Camera pull-down menu in the Front Projection Texture options. What is more relevant to front projection is the image resolution and pixel aspect ratio. Front projection images are always the size and pixel aspect ratio as if the image were loaded as the background image, so changing the resolution and pixel aspect ratio of the camera in the Camera Properties panel ("p") will also affect the front projection. It is best to match the camera resolution to that of the background plate used in front projection to ensure a perfect match.

Speaking of match… matching or aligning geometry to be used for the front projection is probably the most challenging part. You need to ensure that the geometry that has the front projected surface matches as closely as possible the background plate; otherwise, you might lose the effect.

Also keep in mind that you don't want any kind of shading on your front projected objects. To correct this, set the surface Diffuse value to 0% and Luminosity to 100%. You may need to change other values for the surface, depending on what you are trying to achieve.

In the Texture Editor, when using front projection, you will see a check box to turn on or off an option called Fixed Projection. What this does is "stick" the projection of the camera. It is best to keep camera motions subtle since you can go only so far using 2D images in a 3D camera move. When you activate Fixed Projection, the Time options become active. Here you can enter a frame or time where you want the texture to be pin-registered to the background (front projected); for the rest of the frames the texture will be Fixed Projected. Figure 15-67 shows Lady Liberty getting a visit from some friends.

Figure 15-67

# CHAPTER 16

# UV Mapping and Editing

## Preparing Your Model and Creating UV Maps

### Introduction to UV Mapping

And now we move on to UV mapping. If there were such a thing as a Holy Grail of texturing that was greatly sought after by artists, then UV mapping would probably be it. The fact is that all too often there seems to be this shroud of mystery surrounding the use of UV mapping, which makes it appear as a scary, difficult process that requires some kind of genius to master.

The truth is that UV mapping is actually very simple. However, it is an occasionally painful process that can, more often than not, take ages to complete. This is not because it is a very complicated process, but simply because of the nature of editing the actual maps, which is a pretty tedious and usually rather lengthy process.

However, do not despair at the thought of such tedium. Once you understand how the process works, it can actually be strangely enjoyable, as it is a refreshing break from the often mind-bending techniques involved in other areas of the 3D creation process. I always feel a tremendous sense of satisfaction when looking at the results of hours of tweaking a UV map and seeing that it is perfect!

Let's begin to work our way through this shroud of awe and wonder that surrounds the subject.

UV mapping is, in essence, simply a way of converting the topographical information of your model into a flat 2D layout that is then used as a template for painting textures. UV mapping is just another method of placing textures onto your models, except that in this case, a little more work is required in Modeler.

The U and V refer to coordinates in 2D space, just as the letters X, Y, and Z refer to coordinates in the 3D space that you are used to working with when modeling. Basically, you could say that when you flatten X, Y, and Z, you get U and V. So they are not letters that refer to some secret code that could unlock some deep mystery; they are just simple coordinates. The u-axis is the horizontal one, and the v-axis is vertical.

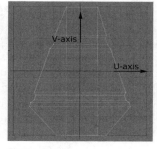

Any point within the UV map has both U and V values that you can adjust using the UV tools within Modeler.

You make a UV map by selecting the model you wish to unwrap, or a section of it, and click-

Figure 16-1

ing on the New UV Map button under the Texture section on the Map tab in Modeler. When creating a UV map, you are presented with a number of options, discussed later in this chapter.

> **NOTE:** You cannot make or edit UV maps in Layout. All mapping tools are found in Modeler.

## The UV Editor

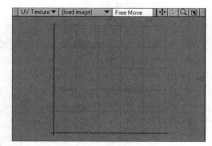

Before we begin unwrapping and editing UV maps, let's take a look at the LightWave Modeler UV Texture Editor.

Each Modeler viewport has three buttons at the top-left corner, two of which are drop-down menus with several view mode options. To open the UV Texture Editor, all you have to do

Figure 16-2

is select the UV Texture option under the viewport's first drop-down menu, the same one you use to select the many different view modes for that particular viewport.

In the second drop-down menu, you can select a background image currently loaded in the Image Editor. If you don't have any images loaded, you have the option to load one from disk. I usually start with a generic checkerboard grid to edit my UV layout, constantly checking it for correct placement, overlapping, and distortion.

The next button is the Free Move button. This handy option allows you to detach the currently selected faces from the laid out mesh and move them to a different location in the UV space, like an instant unweld operation! This is extremely useful since it will decrease the amount of unwelding you do during the UV creation process. I'll discuss the Free Move option in depth in Chapter 17 in the "Understanding Discontinuous UV Maps" section.

**399**

In the UV Texture viewport you'll see a UV grid. This is where you will lay out your, well, you guessed it, UVs! It is recommended (especially for organic models) that you keep your layout inside this grid; any parts of your UV layout falling outside of this grid will have the texture tiled. Tiling UVs are more often used in hard models, such as an asphalt road or a concrete wall. Keep in mind that your texture has to be seamless; otherwise, you'll find seams when the texture tiles over your object. (This might be obvious to some, but I thought I should mention it for those who are new to LightWave and texture mapping in general.)

> **NOTE:** The Free Move function has been available in LightWave since version 8.2.

## Planning Your UV Maps

One of the most important things about using UV maps is that you need to plan them properly. If you have ever tried to unwrap an entire character model (as many people often try to do) and seen the resulting chaos that appears in the UV map viewport, you will know that there is a certain trick to getting a decent result from the command.

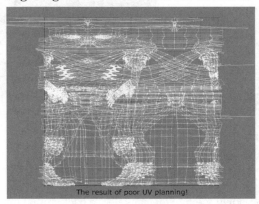

The result of poor UV planning!

**Figure 16-3**

The trick lies in planning where and how you will unwrap the model. Obviously, some types of UV maps are better suited to certain shapes than others. You have to figure out which ones are suited to your needs, and execute them as such.

In most cases, a number of UV maps are required for any object that is more complex than a box. That is because even though UV mapping does flatten things out into a nice template that you can do whatever you want with, you still have to start with logical shapes.

For example, if you are unwrapping a human character, you cannot simply unwrap the entire model. You have to plan where to create the different UV maps, depending on the shapes found in the model. In this instance, it would be most efficient to unwrap the head, torso, arms, legs, hands, and feet separately, using unwrap projections most suited to the rough shape of the part.

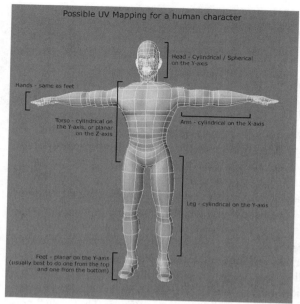

Figure 16-4

Sure, this is quite a lot of work, but it is more efficient in the long run because editing an unwrapped map of an entire character would give endless problems. Planning your unwraps logically is therefore the best option. If a part of a model is more or less cylindrically shaped, then unwrap it cylindrically, whereas if another part is flat and more suited to planar unwrapping, then do that section with a planar unwrap. Simple.

All you need to do is take a good look at your model and divide it up into logical sections to unwrap, based on their shapes.

Another thing to consider is whether UV mapping is really necessary. In many texturing cases, the standard projection techniques discussed earlier will suffice, so why use UV mapping?

One of the interesting things about UV mapping is that technically it isn't as accurate as the standard projection methods. Whereas the standard methods simply project the image straight onto the model without any regard to the actual polygon structure, and more importantly, the actual positions of vertices within the model, UV mapping uses the vertices in the model to place the map. Basically, the vertices are used like pins to attach the map to the model. Because of this, the areas between these points are interpolated, which, in basic terms, is an estimation. So the map is only technically accurate at the points, while the rest of the map is positioned as an estimation of where they should be, in relation to the positions of the points. A well-edited map will place the image nicely onto the model, but it will still not be as technically accurate as a normal planar projection, or any other kind of standard projection.

However, since standard projections are almost impossible to use when texturing very unevenly shaped objects, such as most organic objects, UV mapping is the best option.

It is important to only begin unwrapping when your model is complete. Making changes to a model after you have unwrapped it can often result in a lot more editing having to be done, and sometimes also requires changes to any texture maps you may have already made. It is extremely annoying to have to go back and re-edit parts of your map and parts of your actual textures, so be sure that you are 100% happy with your model before unwrapping and texturing.

## Tips for Better UV Maps

### To Freeze, Or Not to Freeze?

Bearing in mind what we have discussed regarding the manner in which the points within a UV map pin the texture to the model, it is only logical that the more points a model has, the more accurate the map is. This leads to a dilemma. Sure, you can increase the density of the mesh very easily, either by freezing it or by subdividing it further before unwrapping it, but do you really want to do that? We all know that it is good practice to keep the polygon count of a model as low as possible, even when working with high-resolution models, since, among other advantages, it keeps render times down and is easier to animate. However, if the model has a higher poly count, the UV map will be technically more accurate.

The thing to consider here is that a UV map of a dense mesh is a real pain to edit. Since it is almost impossible to use a UV map that has had no editing whatsoever (for the simple reason that it is highly unlikely that your initial unwrapping effort will be perfect), you have to remember that editing a UV map with a lot of polys is going to be a lot of work and, frankly, a bit more of a pain than is really necessary. Most UV maps need pretty extensive editing, and moving large chunks containing lots of polys around in your UV map is going to be really cumbersome and irritating, especially when you have to do it point by point, which is most often the case.

So you need to consider if it is really worth the effort. In my experience, I have never increased the poly count of a model simply for the sake of UV mapping, and I have never really felt that the resulting UV map was not accurate enough once I had edited it. So it is really up to you to decide on this one.

### Multiple UV Maps in a Single Surface

Another problem encountered by many artists is the problem of using multiple UV maps on one surface. Using more than one UV map on a surface often results in oddities when rendering, and often also results in some of the maps not appearing to work at all. Although there are ways to fix this problem, I find that the easiest solution is simply to assign each UV map to a separate surface, if that is possible. While this method does indeed have drawbacks, such as the slight confusion of having so many surfaces applied to a model, it is sometimes nicer not to have to bother with covering up the problems of using multiple maps.

Another advantage of using separate surfaces is that, practically, it is easier to divide a model up into sections for mapping by initially assigning separate surfaces to each section that is to be unwrapped. This makes it easier to keep track of which part is which, especially if you assign a different color to each surface. Simple, yet effective.

## Initial Placement of Seams

Choosing the correct center point for your unwrap is also important. If you have to unwrap a head, for example, the best way of unwrapping it would be to have the center of the UV map in the center of the model as well, so that the model is unwrapped from the center of the back to the front. Unwrapping the model in this fashion will ensure that the main seam for the map will run along the back of the head. A trick for doing this is to place your cursor at 0 (in the center, basically), rotate the model 90°, then unwrap it and rotate it back into position. This guarantees, in most cases, a seam that runs along the back of the model.

Figure 16-5 shows a head that has been unwrapped while facing forward. Notice the way that the seam is placed down the side of the face, just behind the left ear.

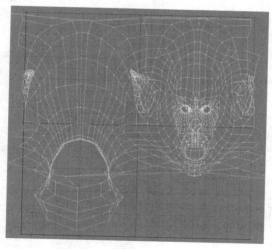

Figure 16-5

Now take a look at Figure 16-6. Here, I rotated the head –90° and unwrapped it. This resulted in the seam being placed down the back of the head, which is preferable since it is easier to conceal this seam when painting textures. This also makes the neck area easier to texture, since it is no longer separated from the lower jaw area, as in the previous example.

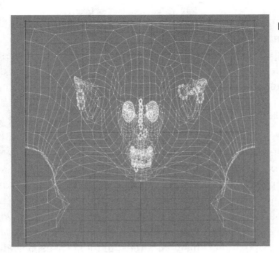

Figure 16-6

## Using Parts

Another little something that makes the whole process a bit easier is to break your model up into parts. This makes for easier selections when unwrapping. I mentioned earlier that it is easy to keep track of your different sections by applying different surfaces to them, but another way is to select the polys that you wish to unwrap and assign a part name to them for easy selection at a later stage.

To group polygons into a part, you simply select them, go to the Display tab, click on the Grouping button, and select Change Part Name. By giving the selection a name, you can then easily select it again from your Polygon Statistics window (which you open by pressing "w") by clicking on the Part button and selecting the part you want.

Little things like this just make the whole process easier.

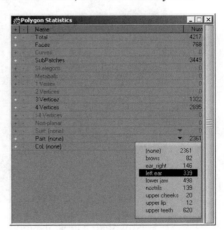

Figure 16-7

## UVs and Subdivision Surfaces

Something that a lot of people complained about — and has been fixed — is the distortion that happened when unwrapping sub-d models. Now it really doesn't matter if you unwrap your models with subdivision on or off since NewTek has added a feature called Subpatch Interpolation. UV maps used to get interpolated linearly even if the mesh was subpatched, which caused distortion of the textures. Now you have a total of five different UV interpolation options that will help get rid of the distortion problem once and for all.

Take a look at Figures 16-8 and 16-9. The first head was unwrapped with Linear interpolation, while the second is using Subpatch UV interpolation. Notice that the distortion is completely gone with Subpatch UV interpolation.

Figure 16-8: Linear interpolation      Figure 16-9: Subpatch UV interpolation

See "Fixing the Annoying Subdivision Distortion Problem — Interpolation Options" in Chapter 17 for more information on this wonderful new feature.

## Don't Panic!

Yes, UV mapping can seem very daunting at first, but do not worry — once you are comfortable with the whole process, you will realize that it is actually really not so big a deal. All in all, UV mapping is something that, once you have done it quite a lot, becomes extremely simple. You should find that you begin to develop your own habits and ways of doing things that make the process much simpler for yourself. Later on we explore all the tools that are used in the process, and many of them can have a number of interesting uses other than what they are specifically for.

Now that we are comfortable with the concepts of UV mapping, let's move on to the actual types of UV mapping and start doing some unwrapping!

# Planar UV Maps

## Using Planar Maps

Planar UV mapping, much like its standard projection counterpart, is probably the simplest method of unwrapping. This is because it is generally quite predictable, in the sense that you know more or less what the resulting map will look like and what sort of editing it will require.

As a general rule, anything can be planar unwrapped. Although some maps might need a lot more editing than others, depending on their shape, planar unwrapping can often be the most efficient way of unwrapping objects. If you have the patience to edit it, you could even unwrap objects like heads or torsos or even limbs in a planar fashion, even though these sorts of objects are generally not flat in shape, which is what a planar solution is usually used for. This is the beauty of UV maps, that they can be edited, unlike standard projections that have problems of stretching along uneven topography, as in the case of the standard planar projections that we explored earlier.

Since we already have an understanding of how planar mapping essentially works (provided you have read the previous section of this chapter), learning how to make planar UV maps is pretty simple.

Basically what planar unwrapping does is it looks at the model along the axis that you specify and simply gives you a nice big flattened version of it along that axis. Of course this means lots of overlapping polygons in most cases (well, in any case that isn't simply a one-sided box or something equally simple), but as mentioned before these can be fixed through editing.

As I mentioned at the start, practically anything can be unwrapped in a planar fashion, but of course this method is more suited to objects that are more or less flattish and lie predominantly along a single axis. So objects like swords, hands, books, walls, and the like are prime candidates for planar unwrapping.

Remember that because you can assemble a number of different UV unwraps into a single UV map, things like buildings work well using planar unwraps because you can unwrap each wall individually along its axis and assemble all the walls into a single UV map. This eliminates the need for loads of standard projections or boring repeating textures since you can then create the textures for each wall in one big image that is far more practical and convenient. (The Atlas unwrapping type that we look at a little later on is also useful for simple architectural unwrapping like this.)

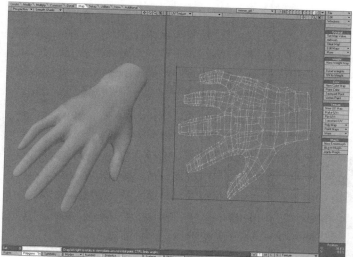

**Figure 16-10**

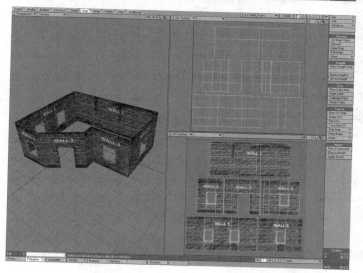

**Figure 16-11**

The example shown in Figure 16-11 was laid out in a matter of minutes by simply unwrapping each wall individually along its own axis and adding it to the UV map. Having each wall separate on a template then gives you the ability to easily paint individual textures for each wall without the hassle of using loads of different layers projected from different directions within the Texture Editor. This is a classic example of why UV mapping can be a convenient solution for texturing, even for relatively simple objects like buildings.

## Planar UV Map Tutorial: Unwrapping a Sword

Let's explore the process of creating a simple planar unwrap of a model, the object in this case being a sword.

1.  Open Modeler and load the 4.2.2-sword.lwo object from the companion CD. A relatively simple sword model should now be showing in your viewports. As you can see, the model faces along the z-axis in Modeler and is fairly flat. This makes it an ideal candidate for planar UV projections.

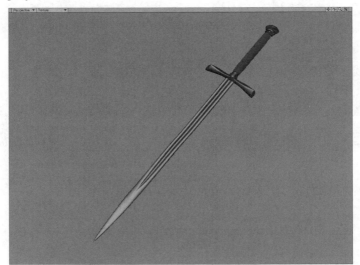

Figure 16-12

2.  Make sure that one of your models is showing the UV map template. To do this, simply click on the viewport view type at the top-left corner of any viewport, and select UV Texture. This is important because once we make our UV map, we can manipulate and edit the map itself within this particular viewport.

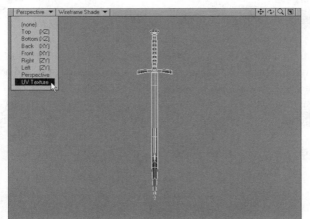

Figure 16-13

3.  Select the polygons of the entire model. Go to the Map tab and under the Texture heading, select New UV Map. A new window pops up with a bunch of options for you to choose from, including what type of UV projection you would like, a field to enter in a name for the UV map, and some options for manually setting up the position of the map itself. By default this window is set to create a planar map, so all we need to do is enter in an appropriate name (just use "sword") and make sure that the projection axis is set to the z-axis. Leave the other settings as they are, and click OK.

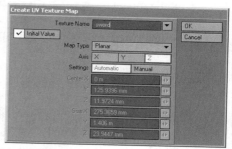

Figure 16-14

You might get a fright now when you see the projection appear in the viewport as it will appear squashed. Don't worry — this is perfectly normal, and is easy to fix.

> **NOTE:** When editing UV maps, it is very important to make sure that your mouse is within the UV Texture viewport only. Doing this will ensure that your changes will only be applied to the UV map, and not to the model itself. Anything that you do to the points and polygons within the UV Texture viewport will apply to the UV map *only*.

4.  Now, while the polygons are still selected, select the Stretch tool (press "h") and, ensuring that your mouse cursor is hovering within the UV Texture viewport, stretch the sword UV map until its dimensions more or less match those of the model itself. This is an adjustment that is approximately 20% horizontal and 120% vertical scale. Now select the Size tool (press Shift+h), and scale down the UV map so that it fits inside the square template within the UV Texture viewport.

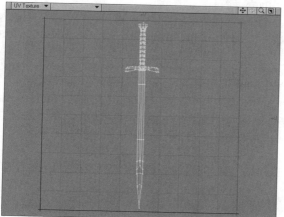

Figure 16-15

We are left with one slight problem. Since we have unwrapped the object straight along the z-axis that the model lies along, parts of the model are now overlapping in the UV map. Essentially what we have is both sides of the model being treated as a single projection within the UV map. So if we were to now paint a texture onto this UV map the way it is, both sides would look the same since the image would be projected straight through the front and back of the sword. So how can we fix this? Well, this is where the editable nature of UV maps really shines.

Before we do any editing, it's always best to unweld all the points in your model. This is simply to prevent slight oddities that can occasionally occur within UV maps. As you can see, the sword is perfectly symmetrical, both on the x-axis and the z-axis.

5. Go into your Right viewport and select all the polygons on the right-hand side of the center line to select the "back" side of the sword.

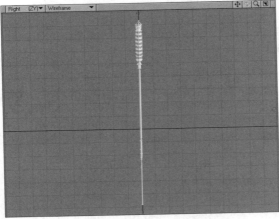

Figure 16-16

If you now hover your cursor over the UV Texture viewport and drag your mouse to the left, you'll see the entire back side of the sword move over the left side of the UV map, leaving the front side on the right, as shown in Figure 16-17.

This now means that because of the way in which the UV map is laid out, we can paint a different texture onto the front and the back of the sword because they are separate in the UV map, instead of overlapping one another. Don't forget to hit "m" again to remerge all the points in the model that we unwelded!

This sword is now ready for some texturing, so go ahead and paint a nice texture for it. If you are not sure how to go about creating metal textures, then take a look at the tutorials in Part 7 for some tips!

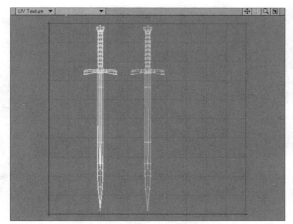

Figure 16-17

## Cylindrical and Spherical UV Maps

### Using Cylindrical and Spherical UV Maps

Cylindrical UV mapping is pretty much identical to its standard mapping counterpart of the same name. Just like we saw with standard cylindrical projections, the cylindrical UV mapping type splits the model along a seam that runs along a defined axis and spreads the rest of the model out from that point in a cylindrical fashion.

I use this type of mapping almost as often as planar mapping, since it is actually very versatile and highly suited to many organic shapes, especially in characters' heads, arms, hands, and even torsos.

Spherical UV mapping, in practice, works in very much the same fashion as cylindrical mapping, which is why I am covering these two UV types in the same section. I have to admit, though, that I have actually never used a spherical UV projection, simply because cylindrical UV mapping always does the trick. Let's face it — how often do you actually have to UV map a round object? A piece of fruit? A planet? A ball? All these can be done with standard spherical projections, and generally wouldn't actually require UV mapping.

Let's take a look at the same model unwrapped using the default settings of cylindrical mapping (on the left) and spherical mapping (on the right). See Figure 16-18.

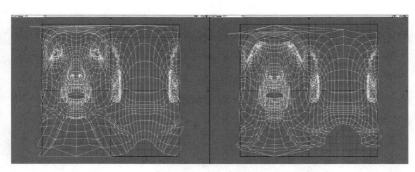

Figure 16-18

As you can see, they are almost identical. The main area of difference is toward the poles, where the spherical map has a more pronounced distortion.

## Placing the Initial Seam

Probably the most common use of the cylindrical projection is in unwrapping human heads. Most people model heads facing forward on the z-axis, and find that upon unwrapping the head, the seam (created by the manner in which cylindrical unwrapping works by splitting the model along the axis) is placed down the side of the face, usually just in front of one of the ears.

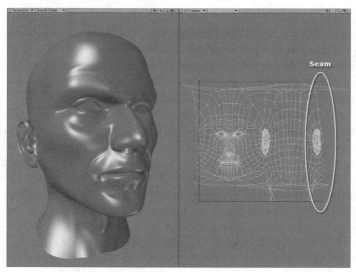

Figure 16-19

While we can obviously easily reposition this seam by moving the polygons in the UV map viewport, it can save a bit of hassle to place the seam in a more appropriate place initially.

The easiest way to do this is to rotate the object before unwrapping it.

Simply select your model, hit "y" to activate the Rotate tool, and then hit "n" to open its numeric control panel. It is better to do this operation with the numeric panel instead of rotating manually in the viewports because you have more precision this way and won't risk changing the position of the model, which can happen when you rotate things by hand.

If your head is facing forward on the z-axis, enter a value of −90.0° along the y-axis.

Hit the Apply button, then unwrap the model cylindrically on the y-axis. Then go back to your Rotate numeric panel, and rotate the model back 90.0° on the y-axis and apply the transformation.

The seam is then placed along the back of the head, a far more convenient place for it to be, since it will likely be covered with hair.

Figure 16-20

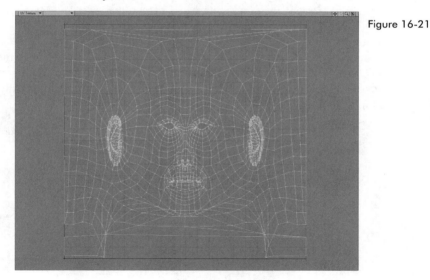

Figure 16-21

## Cylindrical Map Tutorial: Unwrapping a Human Head

I thought it would be nice to do a fairly advanced UV mapping tutorial for this chapter, and since cylindrical mapping is so useful for human heads, let's unwrap one of those.

1. Open the 4.2.3-head.lwo model from the companion CD in Modeler. This is a slightly Oriental male head, and I should mention that the ears were modeled by the fantastic South African LightWave artist Werner Ziemerink.

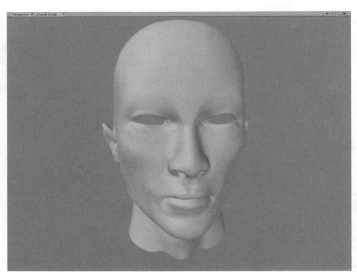

Figure 16-22

2.  Rotate the head using the method described previously, using the numeric panel to rotate it –90.0° along the y-axis. Go to the Map tab and click on New UV Map. When the Create UV Texture Map panel pops up, give it a logical name like "Head" and select to unwrap cylindrically along the y-axis.

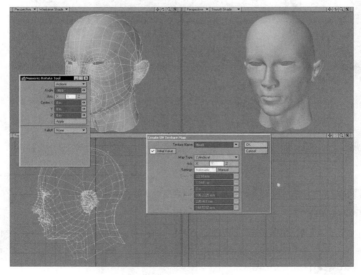

Figure 16-23

Rotate the head back 90.0° on the y-axis before continuing.

3. Now it's time to edit. Go to your Display options (hit "d") and change the Layout to Double Vertical.

4. Set up your two viewports so that one of them is a Perspective viewport that is set to Texture shading (top left of the viewport) and have the other viewport set to UV Texture.

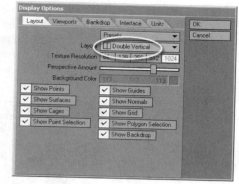

**Figure 16-24**

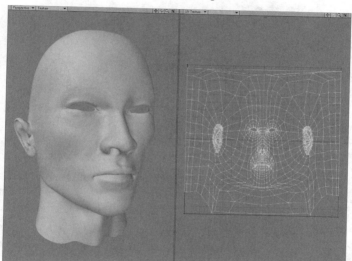

**Figure 16-25**

5. Open the Image Editor (Ctrl+F4) and load the _uv_checker.jpg image into Modeler. This loads a fairly large square image with a red and white checkerboard pattern.

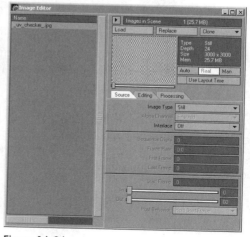

Figure 16-26

**415**

6. Open the Surface Editor, go to the Skin surface, and open up the Color Texture Editor by clicking on the "T" button next to Color. Using the default layer that is created, change the Projection to UV, select the UV map you created for the head from the UV Map list, and select the _uv_checker.jpg image as the image. You'll now see the image applied to the model in your Perspective viewport.

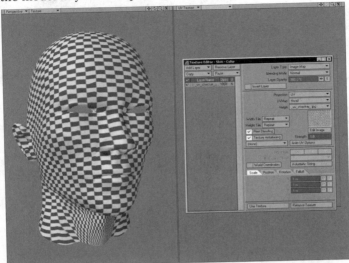

Figure 16-27

Looking now at the texture applied to the head in the viewport, we can immediately see where we need to adjust the vertices in the UV map to eliminate the stretching. (See Chapter 17 for more information about stretching and squashing in UV maps.)

7. Let's start with the neck area first. As you can see, the checkerboard image is becoming squashed here, which means that the polygons for this area in the UV map are too large — hence they are allowing too much of the checkerboard image into that area.

So we need to move the points for this area inward to fix this problem. Go to your UV viewport, select the points immediately surrounding the middle points in the neck area, and move them inward so that they look like those in Figure 16-28.

Notice how this affects the texture applied to the model. The aim of editing this UV map lies essentially in getting the checkerboard as distortion-free as possible through adjusting the vertices. What it really comes down to is that you need to get the shape and size of the polygons in the UV map to proportionally match those in the model itself.

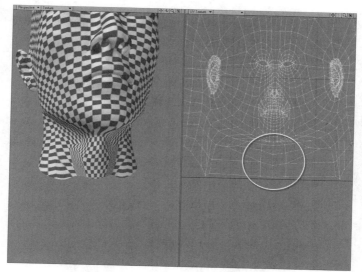

Figure 16-28

8. Let's look now at the underside of the chin. Rotate your Perspective viewport, and you'll see that the image has become very stretched under the chin.

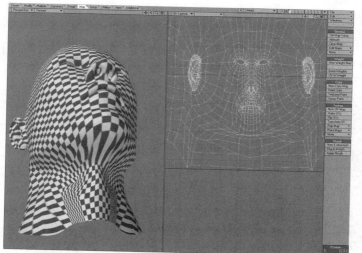

Figure 16-29

When we look at this area in the UV map, it becomes obvious why this stretching is occurring. The polygons that form this part of the model have become totally squashed in the UV map, as shown in Figure 16-30.

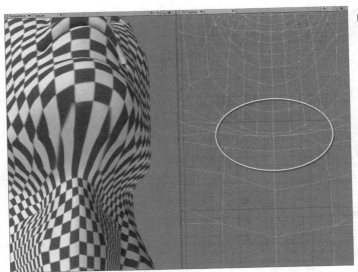

Figure 16-30

9.   So what we need to do is pull these polygons downward to fix this area.
     Figure 16-31 shows how I have edited the area so that the image has
     become less stretched. It's not always possible to totally eliminate
     stretching and squashing, but we should always try to eliminate it as
     much as we possibly can. I have drawn over the polygons in the image to
     make the editing a bit more obvious. Notice that I have also made some
     adjustments slightly lower down to reduce some of the previous distor-
     tion in the neck area.

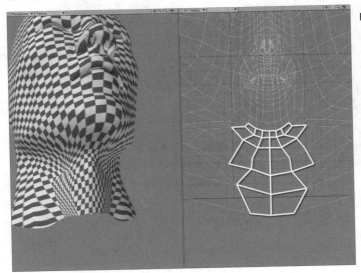

Figure 16-31

10. A little more tweaking, and the entire front of the neck area begins to look correct. This involved not only shifting and arranging the vertices inward, but also selecting the polygons in the UV map themselves and actually using the Stretch tool to stretch them inward.

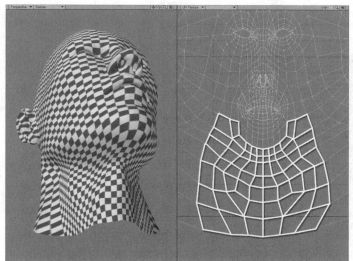

Figure 16-32

This editing has now caused areas on the side of the neck to become squashed. This is simply because I have been shifting things inward, and the polygons on the neck that now look squashed in the Texture viewport look like that because they have become too large in the UV map, thereby causing too much of the image to become squashed into that area.

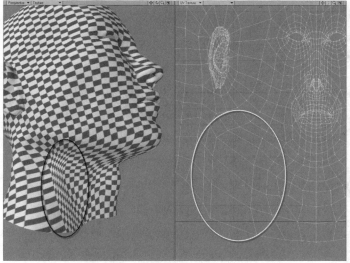

Figure 16-33

11. All we need to do to fix this is obviously continue to move the vertices in this area inward so that the polygon in the UV map is no longer so stretched. You'll find that as you edit certain areas, you'll also need to readjust areas directly surrounding them to allow everything to shift smoothly into place. Remember, don't panic if you cannot get the checkerboard 100% perfect on the model; you just need to remove the major stretching and squashing.

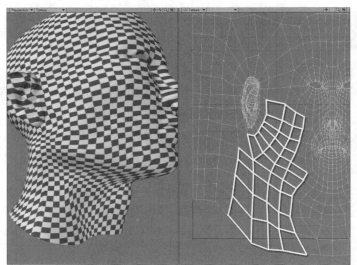

**Figure 16-34**

12. Zoom in on the parts of the texture where it has little wiggly distortions in it, as shown in Figure 16-35.

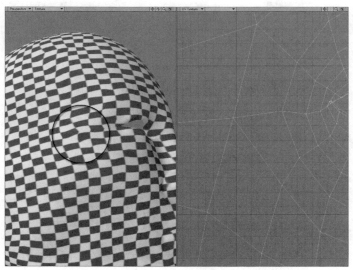

**Figure 16-35**

These distortions are caused by the subdivision of the model and cannot actually be perfectly fixed, since they are an artifact of LightWave's subdivision algorithm. So don't worry about them too much.

13. If we zoom out of the model now and take a look at the entire thing, it becomes obvious that the whole map is a little too stretched along the y-axis. In the UV map, this is the v-axis, and we need to scale the map down along this axis to fix this.

    However, because of the nature of discontinuous UV maps in LightWave, we need to unweld the points in the model before scaling them; otherwise, parts of the model are going to remain stuck in place.

14. Press Ctrl+u to unweld all your points. The model will look a bit odd in your viewport if you were displaying your model in Subpatch mode (Tab), so generally I just press Tab again to go to normal Polygon display mode.

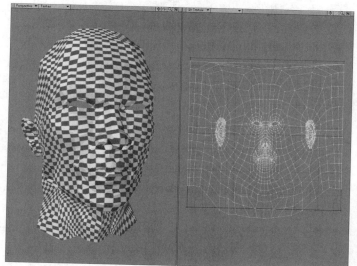

Figure 16-36

15. Now go to your UV viewport, select all the polygons, and press the "h" key to activate the Stretch tool. Holding down the Ctrl key (to constrain the stretching to a single axis), squash the polygons *downward* to squash them along the v-axis. Squash the polygons until the squares in the texture begin to look more square instead of rectangular.

**421**

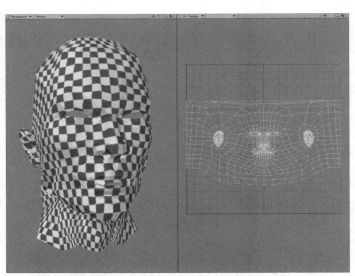

Figure 16-37

16. Press the "m" key to merge your points again before continuing.

Of course, this squashing altered some of the editing we did previously, but you don't really need to worry all that much about it, because the squashing now on the neck is relatively minimal and is not likely to cause problems when you paint a texture for it later on.

17. Let's now focus on the top of the head. Rotate your Perspective viewport so that the top of the head is visible. You'll see some nasty pinching at the pole where the cylindrical map comes to a point.

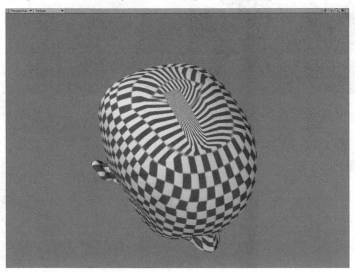

Figure 16-38

To be honest, there is no real point in spending much time actually editing this to fix it because you'll more than likely cover this area with hair, using Saslite or Sasquatch, or even modeled hair. If you want the character to be bald, it would be better to create an additional planar projection along the y-axis (just a standard projection; no UV map necessary) of the top of the head, and blend the two textures together using an alpha channel or Falloff settings in the Texture Editor.

So this pretty much concludes the process of editing the UV map for a head. Some people like to create additional projections for the ears as well, but that isn't always entirely necessary, as ears generally don't tend to have much texture detail on them. It's up to you, and since you now have this model, you're free to do with it as you please.

## Atlas UV Maps

### Using Atlas Maps

Aaaah, the ever-tempting Atlas unwrap option. This often looks extremely alluring to use since it gives the impression of being an ideal option for anything. Let me quickly banish that idea. Although the idea of an atlas unwrap seems like a great one, more often than not the result is a disjointed mess, especially when unwrapping organic models. In my experience, this option is not really suitable for characters (or any organic objects, for that matter) unless you want to spend a really, really, really long time editing the map.

The following image demonstrates the fragmented chaos that results from unwrapping a simple head object.

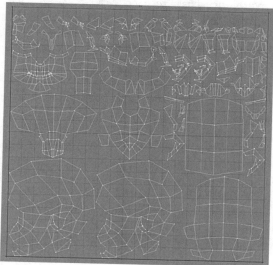

Figure 16-39

Figure 16-40 shows the same map after about an hour of editing, and it still needs a lot more editing before it can be of any use.

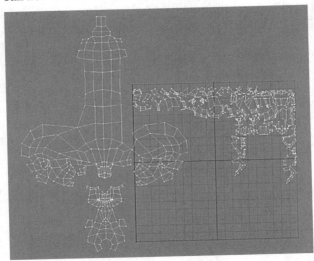

Figure 16-40

The fragmentation that occurs from unwrapping using the Atlas unwrap option makes it disastrous for anything other than structures such as buildings, cars, or anything else that has mostly retained simple shapes (primitive shapes).

Atlas unwrap does have one main advantage: It can be used to unwrap an entire object, regardless of the orientation of any part of that object. This is because atlas does not use an axis to unwrap; it simply flattens out the entire object along an arbitrary axis. Pretty cool!

So basically, you do not have to worry about choosing the right axis along which to unwrap, depending on what sort of alignment the different parts of the model have. Instead, it is simply a matter of clicking to unwrap, and then dealing with the resulting map as it turns out.

In the case of atlas mapping, editing is essentially the key to success, as the result of the initial unwrap is so very unusual. Atlas maps are always very fragmented, no matter what settings you use. Of course, as we know, editing is essential in all unwrapping methods, but in this case it takes on more importance since the initial unwrap is, in almost every case, *totally* unusable without extensive editing. This only really excludes extremely simple buildings, which, although they can definitely be improved by editing, can use the initial map obtained in many circumstances.

When editing atlas unwraps, one tends to use tools such as Flip UV Point Map a lot, since many polys often become flipped when using this method. We explore all the UV editing tools in great depth in Chapter 17.

## Making an Atlas UV Map

To make an atlas UV map, select the model that you wish to unwrap, click on New UV Map on the Map tab in Modeler, and select Atlas.

You'll notice that the Atlas UV mapping type has a different setup of options compared to the Planar, Cylindrical, and Spherical types.

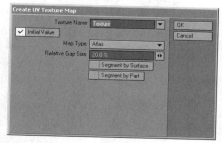

The Relative Gap Size option defines the distance between the fragmented sections of the map. Larger values will cause the sections to be farther apart from one another in the map, but remember that since the entire map needs to

**Figure 16-41**

fit into the square UV template that is a finite size, increasing this value also means that each part will be smaller in the UV map. If you want to paint really fine details into your textures, you are going to have to create much larger images for your textures since each part is so small within that map.

The following image shows an unwrapped cube with a Relative Gap Size value of 20% (on the left) and one with a value of 80% (on the right). I have drawn over the map with bolder lines to make the details clearer.

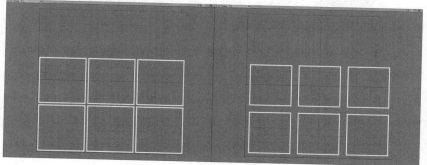

**Figure 16-42**

The Segment by Surface and Segment by Part options allow you to specify whether the discontinuities in the UV map will be positioned according to different surfaces or parts assigned to the model that you are unwrapping. For more information on discontinuous UVs, refer to Chapter 17.

So if you have, for example, three different surfaces assigned to the model, you can choose to have the fragmentation defined by these different surfaces. The same would apply to any parts that you have created in your model (parts are groups of polygons that you can define under the View tab in Modeler).

**425**

## Atlas UV Map Tutorial: Unwrapping a Small Building

This tutorial demonstrates the use of Atlas UV mapping to unwrap a small building. We will unwrap the outer walls first, and then do the inner walls.

1. Open the 4.2.4-small_house.lwo object from the companion CD in Modeler.

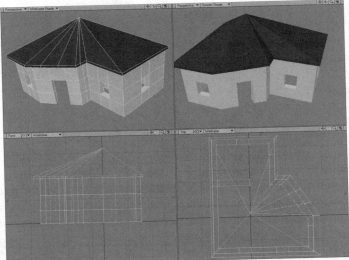

Figure 16-43

2. The roof and the walls are on two separate layers. Let's go to the wall layer and concentrate on that one first. Select all the outer walls of the house. I have already assigned a separate surface to them for ease of selecting, so all you have to do is open the Polygon Statistics panel (hit "w") when in Polygon mode (Ctrl+h), go down to where it says Surf, and select the Walls Outer surface. Click on the little + symbol to select the polygons to which this surface is applied.

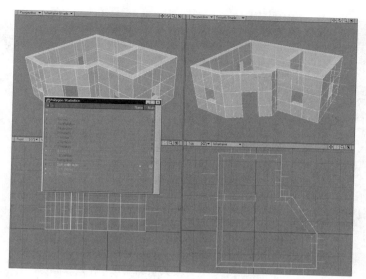

Figure 16-44

3. Go to the Map tab and click on New UV Map. Select Atlas as the Map Type and give it the name "outer walls." Leave the other values as they are and click OK.

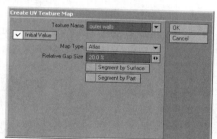

4. Change one of your viewports to UV Texture, and the map should automatically be displayed in the viewport. As you can see, all the walls are nicely flat in the UV template.

Figure 16-45

5. Open the Image Editor and load the _uv_checker.jpg image from the companion CD.

6. Open the Surface Editor, go to the Walls Outer surface, and open the Color Texture Editor. Change the default layer Projection setting to UV, select the "outer walls" UV map from the UV Map list, and load the checker-board image.

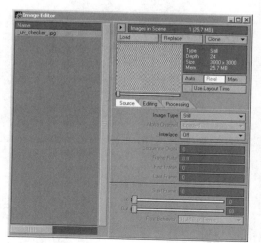

Figure 16-46

427

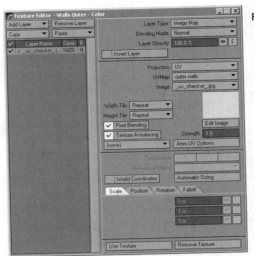

Figure 16-47

Make sure that your Perspective viewport is set to display textures, and you'll see the checkerboard image applied to the model. The outer walls, as you can see in Figure 16-48, are almost perfect.

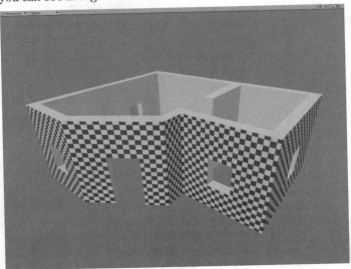

Figure 16-48

If we look at the area immediately to the right of the doorway, we can see that the checkerboard image is slightly squashed in this area.

Figure 16-49

7. These polygons are slightly too wide in the UV map, so we need to use the Stretch tool to fix this. You will have to unweld the vertices before doing this though, as this area is discontinuous, so press Ctrl+u to unweld the points before using the Stretch tool.

8. Now select the polygons that we need to squash, go to the UV viewport, select the Stretch tool ("h"), and squash the polygons inward along the u-axis (horizontally) until the patterns become square instead of rectangular, as shown in Figure 16-50.

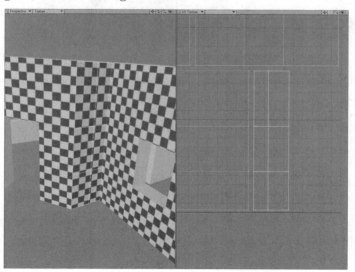

Figure 16-50

Leave all the points in the UV map unwelded for now.

At the moment, the walls in the map are not positioned alongside their correct counterparts. In other words, the walls in the UV map are not necessarily flanked by the walls that are actually next to them in the model. So ideally we need to arrange them correctly in the UV map to make the texture painting simpler, since there will be fewer seams to deal with.

9. Let's start with the door area and the piece of wall to its left. Select the polygons in this area. You'll notice that in the UV map, these two parts of the wall do happen to lie alongside one another. In Figure 16-51 I have made the selection in the UV map bolder so that you can see more clearly what you need to be doing.

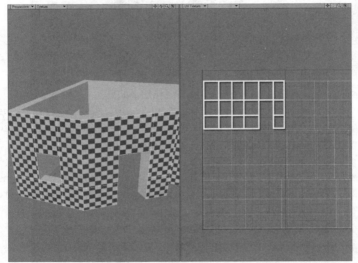

Figure 16-51

10. Move these out of the actual UV area so that we can start arranging things correctly. Move them up and position them above the actual UV map. When you select the polygons to move them, do so in Point mode (Ctrl+g) instead of Polygon mode. Moving the polygons around in Polygon mode sometimes leaves points behind.

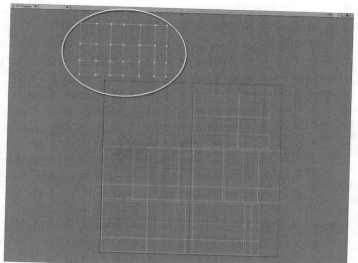

Figure 16-52

11. Now let's move clockwise around the house and move the walls in the UV map into place. Rotate your Perspective viewport around so that you can see the walls to the left of the section we just moved. Select them in your viewport so that you can see where they are in the UV map. We want to have these positioned directly to the left in the UV map as well, so select the points of this section in your UV viewport, and move them up and to the left of the area we moved previously.

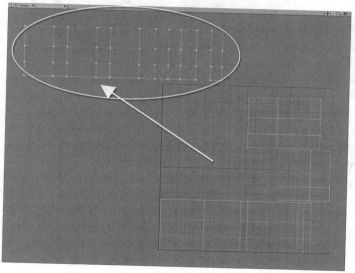

Figure 16-53

Rotate your Perspective viewport now so that you can see the back of the house.

You'll notice something a bit odd. In your Perspective viewport, select these polygons from left to right and watch how they are selected in the UV viewport at the same time. Notice something a bit odd? Yes, they are backward!

12. No need to panic — this is a common occurrence in atlas UV maps. All we need to do is use the Flip UV command to fix it. Select all the points of that section of wall and click on the Flip UVs button. Select Flip U and click OK.

Figure 16-54

This flips the points horizontally, so that they now flow correctly.

13. Select the points for this section and move them into place on our row of walls. Move them up to join with the new row of walls we are building at the top of the UV map.

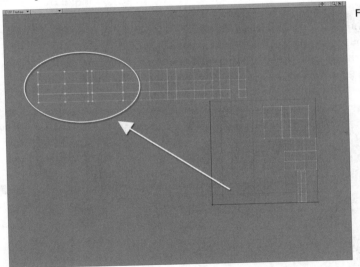

Figure 16-55

14. Swivel your Perspective viewport around to the side of the house now, and select the walls there. Move them into position on the new row at the top as well, and then repeat this process for the next section.

15. Last, we have the little piece that we squashed earlier. If you select these polygons from left to right in the Perspective viewport while looking at the UV viewport, you'll notice that these polygons are also flipped incorrectly. Once again, simply select the points of this section, hit the Flip UVs button, and select Flip U. Then, move this section into place on the row of walls.

16. Now select all the points in this long row of walls, scale them down, and position them back into the actual square template of the UV map.

17. Because they are so small in the UV map now, you will need to create a very large texture map to get detail into these small areas. Since we still have so much room going to waste in the UV map, select the points of the polygons forming the front and left facades of the house and move them below the other row. You'll ideally need to rearrange the sections forming the front part a little, so that the part that is to the right of the door part is now to its right in the UV map (previously it was on the other end of the row from that section).

18. Scale these sections up as much as you can in your UV map now, and it should look like Figure 16-56.

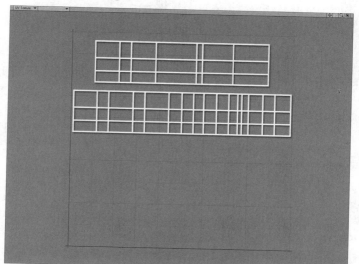

Figure 16-56

19. Okay, so let's move onto the inner walls of the house. Select them by surface from the Polygon Statistics panel ("w"), and click on New UV Map. Select Atlas and call the map "inner walls." Leave the other settings as they are.

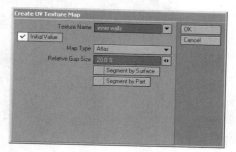

Figure 16-57

**433**

20. You'll get a nice big fragmented map looking like Figure 16-58.

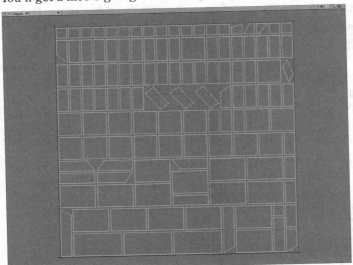

Figure 16-58

You are probably freaking out right now, but relax because I have some good news for you. Remember when we unwelded the points earlier? Well, because the entire model was unwelded, LightWave has assumed that all the pieces are separate, and so it has not kept them intact when it unwrapped the model.

21. So press Ctrl+z to kill the UV map.

22. Merge all the points in the model again by pressing "m." Now create the UV map again, using the same settings I described in step 19. Ahh, that's much better.

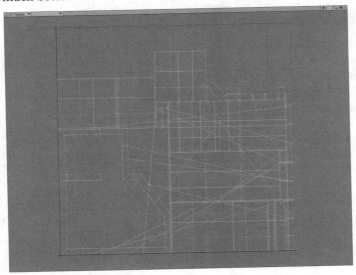

Figure 16-59

Don't worry about all the criss-crossing lines everywhere; they are only there because pieces of wall that should be alongside each other currently are not. Once we have edited the map, those lines will no longer be there.

23. Go to the Surface Editor, select the Walls Inner surface, and load the _uv_checker.jpg image into the Color Texture Editor, using the "inner walls" UV map.

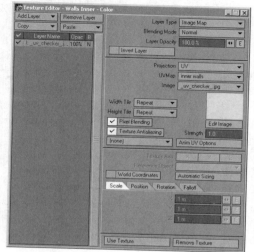

24. Now we need to unweld again because we don't want to be bothered with discontinuities while editing. So press Ctrl+u to unweld all the points.

25. Now simply do the same as we did with the outer walls by selecting each section, moving it up to the top, and

**Figure 16-60**

arranging a nice long row of wall sections. Watch out for flipped polygons, as a few of the sections in this map are flipped the wrong way on the u-axis in the UV map.

Figure 16-61 shows the long row I made, starting from the left side of the back inner wall on the left end of the row.

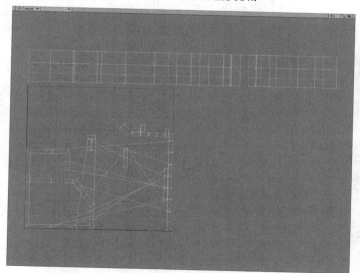

**Figure 16-61**

**435**

26. Once you have them all in a row, split the row into two again, and arrange them so that they will fit into the UV map space.

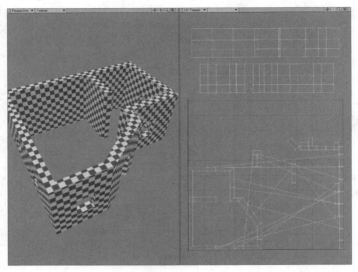

**Figure 16-62**

27. Okay, now we are left with a bunch of polygons that form all the horizontal parts of the model. First, we can get rid of the top row that runs along the top of the walls because the building has a roof and we will therefore never see those polygons. Select them in your Perspective viewport, and then click on Clear Map. This will remove them from your UV map. They will leave some points behind in the UV map — select those points and click on Clear Map again to delete them from the map.

**Figure 16-63**

28. Now we are left with the window ledges, the inner doorframe, and a mess of weird, distorted polygons. Let's deal with the weird ones first. Select them in your UV viewport.

    You'll notice that they are actually polygons on the outside walls, so we don't need them here either. Click on Clear Map again while they are selected. Select any points that they leave behind and clear those as well.

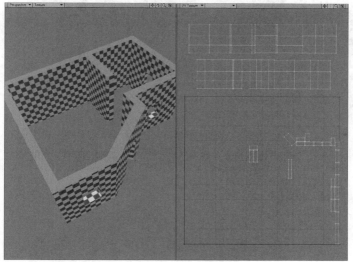

**Figure 16-64**

29. All that we have left now are the doorframe polygons and window ledges. You are really free to arrange these to your own personal prefer- ence. Personally, I really couldn't be all that bothered about them, so I just arranged them all along the bottom of the UV map. If you really want to, you can arrange them inside the window holes in the appropriate sec- tions in the parts you've been editing. Now arrange everything snugly into the UV space.

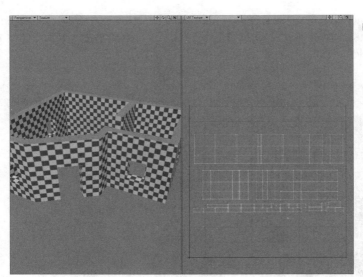

Figure 16-65

And that's atlas UV mapping. A lot of moving things around and rearranging, but useful for situations like this.

30. Merge your points by pressing "m." And that's it!

# CHAPTER 17

# Map Transformation and Editing Tools

## UV Map Editing Tools

Of course, creating UV maps is not just about unwrapping the model and taking it into Photoshop (or whatever paint package you are using). The majority of the time that you spend on UV maps is spent on editing the darn things so that they are actually usable. Once we have made a new UV map, we look to the UV tools in Modeler to start fixing up the stretching and weird distortion that invariably creeps into your unwrapped template.

All the tools that we need are found within the menu under the Map tab in Modeler.

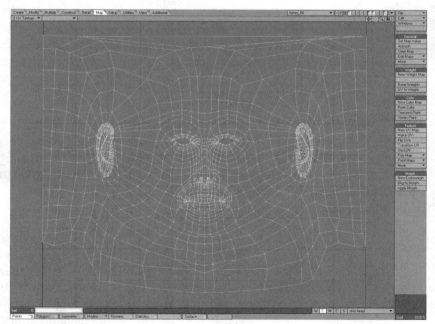

Figure 17-1

Not all of the options we find here are for UV maps, as this tab is for working with all *vertex* maps, of which UV maps are only one particular type. So if you find yourself wondering why I have ignored some of the buttons on this panel, now you know. This chapter only deals with UV mapping tools.

## General Commands

The first bunch of options we encounter under the Map tab are basically just the usual Copy, Delete, and Rename functions that we are accustomed to elsewhere in the LightWave package, as well as a couple of other, perhaps unfamiliar terms. You can click on the Edit Maps and More buttons to access a few other commands as well.

Figure 17-2

Let's look at each of them, one by one.

### Set Map Value

To use this function, you need to select points within your currently active UV map (the one that is show-
ing in your UV map viewport). By selecting points and enter-ing in any U or V value, those points will be moved to those coordinates within the UV map.

Figure 17-3

The first value represents the U coordinate, while the second value represents the V coordinate.

This is great for fine-tuning your UV maps, especially if there is any fragmentation (such as the fragmentation that occurs in atlas maps) and you need to place points back together with a high level of precision. I use this tool a lot when editing UV maps.

### Copy Vertex Map

Click on the Edit Maps button to access this command. This option copies the currently selected UV map, just as its name suggests. Copying a UV map cre-ates a new one that you can name as you wish.

Figure 17-4

You can use this option to create one big UV map from a bunch of differ-ent maps that you have already made. Simply select the maps one by one, and when the Copy Vertex Map window pops up, simply enter in the name of the UV map that you wish to copy it to. This is useful for when you are working with models like game models, where you are limited to the num-ber of images that you can use on a character, so you can unwrap all the different parts separately and then simply put them all together in a single map and arrange them so that you can texture all the different parts in a single image.

### Delete Vertex Map

Click on the Edit Maps button to access this command. This option deletes the currently selected UV map. Use this one cautiously as there is no further prompting to confirm the deletion.

### Rename Vertex Map

Click on the Edit Maps button to access this command. Use this option to rename the currently selected UV map. A new window pops up for you to enter in the new name.

Figure 17-5

### Clear Map

If you wish to remove certain polygons from within a UV map, use this option. Simply select the polygons that you wish to remove, and press this button.

If no polygons are selected, the entire contents of the UV map are removed.

Be aware that due to the nature of UV maps, removing polygons from the map removes the immediately surrounding polygons as well. Be sure to *unweld* (Ctrl+u) the points in the map before using this if you wish to keep all the surrounding polygons intact within the map. Just don't forget to remerge the points again afterward by pressing "m."

### Cull Map

Click on the More button to access this command. Since I have absolutely no mathematical abilities whatsoever (I can barely count over 10), I have a little trouble really fully understanding this tool's function and usefulness since the explanation of it in the LightWave manual left my brain reeling somewhat.

However, after researching it a little, I have a decent explanation of it for you. This tool affects points in a region of your UV map that you specify by entering in a value for the Threshold Magnitude setting below which all points will be selected or deselected, depending on which option you choose.

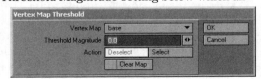

Figure 17-6

This value is reached by using a calculation to determine the region that will be affected by the action, namely the addition of the square root of the U value to the square root of the V value.

All that said though, I have never used this option! When I want to remove points or polygons from a UV map, I generally just select them and hit Clear. It's more straightforward.

### Normalize Map

Click on the More button to access this command. This function scales the selected vertex map from the Source VMap list according to the Minimum and Maximum values specified in the respective fields.

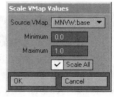

This is handy for ensuring that the map makes the most of the UV map space provided. I usually just scale this by hand, as I sometimes want to have differ-

Figure 17-7

ent areas in a UV map scaled according to how I want to paint them later on, but this can save you time if it is a simple projection that you have been editing, and you now want to simply size up to fill the space with the touch of a single button. Just be careful that it does not distort any areas that shouldn't be distorted (although this isn't all that likely to happen).

## Using the UV Mapping Tools

Under the Texture heading on the Map tab, we find the tools for creating and editing our UV maps for texturing.

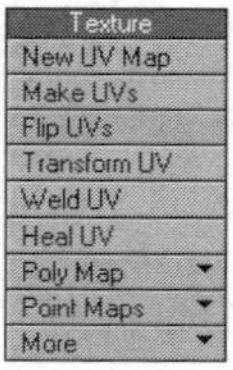

### New UV Map

This particular function creates a brand new UV map for the currently selected polygons or object in Modeler.

Figure 17-8

Clicking on the button opens a window from which you select your projection, name your new map, and specify a few other options.

From the Map Type drop-down, you can select the type of projection that you wish to use for your UV map. For more information on each of these projection types, take a look at Chapter 15.

Next we have the Subpatch Interpolation drop-down. Here you have some options to help you with distortion of textures on SubD objects. See "Fixing the

Figure 17-9

Texture Projections and Mapping

Annoying Subdivision Distortion Problem — Interpolation Options" later in this chapter for more information about the options in this drop-down menu.

Once you have selected a type of projection and a method from the Subpatch Interpolation drop-down, select the axis that you wish to apply that projection along by clicking on the desired axis button.

Below the interpolation options is a button called "move control points (old)" that is used to turn on or off the "classic" way LightWave worked with subpatched UVs. I supposed that's there for backward compatibility because I still haven't found a use for this option in my daily work, but there you have it if you need it for any reason. Just be warned that unlike the interpolation options, this is one you cannot turn on or off interactively; if you don't like the results, you'll have to start over.

You can have your UV settings automatically calculated for you, or you can manually enter your own settings for the placement and scale of the UV map by clicking on the Manual button next to Settings and entering your own values. Since you can edit your UV map once it is made, changing these settings is not always necessary.

## Make UVs — Assign UV Coordinates

Another way of creating a UV map is to click on the Make UVs button. This brings up a window similar to the one you get when selecting the New UV Map button. Apart from creating new UV maps with this command, you can also use it to edit the settings of an existing UV map by selecting that particular map from the Texture Name list, which lists all UV maps currently assigned to that model.

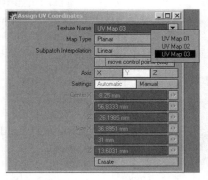

Figure 17-10

This allows you to change the projection type, axis, scale, and position of the existing UV map, which can be particularly useful if you created that UV map without using the Initial Value option in the Create UV Texture Map window.

The Make UVs command can also be used to add additional polygons to an existing UV map. Select the polygons you wish to add to the map, click on Make UVs, and select the map's name from the Texture Name list.

This is a useful way of making a single UV map out of a few maps without using the Copy Map command.

In this window you also have the option to select an interpolation method for your UVs.

## Flip UVs

This command is needed on occasions where, for whatever reason, you have polygons that are facing the wrong way in your UV map. You can flip the polygon along the U (horizontal) or V (vertical) plane, or both.

**Figure 17-11**

Generally, it is advisable to unweld your vertices before using this command since it can mess around with the discontinuous nature of UV maps.

When using the Atlas unwrap command, it is quite common for polygons to have some of their polygons flipped incorrectly, so instead of carefully selecting points and flipping them manually and then trying to carefully reposition them, using this command saves you time and effort.

## Transform UV

Clicking on the Transform UV button brings up a panel from which you can numerically adjust the Offset, Scale, and Rotation values around a specified Center of your currently active UV map.

Remember that UV values are defined by percentage values from within the UV space, so you would enter values from 0% to

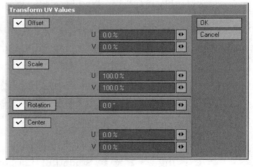

**Figure 17-12**

100% for these options. Use the Center value to define the point from which these values are calculated. By default, the Center value is 0% for both U and V coordinates, which means that all Offset, Scale, and Rotation values will be calculated from the lower left-hand corner of the UV map outward. If you wish to make these changes from the actual center of the UV map, you would enter values of 50% for both U and V in the Center fields.

I don't ever use this command, since I have a tendency to do everything by hand as much as I can when editing my UV maps.

## Weld UV

Weld UV will evaluate the points in the UV map and determine which points are on top of each other and then weld them. This is useful when you have several detached pieces that you move into place and wish to join them with the other pieces (or islands) of the map. For example, if you detach a portion of the UV map mesh using Free Move you will notice that the points of the outer edges will become red on both the section you detached and the mesh you detach it from. If for some reason you want to place it back where it was without using Undo, just move the piece back; the red points will subtly snap, and you can then use Weld UV to make the separated pieces one single mesh again.

### Heal UV

Using this tool is similar to sewing points back together automatically. It is important to note that Heal UV averages the position of the offending discontinuous points and will place the continuous points in that averaged location. Use this tool with caution; if you run it on your whole UV mesh, it might jumble it all up. I have rarely used this tool.

### Poly Map

As these options are no longer used, they are not discussed here.

### Point Maps

Looking under the Point Maps drop-down, we find two commands — Spread UVs and Quantize UVs.

Spread UVs works with quads (four-sided polygons) only, and basically allows you to size them by using numeric values within the UV space.

Figure 17-13

Figure 17-14

The Quantize UVs command snaps selected points in the UV map to the grid using the values entered into the appropriate fields.

Figure 17-15

Again, these are options that I never really use. In fact, I don't think I have ever used them because of my tendency to eyeball everything and move points around by hand.

### Set UV Value

This command is accessed from the More drop-down. The Set UV tool is for numerically positioning points within the currently active UV map. It basically does the same thing as the Set Map Value command we looked at earlier except that this tool is specifically for UV maps, so you have options for entering in values for U and V instead of X, Y, and Z as with the Set Map Value command.

Figure 17-16

**445**

This tool is particularly useful for ensuring that points meet where they are supposed to when you've been editing a UV map with the points unwelded.

Click on either the U or the V button and enter a desired percentage value within the UV space onto which you would like to position the selected points. This is a very useful tool for precision, especially in those pesky UV maps where things have become horribly fractured (such as an atlas UV map).

## Polygon Normal UVs

This command is accessed from the More drop-down. The command projects the texture UVs along the polygon normals, mapping the image flat on the normal.

Figure 17-17

It is a tool that works with poly maps, which is the predecessor to the discontinuous UV maps that we work with now. Since we don't really need poly maps anymore, this tool (along with the other poly map tools) has really outgrown its usefulness, and I am guessing that the only reason it is still in the program is for the off chance that you may happen to be given a really old LightWave model to work with that uses them. Otherwise, you can ignore it.

## UV Spider

This command is accessed from the More drop-down menu. When you select a polygon, the UV Spider crawls along and adds a row of polygons to the UV map. The UV Spider tool is similar in a way to the BandSaw modeling tool.

The following image shows the result of using the UV Spider tool. Two polygons were selected and the tool was activated. In the UV viewport you can now see the entire row (edge loop) of polygons following those selected polygons has been added into the UV map.

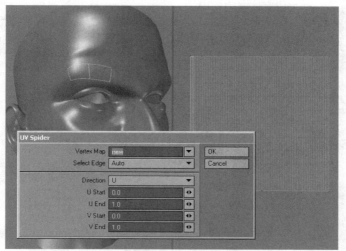

Figure 17-18

You will notice that the polygons are stretched to fill the entire space of the UV map, but this can be adjusted using the settings for the tool.

At the top of the panel, where it says Vertex Map, you can enter a new name to create a new UV map for the tool to work with, or you can select an existing UV map to which the UV Spider will add its unwrapped polygons.

The Select Edge options allow you to specify the direction along the actual topography (the model's surface) that the UV Spider runs along. Selecting Auto will let the tool decide for you.

The Direction option (either U or V) determines the actual direction *within the UV space* that the polygons will be added to the UV map. If the Direction is U, the band stretches in the U direction (horizontally in UV space) with a top and bottom in the UV plane determined by the U Start and U End values.

The following image shows the UV Spider applied along the U direction with the default U Start and U End values, which stretches the band of polygons across the entire UV space.

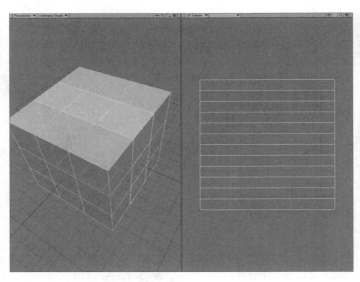

Figure 17-19:
UV Spider
applied along
the U
direction

If the Direction is V, then the band goes in the V direction (vertically in UV space), using the V Start and V End values to determine the beginning and ending values for the scaling of the polygons in the map.

This next image shows the UV Spider applied along the V direction with the default V Start and V End values, which stretches the band of polygons across the entire UV space.

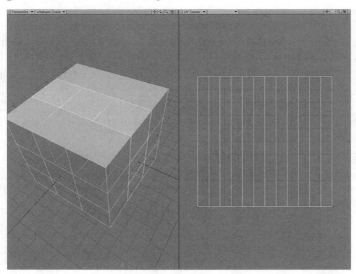

Figure 17-20:
UV Spider
applied along
the V
direction

This tool is quite useful for additional control when unwrapping edge loops (loops of polygons used when modeling organic surfaces), although in some cases you may find it a little more time consuming than using a regular projection.

## Guess Viewport UV Image

This command is accessed from the More drop-down. To use it you should have the surface of which the currently active UV map is a part selected in the Surface Editor. Selecting Guess Viewport UV Image then lets Modeler attempt to guess the appropriate backdrop image for the UV map (to be placed as a backdrop in the UV viewport) by looking for the image that the UV map is projecting in the surface.

Figure 17-21 shows the result of this action when working with a skin texture applied using the UV map. As you can see, the command has placed the painted head texture into the backdrop of the UV viewport.

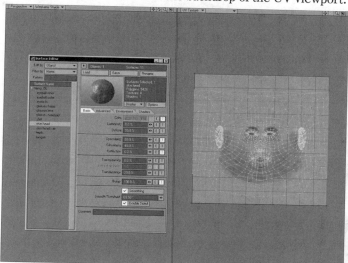

Figure 17-21

This is very useful for making adjustments to the UV map when you need to be able to see the actual image applied while editing, especially when matching a UV map to a premade texture. This option is basically the same as going to your display options, going to the Backdrop tab, and loading the image in there; it simply saves you that effort.

## Texture Guide

Click on the More button to access Texture Guide, an interactive tool for creating texture projections on your model. This tool can adjust existing standard projections, as well as create UV maps from them.

To use the Texture Guide, you should have the surface that you wish to work with already selected in the Surface Editor, and generally it

Figure 17-22

makes sense to already have an image applied to the surface. Select the Texture Guide tool and press "n" to open its numeric panel so that you can adjust the settings.

It is very much like a more interactive version of the options that you find within the Texture Editor in the Surface Editor itself.

You can select your projection type, adjust the axis along which the image is projected, and alter its scale, position, and rotation. Adjusting the position and rotation of an image is made simpler by the appearance of a bounding box shape with a crosshair in your viewport that shows the shape and size of the image (with the crosshair in the center), as well as the rotation of the image.

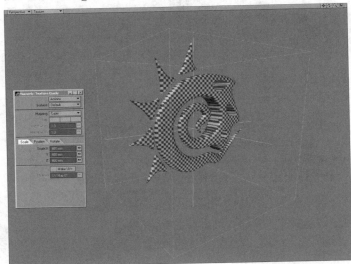

Figure 17-23

Clicking on the Make UVs button and entering a name for the new UV map allows you to see, in real time, what the resulting UV map will look like in your UV viewport.

If a UV map has already been created for the object, the Texture Guide can sample the projection into the UV map interactively. This can greatly increase the speed of creating your initial UV projections since you can immediately see what the resulting map will look like.

I never really use this tool, as I am so familiar with the projections that LightWave has, and so I generally know what to expect when selecting the New UV Map option and choosing a projection type. However, this tool is useful for those of you who are still getting a grip on different projections and want a more intuitive method of working with them. But chances are that you will eventually outgrow this tool once you become a UV mapping expert!

# Tips for Editing UV Maps Successfully

## The Necessity of Editing UV Maps

If I had a dime for every occasion that someone has told me, "I don't under-stand UV mapping," I'd probably have ... well, a lot of dimes. In all honesty I am not sure why it is that people struggle so much to understand the con-cepts of UV mapping when they are actually so very simple. All you need to do is use your brain. If you can make a model in 3D, then you certainly have enough brainpower to handle UV mapping properly, trust me.

As I have mentioned before, one of the really handy things about using UV maps, as opposed to using standard projection techniques to apply your textures to your models, is that UV maps can be edited. This means that you have vertex-level control over the exact placement of your textures since you can adjust the map to suit your needs. Essentially, you can create a UV map using any particular axis and projection type, and with time and effort you can adjust it to look completely different.

Take a look at the following image. As you can see, the unwrapped map of this armor (done along the y-axis using a Cylindrical projection) would be difficult to use as a template for a texture because, well, frankly it's a little crazy.

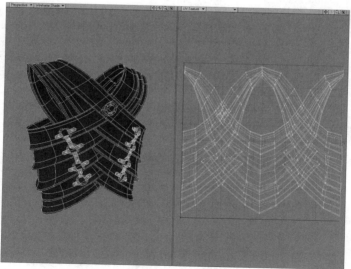

Figure 17-24

This was an armor model I made for an elf character, and I wanted to paint very intricate patterns onto the armor plating. Because of this, I needed to find a more ideal way of laying out the UV map so that the pro-cess of painting patterns would be simplest. I decided to edit the UV map so that each of the strips of armor formed a horizontal band that would be easy to paint rows of patterns onto.

After a bit of tweaking I ended up with the following map instead, a far more convenient layout onto which I could paint patterns.

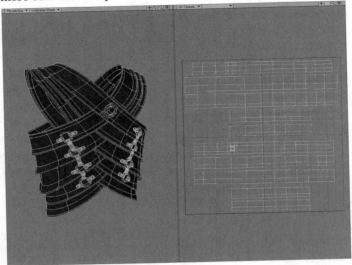

Figure 17-25

In doing so, I've also eliminated all the overlapping polygons, which cause problems once a texture is applied. Overlapping polygons are one of the biggest reasons for editing UV maps, since most UV maps that you create, especially for organic surfaces, will initially have overlapping polygons appearing in certain areas.

This very clearly illustrates the benefits of taking some time to edit your UV maps to make the process of painting your textures so much simpler and straightforward.

But before we look at the actual nitty-gritty of editing UV maps, it's important to understand how UV maps in LightWave actually work.

## Understanding Discontinuous UV Maps

UV maps in LightWave are created in a *discontinuous* manner. This means that when the polygons are unwrapped and flattened to create the UV map, areas where the model has become "split" by the unwrapping process will remain locked in place to ensure that they do not become very badly misaligned during the editing process.

When you try to select all the vertices within the UV map, only a certain number of them can be selected.

In previous versions of LightWave, these vertices could not be selected or even be seen in the UV Editor at all.

The reason the vertices can not be selected or seen is because they are essentially attached to one another on the model itself, despite being in different places within the UV map.

In the following image, I have selected two polygons that are directly alongside each other on the model. However, as you can see, in the UV map they are on opposite sides, and because of that, the polygon on the top right has no selectable vertices in the UV map because those particular corners are joined to other polygons where the points are selectable.

**Figure 17-26**

Since these polygons are all connected to each other, what will happen if I select that polygon marked "1" and try to move it within the UV map? Take a look at Figure 17-27. I've added the arrow to show the direction in which I tried to move the polygon.

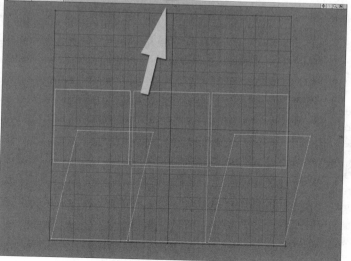

**Figure 17-27**

As you can see, the polygon I selected cannot actually be moved within the UV map because its vertices are locked to the polygons to which it is selected. And it is the polygons to which it is selected that move instead. This demonstrates the discontinuous nature of the UV map.

Starting with version 8.5, however, you can see the vertices in a discontinuous UV map and you can also edit them! Once you open the UV Editor and you have a map made you will notice some red points on your map which are the shared vertices of the discontinuous map. Having those points in red makes it easier to see where the seam is within that map. Just make sure that the vertices of the seam match up for a good, clean map.

## Using the Unweld Command

While this discontinuous property of UV maps can be useful to remind you where the seams lie within a UV map, you will probably find that most of the time you'll want to work without this happening, since you invariably want to be able to shift around all the points you need to when editing your maps.

Thankfully, we now have a new option to help with this problem! When you enter the UV Editor you will now see a button called Free Move on the top navigation bar, which when activated will allow you to edit vertices and polygons whether you are in SubD mode or not. This helps tremendously when editing UVs. You can select a group of polygons and move them to a different area of the UV map without having to unweld first, a huge time saver.

While we now have the Free Move option to help with discontinuous UV maps, you will occasionally get in a situation where unwelding the vertices would be a better solution.

Unweld (Ctrl+u, or Detail>Points>Unweld) will disconnect the polygons within your UV map from one another while maintaining the points that connect them on each polygon. The points are duplicate copies of those selected points (or of all the points in the model if none are selected) so that none are shared by two polygons.

Each polygon is given its own copy of the selected vertices, and VMap values for the polygon are made continuous over the new vertices. This command is essential to being able to edit discontinuous UVs correctly and efficiently when Free Move alone won't do. For example, if you are editing a UV map with Free Move activated, you might see interconnecting lines due to the nature of discontinuous UVs. A better solution for this case would be to make a new set of UV maps for each part you are mapping and merge them all together using the Copy Vertex Map command, as discussed earlier, or simply unwelding your mesh, so keep this technique in mind every time you are editing UV maps.

Just remember to merge (press "m" or Construct>Reduce>Merge Points) the points again once you are finished editing! If you have moved points around in the map that were previously discontinuous, merging the points will keep the changes you have made. This is useful since it allows you to place seams where you want them.

 **NOTE:** Separated groups of polygons in the UV Editor are also known as "islands."

## Fixing the Annoying Subdivision Distortion Problem — Interpolation Options

Many LightWave users, especially the seasoned ones, know about this "little" problem that LightWave's subdivision surfaces have had since their introduction. When UV mapping subdivision surfaces in Modeler, you would encounter a strange phenomenon whereby you find little distortions on your surface when applying textures with UV maps. While some of the distortions might be visually inconspicuous once the texture had been applied to the model, these distortions were sometimes quite obvious, such as when your texture is required to have lines, logos, or letters. This could be quite frustrating and annoying to solve.

Figure 17-28 shows examples of this distortion. I have circled some of the areas affected by this problem, and as you can see, the texture has little jiggles in it in these areas.

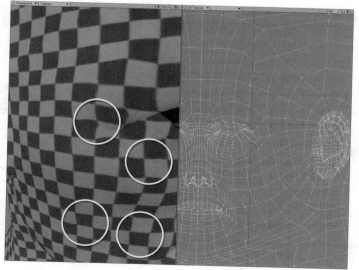

Figure 17-28

In the past we used to have workarounds to help reduce this distortion, including increasing the poly count, but as you know, by doing so you would also be increasing physical size and render times. You could also use morph maps or endomorphs to help alleviate the problem. Of course the last method of dealing with highly problematic situations is simply to opt for using standard projections instead of UV maps.

To correct this problem, LightWave now has Subdivision Interpolation options from which you can select the most appropriate method for your mesh. These options are accessible when you create a new map via the New UV Map button, the Make UVs button, or the Vertex Maps window. You can also customize the Map tab of your GUI and add the interpolation buttons to the UV Texture group of buttons. You can select from the following options:

- Linear — This option is most frequently used when you are creating UVs for polygonal objects. Since there is no smoothing of the geometry like in SubD models, the interpolation is calculated in a linear fashion, point A to point B. Some users like to unwrap their SubD objects while in Polygon mode; however, you will get somewhat less distortion if you unwrap your SubD models while in SubD mode, which leads us to the next option.

- Subpatch — This one is a godsend. This option practically eliminates distortion of your textures on SubD models. I say practically because some distortion may still occur, but it is most likely due to texture stretching or overlapping UVs than the actual conversion from polys to SubDs. LightWave used to have only one method of UV interpolation, Linear, so when you converted your polygons to SubD, the interpolation solution wouldn't take into account the smoothing of the polygons; it would still calculate from point A to point B, ignoring the curve between these two points, and therefore distortion would occur. With this option, the interpolation between points will be weighted, as if the UV mesh was a SubD mesh as well, taking into account the smoothed geometry of a subdivision surface and thus solving the annoying distortion problem. It is also important to mention that the discontinuous edges that you might have will not be aligned.

- Linear Corners — This option will interpolate the corners of the mesh and the pieces you separate using Free Move. The edges between these corner points get Subpatch interpolation. The discontinuous edges do not line up with this option either.

- Linear Edges — Very similar to Linear Corners, the main difference is that the corners and the edges in between get interpolated linearly. The discontinuous edges will meet up, but distortion might still happen as a result.

- Across Discontinuous Edges — This option is very similar to Subpatch with the biggest difference being that unlike Subpatch, the discontinuous edges will line up, thus decreasing the distortion on the discontinuous edge. I usually stick to this option or Subpatch for all my SubD meshes.

When you have the UV Editor open and a UV set selected, you can change between these options interactively and see their effect in the viewports. You can do this with the Vertex Maps window or by adding the buttons to the GUI, as I described earlier. You can also assign wireframe colors to different UV maps, making it easier to tell what's what in the viewport when more than one UV set is selected.

## Eliminating Stretching

For most organic models, as well as some nonorganic ones, you are going to encounter a certain degree of stretching when creating UV maps. This is simply because the unwrapping process is bound to make some changes to the sizes of some of the polygons when it lays them out flat. One of the best ways to check how much stretching is occurring in your map is to apply an image with a checkerboard pattern to the model using the UV map. This immediately shows you where the map is stretching or pinching.

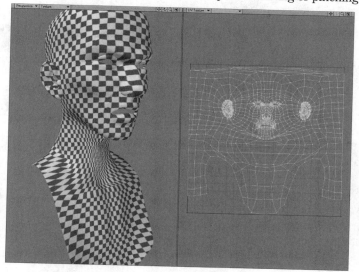

Figure 17-29

Eliminating this stretching is generally quite straightforward. All we need to do is go to those areas of the UV map and push and pull the vertices around in order to size the stretched polygons correctly in relation to the other polygons.

Interestingly enough, this way of eliminating stretching requires you to almost think backward. This is because the way that you move vertices to eliminate it is actually opposite to what may seem logical to you.

For example, let's look at the following area on this unwrapped head, where we can see a lot of stretching occurring.

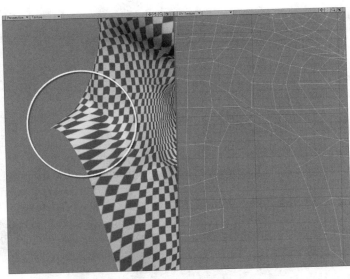

Figure 17-30

The reason that I say we need to think backward is because stretching in a UV map does not occur because the texture is stretched over too many polygons (as would seem logical to those of you who are not UV-savvy), but because the texture is actually stretched over too few.

Let's look again at the model, and focus specifically on the areas where the stretching is particularly bad. I have circled the polygons in the UV map where the stretching is occurring.

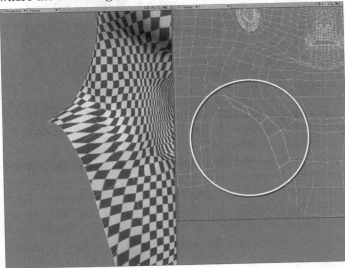

Figure 17-31

Now, the reason that this area is stretching so badly is because the little checks in the image are being stretched over too small an area within the polygons in the UV map. A good analogy to describe this is that the polygons in the UV map basically act as a container into which that particular portion of the image that lies beneath it fits. Sometimes we need to adjust the size of that "container" in order to allow more of the image to fit into it, and sometimes we need to adjust it so that less of the image fits into it, and instead overflows into the surrounding "containers."

So what we need to do to fix this is to stretch the polygons in the UV map *outward* so that *more* of the image is contained within them, instead of a small area of it being stretched to fit inside the polygons.

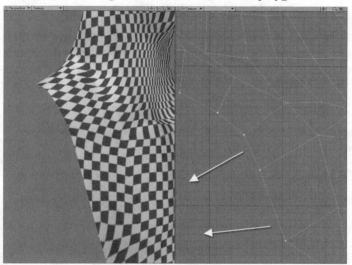

Figure 17-32

Likewise, in areas where the texture is being squashed, as shown in Figure 17-33, we need to do the opposite to eliminate it, since essentially the squashing is caused by *too much* of the image being put into the "containers" of the polygons.

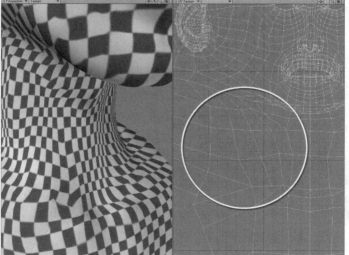

Figure 17-33

459

So in a case like this, we simply push the polygons in the UV map *inward* so that the image overflows into the surrounding polygons instead. In doing so we have *less* of the image fitting into the polygon.

Basically, we need to look at the sizes of the polygons in the actual model, and ensure that they are relatively proportional to one another within the UV map as well. This is probably the most time-consuming part of editing UV maps.

## Combining Different UV Maps

Sometimes you may have a number of different UV maps assigned to a single model that you wish to combine into one UV map once they have all been created. This is something that is particularly common when working with game models, since it means that you can essentially apply textures to an entire character using a single image.

To do this in LightWave, you can start off by making as many different UV maps as you like and then making one final one into which you will combine all the maps already created. When you make the final map, click on the New UV Map button and simply deselect the Initial Value option in the Create UV Texture Map window. This creates a blank UV map.

Figure 17-34

Of course, you don't necessarily have to make a new map. You could just take one of the existing maps and combine all the others into that one. But for the sake of example, let's just use the new blank map.

To get all the UV maps into the single map, all you need to do is use the Copy Vertex Map command, found in the Edit Maps drop-down list.

Go to each of the maps that you have made, click on the Copy Vertex Map option, and in the text field in the window that pops up, simply type in the name of the blank map that you created.

Figure 17-35

Doing this to each of the maps you have created will add the information from each UV map into the one whose name you enter into the text field when copying them.

Figure 17-36

Eventually you will end up with a nice big UV map that contains all the maps for your character, which you can then go into and size and arrange each part to suit your needs.

## Patience

The most important thing you need to have when working with UV maps, apart from using your brain, is a lot of patience. And I'm not talking about the card game.

UV mapping is almost always a fairly time-consuming process, but in the end it's generally worth it since working with a well-edited UV map makes the process of painting textures a lot smoother and more enjoyable because you don't have to worry about stretching or distortion issues when you finally apply your beautifully painted textures to your model. Getting a great UV map can take one hour, or it can take ten hours. Sometimes even more. The more you get used to it, the quicker the process will become as you refine your techniques and habits, but you will still find yourself occasionally sitting for hours on a single map. Just grin and bear with it.

# PART 5

## Animating Textures

# CHAPTER 18

# Enveloping Basics

Enveloping is the simplest form of animating numerical values in LightWave. If you look at the Surface Editor panel or nodes in the Node Editor, you'll notice that each surface attribute has a little button labeled "E" next to it.

This button allows you to *envelope* its value over time. Enveloping simply means that the value no longer remains static.

Clicking on an envelope button opens up LightWave's Graph Editor, as shown in Figure 18-2. The Graph Editor can appear rather frightening at first, but it is actually very simple to use.

LightWave's manual has an entire section devoted to the Graph Editor, so no detailed investigation is required here, but I'll run through the basics.

Basically, the way the Graph Editor works is that you simply create points (keys) on the graphs, and then alter the values of those keys.

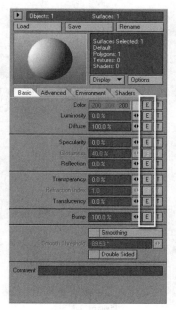

Figure 18-1

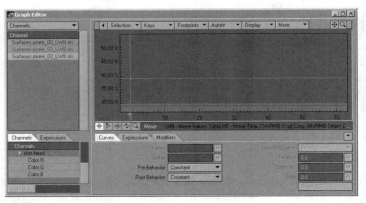

Figure 18-2

At the bottom of the graph window are displayed the frame numbers in your scene. So if you want to create a new key at frame 40, simply hover your cursor in line with the number 40 and create a key on the graph.

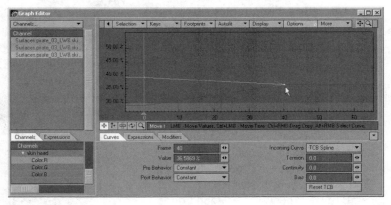

Figure 18-3

Below, on the Curves panel, the Frame field shows the frame number at which you have just created the key, so you can fine-tune things there.

Below the Frame field is a Value field. You can manually enter new values to change the current value, or you can click and drag the key around on the graph itself to adjust the value.

You can adjust the way that the keys are interpolated between one another by changing the Incoming Curve value.

For more information regarding the options for keys on the Graph Editor, refer to the LightWave manual.

# Animatable Surface Parameters in LightWave

When animating surfaces, the only attributes that you can animate in the Graph Editor are:

- The RGB color value of a surface
- The overall values of each of the basic surface attributes (Reflection, Specularity, etc.)
- The Color Highlights, Color Filter, Additive Transparency, and Diffuse Sharpness values under the Advanced tab of the Surface Editor
- The Image Seam Angle, Reflection Blurring, and Refraction Blurring values under the Environment tab
- The Blend Opacity value in the Surface Mixer shader
- The Layer Opacity value of all texture layers in the Texture Editors of all surface attributes
- The Scale, Position, Rotation, and Falloff values of all layers in the Texture Editors of all surface attributes
- U and V coordinates on surfaces that have UV maps applied to them. To animate UVs using the Node Editor you need to use Layer nodes.

Note that gradient keys and most node attributes can be animated using the Node Editor. To gain even more control over your texture animation, use the Node Editor to create your shaders. The Node Editor offer options for animating texture nodes that are not available in the "classic" Texture Editor. Now you have control over settings like Frequency, Contrast, and Small Scale. This is a very welcome addition to LightWave.

# PART 6

# Effects Processing

# CHAPTER 19

# Image Filters in LightWave

The Effects panel in Layout contains a few options for applying effects to your renders. To open this panel, click on the Image Process button under the Scene tab, or press Ctrl+F8.

Most of the functions and settings on the Effects panel fall within the realm of rendering, so we do not need to deal with all of them here. In terms of texturing, however, we find some use for certain image filters that can be added to the Image Filters list. To add an image filter, simply click on the Add Image Filter button and select the filter that you wish to use.

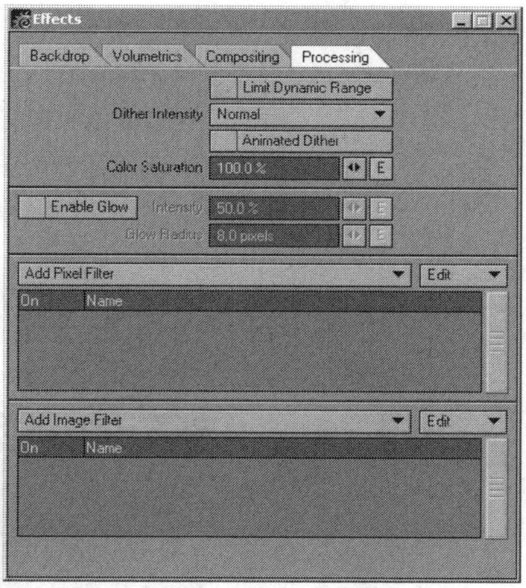

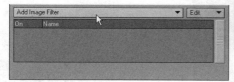

Figure 19-1

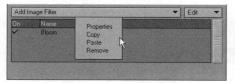

Figure 19-2

Figure 19-3

You can copy, paste, or remove filters from this panel by right-clicking on them in the list, or by clicking on the button labeled Edit.

## How Image Filters Work

Image filters are applied during post-processing. This means that they are added to the rendered image once the actual rendering process is complete. Because of this, they have certain limitations. For example, hair created using a filtering process (such as Saslite or Sasquatch, which uses a pixel filter that is also created during post-processing) does not normally show up in reflections because the hair fibers are created after rendering and are therefore not included in the reflection ray tracing during rendering.

## Using Image Filters to Enhance Surfaces

Although most of these filters are not texturing related, a few of them can be used to create some very cool effects on your surfaces. You can use these globally, by simply assigning them to this list and setting them up as desired, or you can use them in conjunction with Special Buffers, which are discussed in depth in Chapter 5, to have them affect certain surfaces only.

### Bloom

This particular filter helps to create those extremely bright spots or halos that we observe in highly reflective surfaces when they are brightly lit, especially in sunlight. It is particularly useful for enhancing realism in surfaces like highly polished car paint, very reflective metals, glass, and water, which have a tendency to almost sparkle in sunlight.

Figure 19-4 shows an example of this in real life. Look at the extremely bright spot on the edge of the glass where the sun is hitting it.

The shader is very simple to set up, since it only has three controls.

Figure 19-4

Figure 19-5

The Threshold value determines how bright a pixel must be before the Bloom effect will actually affect it. The lower this value, the more of your surface will bloom. Since the bloom effect in real life is usually quite small and focused, higher values tend to be more appropriate here.

The following image shows a fairly reflective and highly specular surface with increasing values of Threshold. The logo on the left does not have Bloom applied to it at all, while the one in the middle has a Threshold value of 25% and the one on the right has a Threshold value of 80%.

Figure 19-6

As you can see, the higher the value becomes, the tighter and more focused the Bloom effect becomes since it only affects the pixels that are far brighter.

The Strength value determines the strength of the Bloom effect compared to the pixel that it affects. Basically, this value controls the overall brightness of the blooming effect on the bright areas of the surface.

The following image shows the increasing effect of this value. The logo on the left has a Strength value of 25%, while the one in the middle has a value of 50% and the one on the right has a value of 100%.

Figure 19-7

Size, the last option, controls the actual pixel radius of the blooming effect at a resolution of 640 × 480. If the resolution changes, the size is automatically adjusted so that the effect always appears the same, despite any changes in resolution.

In the following image, the logo on the left has a Size value of 25 while the logo on the right has a value of 80.

Figure 19-8

Increasing the Size value can increase rendering times quite dramatically.

## Corona

The Corona filter produces the same type of effect as the Bloom filter, except that it gives you more control over the look of the effect by offering more options.

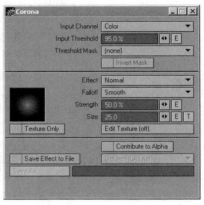

Figure 19-9

The Input Channel drop-down list allows you to specify a particular internal render buffer that the effect will be applied to, while the Input Threshold value determines the threshold level of that input after which to apply the effect.

This is the biggest difference between the Corona filter and the Bloom filter, since Bloom is applied to pixels in all the buffers. This basically allows you to apply the effect to only one particular aspect of the surface, such as its specularity or its reflectivity.

Clicking on Input Channel gives you a rather long list of internal buffers from which to choose.

Color uses the actual raw hue of the pixels to determine which areas are affected by the effect, so that the brighter colors will bloom. Alpha uses the brightness values of the render's alpha.

Specular Shading uses the specular shading values as an input, so that the areas with higher values of specularity bloom, while Diffuse Shading uses the Diffuse channel's shading.

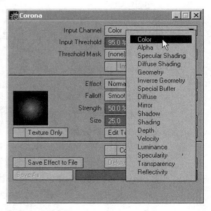

Figure 19-10

These two shading options are different from the Specularity and Diffuse input types in that the shading values vary across the surface, from 0% to 100%, while the Specularity and Diffuse options take their input values directly from the values assigned in the Surface Editor and are therefore uniform across the surface.

Essentially, this means that when using Specular Shading or Diffuse Shading (which are influenced by the lighting in the scene), the bloom effect will appear where there are brighter spots of specular or diffuse shading on any particular area of a surface, while using Specularity or Diffuse will apply the effect to any surface that has a specularity or diffuse value in the Surface Editor that exceeds the input threshold *as a whole*.

Geometry uses the normal angles of the object's surface to trigger the effect. This is an incidence-based (Fresnel) effect, where an Input Threshold value of 100% places the blooming on areas that face the camera directly. Inverse Geometry is the opposite, whereby the normals that are perpendicular to the camera (in other words the edges) trigger the blooming effect when using an Input Threshold value of 100%.

The following image shows the Geometry option on the left and the Inverse Geometry option on the right.

Figure 19-11

Special Buffer uses the Special Buffers feature in the Surface Editor as the input for the effect. This is useful for applying the effect to specific surfaces only. For more information on using the Special Buffers feature, refer to Chapter 5.

Mirror and Reflectivity use reflection information from the surface as the input. Although similar to the Specular Shading versus the Specularity input options we looked at a moment ago, the Mirror and Reflectivity options differ in that Mirror uses the flat reflection value assigned to the surface in the Surface Editor, while Reflectivity uses the reflection shading information.

The Shadow option uses shadows on the surface to trigger the effect, while Shading uses the actual light on the surface as the input. This means the Input Threshold value determines how brightly lit an area of the surface must be before it blooms.

Depth applies the effect according to the z-depth buffer, using the values ranging from 0% to 100% to represent the transition from black to white in the buffer. Velocity uses movement of the object as a trigger.

Luminance and Transparency use the appropriate values set in the Surface Editor as the input for the effect.

You can mask the blooming effect using one of these buffers as well, by selecting it from the Threshold Mask drop-down list.

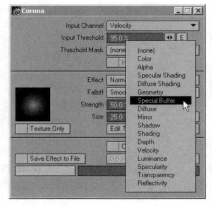

Figure 19-12

This buffer now acts like an alpha channel for the effect. The mask can also be inverted.

The Effect drop-down list gives you three different blending modes for the effect.

Figure 19-13

The Additive mode creates an effect that looks extremely hot (white) where blooming pixels are closely grouped. This is useful for effects like heated metal. This mode creates an effect that is very strong in the middle and much less so on the edges.

Normal (the default) is similar to, although not quite as strong as, the Additive mode, since the effect at the center and the edges tends to grow more evenly, as opposed to being concentrated in the middle only.

Maximum takes the maximum of contributive pixels, creating a strong bloom effect where the blobs of light on the surface actually tend to merge where they meet one another (most noticeable when the Size value is set fairly high).

Figure 19-14 shows each of the different modes, with all other settings the same for each. From left to right, we have Normal, Additive, and Maximum.

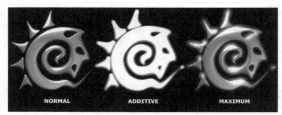

Figure 19-14:
Effect options

The Falloff drop-down list allows you to select an option for how the Bloom effect falls off (at its edges). Refer to the little preview window to see how the different Falloff options work. You can achieve some really bizarre effects by playing around with this setting.

The Linear falloff type simply has a straight falloff in the Bloom effect, from solid white in the middle to fading away completely at the edges.

Smooth produces a slightly tighter effect, with the falloff occurring sooner from the middle, while Center Bias creates an even tighter falloff from the middle. Figure 19-16 shows the Smooth falloff on the left and the Center Bias falloff on the right. As you can see, they are very similar.

Figure 19-15: Linear falloff

Figure 19-16:
Smooth and
Center Bias falloff

Solid Box causes the blooms to appear square, and Ring forms halos of light instead of blooming spots. In Figure 19-17, the Solid Box falloff is shown on the left and the Ring falloff on the right.

Figure 19-17:
Solid Box and
Ring falloff

Just as we have in the Bloom filter, the Strength value is the strength of the Corona pixel compared to the source pixel, and the Size value is the radius in pixels of the brush at a 640 × 480 resolution. If the resolution is different, the brush is adjusted so that the effect always looks the same.

Use the Edit Texture option to add color and modulation to the effect using a texture, which can be a procedural texture, an image, or a gradient. Clicking on this button opens a Texture Editor just like we find in the Surface Editor, where you can create layers of textures.

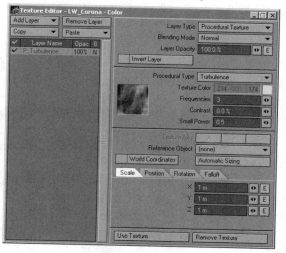

Figure 19-18

When using gradients with the Corona filter, you'll find some unusual input parameters that are only found when using them with this particular filter.

The Previous Layer, Depth, Distance to Center, and LW_Corona Input Channel options allow you to alter the way in which the Corona effect is applied to the surface.

When the Texture Only option is active (checked) and there is also a texture color, the effect uses the value of the texture only.

The Corona filter will be added to your alpha channel when the Contribute to Alpha option is selected. Use the Save Effect to File option to save just the Corona effect to a separate image file (or image sequence) when rendering, and select an appropriate file format in which LightWave should save the images.

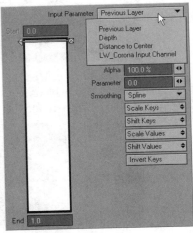

Figure 19-19

And that's it for the Corona filter. Since it offers so many more controls than the Bloom filter, you will probably find that it can take a little longer to set up, but the results often have a greater effect than using Bloom. Use Bloom when you need a quick and easy overall effect, and Corona when you need to limit the effect to certain aspects of the surface.

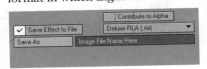

Figure 19-20

## Soften Reflections

This filter creates soft-looking reflections by simply blurring them somewhat. It is a faster rendering option than using the Reflection Blurring option in the Surface Editor, which greatly impacts rendering times.

Take a look at Figure 19-21. The logo in the background has Soften Reflections applied to it (using the filter in conjunction with Special Buffers, discussed in a moment), while the logo in the foreground does not have the

Figure 19-21

filter applied to it. Notice how the reflections in the front logo are sharp, while the reflections in the back logo are softened by the filter.

The filter is simple to control, since it only has a few adjustable options.

The Softness value controls the strength of the effect, while the Blending mode determines how the effect is applied to the surface.

Figure 19-22

The Replace mode (the default) replaces the original rendered reflections with the blurred pass, while Average calculates an average percentage between the original render and the blurred pass to create a more subtle effect. Maximum takes the maximum of the replace result and the original value to create a slightly lighter effect to avoid any dark halo around the reflection.

Alpha uses the alpha channel of the surface to blend the effect, while LumaBlend blends according to the intensity of the actual reflection.

You can select the Scale By Surface Buffer option to use the effect of the filter together with surfaces using the Special Buffers feature in the Surface Editor. This limits the effect so that it only affects surfaces using Special Buffers. For more information on using this feature, refer to Chapter 5.

# CHAPTER 20

# Creating Hair and Fur with Worley Labs' Sasquatch

This isn't texturing, is it? Well, no, strictly speaking, hair and fur are rendering affairs, but since they are intrinsically linked to surfacing as a whole, I thought it would be good to have some coverage of an excellent hair and fur solution for LightWave, Worley Labs' Sasquatch plug-in.

Figure 20-1

Sasquatch is a very vast and powerful plug-in, and to really discuss it in depth would require an entire book, but we'll take a cursory look at its uses here.

> **NOTE:** LightWave ships with a limited version of this plug-in called Saslite. For the purposes of this chapter, we will be looking at the full version of the plug-in, as it contains all of the Saslite options as well as a host of other controls for creating great-looking hair.

## Adding the Plug-in to Your Scene

Once you have installed the plug-in, Sasquatch works in Layout as a displacement on your model, and as a pixel filter for the rendering stage. To assign it to a particular layer in your scene, you simply open the Object Properties window (press "p") and assign it to the Add Displacement list under your Deform tab.

To open the plug-in's control panel, double-click on the Sasquatch name in the list. The initial panel that opens can be quite daunting at first!

Be warned that this is just one of nine such panels. Sasquatch, like G2, comes with a superbly written manual, so there is no need for me to go into every one of these options here.

Figure 20-2

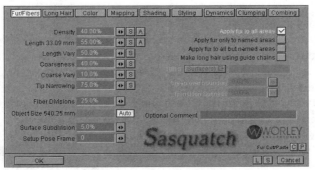

Figure 20-3

## Sasquatch Features at a Glance

Let's look at the shading options of the hair.

The Shading panel in Sasquatch contains a number of settings that you'll find familiar, since they are very similar to the surface attributes that we deal with in the Surface Editor.

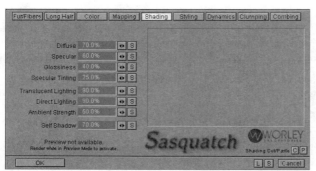

Figure 20-4

The Diffuse, Specular, and Glossiness settings work much the same as their standard surfacing counterparts in the Surface Editor. Use the Diffuse setting to brighten or darken the hair, and use the Specular and Glossiness values to determine how shiny it is. Taking the latter two values up very high will give the hair a wet look. The Specular Tinting option works like the Color Highlights option we have in the Surface Editor — it tints the specular highlights with the color of the surface.

The remaining controls on the Shading panel give us options for controlling how light affects the hair.

You can place hair on the model using a number of different options. You can apply hair to the entire model, you can apply it to a certain surface, you can attach it to guide chains (splines) that you model, or you can use weight maps or alpha images to determine where it appears as well as how it looks, in terms of density, coarseness, etc. Using weight maps is probably the most interactive way of controlling short- to medium-length hair, and is my favorite way of using Sasquatch.

Simply create a weight map in Modeler for whichever attribute you want to control, such as Density, Coarseness, Length, etc., and use high weight values to specify higher values of that attribute or lower weight values for lower values of the attribute.

Density also acts as a method of actually determining where the hair will appear. For example, if you were creating a weight map for Density, you would make the areas where you want a lot of hair a very bright orange in the weight map, and where you didn't want any hair at all you could leave those areas green, or even make them blue.

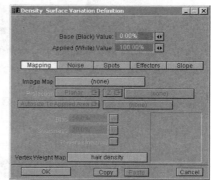

Once you use a weight map within Sasquatch, you can determine how those values are then taken into account when the hair is rendered.

Figure 20-5

To give the hair color, the Color panel offers a number of controls for us to play with.

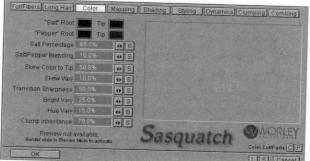

**Figure 20-6**

You can set basic color options here, as well as determine how the color changes along each strand of hair and how the color is randomized through the hair, so that it is not simply a single, unchanging color (which looks very unnatural).

You can also apply mapping to your hair in the Mapping panel.

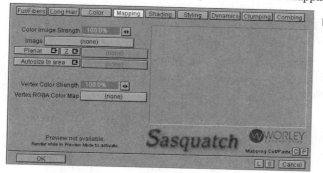

**Figure 20-7**

This allows you to use either an image or a vertex color map to color the hair. Very handy indeed! Sasquatch comes with a number of demo files that demonstrate each of these options.

Apart from shading options and mapping options, Sasquatch offers a vast array of styling tools and dynamics tools as well. While the plug-in can take some time to fully master, it is easy to get started, and since it provides such a great hair solution for LightWave, I highly recommend it to anyone who is serious about character work, since hair is such an important part of that facet of 3D.

Visit Worley Labs' site at www.worley.com for more information about Sasquatch, as well as demo files, a gallery, and tutorials.

# PART 7

# Tutorials

This section of the book runs through some brief tutorials designed for beginning to intermediate users who need a few pointers for creating basic textures and shading. All the models and scene files for the tutorials are on the companion CD.

At the end of each chapter I have summarized some basic tips for those particular types of surfaces for quick reference.

For all the texture painting in this book, I used Adobe Photoshop CS. I chose to use Photoshop since it is the most widely used painting package, although if you are using another package, I am sure that you will find that all the Photoshop tools have an equivalent option in your chosen package, since I don't really use any of the fancy tools unique to Photoshop in these tutorials.

Always build all your different texture layers in a single PSD file, and arrange your layers logically, preferably using layer sets. This makes the process of copying details between the different textures for different surface attributes much simpler.

While many of the tutorials require a painting program to paint textures, some tutorials don't use painted images at all; the texturing is done with the built-in procedural textures that come with LightWave.

Chapter 11 has a small section on good file habits that I think is worth reviewing before moving on to the tutorials.

# CHAPTER 21

# Metal Surfaces

Metal surfaces can be one of the trickier types of surfaces to get right. This is because people often neglect to set up adequate environments for their metals. Most of the realism for metal lies in the reflections, so it is essential to give your metals something to reflect; placing them in a featureless black void and then pumping up their reflection is not going to do anything at all.

Of course, there are many kinds of metals that we encounter and may have to create at some point, and each requires a different approach and different detailing.

Generally, in LightWave, you should set up your metal with relatively low Diffuse, a medium to high Specularity, a low Glossiness (unless it has a coating, like car paint), and a medium to high Reflection. Depending on the type of metal, reflections often look more realistic when blurred, especially if the metal is slightly older and worn.

The first two tutorials in this chapter are very basic ones, involving mostly shading (as opposed to actual texture creation). I have designed them to demonstrate to you how to work with your environments, and to set up the basic shading parameters for a few different types of metal. The third tutorial is not a step-by-step tutorial, but rather a rough guide to painting rusty metal textures.

## Metal Tutorial 1: Car Paint and Chrome Shading

Cars are very popular things to create in CG — I am sure you have seen loads of 3D cars before, and possibly even made a few yourself. So let's take a look at setting up basic car paint. For this tutorial we'll be working with a lovely Mini model created by a talented South African artist, Brendon Goosen. Thanks for the model, Brendon!

1.  Open up Layout. Load the 7.1-mini.lws scene from the companion CD.

Figure 21-1

The scene already has an environment added to it in the form of an HDR image loaded into Image World. This ensures that the metal and glass of the vehicle will have something to reflect.

Let's start with the car paint. There are two different colors of paint currently applied to the car — a green and a light cream color. I chose these two colors because they are classic colors for these cars, but by all means go ahead and change the color if you so wish.

Figure 21-2

2. Open the Surface Editor and select the "car paint green" surface. Set up the surface values as follows:

RGB: 13, 36, 6 (this should be applied already)
Diffuse: 80% (This lower value prevents the surface from becoming oversaturated when we apply reflections to it.)
Specularity: 100%
Glossiness: 80%
Reflection: Leave at 0% for now, as we will use a gradient for this later.

3. Leave all the other values as they are, as shown in Figure 21-3.

4.  Go to the Advanced tab and give the Color Highlights a value of 70%. This is to prevent the surface from becoming overly bright when we add reflection to it, since it tints the specularity as well as the reflections on the surface.

5.  Go back to the Basic tab now, and click on the "T" button for Reflection to open up its Texture Editor. Change the default layer to a gradient layer by clicking on the Layer Type pull-down list and selecting Gradient.

6.  Change the Input Parameter of the gradient to Incidence Angle. This gradient will allow us to control the amount of reflectivity based on the angle at which we view the painted car surface. Varying the reflectivity helps to create a sense of realism, since having a constant value of reflectivity across the entire surface is overwhelming and tends to look really CG.

Figure 21-3

7.  Select the top key on the gradient ramp that is automatically created when you create a gradient layer. Change its Value to 45%.

8.  Now create a new key at the bottom of the gradient at 90.0 (you can tweak this with the Parameter value to be sure). Change the Value of this key to 5.0%.

This gradient now makes the surface 5% reflective in areas that are directly facing the viewer (in other words, the areas that are directly perpendicular to our line of vision), and gradually increases to a value of 45% reflectivity on areas of the surface that slope out of our line of vision, this being 90°.

We are now finished with setting up the basic parameters of the green paint. However, the paint still doesn't look quite right yet.

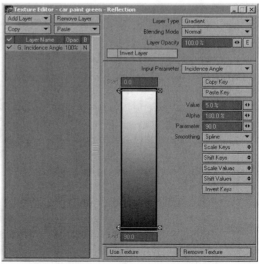

Figure 21-4

9. Go to the Shaders tab and load the BRDF shader.

10. Double-click on the shader's name to open its panel. Set up the Layer 1 tab with the following values:

Specular Reflection 1: Regular
Color: 150, 150, 150
Specular: 60%
Glossiness: 10%

This creates a fairly strong yet broad specular highlight on the surface. This sort of highlight is suitable for a dull metal.

Figure 21-5

Now we need to create another specular layer on top of this one to create the effect of a coating on the surface that has different specular properties.

11. Go to the Layer 2 tab. Set up the values on this tab as follows:

Specular Reflection 2: Regular
Color: 255, 255, 255
Specular: 150%
Glossiness: 80%

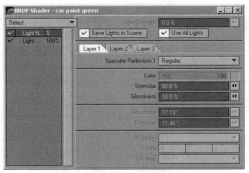

Figure 21-6

This creates a two-layer effect in the specularity of the surface. The first layer we created was suitable for metal, while the second layer acts like a lacquer that has been applied to the metal, giving it a nice shine and coating.

The preview pane in your Surface Editor should now be showing a rather reflective, shiny-coated-looking material.

Now it is time to create the cream colored paint. Since we have already set up a good-looking paint for the green, all we need to do is copy those settings into this surface and change the color to cream.

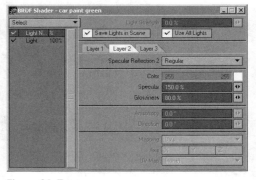

Figure 21-7

Figure 21-8

12. Select the green car paint surface, right-click on it, and select Copy. Select the cream car paint surface, right-click, and select Paste. Then change the cream paint surface RGB values to 240, 238, 198.

13. Check the Double Sided option for the cream paint; otherwise we'll be able to see through the roof of the car!

    Now let's set up the chrome surface. Chrome is highly reflective, and for the purposes of this tutorial, we'll be making it look brand spanking new. The chrome surface is applied to the bumper, the front grille, the mirrors, and all the metal trim on the vehicle's body.

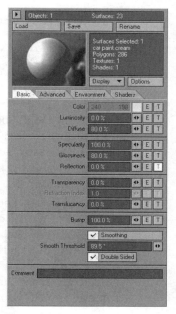

**Figure 21-9**

14. Select the "chrome" surface in the Surface Editor list and set up the basic parameters as follows:

    RGB: 32, 32, 32 (This should be applied already.)
    Diffuse: 50% (We need to make this value very low since the reflections will be quite strong.)
    Specularity: 80% (Specularity is generally unnecessary when using a lot of reflection, but I usually assign a value out of habit, and frankly it can't hurt to have a bit of specularity anyway.)
    Glossiness: 60%
    Reflection: Leave at 0% for now, as we will also be creating a gradient here again.

    Leave all the other values as they are.

15. Go to the Advanced tab and give the Color Highlights a value of 30%. Once again, this is to prevent the surface from becoming overly bright when we add reflection to it.

16. Go back to the Basic panel, and open the Texture Editor for the Reflection attribute by clicking the "T" button. Change the default layer created to a gradient layer by changing the Layer Type from Image to Gradient. Once again, this will

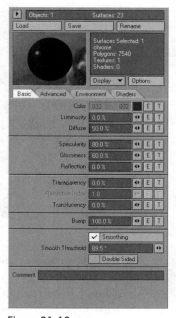

**Figure 21-10**

be an incidence-based gradient, so select Incidence Angle as the Input Parameter for the gradient.

17. Select the top key that has been created on the gradient ramp, and change its Value to 60%. Create a key at the bottom of the gradient ramp now, at 90.0, and change that key's Value to 20%.

18. Now render! As you can see, I had already set up the surfaces for the other parts of the car. Feel free to experiment with the model, set up your own surface ideas, and make something really cool out of it.

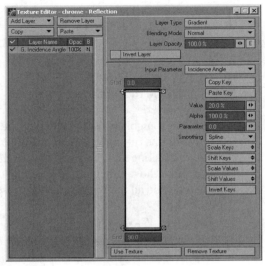

**Figure 21-11**

**Figure 21-12**

Of course this car looks very, very new with perfect chrome reflections and such, so it doesn't have much realism at all, but this was just a simple tutorial to demonstrate shading with reflections and to get started working with metallic surfaces.

Later on in this chapter we'll be looking at rusty metal, so I would recommend that you have some fun with this car and rust it up a whole lot once you're more comfortable with the techniques.

## Metal Tutorial 2: Desert Eagle Pistol

Now that you are comfortable with basic metal shading, let's move on to something a little more involved — creating metal textures and applying them to your model.

The model we will be using is a Desert Eagle pistol, also modeled by Brendon Goosen. Unlike the previous tutorial, where we made a nice, new-looking surface, we'll be scratching this surface up and learning how to make mottled, noisy reflections and specularity for steel.

1. Open Modeler and load the 7.1-desert_eagle.lwo model from the companion CD.

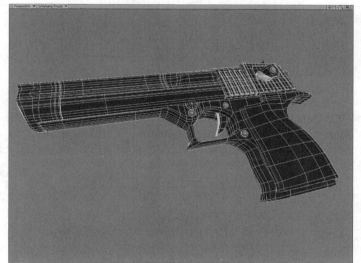

Figure 21-13

2. Go to your Top viewport where you can see the pistol from above. Zoom in so that the pistol fills the viewport rather snugly, and then take a screen shot of it by pressing Prt Sc (on a PC). Close Modeler.

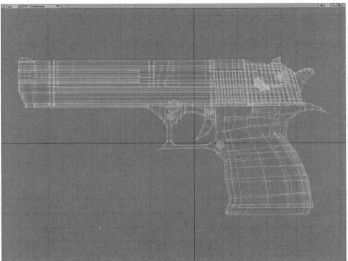

**Figure 21-14**

3.  Now go into your favorite paint application. Create a new file, which should automatically be the size of your screen (your current screen resolution in pixels). When the new document has been created, simply paste the image from your computer's clipboard into the document.

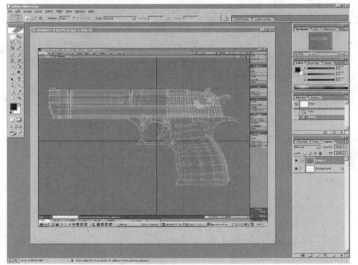

**Figure 21-15**

4.  Now crop this image so the pistol fills the image on all sides. Basically, find the topmost and lowest points of the model, and the farthest right and farthest left parts, and crop the image to that, so that there is no surrounding space around the pistol. This is so that when we finish creating the textures, we can use the Automatic Sizing option to perfectly fit the image to the model.

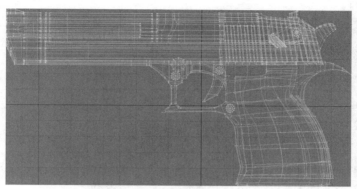

Figure 21-16

5. Before you do anything else, resize this image so that we have more room to work. Size the image up to a minimum of 2000 pixels wide. If you cropped your image to the pistol size correctly, you should have a size that is close to 2000 × 1050 pixels.

6. If your paint program has the option, lock the layer with the screen shot. This is to avoid accidentally painting on it. In Adobe Photoshop you lock a layer by clicking on the tiny little lock icon in the Layers panel where it says "Lock."

7. Create a new layer on top of the layer with the screen shot. Paint the entire area of the pistol with the RGB color 37, 42, 45. This is a dark gray-blue color.

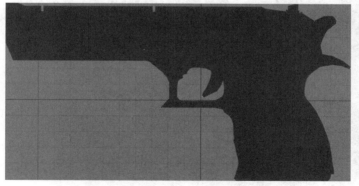

Figure 21-17

What really helps me position details when I am painting textures is to create a copy of the screen shot (or UV map shot) and place it above what I am doing so that I can see all the contours of the model, as shown in Figure 21-18.

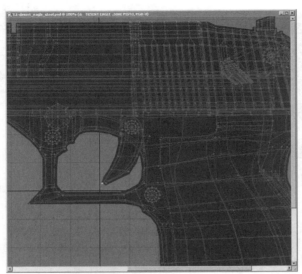

**Figure 21-18**

I copy the layer with the screen shot and increase its contrast until it is pure black and white.

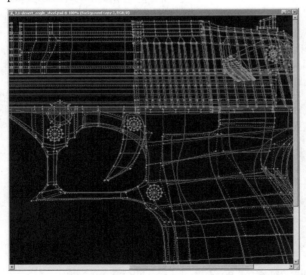

**Figure 21-19**

I then change the blending mode of this layer to Screen. This makes all the black areas of the layer transparent. I keep this layer on top of all the other layers in my Photoshop file, on a low opacity, so that I can always see what shapes I am painting onto.

8. Now comes the detailing part. Set your paintbrush to black, and on a medium to low opacity with a soft edge, paint darker areas on the gun

surface, especially following the contours of the different pieces that make up the gun. Don't overdo it though; just build up the darker tones carefully and subtly. Then use a white paintbrush, also on a low opacity with a soft edge, and gently build up a few lighter areas here and there.

Figure 21-20 shows the areas that I darkened and lightened — please note that I have brightened the image solely to make it clearer to you what I have done, and that my texture is not mysteriously a whole lot lighter than yours.

Figure 21-20

This is simply to create some color variation. If you look at the contours of the model, you'll see that I darkened areas at the edges of pieces and the area around the plastic grip, as these are areas that often tend to become worn or gather grime. Steel tends to become blackish in areas from the oil from people's fingers over a long period of time. So these darker areas create that effect. The lighter areas simply offset the darker areas here and there, solely for the purpose of variation.

The important thing is to do this carefully. Don't go and simply paint big splotches of dark and light tones. Build up your tonal variations subtly and cautiously.

9. Create a new layer. Fill this layer with the same color that you initially painted the gun. Now create some noise. In Adobe Photoshop you can do this by going to Filter>Noise>Add Noise. Set the Amount to 100%, leave the Distribution on Gaussian, and make sure that the noise is Monochromatic.

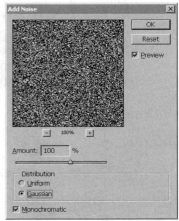

Figure 21-21

10. Now add Motion Blur to the noise. Go to Filter>Blur>Motion Blur, set the Distance to 250 pixels, and leave the Angle at 0.

Your layer should now look like Figure 21-23. I have cropped my layer to the shape of the pistol, although it isn't strictly necessary. I have also increased the contrast in this image so that the detail is clearer for you to see.

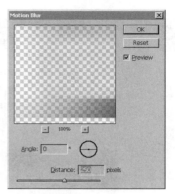

Figure 21-22

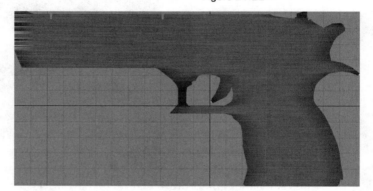

Figure 21-23

11. Change the Blending Mode of this layer to Darken. Doing this now blends the brushed layer with the layer beneath it, so that it just adds a hint of detail to the color map so far.

12. Time for some scratches. Create a new layer and set the color of your paintbrush to a light gray, around 140, 140, 140. Make your paintbrush size 1 pixel. Now paint some scratches around the barrel, on the tip of the muzzle, and around the trigger. These are areas that are likely to become scratched since they come into contact the most with other things such as the owner's hand and the holster. You can paint the scratches fairly roughly, in a criss-crossing pattern.

Figure 21-24 shows a close-up of the scratches I created around the trigger area.

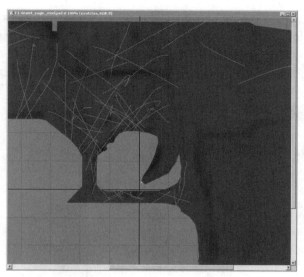

Figure 21-24

13. Now change the opacity of this particular layer to 20% or thereabouts, so that they are only faintly visible.

14. Desert Eagles have some text on them, so let's add that next. Use Arial, at size 36 for this text, and type "® DESERT EAGLE .50AE PISTOL" and below that line, type "ISRAEL MILITARY INDUSTRIES LTD (I.M.I)." Set the text to center justification and place it on the shaft of the pistol, as shown in Figure 21-25.

Figure 21-25

15. Change the text color to black and set the layer's opacity down to 40%. That's it for the color layers. Save a copy of this out as your color image texture.

16. Create a new layer. This will be the base layer for your bump texture. Make it a medium gray, using 100, 100, 100 as the RGB values.

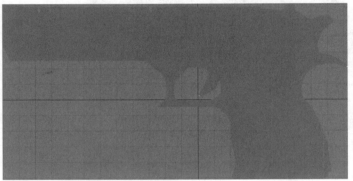

**Figure 21-26**

17. Copy the scratches layer you made earlier and place the new copy over the bump base layer. Change the brightness of the layer (go to Image>Adjustments>Brightness/Contrast) so that the scratches are a shade of gray just slightly darker than the gray of the base bump layer. We don't want these to look like giant scratches in the surface, just very shallow abrasions on it.

18. Copy the text layer that you made earlier, and place it above the scratches layer. Change the color of the text to 157, 157, 157. This is so that the text will appear slightly raised on the surface of the pistol.

**Figure 21-27**

19. Next, copy the brushed layer that you created with the motion blurred noise and place it in between the scratches layer and the text layer. Change the blending mode of the layer to Screen. It will go much lighter, adding the brushed grain to the underlying layers. This will help to

create some texture to the bump map so that the metal does not appear totally smooth.

20. Your bump layers are now complete. Save a copy out as a file to use as a texture in LightWave.

21. Now we move on to the specular layers. Create a new layer and fill it with a medium gray, RGB 60, 60, 60. Now go to Filter>Noise>Add Noise. Enter an Amount of 20% and leave the other settings as they are.

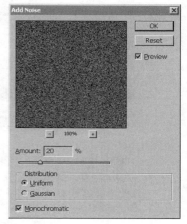

Adding noise to the specularity softens the specular highlights somewhat, and gives the metal that mottled, grainy look that steel generally tends to have.

22. Now, as you did before with the color layers, create a new layer, and taking a dark paintbrush on a low opacity with a soft edge, paint some darker areas on top of the noisy specular layer to create some variations. Do the same with a light color as well, so that some areas have slightly stronger specular values.

**Figure 21-28**

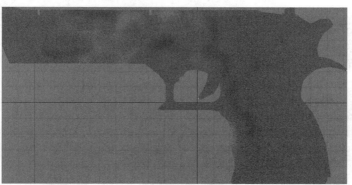

**Figure 21-29**

23. Copy the scratches layer from the bump map, and place it above the layer you just created. Adjust the brightness of the layer (Image>Adjustments>Brightness/Contrast) so that the scratches are a very light gray (not white, but close to white).

Figure 21-30

And now for the final little detail in the specular map. This one is optional, and is rather over the top, but it's the kind of detail that I love adding — fingerprints. Fingerprints are really great to add to the specular maps of shiny materials like metals and plastics since in reality we see them all over everything. In this particular example, I will use fingerprints to lessen the specularity, although in some cases a fresh fingerprint will actually increase the specularity because of its oily residue.

Making a fingerprint is simple. You can try to find an image of one on the web (do a Google image search for "fingerprint"), or you can even take your own prints and scan them in. However you choose to do them, make sure you edit the image to get a nice, clear, contrasted fingerprint like the one in Figure 21-31.

Figure 21-31

24. Add a few fingerprints to the barrel of the pistol.

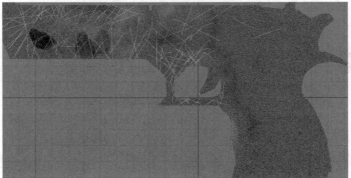

Figure 21-32

What's really great about a detail like this is that you can brag about it. You can go around saying, "I even added fingerprints to the textures — aren't I a great texturing artist?" and everyone will be suitably impressed. Or maybe not. Well, it's up to you really. Save these textures as a copy to a file that you will use as a specular texture.

25. Moving on to the reflection layers now, the reflection map will be the last map you create for this particular model. Start off by copying the noisy layer you created as the base texture for the specular map. Darken it considerably (by about 65% in the Brightness/Contrast panel), as we don't want the pistol to be too reflective, so darken it until it becomes a dark charcoal gray, almost black. The noise in the layer will give us a nice grainy reflectivity for the pistol.

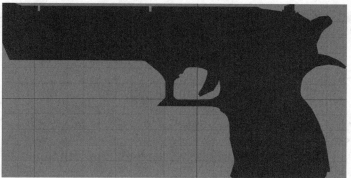

**Figure 21-33**

26. Just as we have done before with the color and specular layers, create a new layer now and paint some lighter and darker areas here and there to create a little variation. Make sure that the light areas are not too light though, as we want to keep the overall reflectivity quite low.

**Figure 21-34**

27. Finally, copy the scratches layer and place it above this last layer, and take the opacity down slightly so that the scratches won't be too reflective. We just want the scratches to be slightly more reflective than the rest. Save these layers to a file to use as a reflection texture.

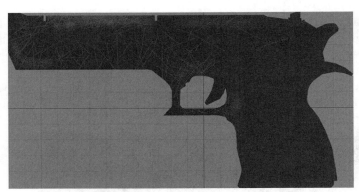

Figure 21-35

And now we are done with the texture painting!

28. Load the 7.1-desert_Eagle.lws scene from the companion CD in Layout. I have already set up a basic light in the scene, as well as a light that is purely there for adding specular highlights. You'll notice that the spotlight has the Affect Diffuse option turned off, while Affect Specular remains checked. Having lighting that is there purely for specularity can help to enhance shiny objects without making their surfaces overblown from high diffuse levels.

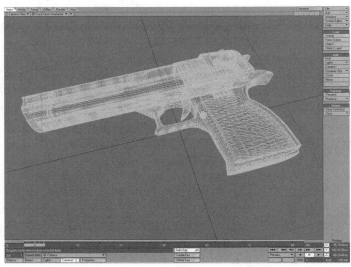

Figure 21-36

29. Open the Surface Editor, and select the "steel" surface. Set up the basic parameters as follows:

RGB: 37, 42, 45 (not really all that necessary though, since we are going to be using a texture for the color)
Diffuse: 70%
Specularity: Leave at 0% (since we are mapping it)

Glossiness: 3% (so that the specular highlights are broad, creating a duller, cold metal
look)
Reflection: Leave at 0% (because we've
made a texture for it)

Leave all the other settings as they are.

30. Open the Texture Editor for the Color
attribute by clicking on the "T" button
next to it. The default layer that is created
is for an image map, so simply load your
color map that you saved into this layer by
loading it from the Image pull-down list.

Select Y as the Texture Axis since we
are projecting the image downward onto the
model. Hit the Automatic Sizing option.
Since you cropped the screen shot of the pistol earlier to the exact proportions of the
model, the image should project perfectly
onto the pistol. (See Figure 21-38.)

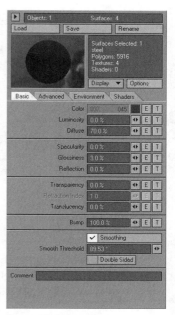

**Figure 21-37**

31. Now do the same thing
for the Specularity,
Reflection, and Bump
channels, loading the
appropriate texture that
you created into each of
their Texture Editor
panels.

32. Render! You'll notice that
I have activated radiosity
in the lighting, simply
because it looks so nice!
If you are finding the rendering too slow, you
might want to consider
switching the radiosity off
or changing the quality of
the radiosity to speed it
up.

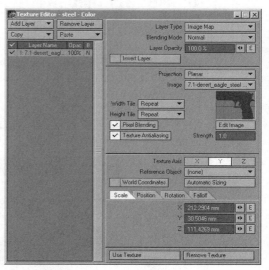

**Figure 21-38**

Your render should look something like Figure 21-39.

**Figure 21-39**

If you find that the reflections or specularity has come out a little too bright, simply adjust the Layer Opacity of those textures in their respective Texture Editor panels.

## Metal Tutorial 3: Rusty Metal Textures

The previous two tutorials were basic ones that explained every single step in detail. For the advanced tutorials in this book, the steps won't be explained as explicitly (in fact, the steps aren't even numbered), but are rather shown as a guide for building your own textures. This is to encourage you, the artist, to develop your own initiative in creating and painting textures.

The example that we are looking at is a beaten iron goblin helmet that is in some dire need of rust and aging, and more realism.

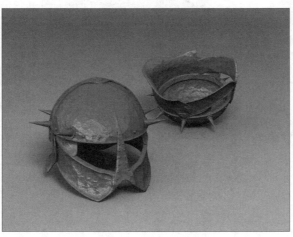

**Figure 21-40**

I have set up all the UV mapping for this model already, and you'll find it on the companion CD as 7.1-helmet.lwo. Load it up, export its UVs into your paint program, and follow along.

Before we get started, I want to explain that since we are going for a relatively realistic look (compared with the previous two tutorials), we will create no specular maps for this model. Instead we'll stick purely to reflection mapping, a color map, and a bump map. Simple, yet you'll be surprised at how effective just these three textures can be. I literally painted the maps for this model in less than 15 minutes, and you should be able to do the same once you are comfortable enough with the process.

When I open the UV map (which I exported from Modeler as an EPS file), I have the following image. I set the UVs out in such a way as to make the painting really, really simple.

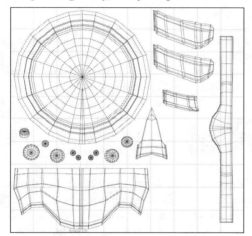

Figure 21-41

I start off by painting a wash of color, using a dark brown (actually it is the same shade of brown that was assigned to the model initially, as shown in the previous image of the helmet render). This particular shade of brown has RGB values of 55, 46, 38 and works really well as a dirty iron color.

Once I have painted by wash of color, I do the usual step of taking light and dark paintbrushes and painting lighter and darker areas for some variation. Figure 21-42 shows this, although please note that I have brightened this image so that the variations will be a little more apparent to you.

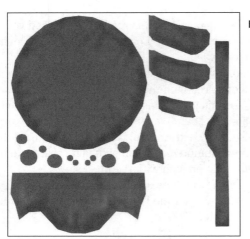

**Figure 21-42**

As you can see, I have created mostly dark areas around the edges. This is mostly due to habit, but is based on the premise that grime tends to collect toward edges of things a lot more than on the open middle areas.

Next I want to add some rust. Now the really cool thing about painting rust textures is that generally there is no necessity to paint them by hand. This is because there is an ample supply of rust photos available on the web and in texture collection CDs. And because rust isn't particularly reflective, it is easy to get photographs of it that can be used as textures, since it is so dull and doesn't tend to pick up any highlighting when you take a photo of it.

I have a massive collection of rust photos that I have collected over the years, and when I am painting rusty textures, I always use a couple of different ones to create subtle variations in the rust color.

So basically all I do is drag a couple of different rust photographs into the texture file, and using a combination of a soft-edged eraser and the Rubber Stamp (clone) tool, I place some rust all over the texture. Once I have roughly positioned all the rusty bits, I take down the opacity of the eraser and work some areas so that the rust is a little less solid, purely for the sake of variation.

Figure 21-43 shows the rust that I have created on the different parts. I have left the lower layer brightened in this image so that the rust is a little clearer to you.

Zooming into an area now, as shown in Figure 21-44, you can see the three different rust images I used. The first rusty image has a relatively dark, powdery rust in it, the second image is coarser with larger details, and the third is a streaky rust.

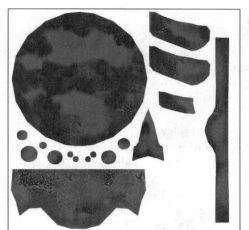

Figure 21-43

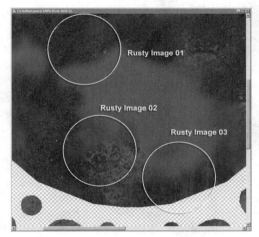

Figure 21-44

It is really important to ensure that you don't use a tiny little photograph of rust and then simply clone it all over the place. This always looks nasty since it creates a patchy look with no real detail. Use large images and use a few different ones, so that you can create a variety of different rusty types and tones.

As always, vary the opacity of your tools while you erase parts, and use the Rubber Stamp (clone) tool carefully so that your texture does not look overly repeated. And remember to use soft-edged brushes!

Believe it or not, this is the finished color map. Just two steps, one to create the base and the second to create the rust. Because we'll be using reflection maps on this, the surface will pick up a lot of detail from its environment, as metal does in reality, so the model won't look plain, trust me.

Moving on to the reflection maps, I simply create a new layer that has a gray value of 3%, so that the overall reflectivity of the metal will be 3%. As low as that is, it will be absolutely adequate for this type of metal. We also don't want the metal to be too reflective, since it wouldn't make sense if some parts of it were really shiny while other parts were all rusty. If something is rusty, logic dictates that it is probably quite old or has seen a lot of action.

To this layer of 3% gray I add some noise on a very low level, just to have some graininess in the reflectivity. I also take my Burn tool and make a few areas slightly darker, for an overall variation. Figure 21-45 has been brightened so that you can see the details more clearly.

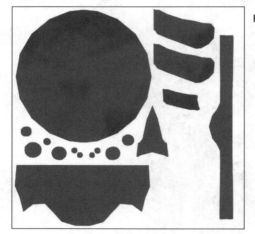

Figure 21-45

Of course, now we need to make sure that the rusty areas are not reflective, so all I do is copy the rusty layer over, place it above this layer, and darken it until it is black. Figure 21-46 shows the result, with the lower layer kept brightened for you to see.

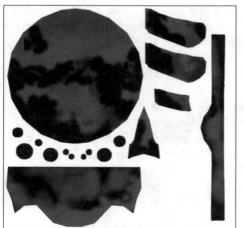

Figure 21-46

The final reflection texture looks like Figure 21-47. While it is almost impossible to see the difference between the rusty parts and the reflective parts with our eyes, LightWave will definitely see the difference.

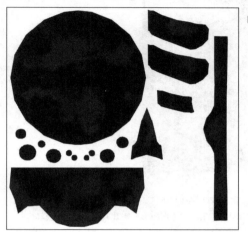

Figure 21-47

Last comes the bump map. As the basis for my bump map, I baked a Crumple procedural out to the model's UV map. This Crumple texture creates a look of the surface having been beaten into shape with a hammer.

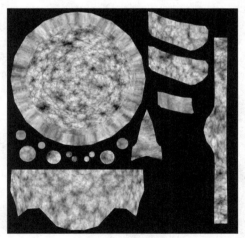

Figure 21-48

On top of this layer I simply drag a copy of the rust color layer and desaturate it. It couldn't possibly be simpler.

Figure 21-49

Of course, I am lucky since the rust textures I am using actually appear to work correctly as a bump map when desaturated. I know that I have said before that simply desaturating a color map is usually wrong since the details are rarely correct, but this is one of those times when it actually does work, mostly because there are no shadows in the photo and the lighting is so even.

I now load up Layout and set up my scene. Of course, as always, I start off by bringing an HDR image into LightWave and loading it into Image World.

I then set up a single area light and activate radiosity. I apply the textures to the model, render, and get the image shown in Figure 21-50.

Figure 21-50

Now who said that metal textures were difficult, eh?

As you can see, the reflections in the surface create some great details on it that liven up the otherwise rather plain brown areas that I painted in the color texture. Of course, as always, it could certainly benefit from some tweaking, but considering the fact that this took less than 15 minutes, you have ample time to tweak it.

## Summary of Tips for Creating Metal Surfaces

- Always place metal surfaces in an environment that they can reflect.
- Use low Diffuse values.
- Use medium to high Specular values (for quick rendering results).
- Use low to medium Glossiness values (if you're using specular mapping).
- Use low to high Reflection values in reflection maps for more realistic effects (instead of specular maps).
- Scratch the metal up, especially in areas where it is touched a lot.
- Scratches in steel and other duller metals are generally more specular/reflective than the surrounding metal. Once the metal has aged a lot, place rust into the cracks and scratches.
- Use the Color Highlights option to prevent high levels of reflectivity from becoming blown out.
- Create mottled reflection and specular maps to give a sense of wear and tear.
- Blur the reflections for slightly older metal, especially steel.
- Use noisy images or procedurals in the specular and reflection maps to create a grainy effect.
- Use the BRDF shader for anisotropic effects. Worley Labs' G2 plug-in also has great anisotropic effects and can produce very realistic results.

# CHAPTER 22

# Wood Surfaces

Wood surfaces are one of the surfaces that I am generally quite lazy with. Ordinarily I love painting textures, but wooden surfaces are just a pain because the burls and knots are tricky details to paint. So I always tend to use photographs to create them instead. What's the point in struggling with painting textures when a photograph is perfectly adequate? And the cool thing about wood is that there are loads of photos available, and, like rusty metal, many are highly suited to being used as textures since they don't tend to have lighting information in them, especially in the case of finished woods such as wood parquet and other household woods that tend to be smooth.

Most texture CD-ROM collections have hundreds of great high-resolution wood images that you can incorporate into your textures with the greatest of ease. I have a couple of texture collections that contain loads of fantastic wood images that I use all the time while creating wood textures and will be using in these tutorials. Since I cannot redistribute these images, you'll have to locate wood images of your own, but they are relatively easy to find for free if you are not in a position to purchase a texture collection.

Depending on the type of wood, the shading of the surface can differ rather vastly. Finished woods can be very reflective and smooth, while older wood or untreated wood, such as raw planks, crates, etc., can be very dry and sometimes quite rough.

## Wood Tutorial 1: A Guitar

This tutorial covers the very quick and easy process of creating a suitable wood image for a guitar, specifically a detailed Gibson Les Paul guitar model.

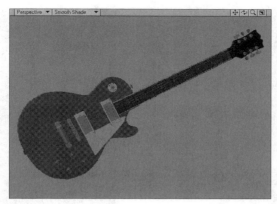

Figure 22-1

We will only be creating a color map for this particular model, since the wood is varnished and totally smooth. For the varnish, I have created an actual layer of polygons surrounding the body of the guitar that we'll shade as a lacquer to add a great shine to the wood beneath. Doing the lacquer as a separate layer of polygons creates a far better effect than simply trying to create a two-layer effect by shading.

1.  Open the 7.2-LesPaul.lwo model from the companion CD in Modeler. Go to your Front viewport, zoom into the body part of the guitar, and take a screen shot of it.

2.  Open up your paint program and paste the image from your computer's clipboard into a new document. Crop the image to the size of the model so that the edges of the model's body touch the edges of the image. This is to ensure that we can use the Automatic Sizing option to fit the texture to the model once it is done.

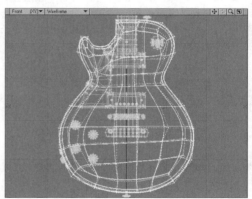

Figure 22-2

3.  Size the image up to at least 1000 pixels in width before continuing. This is to ensure that the texture will look right when viewed up close.

4.  Find some images of wood that are large enough to be used in a texture. Do a Google image search or look through web sites such as www.imageafter.com to find loads of images that are suitable.

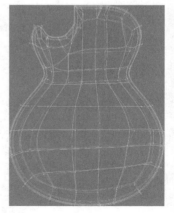

Figure 22-3

**515**

These particular guitars are often made from maple, so I found an image of maple to use. I specifically wanted something with a bit of a pattern in it, since it makes the guitar a little more interesting to look at. If the image you have found is not large enough to cover the guitar body, then clone it around a bit to cover it all. Make sure that you don't clone any small details too many times, since that can be a dead giveaway that it is fake.

The grain of wood on a guitar runs along the length of it, not across the width. So make sure that any visible grain in your wood image is vertical in your texture.

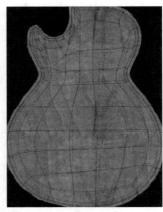

Figure 22-4

5.  If your wood is relatively plain, try to find an image of a wood knot to add to your texture. I found the image shown in Figure 22-5.

6.  Mixing a detail like this with the rest of your texture is simple. Start off by desaturating it to gray and place it over the rest of the wood that you have so far to position it where you would like it to be. Don't place it too near the edge because you'll be doing some spray painting there in

Figure 22-5

a moment. Erase the edges so that you are simply left with the knot or burl or whatever detail you are adding to the texture. Remember to use a soft-edged eraser so that the edge of the image will blend with the layer below it. See Figure 22-6.

7.  Now you need to use your eyes. Go to Image>Adjust-ments>Hue/ Saturation (or whatever the equiv-alent is in your painting application) and adjust the color and saturation of the image until it blends with the layer beneath it. See Fig-ure 22-7.

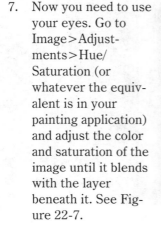

Figure 22-6

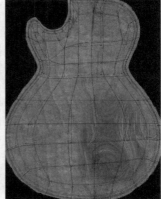

Figure 22-7

If you have ever worked in compositing or grading, then this type of color and saturation adjustment will be easy for you to do. For the rest of you, just use your best judgment. This is something that you will get better at over time.

Try to get the overall color of the wood to be quite a bright orangey red.

> **NOTE:** I have included this texture on the companion CD in case you couldn't find any decent wood images. Look for it in the Images folder in the Tutorials directory — it's called 7.2-LesPaul_wood.tga, a 24-bit Targa file.

8. Now it's time to add the spray paint work. Take a look at the photograph in Figure 22-8.

This is the type of finish that we are aiming for. The design of the paint along the edges, showing the wood grain in the middle of the body, is called a sunburst — a popular paint finish for guitars.

9. Mix up a nice deep red color using the RGB values 36, 6, 0. Now, carefully following the contours of the screen shot, spray with a soft-edged brush along the edges of the guitar to create the sunburst design. See Figure 22-9.

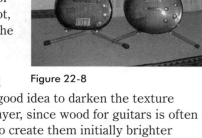

Figure 22-8

10. Now that we have the paint work and the wood looking fine, it is usually a good idea to darken the texture using a Hue/Saturation Adjustment layer, since wood for guitars is often stained to be darker (it's just easier to create them initially brighter since we can see the details better). Adjust the texture so that it is darker but still saturated enough. You should ideally end up with a medium to darkish brown that still has a strong hint of red in it. See Figure 22-10.

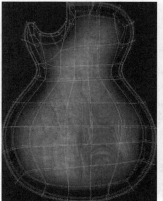
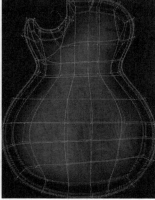

Figure 22-9                    Figure 22-10

11. Open Layout and load the 7.2-LesPaul.lws scene from the companion CD.

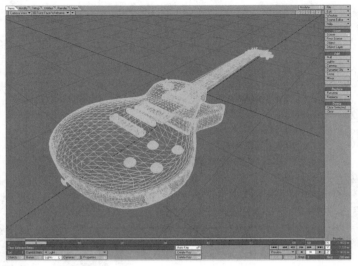

Figure 22-11

I have already set up the scene to include an HDR image in Image World for the reflections in the metal and the wood finish.

12. Open the Surface Editor and set up the wood surface first. Select the "wood inner" surface and set up the basic parameters as follows:

Color: 96, 78, 43 (although this doesn't really matter since we're applying a texture to it)
Diffuse: 80%
Specularity: 80%
Glossiness: 60%
Reflection: 2%

Leave all the other settings as they are.

13. Open up the Color Texture Editor by clicking the "T" button next to it. Using the default image layer that is created, load the texture that you made. Using Planar as the Projection type, select the z-axis as the Texture Axis and click on the Automatic Sizing option, as shown in Figure 22-13. This should fit your image perfectly onto the model.

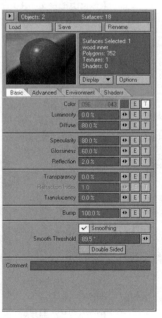

Figure 22-12

Figure 22-13

Now to set up the lacquer surface. This will give the body that nice varnished two-layer effect.

14. Select the "lacquer" surface and set up its basic parameters as follows:

Color: 0, 0, 0 (since we want it to be clear)
Diffuse: 10% (a surface should usually have at least a little diffuse applied in order for it to have shadows cast onto it)
Specularity: 80%
Glossiness: 60%
Reflection: 0% (we'll map it with a gradient in a moment)
Transparency: 95%
Refraction Index: 1.2
Select the Double Sided option.

Leave all the other settings as they are.

15. Go to the Advanced tab and change the Color Highlights value to 80%. This is to prevent the surface from becoming too blown out when lit.

16. Go back to the Basic tab and open the Reflection Texture Editor. Change the default layer to a gradient texture by selecting Gradient from the Layer Type pull-down list at the top right of the panel.

Figure 22-14

**519**

17. Change the Input Parameter of the gradient to Incidence Angle. We'll use this gradient to vary the amount of reflectivity based on the angle at which the surface is viewed.

18. Select the top key that is made on the gradient ramp and change its Value to 30%. We don't really want the reflections on the lacquer surface to be too strong, so 30% is an adequate amount.

19. Create a new key at the bottom of the gradient ramp and change its Value to 2%. The way the gradient is now, areas that are viewed directly at 90° will appear to be 2% reflective, while areas that are sloping away from our vision increase to a maximum of 30%. However, in this particular instance, a linear increase from 2% to 30% is a little too strong overall, so add a third key to the gradient a little way above the middle.

20. Tweak its Parameter setting to 30.0 and change its Value to 4%.

    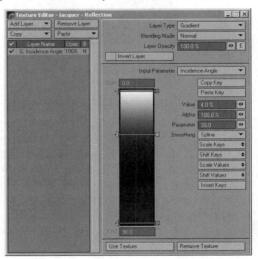

    What this key now does is it keeps the overall reflectivity to a maximum of 4% until shortly before the surface slopes away, at which it rapidly increases to 30% reflectivity.

    This isn't strictly realistic at all, but artistically it creates a more pleasing result for our purposes.

21. Render! Your guitar should look similar to Figure 22-16.

    This is a decent enough start for the texture. Feel free to go wild by adding fingerprints and smears and whatnot to your reflection map to make it more realistic.

**Figure 22-15**

**Figure 22-16**

# Wood Tutorial 2: An Old Crate

This is not a step-by-step tutorial, but rather a guide to creating rougher, more messed up wooden textures using an old wooden crate as an example. Figure 22-17 shows the crate we'll be looking at. (All three crates in this render are actually the same crate, just cleverly rotated to keep that from being too noticeable.)

**Figure 22-17**

This scene (and object) is on the companion CD, so feel free to load it up and follow along. The scene is called 7.2_crate.lws and the object is called 7.2_crate.lwo.

I have already set up the UV maps for this crate, exported them from Modeler, and opened the template up in Photoshop.

I start off my texture by scrounging through my vast texture library and finding some appropriate images of planks. I carefully place these planks around on the template, being careful to ensure that no repeated details appear close to one other.

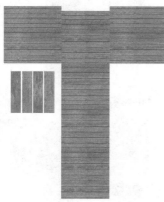

**Figure 22-18**

You may have noticed that I have left dark lines between each of the planks. This is because dirt and such tends to build up between planks of wood like this, so having these areas darker is not necessarily a problem.

Next up I want to make the paint layer. Since I want this crate to look like it's had a pretty eventful life, I want to have paint that is chipped away in a lot of places. To do this most effectively, I can use a grunge mapping technique (as discussed in Chapter 11).

Once again, I go through my collection of texture images, looking for some ideal images for this situation. See Figure 22-19 on the following page.

**521**

What I do now is desaturate it and increase the contrast, until it looks like Figure 22-20.

Figure 22-19

Figure 22-20

I then clone this around on top of my previously made wood base layer. I also take a white paintbrush and paint very lightly onto some areas to create small patches that don't have as much gritty detail. See Figure 22-21.

All I have to do now is colorize the layer using Hue/Saturation, which I use to color this layer a fairly bright red, as shown in Figure 22-22.

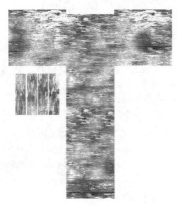

Figure 22-21

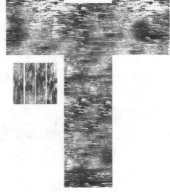

Figure 22-22

I then change the blending mode of the layer to Color Burn and decrease its opacity by 40%, which allows the underlying wood texture to show through the white areas of the texture. This creates a perfect peeled and chipped paint look that actually looks like a thin coating of wood stain.

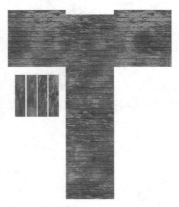

Figure 22-23

Well, that is the wood part sorted out. You see how easy it is to create details like chipped paint simply from another image of wood? Always remember to think outside the box. Images can be altered to serve many purposes.

All I add now is a little "EXPORT" label to the crate, and use an eraser to eat away at parts of the letters so that they too look old and chipped. See Figure 22-24.

Moving onto the bump map now, I use a very quick and easy method for making the bumps — simply copying the color textures and altering them slightly. I start off by copying the base layer of the color texture and altering its contrast slightly, as well as desaturating it to gray, as shown in Figure 22-25.

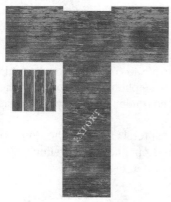

Figure 22-24

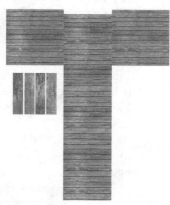

Figure 22-25

Again, this is another rare situation where it is actually possible to use the desaturated color map as the base for the bump map, since there are no highly contrasted, specific details that will create the wrong effect.

I want the paint to appear very slightly raised off the wood, so I copy the paint layer and place it above this bump base layer. Inverting it now makes the paint parts lighter while the other parts appear to go darker. This is the exact effect I need since it will indeed raise the painted parts slightly off the surface.

Figure 22-26

And that's all I need for the bump texture. This leaves only the specular texture to be created.

Since this wood is old and dry, it won't really have much specularity. In fact, the paint will have a very slight specular value while the wood itself will have almost 0%.

I copy my bump textures and reblend them to create the specular map, darkening both considerably. The image in Figure 22-27 shows the specular map; however, please note that this image has been lightened so that you can see more clearly what I have done.

**Figure 22-27**

And that's it really. As you have seen, wood textures are definitely one of the simpler types of textures to create because of the way that we can use photographs to create them.

I load up my crates into Layout and render them to get the image that you saw in Figure 22-17.

As I demonstrated in an earlier chapter, I can make the clones of the crate within the scene appear different from one another simply by adding a procedural diffuse map to them, as shown in Figure 22-28.

**Figure 22-28**

## Summary of Tips for Creating Wooden Surfaces

- Finding and using suitable photographs for your textures is usually quicker than painting wooden images.

- Make sure that the direction of the grain in the wood is correct. For example, you wouldn't have the grain running horizontally across the width of a long plank — the grain would run along the length of it.

- For lacquered, finished wood objects, model an additional layer surrounding the wood and shade it as you would clear plastic.

- For older or dry woods (such as trees, crates, driftwood, or rough planks), use little to no specularity and no glossiness. Using reflection for highlights on dry wood is a waste of rendering time, so stick to specularity in small quantities.

- If you are working on a tree with coarse, chunky bark, use displacement mapping for the bark instead of just a bump map. A bump map will most likely end up looking fake.

- Details such as fingerprints make lacquered wood duller. Add dark streaks from fingerprints to your reflection or specular maps to lessen the effect in those areas.

- When lacquered wood has just been polished, it shows streaks of variations in the reflection map, usually in circular patterns, since this is the pattern in which most people tend to polish. If you really want to be a detail freak, add these patterns to your reflection maps.

- Whatever you do, don't use that cedarfence.jpg image that every single 3D user on the planet has used at some stage or another as a wood texture. It has been used to death, and it is about time that it is retired from its long-standing run in the 3D world.

# CHAPTER 23

# Organic Surfaces

Organic surfaces are probably the toughest surfaces to create, because not only do you have to make them look realistic, but you also need to make them look alive, and that is by far the trickiest thing to do in texturing.

I tried, I really did, to write a step-by-step tutorial on painting human skin for this book, but failed miserably. You cannot give somebody a paint-by-numbers tutorial on painting human skin because a lot of artistic technique is involved, and it requires an approach and a certain delicacy that cannot be taught, only developed over time and with practice.

And the same really applies to any organic surface. This is because organic surfaces require a subtlety that can be demonstrated but not laid out in a series of instructions. I cannot teach you to be an artist; I can only show you my own examples and hope that by observing, you will understand what it is that is required and subsequently develop your own technique of creating what you know is needed.

As I have said time and time again, references are essential when creating textures, and this is probably the single most important piece of advice I can give you when it comes to organic substances. If you have lots of references, you simply cannot go wrong. Paint what you see and paint what you need. This is a simple philosophy, but it usually requires a lot of work.

By now you should have a clear understanding of why and how surfaces work, and what you need to manipulate in your settings in order to achieve certain effects.

If, for any reason, you are still trying to get a handle on texturing, I recommend that you stick to simpler surfaces until you have a finer grasp of them before trying to tackle organic surfaces; otherwise, there's a good chance you will simply end up disappointed. Organic surfaces, above all, require patience, an artistic eye, extreme attention to detail, and very good painting and color skills.

There are two tutorials in this section. The first is that of an eyeball. The eyeball is a step-by-step tutorial; however, it does not involve texture painting (I have supplied an iris image for you to use). I included this tutorial solely because eyes are one of the most essential parts of a character, and all too often I see dead-looking eyes in digital characters.

The second tutorial is a guide to human face painting. The same ideas can be applied to any type of skin. As you will see, it all comes down to observation and recreation, with a large dose of careful painting and use of color.

Good luck!

## Organic Tutorial 1: An Eyeball

Eyes are the windows to the soul. Well, some people say so anyway. By creating eyes that have a sense of depth, we instantly impart life to our characters, and this is why it is so important to ensure that your character's eyes, whether they are human, alien, or animal, are believable and have a spark of life in them.

The first essential thing for eyes is to model them with details. At the very minimum, model your eyeballs in three parts: the inner eyeball, the outer liquid layer covering the inner eyeball, and the lens.

Modeling your eyes to have these three parts is the first step to a successful eyeball. I am supplying an eyeball model for this tutorial anyway, so feel free to use it as much as you like on all your characters if you've simply been using spheres up to now.

Some people also like to model the actual pupil separately as well, but that is only really necessary when you are going to be doing a lot of close-up animation and want to have control over animating the size of the pupil according to lighting changes.

1.  Load up the 7.3-Eyeball.lws scene from the companion CD. You'll see a lonesome eyeball staring up at you.

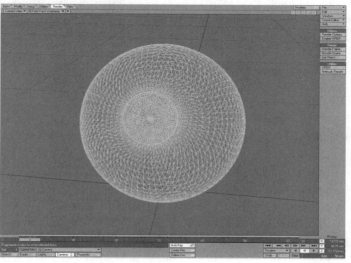

Figure 23-1

As always, I have already set up Image World in this scene to create an environment with an HDR image so that the eyeball has something to reflect.

I have already painted the textures for this eyeball, but let's quickly take a look at each of them. (You'll find the Photoshop file of this eyeball texture with a few different colored irises on the companion CD.)

First, let's examine the color texture.

It really couldn't be simpler. I took a photo of an iris, worked it a bit to remove lighting (this involved cloning areas onto the areas where there was light), and positioned it correctly onto the image. If you look at the Photoshop file I have included on the CD, you'll find a blue and a brown variation of this iris as well.

Immediately surrounding the iris we have a white area with faint pink coloring in certain areas, just to offset the white slightly. And surrounding the white is a pink border, with veins of varying intensity. The pink edges and the veins are on separate layers and can therefore be adjusted separately. Please feel free to go ahead and alter these to your tastes.

Secondly, we have a bump map.

As you can see in Figure 23-3, the bump map is solely for adding a bit of bump to the veins on the eyeball. Again, the veins are on separate layers so they can be adjusted to suit your taste.

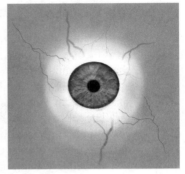

Figure 23-2

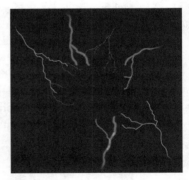

Figure 23-3

2. Back to the scene. I have already added the textures to the eyeball's "eyeball inner" surface, which is the actual inner sphere forming the bulk of the eye itself.

Set up the rest of the basic parameters as follows:

Diffuse: 50%
Reflection: 3%
Translucency: 50%

Leave all the other values as they are. This creates a reasonably fleshy eyeball that is somewhat reflective. Having a bit of reflection on the inner eye helps to create a deeper look to it since it appears to form more layers.

3. The eyeball lens and the outer eyeball surfaces require the same settings, so all we need to do is set one up and then copy it to the other.

Select either one of them and let's get started. Set up the basic parameters as follows:

Color: 255, 255, 255 (pure white)
Diffuse: 40%
Specularity: 80%
Glossiness: 60%
Reflection: 0% (we'll map this in a moment)
Transparency: 0% (we'll be mapping this one too)
Refraction Index: 1.2

Make sure that both Smoothing and Double Sided are checked. See Figure 23-4.

4. Open the Reflection Texture Editor by clicking on the "T" button next to it. Change the default layer to a gradient texture by selecting Gradient from the Layer Type pull-down list at the top right of the panel. Change the gradient's Input Parameter to Incidence Angle.

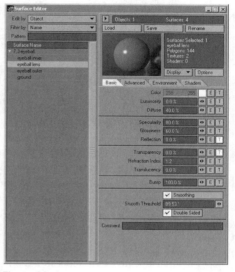

Figure 23-4

5. Select the top key on the gradient ramp and change its Value to 5%. Now create a second key at the bottom of the ramp and set its Value to 1%. This applies a very low level of reflectivity to the surface; however, even such a low level is sufficient for this example. See Figure 23-5.

6. Open the Texture Editor for Transparency. Change this default layer also to a gradient texture and select Incidence Angle as the Input Parameter.

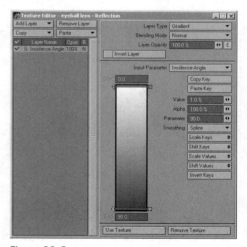

Figure 23-5

Select the top key that was created on the gradient ramp and change its Value to 80%. Create a second key at the bottom of the ramp and change its Value to 100%. See Figure 23-6.

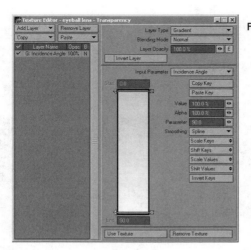

Figure 23-6

7. Copy this surface to the other surface (either the lens one or the outer eyeball one, depending on which one you just set up) by right-clicking on its name and selecting Copy, and paste the settings into it by right-clicking and selecting Paste.

Your surfaces are now set up. Rendering the eyeball should give you something like Figure 23-7.

And now you have a decent eyeball for your characters. Depending on the lighting in your scenes, you may find that you'll have to change some of the parameters from scene to scene (especially the Diffuse parameter), but as I mentioned before, it is the modeling of the eyeball that makes all the difference.

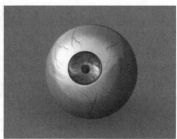

Figure 23-7

## Organic Tutorial 2: A Human Face

I chose a pirate for this exercise because such a character has the potential to have many of the kinds of details that you'll encounter when you texture heads, such as scars, pimples and blemishes, wrinkles, dark circles under the eyes and so on. Basically he's the ultimate exaggeration of skin texturing!

So let's get started. When I'm texturing skin I like to start off the entire process by taking the model into Layout and setting up the lighting and the basic shading of the model. We all know what lighting is, but let me quickly explain what I mean by shading. Shading, as discussed previously, is the stage when I set up all the basic surface parameters — diffuse, specularity, reflection, translucency, and colored highlights — to get the basic look of the surface simply by assigning overall values to each so that it more or less begins to look like skin. I also add a rough procedural grain to the skin to give it some texture.

While I am doing this I also set up my lighting because the interaction between the surface and the lighting is very important for realism. For this example, I used an area light as the main light, with two spotlights (one behind, one to the side) and Backdrop Only radiosity to soften the overall lighting. I mix a little bit of red and blue into the lighting as these colors go well with skin.

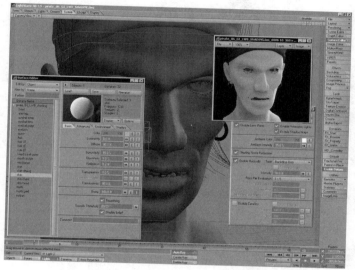

Figure 23-8

You'll find that when working with skin, the shading values you assign can vary quite a bit depending on the lighting setup. There is no foolproof surface setting for each surface attribute that will always work in any light-ing situation. However, what generally does always work is to make the skin look overly soft to begin with. Take a look at the flesh on your cheeks and try to make the entire head look like that — in other words, make it look really soft, fleshy, and, well ... almost squishy. You can create specular and reflection maps later on to "harden" the areas that shouldn't look that soft.

Once you're happy with the way the skin looks in the shading render, it's time to start painting your texture maps. Ideally, the textures you paint should serve only to add details to the shading you've already set up. In other words, we'll make textures to add color variation, blemishes, wrin-kles, etc., as well as variations in the actual surface attributes like specular, translucency, reflection, etc.

I've already set up my UV map for the head using a cylindrical map on the y-axis that I have edited to eliminate stretching. I then export the UV viewport out of Modeler.

Fire up Photoshop (or whatever you use for painting textures) and let's get going.

I generally start off my texture painting by doing the color map. This is purely out of habit — there is no reason why you can't start off with any of your other attributes. I like doing the color map first simply because I like to start off by establishing the basic look of whatever I am creating textures for, and for me the most logical choice is color. But start off with whatever you feel most comfortable with.

I start off my color map by creating a flat skin tone and then adding subtle variations to it to break up the monotony of the single color.

A nice quick way of creating subtle color variation is to create some noise using the Noise filter. Create some fairly low-level noise (don't use the Monochrome option) and then blur it a lot.

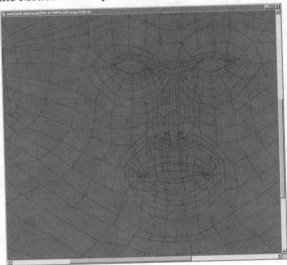

**Figure 23-9**

Skin color can be a tricky thing to paint because in reality skin is actually very plain. It gets most of its perceived tonal variations from two things: its environment (i.e., reflections) and what's going on beneath it. Generally we'll fake what's going on beneath it by adding those particular tones to the color map, and we'll create a reflection map for the surface in order to allow it to reflect its environment a little. So in order to fake what's going on beneath the surface, we basically have to create the illusion of blood beneath the skin, and this means that we add red and blue tones, particularly in the cheeks and just below the eyes where the skin is a little thinner.

The bridge and tip of the nose tend to get a little redder as well.

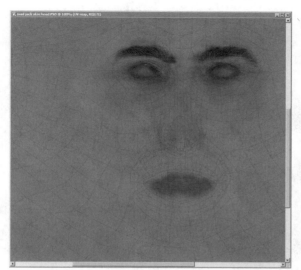

Figure 23-10

The key to creating successful skin textures lies in subtlety. A subtle buildup of tones creates a far more realistic look than big splotches of color. For this reason I tend to use my airbrush on a low opacity (usually around 30%) with 0% hardness (soft edges), and slowly build up my tones by gradually painting over and over certain areas until the blending looks right. I use a Wacom for most of my painting, which does make this a little easier since you have a lot more pressure control, but using an extremely low opacity with a mouse can create exactly the same effect.

I now want to make the scar and some blemishes for the face. I start off with the scar, sketching its shape out in gray using the airbrush and then the Soft Light blending mode, and taking the opacity of the layer down to create the right blend of scar tissue with the underlying skin texture. See Figure 23-11.

I sketch some faint vein details and some subtle blue tones around this area as well, to create a little more "activity" in that area. Each detail is on its own layer.

I also draw some blemishes and pimples on their own layers and find the right blending for them, in this case using the Color Burn blending mode. At this point, I also add some more detail to the lips to give them some nice tonal variations and make them look a little fleshier.

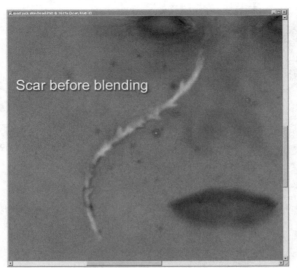

Figure 23-11

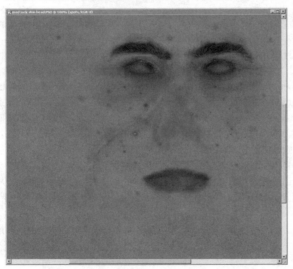

Figure 23-12

Now that I have some blemishes, pimples, and a scar, it's time to focus on the eye areas. These areas are important because the eyes are generally the first part of a CG character that your viewers are going to focus on, so you have to ensure that they look good.

I start off by adding even denser layers of blues and reds to create dark, purplish flesh below the eyes. This is to create a sickly, gaunt look for the character. Having dark rings under the eyes also adds a creepy and danger-ous air to the character. I also add some very subtle wrinkles to this area.

On top of the blues and reds, I create a new layer of little one-pixel spots in light gray. I use the Overlay blending mode for this, and set the Opacity of the layer down to create very faint spots below the eyes.

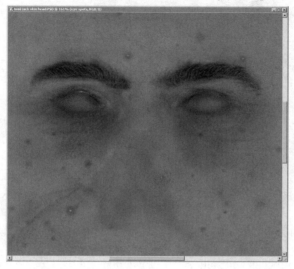

Figure 23-13

This is quite extreme coloring for this area, done intentionally for this type of character. However, you'll see similar coloring, to a lesser intensity, on most people. So when creating textures for "normal" people, you'll still do something along these lines, only to a lesser degree. The cool thing about having these new tones on their own layers is, of course, that should I wish to make him look a little more normal at a later stage, I can simply lower the opacity of this layer to lessen the effect.

Now it's time to create some stubble for him. I'm going to be using Sasquatch to give him facial hair later, but creating some stubble on the actual skin surface helps to ease the transition between the model's skin and the rendered hair.

To make stubble, I make myself a couple of stubble brushes in Photoshop by simply taking a one-pixel size paintbrush and drawing a few points, then selecting them and creating a brush from the selection. I create a few different brushes and constantly switch between them when painting the stubble layer in order to prevent any distinct patterns from developing. When painting the stubble, I don't drag the brush but rather click, move the cursor, click, and so on. Dragging a brush like this creates horrible patterns that we don't want.

Because hair does not generally grow on scar tissue, I avoid painting stubble in the scar area. See Figure 23-14 on the following page.

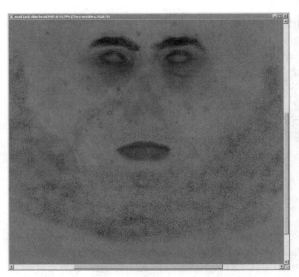

Figure 23-14

The stubble still looks a little sparse on top of the skin though, so it often helps to create a little discoloration below the stubble hairs.

I take the airbrush and paint some brown beneath the stubble layer I just created. I then use the Noise filter to add some low-level noise and blur it. This creates a nice discolored layer beneath the stubble hairs that helps to create the look of rough, older skin. Again, I avoid painting this in the scar area.

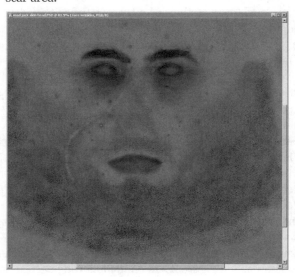

Figure 23-15

The color layers are almost done. All I do now is add some faint blue veins here and there, and also add some strong red tones to the ears to help create the bright color that ears get when lit from behind.

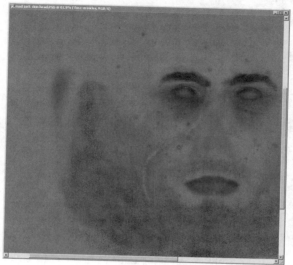

Figure 23-16

Of course this is still a pretty basic texture — I could add loads of tiny details to this to improve it, but for now it'll do the job well enough.

So we move on to the other surface properties. I usually do the bump layers next, so I create a new layer set and create a new gray layer. I choose a neutral value of gray (128, 128, 128) so that I can create a suitable range of both light and dark details over it to create the details necessary for the bump map. Remember that with LightWave, lighter areas in the bump map create the illusion of raised details, while darker ones appear to form indentations.

I start off by adding a little noise to this first layer, and start sketching out some initial details like the eyebrows, eye area, and lips using the air-brush and pencil. I also create the forehead wrinkles using two of my favorite tools in Photoshop: the Dodge and Burn tools. These two tools are awesome for creating subtle details in your grayscale texture maps, as they are very intuitive and allow for the gradual building up of details when used on low exposure levels.

The very fine details around the eyes (crow's-feet) are created using a one-pixel pencil, and the blending detail around them is created with the Dodge tool on the base gray layer I created initially.

I also copy the layers containing the blemishes and pimples from the color layers over to my new bump layer set, desaturate them, and adjust their brightness until I get the right level of gray that I want for them in the bump map.

Copying the layers over like this ensures that all your details remain in the right positions.

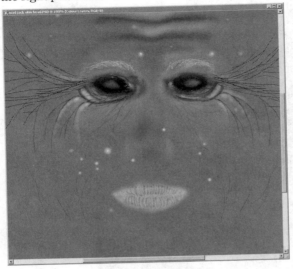

Figure 23-17

Now I also copy the stubble hair layer over from the color layers, desaturate it, and make it a bright white in the bump layer set. This is obviously to make the stubble hairs appear to protrude from the skin. Then I copy the scar layer over and adjust its opacity to get the right look for it as well, as scars can sometimes be quite lumpy and I want it to stick out a bit from the skin.

At this point I also create a new layer with a rougher grain for the skin on the cheeks. Again, I do this by roughly painting some gray, using the Noise filter (using the Monochrome option), and blurring it. This makes a nice, coarse texture for the cheeks to make them look weathered and rough. I also add some faint wrinkles to these areas. As a nice little touch I also add some pore indentations on the tip of the nose with a one-pixel airbrush, as people often tend to have larger pores in this area. See Figure 23-18.

Now it's time to copy the layer where I created the little spots under the eyes into the bump layer set. I do this and desaturate it, then adjust the blending of the layer so that it stands out of the bump map. This will create the slightly coarser grain that our skin has directly beneath our eyes. See Figure 23-19.

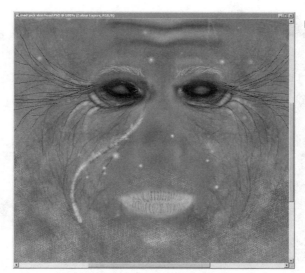

**Figure 23-18**

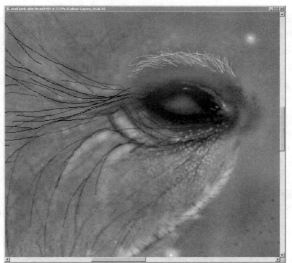

**Figure 23-19**

That's the bump map almost done. All I do now is copy the veins layer over from the color layers, desaturate it, and adjust it to get the right level for the bump map. I also create some other veins on the side of the head. See Figure 23-20 on the following page.

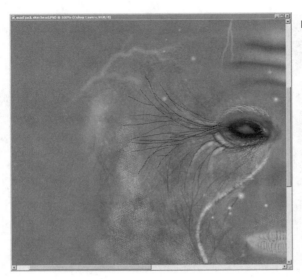

Figure 23-20

Now we move on to the specular map. I usually like to do my specular map next because it helps to enhance the bump map (when rendered) and because it's a nice way of starting to define how the surface feels to the touch. Remember that specularity (in CG) is basically a fake form of reflection, so a properly made specular map helps to create shininess on the surface.

I've already assigned a basic Specularity value to the surface during the shading phase, and you may recall what I mentioned earlier about making the texture maps in such a way as to have them add details only to the surface. So how do I ensure that this map will only add details to the current specularity of the object without changing it completely? The answer is simple. I take a look at the Specularity value that I assigned to the surface when shading it, and use that value as the starting value for the gray specular map.

I take that value, which in this case was 9%, and use that as the brightness value for the gray layer that I initially create for my specular map.

I open the Color Picker in Photoshop, select a gray, and check the HSB values — the B value is the brightness value. I simply enter in a value of 9.

Now I begin to create some basic variations (in other words, some details) to the specular map, starting off with areas like the bridge and tip of

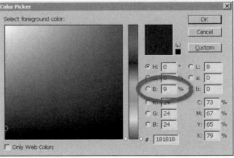

Figure 23-21

the nose, the eyelids, the lips, the forehead, the chin, and the areas directly beneath the eyes. These areas are generally slightly shinier than the rest of the flesh. As you can see, at this stage the map is actually quite rough and very simple.

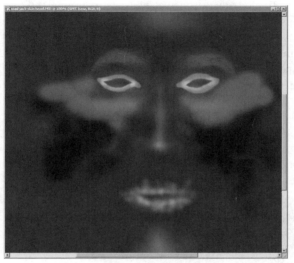

**Figure 23-22**

Once I've roughly established the areas for increased/lessened specularity, I copy some layers over from my bump map (specifically the wrinkles and some grain, and also the scar), and adjust the intensity of these layers to get the right effect. Since scar tissue is generally quite a bit shinier than ordinary skin, I keep the scar quite bright in the specular map, and I use the wrinkles layers to lessen the specularity in those areas simply for the sake of variation.

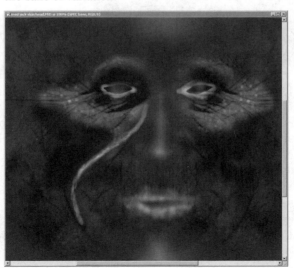

**Figure 23-23**

Believe it or not, this is enough detail for the specular requirements of this particular model. Yeah, it could certainly be improved, but again, sometimes you can get away with quite simple textures.

Okay, so now that we have a specular map, it's also a nice idea to use a teeny bit of reflection on your surface as well. As mentioned before, specularity is just a fake reflection, but I find that adding an actual reflection map to the surface as well helps to really sharpen the highlights and adds a sense of realism to the surface. Skin gets a lot of its color from reflecting its environment and, unless you want to render with a lot of Monte Carlo radiosity, using a teeny tiny bit of reflection on the surface can help to create this effect.

The really cool thing is that you don't necessarily need to make a new reflection map. All I do is simply take the specular map and make it really, really dark (almost black actually) and use that. So I just create a new Brightness/Contrast Adjustment layer over the specular layers, and darken it considerably to create the right levels for the reflection map.

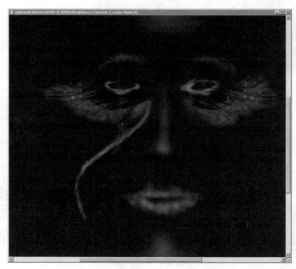

Figure 23-24

So what's left? The only other texture I'm going to create for this model is a translucency map. Translucency is basically the quality that most organic surfaces have whereby light can partially penetrate them. Look at anyone who is lit from behind and you'll see how their ears almost glow. This is translucency in action.

Okay, now translucency can be a bit of a devil at times, and you kind of have to cheat it a bit. In reality, although skin is very translucent, we have muscle and bone directly beneath our skin that prevents light from penetrating beyond a certain depth. This means that in order to create this effect realistically in LightWave, you'd actually have to model a skull and everything inside your head to allow for realistic volumetric translucency, because simply assigning a value to the translucency attribute, or creating a texture map for it, is going to allow light to go all the way through the head. Unfortunately, there is no easy way around that (yet), so in the meantime I just create a translucency map that makes the skin quite translucent anyway.

The translucency value that I assigned to the model when shading it was 30%, so I create a new gray layer in Photoshop and fill it with 30% gray. I then use the Dodge tool to lighten areas like the ears and areas directly beneath the eyes where the skin is thinner and more translucent. I also copy the scar layer over from the specular map and blend it on top of this to let the scar flesh become a little more translucent as well.

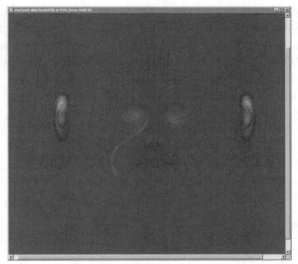

Figure 23-25

And that wraps up the texture painting for this head! As you can see, it's actually all very simple — all you need is a good eye for detail and a decent knowledge of what sorts of details you can expect to find in skin. Over time you'll develop an eye for detail and a collection of photographic references you can use.

As I have demonstrated, you can easily create great-looking textures that work really well simply by adopting good Photoshop/painting habits. Creating your own custom brushes can help a lot (as I showed with the stubble example), as can using tools like Dodge and Burn to gradually build up tonal variations for your grayscale maps.

Photoshop's Adjustment layers are a great way of making tonal adjustments to entire maps if you find that the overall tone isn't working too well when you add them to your model and render.

Of course, I can't stress enough the importance of keeping everything on its own individual layer! I'm sure you've seen the usefulness of this as I have demonstrated, so make sure you do the same in order to avoid having to make destructive changes, and just to generally make life a lot easier.

Remember: Look at your textures, examine them, and compare them to photographic references. Any discrepancies in your textures will be immediately obvious. You have your own face, so look in a mirror if you're unsure about any particular type of detail.

I have managed to get together a couple of character and head models for the companion CD. Please go ahead and create textures for them!

## Summary of Tips for Creating Organic Surfaces

- Use lots of reference materials.

- Subtlety is essential. Don't paint large splotches of color, but rather build up your tones gradually to form new variations.

- Change the opacity and sizes of your brushes constantly while working to ensure a more natural look. Using the same opacity and sizes tends to form subtle patterns that wreck the texture.

- Pay attention to the tiny details, as these make all the difference. Make sure that you always have loads of color and shading variations across your surfaces, and be sure to add many imperfections, whether subtle or obvious.

# CHAPTER 24

# Natural Surfaces

In the previous tutorials you learned how to paint realistic organic surfaces using painting software such as Photoshop. Now we're going to take a look at how to create natural surfaces with procedural textures and nodes. You can achieve the same results with the layer system, but nodes are more flexible. You may want to duplicate the results with the layer system in order to practice with it as well.

## Natural Surfaces Tutorial 1: An Ocean

In our first tutorial we are going to create water. There are several things that you need to keep in mind while creating water. Think about the type of water you would like to create; for example, is it a pond, a river, or an ocean? All of these will look different since the surrounding environment is not the same. You also have to know what kind of weather conditions you'd like your scene to have. This will have a great impact on how the water looks. There are other variables that will affect the look of water such as nutrients, particles, sediment, and any other debris that might be found floating around. The combination of all these things will determine what the water will look like.

Before we begin, we're going to be working with the new Node Editor shading system. We'll be making some simple network connections that you should be familiar with if you read Chapter 14. If you skipped that chapter, I recommend you go back and read it thoroughly. There are a lot of things in the new LightWave shading system that you may not be completely familiar with, such as anisotropic shaders, diffuse shaders, and SSS shaders, to name a few. Since we are going to be focusing more on the texturing aspects of things, I have provided a complete scene on the companion CD for you to work from. If you would like to see the models, just load them up in Modeler. They are all very simple to make on your own.

The ocean that we are going to create is set in the late afternoon with medium winds that are strong enough to get some nice waves, almost like a storm is about to hit.

Load up the ocean_for_tutorial.lws scene. This scene has all the elements already placed and ready to be textured. The scene also contains a sky created with SkyTracer to be used as our background and reflection environment. You can also use your own image, preferably a panorama or an HDRI probe. This background is essential to the scene since water reflects its environment; a good reflection map will make a huge difference in your final render by providing contrast, detail, and mood to the scene. Water scenes tend to look very flat if the reflected environment is poor or has not been added to the scene at all. The NewTek web site (http://www.new-tek.com) also provides some great sky photos that you can use.

> **NOTE:** For more information on SkyTracer, consult your reference manual.

## Creating the Displacement Node Network

In LightWave v9, the Node Editor can be accessed from three different places: the Deform tab of the Object Properties panel, the Volumetric Lights of the Light Properties panel, and the Surface Editor via an Edit Nodes button. In each of these instances, the Node Editor targets that specific area. We're going to be using nodes in the Surface Editor and in the Object Properties as a displacement map.

1. Once you have loaded the ocean_for_tutorial scene from the companion CD, select the ocean and open the Object Properties panel ("p" on the keyboard).

    We're going to be using the first two tabs: Geometry and Deform. For now, we'll leave the Subdivision Order in the Geometry tab at First; we're also going to leave the Display SubPatch Level at 3 and set Render SubPatch to Per Object Level. Later we'll change it to Per Polygon Level to take advantage of the new Adaptive Pixel Subdivision (APS), which will allow us to add a lot of detail to our ocean without getting a huge render hit.

2. Now go to the Deform tab; you will notice there is a button labeled Edit Nodes. Click on this button to open the Displacement Node Editor. Also click on the check box next to this button to actually activate it; otherwise, whatever we do in the Node Editor will not be reflected in the viewport or renders.

    Once in the Node Editor, you'll see the Displacement destination node. That's the final node to which everything will be connected. Beginner- and

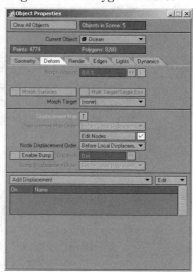

Figure 24-1: Object Properties panel

intermediate-level users might want to try using the Node Editor to repli-cate what could be done using layers alone in older versions of LightWave. This will make for an easier transition. The Node Editor has dedicated Layer nodes that bring the "classic" layers of the Texture Editor into the Node Editor, making it easier to have a smoother transition to nodes (see Chapter 14, "The Node Editor," for more on Layer nodes). In this first tuto-rial, we are going to follow that line of thought to make the beginning of our journey into the Node Editor a snap.

> **NOTE:** Displacement maps are also covered in Chapter 25, "LightWave/ZBrush Workflow."

3.  Here, go to the Add Node menu and add a Scalar Layer under Layers. In this Scalar layer we're going to add layers like we used to do in the "clas-sic" Texture Editor. You will find this to be easier in the beginning. As your skills start getting better with nodes, you're going to find yourself deviating from layers and instead incorporating function-specific nodes into your network.

4.  Now, double-click on your Scalar layer and you'll see a panel that resem-bles the classic texturing system. In this panel, we're going to create the different types of layers that we need for our waves displacement. There should be a default layer in the node. Click on the Layer Type pull-down menu and change this layer to a procedural texture. Once you select Pro-cedural Texture from the list, the layer is converted to a procedural texture layer with Turbulence as the default. Let's make some changes to this texture; leave the Blending Mode as Normal, but change Layer Opacity to 20%. We don't want the texture to be too strong. The trick here is to blend several different lay-ers together and try to get rid of the CG-type look that we often see on images. Change the following set-tings for this layer:

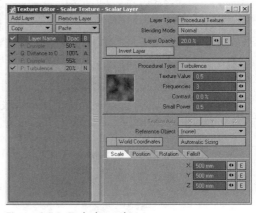

Texture Value: 0.5
Frequencies: 3
Contrast: 0%
Small Power: 0.5
Scale X, Y, and Z: 500mm

Figure 24-2: Turbulence layer

5.  Now we'll move on to the next layer where we'll create the larger waves. At the top-left corner of the Texture Editor, you will see a pull-down menu called Add Layer. Click on this menu and select

Procedural from the list. The default is Turbulence; click on the Procedural Type pull-down menu and select Crumple, which will give a sharper top and smoother bottom to the waves. Change Layer Opacity to 55%, change Blending Mode to Additive, and also change the following:

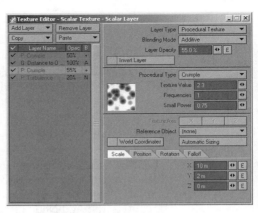

Texture Value: 2.3
Frequencies: 1
Small Power: 0.75
Scale X: 10m, Y: 2m, Z: 8m

Figure 24-3: Crumple layer

6. Next we'll create another Crumple layer. Change Blending Mode to Additive and Layer Opacity to 50%. Changing the opacity in a layer allows you to control the overall look of the waves and how they interact with each other, in essence controlling the size or strength of the wave patterns that they create; higher opacity values will create a more prominent wave while lower opacity values will create a more subtle wave. Here are the layer settings:

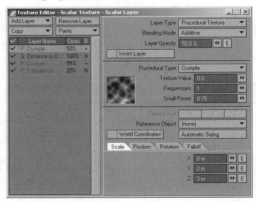

Texture Value: 0.8
Frequencies: 1
Small Power: 0.75
Scale X: 8m, Y: 2m, Z: 3m

Figure 24-4: Crumple layer

7. If you would like to animate this ocean, go to each of the layers and add an envelope. For example, let's go to the first layer we created, the Turbulence layer on the bottom of the stack. Click on the Position tab located at the bottom of the panel. You will see an "E" button at the far right of each of the channels. E stands for Envelope, which lets us animate it. When we select the "E" button, the Graph Editor pops up; this is where we can add keys to the layer and have it animate over time. At frame 30, add a key to the Z position. Change Value to 1.5m. Change Post Behavior to Offset Repeat in the drop-down menu so it repeats over time. We will repeat this process in all the layers with a slight offset. Chapter 18, "Enveloping Basics," has more information on the process of animating textures using envelopes.

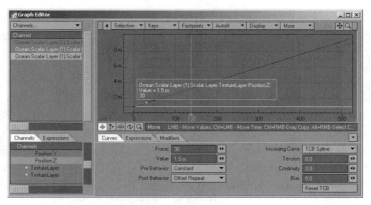

Figure 24-5: Texture animation

8. Go to the second Crumple layer from the top of the layer stack and once again click on the "E" button. In the X position at frame 60, change Value to 3.1m, and then set Post Behavior to Offset Repeat. In the same frame but at the Y position, let's change Value to 3.29m or something close to that and change Post Behavior to... yep, you guessed it... Offset Repeat. Change the Z position with 1.6m as Value and set Post Behavior again to Offset Repeat. By offsetting these position values we can create the illusion of movement; making some waves look big and some small, and moving at different rates gives it a more realistic look.

9. Open the first Crumple layer from the top of the layer stack and offset the values at frame 40 by creating keys on the graph just like we did before. Let's change the X position to 555mm, Y to 333mm, and Z to 166mm. All of the channels should be set to Offset Repeat. The value is incrementally added to the original values and therefore makes it seem like it is moving for however long the animation turns out to be. After some fine-tuning, these patterns will look very nice animated.

10. Finally, we are going to add another layer. This will be a black and white gradient. Click on the Add Layer pull-down menu and select Gradient from the list. The first key should be white, with a Value of 1 and Alpha at 100%. The second key at

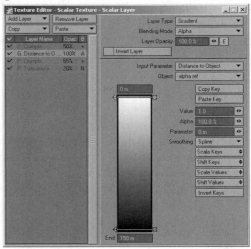

Figure 24-6: Alpha gradient

the bottom of the gradient (the "End" value) should read 150m, with a Value of 0 and Alpha at 100%. These values will make the strongest crumple. Put this gradient between the two Crumple textures we created by clicking and dragging the gradient layer to its new location. This gradient will act as an alpha gradient, so change the Blending Mode to Alpha. The strength of the layer below it (Crumple in this instance) will start to fade toward the horizon line, ensuring that there are no visible high points on the horizon that would kill the depth effect.

11. Now let's make all these layers work together. You will notice that the displacement is a Vector input. That is what is recommended. You can connect other inputs, but the results may vary and may be very unpredictable. In order to have this scalar layer work with a Vector input, we need to add a new node called Scale. Go to the Add Node menu and choose Math>Vector>Scale to add it to the network. You'll notice that you have Vector and Scale inputs and a Result output. We need to tell the displacement which direction to use when calculating the map. Create a spot info node by going to Add Node>Spot>Spot Info. We're going to take the Normal output of the Spot Info node and feed it to the Vector input of the Scale node. Then take the Scalar output of the Scalar node and connect it to the Scale input of the Scale node. This will specify how far and in which direction the displacement should be. Now that these are set up, we can connect the Result output of the Scale node to the input of the Displacement destination node. When you do that you should be able to see the ocean object displaced in the viewport.

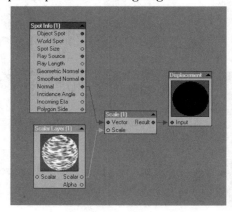

Figure 24-7: Displacement node network

12. Close the Node Editor and go back to the Object Properties panel, then go to the Geometry tab. Now we're going to use a feature called Adaptive Pixel Subdivision (APS), which is new in LightWave v9. As I mentioned earlier, this will let us create an incredible amount of detail in our subdivided object without a huge render hit. Change the Render SubPatch option to Per Polygon Level. Click on the "T" button to open the Texture Editor. Here we are going to set how much detail we want to see while keeping memory and render times at a reasonable level. To do this, create a gradient and change the default key Value setting to 65. Add an additional key and give it a Value of 1. In order to see the gradient working, change the End parameter at the bottom of the gradient to 10m. Now we have a gradient that starts at a value of 65 and ends at a

value of 1. This will create a lot of details where we need it, right in front of the camera, and less detail where we don't need it, farther back toward the horizon line. In order for this to work properly, we need to set the Input Parameter of the gradient to Distance to Object and select the Null object named alpha ref as the controlling object.

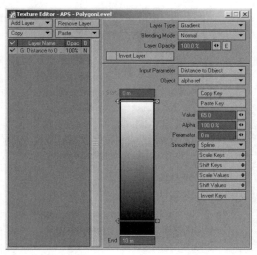

Figure 24-8: APS

That's it for the displacement map. You can make a test render to see the ocean so far.

## Creating the Surface Node Network

We have a good-looking wave pattern going in the scene, but it isn't very convincing yet, is it? Let's fix that now, shall we?

1.  Open the Surface Editor (F5), select the ocean surface, and click on the Edit Nodes button to open the Node Editor. Remember to activate nodes by clicking on the check box next to the Edit Nodes button in order to see the results in the rendered image.

2.  To keep things simple in this exercise we are going to use a Color Layer node and a Bump Layer node, which work just like the "classic" Texture Editor for the color and bump channels of this surface, so go ahead and add them to the workspace (Add Node>Layers>Bump Layer and Color Layer).

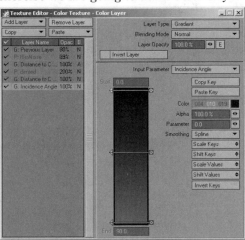

Figure 24-9: Incidence Angle gradient

3.  Double-click on the Color Layer to open the Texture Editor; here we are going to add a couple of gradients. Set the first gradient to Incidence Angle and add

two additional keys, one in the middle and the other one at the bottom of the gradient. Change the key values to the following (top to bottom):

Key 1
Color: 4, 10, 19
Parameter: 0

Key 2
Color: 14, 34, 74
Parameter: 42.6

Key 3
Color: 36, 95, 177
Parameter: 90

4.  The second gradient will make the ocean a bit desaturated toward the horizon line. These two gradients set the overall color of the ocean; if you wish to change the ocean color, start with these two. Set this gradient's Input Parameter to Distance to Camera so the color of the water will change relative to the camera position. Set the End value for the gradient to 200m or so. Here are the rest of the gradient's values:

Key 1
Color: 1, 2, 20
Parameter: 0m

Key 2
Color: 121, 141, 172
Parameter: 200m

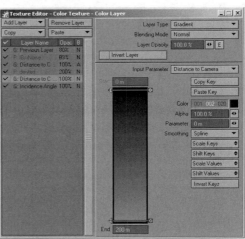

Figure 24-10

5.  All we have left to do for the color layers is create the foam. For this, create a Dented procedural texture with these settings:

Layer Opacity: 200%
Invert Layer: On
Texture Color: 238, 244, 255
Scale: 2.46
Power: 0.806
Frequency: 0.859
Octaves: 6.0

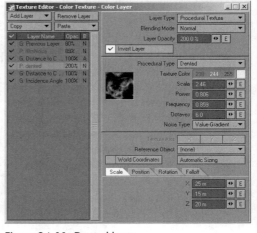

Figure 24-11: Dented layer

Noise Type: Value-Gradient
Scale X: 25m, Y: 15m, Z: 20m

6.  This texture is quite large and strong in order to be seen properly; how-
    ever, toward the horizon
    the water starts to look
    more like snow. To correct
    this, you can add an Alpha
    gradient that will fade the
    texture toward the horizon.
    Add a gradient layer to the
    stack, set the Blending
    Mode to Alpha and the
    Input Parameter to Dis-
    tance to Camera, and set
    the End value to 200m. Add
    the following keys to the
    gradient:

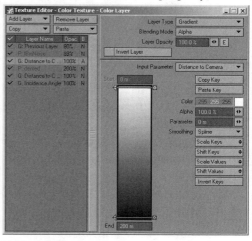

Figure 24-12

Key 1
Color: 255, 255, 255 (white)
Alpha: 100%
Parameter: 0m

Key 2
Color: 000, 000, 000 (black)
Alpha: 100%
Parameter: 200m

 **TIP:** Click and drag on the Dented texture preview to browse
through the patterns. This works on all procedural textures.

7.  Add another layer of foam
    to the ocean, making this
    one an FBM Noise proce-
    dural texture. This layer
    will add some foam specks
    to the water, like leftovers
    from a larger foam area.
        Change this texture's
    values to the following:

Layer Opacity: 90%
Color: 230, 242, 255
Increment: 0.5
Lacunarity: 2.1

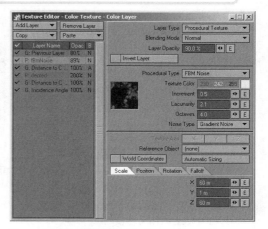

Figure 24-13: FBM Noise texture

Octaves: 4
Noise Type: Gradient Noise
Scale X: 60m, Y: 1m, Z: 60m

8.  To further emphasize the look of
    foam, add another gradient to the
    layer stack to mimic the white
    foam on the tips of the waves.
    Leave its color at white and add
    two additional keys with these
    settings (from top to bottom):

    Key 1
    Alpha: 0%
    Parameter: 0

    Key 2
    Alpha: 0%
    Parameter: 0.8

    Key 3
    Alpha: 75%
    Parameter: 0.96

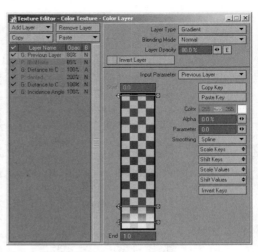

Figure 24-14: Foam gradient, key 1

9.  Now that the Color Layer is finished, connect its Color output to the
    Color input of the surface destination node.

10. Let's add more detail to the waves with a bump map. Double-click on the
    Bump Layer node that you added earlier. Here you can add as many
    bump procedural textures as you
    wish (depending on memory, of
    course). What you are looking to
    do here is build details that
    would be impractical to do with
    displacement maps alone. First
    add a Turbulence texture with
    these settings:

    Layer Opacity: 50%
    Texture Value: 50%
    Frequencies: 3
    Contrast: 0%
    Small Power: 0.61
    Scale X: 3m, Y: 1m, Z: 3m

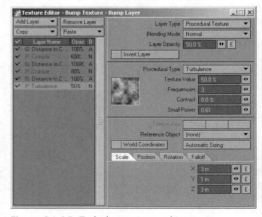

Figure 24-15: Turbulence texture layer

11. Now add a couple of Crumple procedural textures to add smaller details
    to the waves with the following settings:

    Layer Opacity: 80%
    Texture Value: 80%

Frequencies: 4
Small Power: 0.75
Scale X: 2m, Y: 1m, Z: 1m

Layer Opacity: 70%
Texture Value: 90%
Frequencies: 4
Small Power: 0.75
Scale X: 1m, Y: 500mm, Z: 500mm

12. It would be a good idea to add an alpha gradient to these bump textures in order to lessen the effect of texture flickering if the ocean were animated. Add a gradient layer to the stack, set the Blending Mode to Alpha, and set the End value to 200m. Add the following keys to the gradient:

Key 1
Value: 100%
Alpha: 100%
Parameter: 0m

Key 2
Value: 40%
Alpha: 100%
Parameter: 91.2m

Key 3
Value: 14%
Alpha: 100%
Parameter: 169.3m

Key 4
Value: 0%
Alpha: 100%
Parameter: 250m

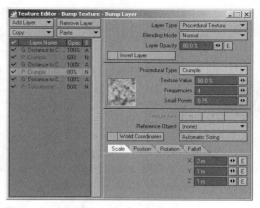

Figure 24-16: First crumple texture

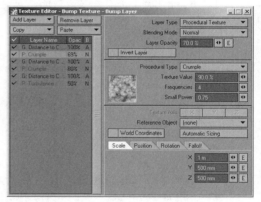

Figure 24-17: Second crumple texture

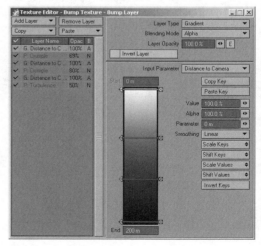

Figure 24-18: Alpha gradient, key 1

13. Since alpha gradients only affect the layer immediately below them, you need to copy this gradient and paste it on top of each of the procedural texture maps. Connect this node's Bump output to the Bump input of the surface destination node. It really doesn't matter when you make the connections, but it is a good idea to make connections right away if you know for sure what you are doing so you can see your changes in VIPER.

14. We need to change other channels of the surface to make the ocean more realistic. Let's change the Diffuse channel of the surface first. In this case, add a Turbulence texture to the workspace (Add Node>3D Textures>Turbulence) and change this texture's values to the following:

Layer Opacity: 95%
Small Scale: 0.5
Contrast: 0
Frequencies: 3
Scale X: 1km, Y: 1m, Z: 1km

15. Connect the Color output of the Turbulence node to the Diffuse input of the Surface destination node. You should have so far a Color Layer node, a Bump Layer node, and a Turbulence node connected to the surface. Don't worry about the dissimilar type connections we made here; all we are doing is using the color information instead of the alpha information of the node to drive the diffuse value of the surface. The node network should look like the one shown in Figure 24-19.

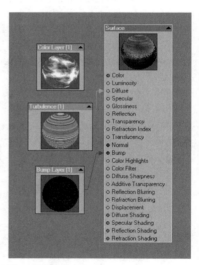

Figure 24-19

16. You have now made a few nodes, changed values, and made connections; let's add another element to the process. Add a Gradient node to the workspace (Add Node>Gradient>Gradient). Open the gradient's edit panel and change these values:

Input: Incidence

Key 1
Color: 255, 255, 255 (white)
Alpha: 100%
Position: 0

Key 2
Color: 000, 000, 000 (black)
Alpha: 100%
Position: 1

17. Connect the Color output of the Gradient node to the Reflection input of the Surface destination node. This simulates the Fresnel effect.

Figure 24-20: Gradient edit panel

18. For the Transparency channel, we can use a Surface Thickness layer to control the amount of transparency according to a specified thickness value. Since we are trying to replicate what we would usually do with the "classic" layer system we need to add a Scalar Layer node to the workspace (Add Node>Layers>Scalar Layer) and connect the Scalar output to the Transparency channel input of the Surface destination node. In this node, create a gradient set to Surface Thickness as the Input Parameter, change the End value to 400mm, and also change these key properties:

Key 1
Value: 0.85
Alpha: 100%
Parameter: 0

Key 2
Value: 0.15%
Alpha: 100%
Parameter: 400mm

19. Instead of a Specular channel we are going to use a Specular Shading channel where we can adjust the specular and glossiness properties at one time. Create a Blinn node (Add Node>Shaders>Specular>Blinn) and change the following:

Color: 255, 255, 255 (white)
Specularity: 85
Glossiness: 55

20. Connect the Color output of the Blinn to the Specular Shading channel of the Surface destination node. Done! If you render frame 139, your surface should resemble something like Figure 24-22.

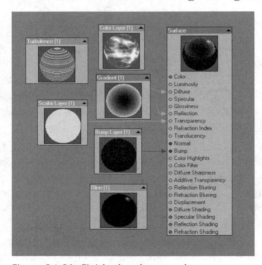

Figure 24-21: Finished node network

Figure 24-22

21. Now, select the Ocean surface and go to the Advanced tab of the Surface Editor. Here, I played with the Color options on the bottom of the panel. I changed Color Highlights to 5% to add a bit of color to the highlights. I also changed the Color Filter and Additive Transparency settings to 50% each. Color Filter will tint transparent surfaces such as our ocean. Additive Transparency will add the color of the transparent surface to objects seen through it. Play with these settings to see what kind of results you get.

You can save this image or sequence and open it in a compositing or painting package to manipulate it further. In Photoshop I composited a picture of clouds that I downloaded from one of my favorite texture sites: http://www.mayang.com/textures.

I also added a layer to create haze. I first made a gray bar that goes across the horizon line. Then I blurred it and tried to match its color to the haze of the cloud picture to blend it further. The horizon line was a little too sharp, so I blurred it with Gaussian blur.

I thought it would be cute to add a couple of paper boats to the image; this will also help the viewer to better determine the size of the ocean. The Photoshop comp can be found in the companion CD if you would like to take a look.

Figure 24-23: Final composite

## Summary of Tips for Creating Water

- Determine the type of environment surrounding the water body.
- Always use a good reflection map.
- Use displacement maps for low-frequency bumps (big waves).
- Use bump maps for high-frequency bumps (tiny waves).
- Gradients are your friend, and can be used for anything from color to Fresnel effects.
- Envelope every texture to give it a more realistic look when animated.

# Natural Surfaces Tutorial 2: Red Rocks

The Ocean tutorial was a great exercise to get a little experience with the Node Editor. We created some simple layered nodes and plugged them in to their appropriate inputs of the Surface destination node in a way similar to what we used to surface with the classic layered system. Let's experiment a little now with a more challenging exercise. Nice rocky terrains are difficult to create with procedurals in the classic layer system because of the number of layers needed to convincingly create such a surface and hide the "computer-generated" look that procedurals tend to have. You could easily end up with 25 color layers on one channel alone, so looking at the big picture, it would be an incredibly difficult task to make edits to this surface. With nodes you can see all of the textures of every channel at once, which is extremely helpful, but the coolest thing is to have the power to use one node to control several properties at once. For example, to reuse a gradient, you do not have to copy and paste the gradient into a different texture channel; you simply connect it to every texture you wish to affect.

Like in the Ocean tutorial, and anything else that you attempt to create, collect as many reference images as possible. Don't just look at it, but study it and observe it. Are the shadows sharp or fuzzy? What color are they? What do you think the time of day was when the photo was taken? What's the weather like? Is the mountain smooth or rough looking? Is it granite or sandstone? Ask yourself as many questions as possible; the answers will help you in the texturing process.

As before, the objects and scene can be loaded from the companion CD, so load the scene and let's get to work!

## About the Canyon Model

If you open the canyon_plain.lwo file from the CD you will see that unlike the ocean, I actually modeled the canyon to follow a very natural realistic pattern. I used the references I collected to model this object. The lines are based on a real-world canyon; I took creative freedom here and there, but the point is that for this kind of terrain it helps if the mesh's edges flow realistically from the beginning. This will help our displacement map as well. This is not to say that a canyon such as this one couldn't be done by displacing a subdivided mesh like we did with the ocean, but I find that it is more difficult and/or time consuming to do. This is totally based on personal preference. You may also create landscapes with programs such as Vue5; in this case I already had in mind exactly what I wanted, so I just modeled it.

The scene called canyon.lws that I provided for you has everything set up... with the exception of textures of course.

## Creating the Displacement Node Network

1.  Once you have the scene loaded, click on the canyon object and open its Properties panel ("p"). Subdivision Order should be set to First. The Render SubPatch drop-down should be set to Per Object Level and 16 and the Display SubPatch Level to 3, just so we can see a hint of what we are doing on the viewport.

2.  Click on the Deform tab of the Object Properties panel, make sure the Edit Nodes check box is selected, and click the Edit Nodes button to open the editor. We are going to use some texture nodes along with some utilities and function nodes. Add a Spot Info node; by now you know that you are going to use the Normal output of this node for every displacement that you do, and the same goes for the Scale node, which is the node that combines the direction normal and the value of the textures we put together. The output result will be plugged into the input of our Displacement destination node.

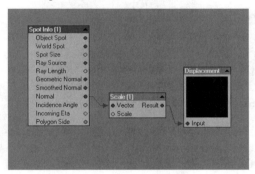

Figure 24-24: Spot Info and Scale nodes

3.  Now add two 3D textures: Turbulent Noise and HeteroTerrain. Double-click on the HeteroTerrain texture to open its attributes. Change Fg Color to white and leave the rest of the HeteroTerrain attributes at their default values with the exception of the texture's Scale, which should be X and Y: 15m, Z: 20m to stretch the texture on the z-axis. You can connect the Alpha output of this node to the Scale input of the Scale node. You should be able to see a change on the canyon object in your viewport since there is something to displace now. To make this texture more random looking, we are going to connect the Alpha output of the Turbulent Noise node to the HeteroTerrain's Opacity input. This is like changing the texture mode to alpha in the classic layer system. Change the Turbulent Noise attributes to the following:

Opacity: 150%
Increment: 0.5
Lacunarity: 2.0
Octaves: 6.0
Noise Type: Perlin Noise

4.  This texture should be somewhat bigger in order to fade large areas of
    the HeteroTerrain texture, so let's change the Scale values to X and Z:
    25m, Y: 2m.

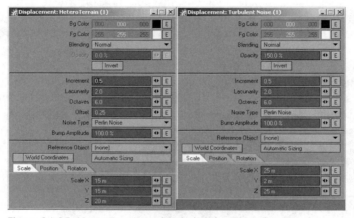

Figure 24-25: HeteroTerrain and Turbulent Noise attributes

5.  So far, so good. At this point I would like to add another two-node net-
    work to this setup to add interest and detail. Add a Turbulent Noise node
    and a Crumple node. Double-click on the Turbulent Noise node to open
    its attributes and change the following values:

    Increment: 0.509
    Lacunarity: 1.8
    Octaves: 6
    Noise Type: Perlin Noise

6.  Let's make this texture stretch a little on the y-axis by changing the
    scale to X and Z: 5m and Y to 10m. Now let's change where this texture
    shows up by connecting the Crumple texture Alpha output to the Opac-
    ity input of the Turbulent Noise that we just created. I very rarely leave
    textures with their default values, so scale this Crumple texture as well
    to X and Z: 30m and Y: 50m. Make the Background color a dark gray, 52,
    52, 52. To give the crumple a more organic feel, change these attributes:

    Opacity: 50%
    Small Scale: 0.75
    Frequencies: 2.0

7. After changing these values, make the connection, setting the Alpha output to the Opacity input of the Turbulent Noise node.

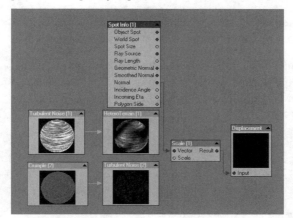

Figure 24-26: The displacement network so far

8. In order to mix these textures together, we are going to use a node called Add. This node is located under Add Node>Math>Scalar>Add. Plug the Alpha output of the HeteroTerrain to the Add A input and the Alpha output of the Turbulent Noise to the B input of the Add node. This basically reads: A+B = new value. The result of this node is plugged in to the Scale input of the Scale node. You should notice a difference in your viewport. You can make test renders after each node is configured and connected into the network to better see what you did to the canyon object.

9. Now, in order to perturb the displacement a little further we can use Function nodes, which are simply curves. The texture is disturbed according to the attributes that make the curve. Add a Noise Function node, a Modulate Function node, and a Crumple texture (you can copy and paste the texture already on the network). Open the Crumple attributes, make sure the background color is black and the foreground color is white, and type in these values:

Opacity: 50%
Small Scale: 0.3
Frequencies: 3
Scale X and Y: 15m and Z: 30m

10. Connect the Alpha output of this Crumple texture to the Amplitude of the Noise and Modulate nodes. Open the attributes of the Noise function and change the value of Clamp High to 0.5, then open the Modulate attributes and change the Frequency to 0.5 as well. Connect the Result output of the Noise function to the Function 1 input of the Modulate node. Modulate allows you to mix Function nodes together, so take the

Result output of Modulate and connect it to the HeteroTerrain node Function input.

> **TIP:** Functions should only be connected to Function inputs. Connecting functions to any other input will have unpredictable results.

11. Make a test render and see the nice rocky displacement that we have created. By changing the Opacity setting of the Crumple node attached to the Turbulent Noise, we can control the amount of displacement of the ridges that go horizontally across the surface.

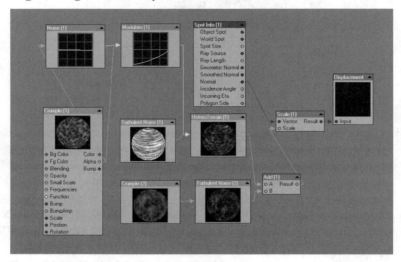

Figure 24-27: Finished displacement network

## Creating the Surface Node Network

We are now ready to texture the canyon's surface. This network will be more complex than the ocean we created earlier, but there is no heavy math hocus-pocus. As your skills develop, you will undoubtedly be experimenting with more math wizardry, but for now we'll keep things simple.

In LightWave v9 we have more diffuse shading models available to us besides the default Lambert. One of those shaders is called Minnaert, which was designed to describe nonatmospherical celestial bodies such as moons. Even though we are not making asteroids or moons, this shader will provide us with a believable surface for the canyon that is close enough to the type of surface that you might find on a moon or maybe even Mars.

1. Open the Surface Editor (F5), select the canyon surface on the list, and click on the Edit Nodes button. Make sure the check box next to Edit Nodes is active; otherwise, the changes will not be seen in the render. Once the Node Editor is opened, we will find the Surface destination

node. We are going to change this default shading model to Minnaert. Add this node to the workspace with Add Node>Shaders>Diffuse> Minnaert. Open the node's attributes and change the Diffuse value to 85%, but leave Darkening at 0.

2. We need to add some color variation to the surface to mimic the layers you would expect to see on rocky mountains. First create a Color Layer node (Add Node>Layers>Color Layer), a Crackle node (Add Node>3D Textures>Crackle), and a Mixer node (Add Node>Tools>Mixer). We are going to make a base color with these nodes and then build the color from there. Open the Color Layer node attributes and make the default layer a Turbulence procedural with these attributes (see Figure 24-28):

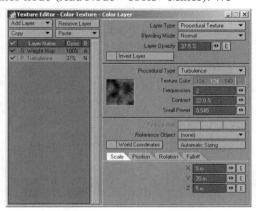

Blending Mode: Normal
Layer Opacity: 37.5%
Texture Color: 124, 124, 143
Frequencies: 2
Contrast: 22%
Small Power: 0.545
Scale X: 5m, Y: 20m, Z: 5m

**Figure 24-28**

3. Add a Gradient layer going from white to black and select Alpha from the Blending Mode drop-down menu. Also, select Weight Map as the Input Parameter and pick the "rough" weight map from the drop-down menu. Figure 24-29 shows the rough weight map. I created a few weight maps to isolate different areas of the canyon. For more information on weight maps, see Chapter 10, "Using Weight Maps for Texturing." Open the Crackle attributes; you can leave the background color as is but change the fore-ground color to a dark orange like 135, 89, 3. Keep Blending Mode set to Nor-mal and change the following properties:

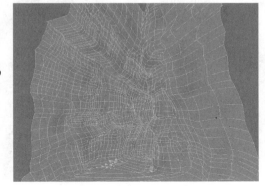

Small Scale: 0.5
Frequencies: 3.0
Scale X: 5m, Y: 15m, Z: 5m

**Figure 24-29**

4. Now we need to mix these layers together using the Mixer node. Connect the Color output of the Color Layer node to the Bg Color input of the Mixer node and the Color output of the Crackle node to the Fg Color input of the Mixer node. Open the Mixer's attributes and change Opacity to 17.5%. Plug the Color output of this node to the Color input of the diffuse Minnaert shader, then connect the Color output of this shader to the Diffuse Shading slot of the Surface destination node.

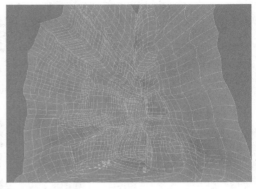

Figure 24-30: Base color network

5. We can now start building detail and interest to our color texture. I would like to have the Crackle texture show only in the areas designated by the "smooth" weight map. To do this, add a Weight Map node to the workspace: Add Node>VertexMap>Weight Map. Double-click the Weight Map node and select the smooth weight from the list, then connect the output of this node to the Opacity input of the Crackle node. At this point you might be asking, "Why take this route when we already have a Color Layer node and we could have added these nodes there?" The answer is because I would like to control the background color of the Crackle texture with a Crumple texture and this would not be possible with the Layer node. Add a Crumple texture to the workspace (Add Node>3D Textures>Crumple), then open the attributes of this node and change the following:

Bg Color: 84, 35, 22
Fg Color: 201, 122, 88
Small Scale: 0.75
Frequencies: 4
Scale X, Y, Z: 5m

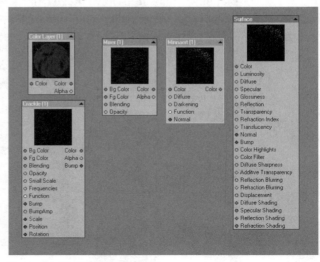

Figure 24-31: "Smooth" weight map

6.  Now take the Color output and plug it into the Crackle Bg Color input. Now the Crackle background color is driven by the Crumple texture. Cool, huh?

7.  The texture is looking good, but it is lacking something very important for achieving a realistic look for a canyon such as this one... the strata, or layers that make the canyon. To do this we'll use a gradient with several different earthy colors. Add a new Gradient node and change the End of the gradient to 25, which is about the height of the canyon. Create the following keys and spread them out almost evenly through the length of the gradient as seen in Figure 24-32:

    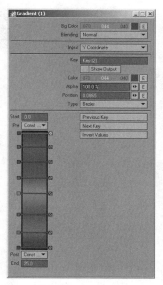

    Key 1: 70, 44, 40
    Key 2: 106, 61, 44
    Key 3: 95, 50, 30
    Key 4: 99, 67, 48
    Key 5: 172, 109, 79
    Key 6: 106, 61, 45
    Key 7: 158, 77, 53
    Key 8: 70, 44, 40

    **Figure 24-32**

8.  After you create these keys, select the third key from the top and click the Show Output button; this will add Key Color, Key Position, and Key Alpha to the Gradient node for that particular key. Now you are able to plug in different nodes to drive that particular key's properties. Here, we are going to drive that key's color with a Crumple texture (Add Node > 3D Textures > Crumple). Open the node attributes and change the following:

    Bg Color: 50, 31, 29
    Fg Color: 139, 74, 55
    Small Scale: 0.75
    Frequencies: 4
    Scale X: 56m, Y: 73m, Z: 90.5m

9.  Now connect the Color output to the Key Color input in our gradient. You can do this for every key in the gradient and have a massive amount of detail. This is possible to do in the classic layer system, but it would consist of a massive number of layers, which could lead to a massive amount of confusion. Being able to drive keys with other textures in the network is a really powerful feature that you will be using often. To finish the color of the surface, connect the Color output of the gradient to the Color input of the Color Layer node. Make a test render and check

the results. All we need now is a little bump detail to finish off the canyon.

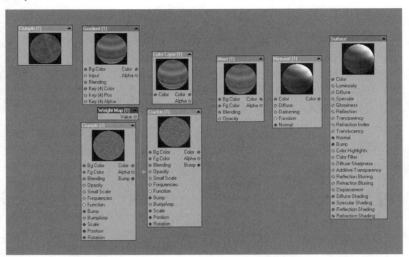

Figure 24-33: Finished color node network

10. For the bump, we are going to take a similar approach to how we did the color textures. Add a Turbulent Noise node and an fBm Noise node to the workspace. Open the Turbulent Noise attributes panel and change these settings:

Increment: 0.5
Lacunarity: 2.0
Octaves: 6.0
Noise Type: Perlin Noise
Bump Amplitude: 35%
Scale X, Y, Z: 800mm

11. Also change the following values for the fBm Noise node:

Increment: 0.5
Lacunarity: 2.0
Octaves: 6.0
Noise Type: Perlin Noise
Bump Amplitude: 40%
Scale X, Y, Z: 300mm

12. Connect the Bump output of the Turbulent Noise node to the Bump input of the fBm Noise node. This is very similar to what we did earlier while working with the color nodes.

13. We are looking to create subtleties on the bump of the surface and break up the "computer made" look that procedurals tend to have, so let's add a couple more 3D texture nodes and blend them all together. Add a Crumple node and a Crust node. Open the Crumple first and change these attributes:

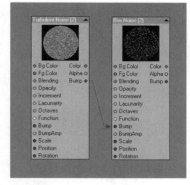

**Figure 24-34**

Small Scale: 0.75
Frequencies: 4
Bump Amplitude: 15%
Scale X, Y, Z: 300mm

14. Open the Crust node's Properties panel to change these values:

Width: 10%
Contrast: 0
Bump Amplitude: 15%

15. Leave Scale at the default 1 meter. Notice how we are changing the Bump Amplitude of every bump node; by doing this, the strength of the bump will be subtle, as we are not looking to overpower the look of the image with a very strong bump. The last two nodes are meant for the ground. There is a weight map already created in the canyon object for this purpose; all we have to do is add a Weight Map node with the ground weight selected from the node's attributes panel and plug that in to both the Crumple and Crust nodes' Opacity inputs.

16. We can control the value of the ground weight a little better by adding a gradient to the network. Add a Gradient node (Add Node>Gradient>Gradient) and make this gradient go from white at the top to black at the end. Connect the Value output of the weight map to the input slot of the gradient, then connect the gradient's Color output to the Opacity of the Crumple, Crust, and Turbulent Noise nodes' Opacity inputs.

17. Since bumps are vector in nature (XYZ), the Mixer node won't do such a good job, so we need a different way to combine these together to be able to connect all the nodes to the Surface destination node Bump input.

One way to do this is with an Add node, which is available as a scalar and/or vector (Add Node>Math>Vector>Add). Now connect the Bump output of the fBm Noise node to the A input of the Add node, and plug the Bump output of the Crust node to the B input of the Add node; the result output can finally be plugged in to the Bump slot in the Surface destination node.

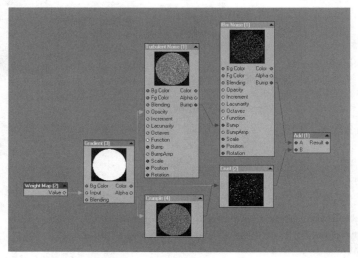

Figure 24-35: Bump node network

18. To finish it off, you can add a CookTorrance specular shader and plug it in to the Specular Shading slot in the Surface destination node, and bring the Glossiness setting down to 5%.

Make a new render to see the results. From here you can experiment by adding more color and bump variation using the techniques that you followed here and see what you come up with. Figure 24-37 shows the final composite in Photoshop; I created a screened bloom layer and added some adjustment layers to do some minor color corrections.

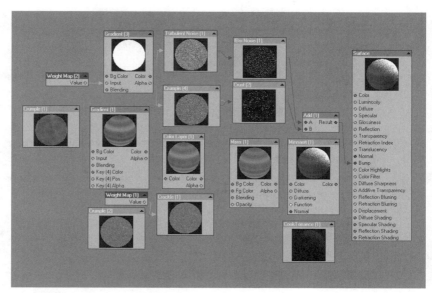

Figure 24-36: Finished surface network

Figure 24-37: Final composite

## Summary of Tips for Creating Canyons and Rocky Mountains

- Study as much reference material as possible; this goes for anything you do.
- Have a clear knowledge of the type of rock that makes the canyon or mountain.
- Make the Bump Amplitude of nodes small and adjust from there; subtlety is key.
- Remember that the colors of the strata will change depending on the type of rock that makes the terrain.

# CHAPTER 25

# LightWave/ZBrush Workflow

In Chapter 11 I gave you a quick overview of ZBrush's features. Now I'll talk about how you can implement ZBrush into your LightWave work so you can take advantage of the displacement maps, normal maps, etc., that are now part of the everyday production pipeline. It might seem at first glance that the steps are quite extensive, but in reality it isn't that difficult or lengthy. Once you know what to do, it'll be a breeze, and working with ZBrush is a lot of fun, too. For artists who are new to ZBrush, I recommend getting used to the interface and tools first since ZBrush's interface is quite different than any other app out there. If you just can't wait and want to dig right in, then follow along; by the time we are done, you should be able to work with your own models from start to finish. Let's get to it!

## Preparing Your Model for ZBrush

The first thing we need is a model to work from. I have provided a base object of an alien head for you to follow along with (in the Tutorials\Alien directory on the companion CD), but you can work with your own model if you prefer. One rule of thumb that you should keep in mind when your model is intended for sculpting and painting in ZBrush is that it is preferable for your model to be all quads. ZBrush subdivides the base object the best when it is all quads. If you find that some triangles cannot be avoided, try to place those triangles in inconspicuous places so if there is any pinching it is not so noticeable. Another "rule" is to cap the holes in your model, such as eye sockets and nostrils. I have left holes in the base object for illustrative purposes; the bottom of the chest will not be seen in our final render, but if you move the camera in Layout you will see a harsh line of the displaced polygons caused by the lack of a cap in the alien bust. I also left the mouth interior out since I wasn't going to open its mouth. When you are working with your own models, don't forget to cap the holes.

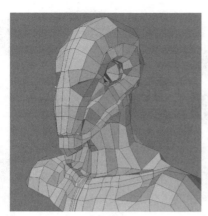

Figure 25-1: The Alien head base object

Figure 25-2: The Alien head unwrapped

A last tip about preparation is about the UV layout. ZBrush has some powerful UV tools that make this part of the creation process a breeze; however, I personally like to unwrap the mesh myself in LightWave. I'll explain why shortly, but for now just remember that if you decide to unwrap your mesh in LightWave, make sure there are no overlapping UVs. If your UV layout has any overlapping UVs, ZBrush may crash upon loading the object, so if you run into this problem take a look at your UV layout first. Taking the time and not rushing through unwrapping pays off at the end.

We are almost ready to export our freaky-looking alien, but one last thing before we hit the Export button… Open the Surface Editor (F5), and then the Color Texture panel, and in the default layer select the UV texture we created. It doesn't have to have an actual image; what we are looking for is that the OBJ Exporter recognize that there is a UV texture being exported with the model. If this step is skipped, the UVs will be skipped as well upon exporting.

Now we are ready to export. Create a descriptive folder in your content directory to avoid any confusion. I usually name mine "OBJ" and then save the OBJ file there with something like "base" somewhere in the name; this way you know it is the base object that you exported from Modeler.

> **TIP:** You can take advantage of Modeler's "parts" in ZBrush since they get exported with the OBJ model. In ZBrush, "parts" will show as polygroups that you can hide on the fly by holding the Ctrl and Shift keys while clicking inside the polygroup you wish to keep on the canvas. Click again while still holding the keys to invert the selection.

# Importing Objects into ZBrush

Now that we have our base object completed, it's time to load it into ZBrush.

Once you open ZBrush, roll your mouse over the Tool menu at the top of the UI. Click on the little orange icon on the far left corner to dock this menu to either the left or right side of the UI. ZBrush calls imported objects "tools" and this is where our object will be after import. Click on the Import button under the Tool menu and browse for the OBJ model we exported; the object will appear as the current tool.

Go ahead and draw the Alien head on the canvas by clicking and dragging. Immediately after drawing the object on the canvas, click on the Edit button right below the main menu. As long as the Edit mode is active, you will be able to modify your mesh in 3D space. The minute you deactivate this button, ZBrush will drop your mesh onto the canvas and it will no longer be an editable 3D object like before. In Edit mode it is "pixols" based, also known as 2.5D. Like I said earlier in the book, pixols are more powerful than regular pixels since they can hold z depth and material information.

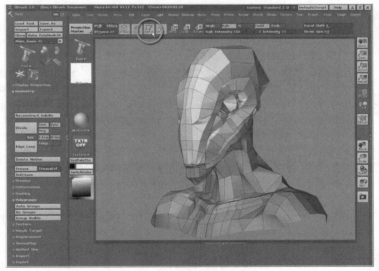

Figure 25-3: ZBrush's UI with our Alien OBJ model

We are not going to experiment with this aspect of ZBrush; just remember to keep the Edit button active and everything will be fine.

On the right side of the UI you will find the tools needed to navigate through the canvas. These tools also have keyboard shortcuts. To move your object, press and hold the Alt key and click and drag your mouse. To rotate the object on its own axis, just click and drag anywhere on the canvas. Scale is a bit trickier. Press Alt, then click and hold on the canvas, and release the Alt key; this might take a little getting used to.

# ZBrush's UV Tools

Let's explore the UV toolset in ZBrush and see the advantages and disadvantages of their use in our LightWave workflow.

There are many options available in the Tool menu when we have an object active on the canvas. We are going to use several of those options, also called subpanels, but for now let's look at the Texture panel, which is accessed by clicking on the Tool menu. Here we have the UV tools; the first three from left to right are the common cylindrical (Uvc), planar (Uvp) and spherical (Uvs) projections that by now you should feel comfortable using. The next one, UVTile, will tile the texture image map to every single polygon of your mesh, taking advantage of tileable texture maps. This option works best when the polygons are pretty uniform across the mesh.

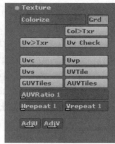

Figure 25-4: Texture panel

Next we have the two options that you will use the most when unwrapping meshes in ZBrush: GUVTiles and AUVTiles. Adaptive UV tiles (AUVs) explode the texture into rectangles of the same approximate size. These match the size of each polygon of the mesh, so the more polygons on your mesh, the more tiles in your AUV.

Grouped UV tiles (GUVs) are very similar to AUVs with the biggest difference being that GUVs try to group areas together so it is easier to read if the texture is later opened in an external program such as Photoshop or Painter. I personally like to unwrap my models myself because I end up getting exactly what I need and they are perfectly readable by anyone who takes a look. This might be very important in large studios where a texture might have to be retouched by someone not familiar with ZBrush. If UVs are not your strongest skill, then either one of these two options will do a great job for you.

ZBrush needs UVs in your object for the creation of texture, normal, and displacement maps. If you are sculpting, you do not need to have one right away, but it is good practice. Also, try to use a power of 2 for textures; for example, 256, 512, 1024, 2048, or 4096. The power of 2 is really important when dealing with real-time render engines like those used for video games. A 1000 × 1000 texture map will use as much memory as a 1024 × 1024 map, so why not use the extra pixels? Also, some engines will round the texture to the next size, so if you have a 1050 × 1050 texture the engine will need the same memory as if a 2048 × 2048 texture was used. Of course this greatly depends on the game engine itself, as some engines do let you use odd resolution figures. For textures intended for broadcast and/or film, the issue is not that important. What would be more important is that UV maps are square, and since you are using UV maps to paint your objects, your ZBrush texture map should be square as well; otherwise, you might have unpredictable results.

Our alien head has a UV map already created in Modeler, but if you would like to try the above mentioned UV options by all means do so. You won't break anything. ;)

## Sculpting and Texturing

You have everything ready to start sculpting… well, almost everything. Before you start sculpting your object, go ahead and open the Morph Target subpanel and click on the StoreMT button as shown in Figure 25-5. ZBrush uses a form of hierarchical subdivisions, and you can go up or down the levels of subdivision at any time. Changes done at any particular level of the hierarchy are propagated through all the other levels of subdivision, so if there are major changes to the mesh, level 1 of our base will get deformed as well. The Morph Target helps us go back to the original base object when it is time to generate our displacement maps and normal maps. However, if the changes are extremely drastic, it is better to create the needed maps from level 1. We'll discuss this in detail later, when we are ready to go back to Modeler. Now let's get started with the sculpting process!

Figure 25-5: Morph Target subpanel's StoreMT button

Open the Display properties subpanel and change the DSmooth option to 1. This is like turning smoothing on in the LightWave Surface Editor. At this point you can subdivide your object. I start by working one level at a time first, adding a level when I feel I have gone as far as possible with the current level. Click on the Geometry submenu and click the Divide button to add a subdivision level to the mesh, then sculpt away until you feel that you need another level of subdivision. Remember that the changes to the mesh will propagate through the subdivision levels.

Having a pressure-sensitive graphic tablet like a Wacom, for example, is a great advantage and I strongly recommend it; it makes sculpting and texturing in ZBrush that much more enjoyable.

Sculpting is very intuitive in ZBrush, but you still need to familiarize yourself with the tools right above the canvas area. Let's just concentrate on those that will allow us to sculpt our mesh. (Remember to keep that Edit button on!) Right next to the Edit button are the Draw, Move, Scale, and Rotate buttons. When you are using Draw, you will be able to paint and/or sculpt your mesh. Move allows you to move vertices very similarly to the Magnet tool in Modeler, where the brush has a falloff and therefore lets you adjust several vertices at once. If you make the size of the brush and its focal shift quite small, you will be able to affect one vertex at a time. The same goes for Scale and Rotate. Notice that some options in this toolbar will be grayed out depending on what mode is active.

This toolbar also contains buttons to turn off or on the channels that you wish to affect: Material + RGB (Mrgb), Rgb (RGB alone), Material (M alone), Zadd, and Zsub. Zadd will add volume to the sculpt, and Zsub will take away volume from the sculpt. These are the two we are going to be using right now. Leave Zadd active and deactivate Rgb or Mrgb if they happen to be on.

Also in this toolbar you will see Z Intensity, which is the strength of the current brush; Focal Shift, which controls the brush's falloff; and Draw Size, which controls the overall size of the brush. Because these are used quite often, Pixologic created some contextual menus to make changing all these options a snap. Press the "s" key to display a contextual menu from which you can change the brush's size. If you also need to change other options at the same time, like Size and Focal Shift, then press the Spacebar to open a contextual menu that displays most of the options available on the top toolbar. This increases productivity since you don't have to break the creative process just to change the focal shift of the brush, for example.

Figure 25-6: The top toolbar buttons and options

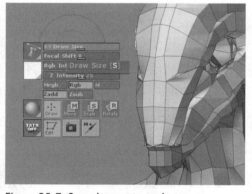

Figure 25-7: Spacebar contextual menu

Another extremely useful shortcut when you are sculpting is the Alt key. By pressing this key your brush will interactively change modes on the fly; for example, if you are in Zadd mode, the Alt key will switch the mode to Zsub! This is so convenient and is one of those little things that make a huge difference when sculpting.

While you are sculpting, you will run into some hard edges. These are common and sometimes even desirable, such as when you're sculpting wrinkles. Press and hold the Shift key to switch your brush to a smoothing brush.

You may reach a point where your mesh has over one million polys and performance suffers a little, even though it's still quite fast for such a high amount of polys. To get better rates you can hide parts of your mesh momentarily. Remember when I mentioned that parts get saved in the export to OBJ from Modeler? Now we can take advantage of those. Click on the Frame button on the top toolbar and you will see the alien head in wireframe shaded view with two different colors. Those colors are the parts

I saved in Modeler; in ZBrush they are called polygroups. This is extremely useful not only because of performance improvement, but also so you can access areas of the mesh that would otherwise be hard to reach or isolate. You can also save your own polygroups right in ZBrush by separating the UV islands of your mesh into groups (if your model happens to have a UV layout, that is). You can also hide the geometry you wish to exclude from the polygroup and then click on the Group Visible button in the Polygroups subpanel.

One thing that I run into a lot in forums is that new users try to sculpt every little miniscule detail on their objects, such as skin pores and tiny wrinkles. I believe that doing so is kind of inefficient and a waste of memory since the mesh needs to be subdivided a lot in order to achieve such fine details and replicating such a high level of detail can be quite difficult and time consuming. It is more efficient to do two passes: a low-frequency sculpt where you sculpt the major changes of the form of the mesh and a high-frequency pass for adding details such as the skin pores as a bump map. The results are excellent and it is far more efficient.

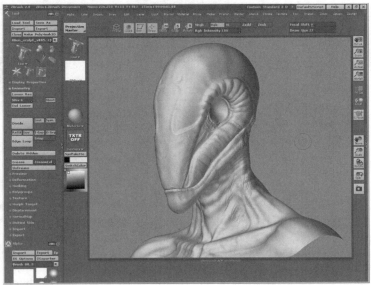

Figure 25-8: Low-frequency sculpt

Texturing is a similar process to sculpting but you usually will work with Zadd or Zsub off, and use Rgb only. As I mentioned before, you need to have UVs present before you start painting. You already know that the alien head provided has a set of UVs, so all you have to do is pick a base color first and then create a texture of the desired size; the new texture will be created and will be filled by the main color on the palette. At this point, ZBrush handles painting like "vertex paint." You paint the vertices of the mesh, so the higher the level of subdivision, the more information there is and the smoother the stroke. Don't worry too much about this right now since we are going to use one of the greatest tools of ZBrush to paint: Projection Master!

## Projection Master

Projection Master allows you to to paint deformations or textures or both at the same time using all of ZBrush's tools and specialized brushes, such as the Deco, Blur, Highlighter, and Colorize brushes. Projection Master will temporarily drop your object in 2.5D space to paint and you will not be able to navigate through the object in 3D space; however, Projection Master will compensate for all the deformations and color information painted. After you are done with one side you move on to the next, and so on, until the complete mesh is detailed or painted. Another cool feature of Projection Master is that you can use alphas as brushes and thus paint and deform an incredible amount of detail very quickly. I have included a folder on the companion CD named SNoWs_ZBrush_alphas that contains alphas for you to use. Let's go through the process of painting deformation details on our alien dude.

Go to the highest level of subdivision in the mesh by moving the SDiv slider on the Geometry subpanel to the far right and then click on the Projection Master button. The Projection Master window pops up. This window is divided in two sections. The top section has to do with color textures and the bottom section has to do with deformation textures. Turn off every color option and turn Deformation on. Once you click on the DROP NOW button, the model will become pixols based until we finish the Projection Master session.

Figure 25-9: Projection Master

Load any of the provided alphas from the companion CD. Set the size and intensity of the brush and make sure Zadd is active. Select a brush from the Tool panel and go crazy! Experimentation is the name of the game at this point. Experiment with different brushes, z intensity, alphas, and strokes and see their effects.

Once you are happy with the results, you are ready to pass all those changes to your actual mesh. Click Projection Master once again; the DROP NOW button now reads PICK UP NOW. Once you hit that button, ZBrush will transfer all that information to your mesh! Easy, right?

The same thing goes for painting textures, but you select the Colors option instead of Deformation. Follow the same steps as before but remember to turn Zadd/Zsub off and turn Rgb on. Again, experiment. Use different colors and alphas, use the Blur brush to blend colors, use the Highlighter, Noise, etc. Go crazy!

> **TIP:** When using Projection Master, stay away from mesh edges. If your brush goes over an edge that is not visible, the texture will get projected through the mesh in a similar fashion as a planar map, causing undesirable stretching or displacement where it was not intended.

Now that we have all the low-frequency deformation and color textures done, we can move on to the high-frequency details. Create another texture filled with a medium gray (128, 128, 128). This will be our high-frequency bump map. Click on the Material ball and load the bumpmatviewer material from the ZMaterials library that comes with ZBrush. This material will be applied to the mesh automatically upon loading and will allow us to view the bump map as it will appear in LightWave when rendered. Drop your mesh in Projection Master and knock yourself out! Pretty cool, right?

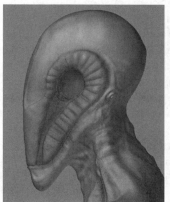 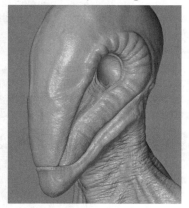

Figure 25-10: Color texture

Figure 25-11: Bump map viewer material

# Rendering and Saving Displacement, Normal, and Texture Maps

Well, that's been fun and all, but we want to go back to LightWave to get our masterpiece rendered.

In order to use all of the texture maps we created, we need to flip the V coordinates of the maps; otherwise, our textures will be mapped incorrectly in our model. This is the most common problem people have when they are starting out incorporating ZBrush into their work. The active texture should be the bump map that we just worked on. Open the Texture panel and dock it. Right below the texture maps is a button labeled Flip V. If you click this button, you will see that the bump map seems to be improperly mapped to your model in ZBrush, but it will show correctly once we load it into Layout. You will have to do this for every texture you save from ZBrush to be used in LightWave. After you flip the bump map, save it as a TIFF or PSD file, whichever you prefer; the file format for bump maps is not as important as it is with displacement maps.

Displacement maps are grayscale maps rendered from the sculpting you painted on your object; essentially they are height maps. This map is then used in Layout to displace the geometry to mimic the ZBrush sculpt.

Let's get our displacement map rendered out. Go to the first level of subdivision of the alien head model and roll out the Displacement subpanel. Here, you set the algorithm to be used and the resolution of the map. Go ahead and change the DPRes to the maximum, which is 4096 pixels, and turn on SmoothUV. Now you need to select the displacement algorithm. You can select from Adaptive Scan or DPSubPix (subpixel). Adaptive Scan should be fine for most of our work and this is what I used for the final displacement of our alien. The main difference between Adaptive and subpixel is that subpixel calculates the number of times the mesh is subdivided before the displacement map is generated. If you went all out and painted in skin pores, for example, this will give you better results than Adaptive since it is more accurate; however, the render times will be dramatically longer — sometimes several hours longer depending on resolution and the level of accuracy you selected. Since we separated the high frequency from the low frequency, we can use Adaptive and save a lot of time without the quality suffering at all.

Click on the Create DispMap button to render the displacement map. A progress bar will appear, informing you of the progress and estimated time. After the map is rendered, it will show up as the current alpha map in the Alpha panel. If it doesn't show as the current alpha, click on the Alpha panel and select it; it should be the last image listed in the panel. Now flip this image's V coordinates and save it as a TIFF file. This is very important since TIFF files saved from ZBrush will be 16-bit per channel instead of 8 like PSD, and therefore will give you greater accuracy and in turn better results.

Normal maps are very similar to bump maps, which are used to add detail without adding more polygons to your geometry. They contain more data and thus provide better results, and they can completely replace the normals of the polygons. Open the Normal Map subpanel in the Tool panel and turn on SmoothUV and Tangent, which is necessary for LightWave v9. Click on the Create NormalMap button to render the

Figure 25-12: Flip V

map and the progress bar will come up again. After the map is rendered, it will show as the current texture; once again you will flip the V coordinates and save it as a TIFF.

If you have painted any other maps, such as specular and diffuse maps, flip and save those as well. They do not need to be TIFF 16-bit and can be saved in PSD format. All of these images will be opened in Photoshop or your image editing software of choice to be converted to PNG format images. PNG will keep file sizes small without sacrificing their quality. Keep the displacement and normal maps as they are; do not convert them to PNG or you will lose the extra data saved in a 16-bit file like those we saved from ZBrush.

At this point export the level 1 object as an OBJ file. We will bring this into Modeler to prep it for Layout.

## Bringing It All Together

Open the original LightWave object and the newly created object. Since our object had major changes I decided to go with the level 1 mesh from ZBrush, but there is one slight problem — our original mesh contained vertex data since it had a morph map. We lost this morph map when we exported the model for ZBrush. Don't worry, though, we just need to pass the vertex position of the new object to the original model so we do not have to recreate every morph map. Copy the object from ZBrush and paste it in a new layer of the original object. We are going to use a Modeler tool called Background to Morph. This is a snap since the vertex order has not been changed; if the vertex order had changed at all, then I'm afraid there is no recourse but to redo all your morphs, weights, etc. Luckily, we don't have to deal with that because we did not add or subtract geometry to the base object.

Make the original object the foreground and the ZBrush object the background layer, then go to Map>Morph and select Bkg to Morph, pick a name, and click OK. Now that we have a morph of the new vertex locations we need to pass this data to the base object. Go to Map>Morph, choose Apply Morph, and make sure you select the correct morph map since every vertex map you have in the file will be listed here. Then click OK, and you're done! All the vertices are now in the identical positions as the base exported from ZBrush. Hit the Tab key to convert your object to subdivision surfaces, and delete the ZBrush OBJ layer and the morph map we just created to keep the file clean and tidy. That's it.

Since we created our UV map right in LightWave, the base object already had it and we didn't have to pass that information over. If you have a ZBrush-generated UV map, then that has to get transferred to the original base object. To do this we need a free plug-in called ZWave, which you can download from www.flay.com. Install the plug-in like any other plug-in in

LightWave, and it will show up in the Additional list. This plug-in is quite easy to use. Just load the original object, the one you want to copy the UVs to, and activate ZWave. Click on the Import File button and browse for the ZBrush exported object. Leave every option as is, making sure that Replace Existing Texture is on, and click OK; the UV data is transferred to the object! Now it's time to jump to Layout.

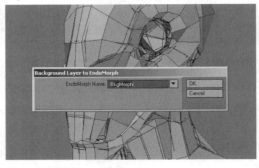

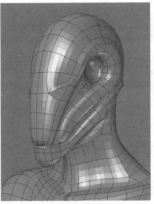

Figure 25-13

Launch Layout and load the scene called Alien_Start.lws. This scene has the object already loaded and ready for displacement and texturing. We are going to use the Node Editor to set up our displacement and texture maps.

Figure 25-14: Finished SubD model

> **NOTE:** For more information about the Node Editor, refer to Chapter 14, "The Node Editor."

First let's get our displacement map working and matched as close as possible to the ZBrush sculpt. Select the object and open the Object Properties panel ("p"). In the Geometry tab, change Subdivision Order to after bones. We are going to revisit this in a minute. Click on the Deform tab and under Add Displacement, select Morph Mixer, then apply the only morph map available in the list. Now we can see that our morphs are still there and working properly. Click the check box next to Edit Nodes to activate nodes and then open the editor by clicking on the Edit Nodes button. If you are unfamiliar with nodes and you don't want to go back to Chapter 14, just follow these steps and you will be fine.

Upon opening the Node Editor window, we see a node already there. This is the destination node. In this case it is a displacement node; we will be plugging our displacement network here. Go to the Add Node drop-down menu at the upper-left of the window and add the following nodes:

2D Textures > Image
Math > Scalar > Subtract
Math > Scalar > Multiply
Math > Vector > Scale
Spot > Spot Info

Double-click the Image node and load the displacement image you saved earlier or load the one provided on the companion CD called Alien_sculpt_ disp.tif. Turn MipMap Quality to Off and under Mapping select UV map and pick Alien; this is our UV map that we used to paint our displacement, normal, and color maps in ZBrush.

ZBrush, unlike LightWave, uses 50% gray as no displacement. We need to change these values for LightWave to displace the mesh properly; to do this we use the Subtract node. Connect the Luma output of the Image node to the A input of the Subtract node, then double-click this node to view its properties and change the B value to 0.5. That will take care of the displacement values; now we move on to the amount of displacement. Plug the Result output of the Subtract node to the A input of the Multiply node. Open its properties by double-clicking on it, and then change the B value to 1.5. This number is dependent on the scale of the object; since our Alien head is quite big, let's start with 1.5 and fine-tune from there.

We now need to tell LightWave the direction and scale we want the displacement to have. We already have the scale figured out using the Subtract and Multiply nodes, so all we need is the direction, which the Spot Info node will give us. We then need to combine the direction with scale, which is the function of our Scale node. Plug the Normal output of the Spot Info node to the Vector input of the Scale node, then plug the output of the Multiply node to the Scale input of the Scale node. The output of the Scale node is then plugged to the input of the Displacement node and our network is finished. You should be able to see the displaced mesh in your viewport.

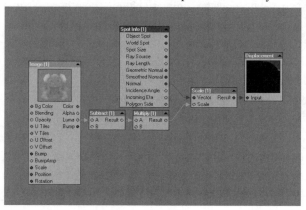

Figure 25-15:
Displacement
node network

In order to get as close as possible to the ZBrush sculpt we need to add more subdivisions to the mesh, but instead of doing that globally we will take advantage of APS (Adaptive Pixel Subdivision). With APS we can tell the LightWave render where more detail is needed and where it is not that crucial, so let's revisit the Object Properties panel and make some changes.

In the Geometry tab in the Object Properties panel, change Render SubPatch to Per Polygon Level and click on the "T" button to open the Texture Editor.

Here we are going to create a gradient with three keys that will control the density of the mesh. Change the value of the first key to 25, make another key and place it on the bottom of the gradient, then make a third key and change its value to 0 and place it on the middle of the gradient.

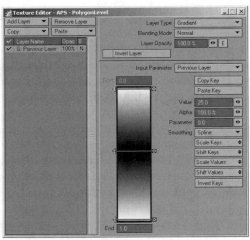

Now you can make a test render to compare your LightWave output to the ZBrush sculpt. After the test I felt I needed to increase the amount of displacement, so

Figure 25-16: APS

in the displacement Node Editor I changed the amount of displacement from 1.5 to 1.75; the results look closer to the ZBrush sculpt at this amount.

Almost done... Open the Texture Editor (F5) and open the Node Editor, making sure that the check box is on. Here you will see the Surface destination node, which is where we are going to plug in the other textures we created in ZBrush.

Create the following nodes:

2D Textures>Image
2D Textures>NormalMap

Load the color texture in the image map like we did with the displacement map. Make sure MipMap Quality is off and that you select the Alien UVs. Do the same for the Normal Map node but load the normal map we created in ZBrush. Copy and paste the color texture image node and replace the image with the specular, bump, and any other textures you may have. Plug the Color output of the color texture image node to the Color input of the Surface destination node. Plug the Normal output of the Normal node to the Normal input of the Surface destination node, and so on, until all your textures are properly mapped to the corresponding input.

Render again. All the textures should show properly on the rendered image with the exception of the bump map, which is very faint. This is due to the mid-gray ZBrush values again. In order to correct this, just increase the Bump Amplitude in the image node that contains the bump map to a very large amount, like 300% or 400%. Now it is just a matter of fine-tuning the specular, glossiness, diffuse, etc., values as needed. You can even add subsurface scattering or any other type of shaders. Experiment!

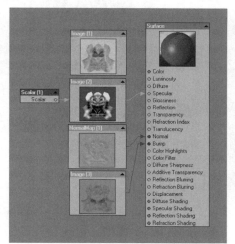

Figure 25-18: The result

Figure 25-17: Finished skin node network

> **NOTE:** Check out Chapter 14, "The Node Editor," for more on creating networks, shaders, SSS, etc.

> **NOTE:** For more on LightWave and ZBrush workflow and techniques I suggest you read the LightWave ZPipeline guide published by Pixologic and written by fellow artist and author Steve Warner. It has some more cool information that I'm sure you will find useful as well. It can be found at http://www.zbrushcentral.com as well as www.pixologic.com.

ZBrush is an extremely powerful application. By combining it with LightWave, you will be able to create stunning characters, landscapes, planets, meteors, and more!

Figure 25-19 shows a comp I created in Photoshop after playing with the node network a little further. If you would like to use this surface, just load it from the Surface Presets folder on the companion CD or load up the scene called Alien_finished.lws.

**Figure 25-19**

# CHAPTER 26

# Architectural Surfaces

Architectural images are extremely popular these days, with entire studios dedicated only to architectural visualization work. You can show clients images of their building's exterior or interior long before a single nail is hammered or walls get painted. FPrime helped bring LightWave to this market mostly due to its sheer speed. You can render images using radiosity at a fraction of the time than you can with LightWave alone. In this tutorial I wanted to do something a bit different from the average room. We are going to texture a daylight-lit basement stairway. Besides good textures, good lighting is essential for architectural renders. Remember that good textures make your models but good lighting makes your scene! Since I would like to use FPrime to render this image, we will be texturing it with the "classic" Texture Editor by adding layers to the surface just like the guitar tutorial. If you don't have FPrime, you can render with LightWave's standard radiosity, but it will take longer.

## The Model

This model is quite simple: a few walls, a ceiling, floor, a window, and of course the stairs. The model contains weight maps that we will use to control certain aspects of the textures. In general, it is a simple model and what makes it look nice is the texturing and lighting. To get a bit of a nostalgic feeling, I modeled a couple of toys to be added to the scene later.

## Surfacing the Room Elements

In this tutorial we are going to use the "classic" Texture Editor using layers. I would also like to use FPrime for rendering this image and since at this point it does not take advantage of nodes, we have to stick with layers.

1. Set the content directory in LightWave to the Stairs folder inside the Tutorials directory of the companion CD ("o" on the keyboard, then "Paths"). After setting the content directory, load the scene called Stairs.lws.

   Most of the surfaces in this room are quite simple. The procedurals used are subtle as well; it is a good idea to build your textures slowly, one by one, and fine-tune from there. The biggest problem with that approach is that it will be difficult to see exactly what the textures are doing separately. So if you think you are going to need four different procedurals or images to achieve the look that you are after, just add the layers one by one and see their effect. Another suggestion I can give you when using procedural textures is to change the texture color to a very bright, vibrant color like a bright red. This makes the procedural really stand out and the patterns will be clearly visible; then after you are happy with the texture, change the color to a more appropriate one.

2. Before you start, if you would like to see what you are doing interactively, activate VIPER, create a new camera in the scene, and leave it at its default settings. Make a test render so the buffers can be saved for VIPER.

   During the surfacing session you can move this camera to the specific area that you are working on and have a clear view of the surface in the VIPER window. Every time you move the camera to a new location you need to make a new render in order to update VIPER's buffers; if you have FPrime a new render is not needed, as the previewer will update automatically.

3. Let's begin with the walls. There is not much going on here, so you just have to decide the type of paint finish that you would like to have for them. In this case I'm going for a semi-gloss finish. I changed the base color of the walls to a beige color: 217, 205, 164.

4. Click on the "T" button to open the Texture Editor of the Color channel and change the default layer to a Crumple procedural texture. Change the texture attributes as follows:

   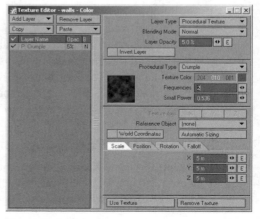

   Layer Opacity: 5%
   Texture Color: 204, 10, 1
   Frequencies: 2
   Small Power: 0.536
   Scale X: 5m, Y: 5m, Z: 5m

Figure 26-1: Color layer

This layer is very subtle, but it breaks up the base color a little so it isn't completely even.

5.  For the Diffuse channel, lower the amount to 95%; semi-gloss paint reflects quite a bit of light so a nice bright color for the surface would be ideal. We can use procedural textures to break it up a little. Click on the "T" button of the Diffuse channel to open the Texture Editor. Add a Turbulence layer with the following values:

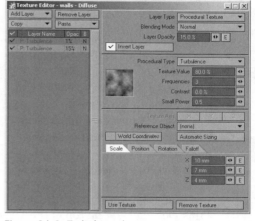

Figure 26-2: Turbulence layer

    Layer Opacity: 15%
    Texture Value: 80%
    Frequencies: 3
    Contrast: 0%
    Small Power: 0.5
    Scale X: 10mm, Y: 7mm, Z: 4mm

6.  To randomize it a bit more, add another Turbulence layer with these values:

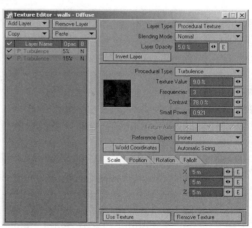

Figure 26-3: Second Turbulence layer

    Layer.Opacity: 5%
    Texture Value: 9%
    Frequencies: 3
    Contrast: 78%
    Small Power 0.92
    Scale X: 5m, Y: 5m, Z: 5m

7.  We need to make exactly the same Turbulence layer for the Specularity channel that we made for the Diffuse channel. Instead of making the layer from scratch again, go back to the Texture Editor of the Diffuse channel by clicking on its "T" button. Select the Turbulence layer on the bottom of the stack, then click on the Copy pull-down menu button above the layer stack and choose Selected Layer(s). Next click on the "T" button of the Specular channel to open its Texture Editor and click and hold on the Paste pull-down menu and select Replace All Layers.

8.  Keep the Glossiness channel with a low value, like 5%. Since the paint that we are trying to mimic is semi-gloss, add a tiny bit of reflection, such as 2%.

9.  The last channel for the walls surface is Bump; again paste the same Diffuse Turbulence layer that we also used for the Specular channel.

10. Next, let's make some imperfections on the wall's surface. Sometimes when you paint walls you'll notice that the wall is not 100% smooth. It might have dents or plaster bumps, or it may have been painted with low-quality tools, such as cheap rollers or brushes that can lose fibers or hairs that get mixed with the paint (I hope my mom reads this). To mimic all these imperfections you can use a Dented procedural texture. Add this Dented layer on top of the Turbulence layer and change the following values:

    Layer Opacity: 100%
    Texture Value: 42.5%
    Scale: 1.45
    Power: 5.0%
    Frequency: 0.75
    Octaves: 3.6
    Noise Type: Perlin Noise
    Scale X: 15mm, Y: 15mm, Z: 15mm

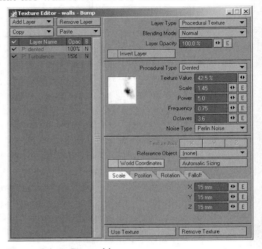

Figure 26-4: Dented layer

11. I didn't spend too much time on the window surfaces since they won't be visible in the final render and any textures added to it will have some impact on rendering time. I thought of just using some basic channel settings, like lowering the Diffuse and increasing Specularity and Glossiness. The only surface that is really important is the glass of the window since the rays produced by Ray Tracing need to go through the glass and into the room. Select the "Glass" surface and change these channel values:

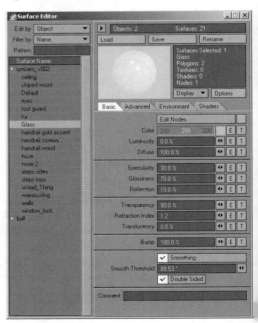

Figure 26-5: Glass surface

Color: 200, 200, 200 (gray)
Diffuse: 100%
Specularity: 30%
Glossiness: 70%
Reflection: 10%
Transparency: 90%
Refraction Index: 1.2
Smoothing: On
Double Sided: On

12. Now let's surface the hand rail. It consists of three surfaces: the painted wood, the gold-colored support, and the screws. I wanted to surface the wood surfaces in the scene other than the steps to make them look like they could use another coat of paint, so I use a very light gray base color, like RGB 240. Click on the "T" of the Color channel to open the Texture Editor and add a Cyclone layer. This is a rarely used texture, and I thought this would be a great example of showing this texture being used in something other than... err, cyclones. After the layer is created, dial in these values:

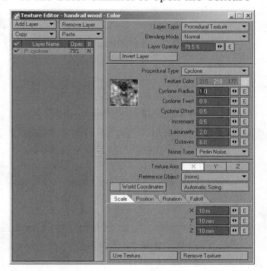

Layer Opacity: 79.5%
Texture Color: 215, 218, 177
Cyclone Radius: 1
Cyclone Twist: 0.9
Cyclone Offset: 0.5
Increment: 0.5
Lacunarity: 2
Octaves: 6

Figure 26-6: Cyclone texture

Noise Type: Perlin Noise
Texture Axis: X
Scale X: 10m, Y: 10mm, Z: 10mm

13. For the other surface channels, just dial in these values:

Diffuse: 90%
Specularity: 10%
Glossiness: 32%
Reflection: 3%

14. For the Bump channel we need to copy the Cyclone layer from the Color channel. Click on the Color channel's "T" for the Texture Editor and copy the Cyclone layer. Now click on the Bump channel's "T" button for the Texture Editor and paste the Cyclone texture layer. Add a Dented layer on top of that for extra detail as seen in Figure 26-7:

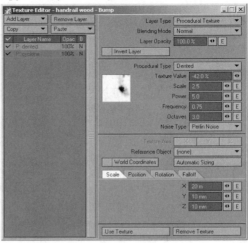

Layer Opacity: 100%
Texture Value: –42%
Scale: 2.5
Power: 5
Frequency: 0.75
Octaves: 3
Noise Type: Perlin Noise
Scale X: 20m, Y: 10mm, Z: 10mm

Figure 26-7

15. The metal details of the handrail are easy enough; just remember that for good metals you need low Diffuse and high Specular values. Make the base color of the gold accent 244, 208, 114. Then click on the Color channel's "T" once again, and change the default layer to a Turbulence procedural with these settings:

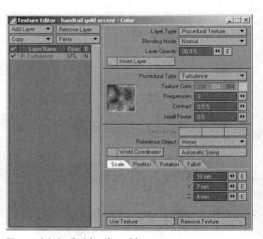

Layer Opacity: 38%
Texture Color: 204, 204, 204
Frequencies: 3
Contrast: 0%
Small Power: 0.5
Scale X: 10mm, Y: 7mm, Z: 4mm

Figure 26-8: Gold-colored layer

16. Use a gradient for the Diffuse channel. Create one extra key and put it on the bottom of the gradient. Make the Layer Opacity 80%, select Incidence Angle as Input Parameter, and set in these values for the keys:

Top key
Value: 79.5%
Alpha: 100%
Parameter: 0

Bottom key
Value: 0%
Alpha: 0%
Parameter: 88

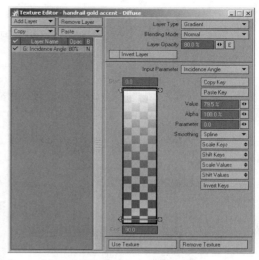

17. This gradient will cause the surface's Diffuse to increase incrementally toward the surface edges, creating the effect of a subtle rim highlight. Now change the following channel values:

Diffuse: 35%
Specularity: 55%
Glossiness: 34%
Reflection: 50%

Figure 26-9: Incidence Angle gradient

18. Now you have a pretty convincing metal. Before we move on to the screws, let's add some bump detail to the metal. Add a Turbulence procedural texture with the following values:

Layer Opacity: 20%
Texture Value: 10%
Frequencies: 5
Contrast: 0
Small Power: 1
Scale X: 7mm, Y: 7mm, Z: 7mm

19. Add a Dented texture layer to add variation to the texture:

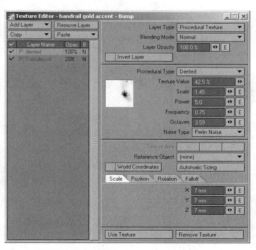

Layer Opacity: 100%
Texture Value: 42.5%
Scale: 1.45
Power: 5
Frequency: 0.75
Octaves: 3.59
Noise Type: Perlin Noise
Scale X: 7mm, Y: 7mm, Z: 7mm

Figure 26-10: Dented texture

**595**

20. These layers combined will create the look of some wear and tear on the surface, but it isn't strong enough to overpower the surface. Use this texture for the screws as well, but change it slightly so it isn't an exact copy. Right-click on the handrail gold surface and copy it, then right-click on the screws surface and paste it. Get rid of the bump map for the screws; they are so tiny that it will not make a difference to the final image and the procedurals won't have to be calculated. Change the basic surface properties to these:

Color: 223, 233, 233 (light gray)
Diffuse: 60%
Specularity: 100%
Glossiness: 24%
Reflection: 5%

21. Add a gradient in the Reflection channel and select Incidence Angle as the Input Parameter. Leave the default key as is and add an extra key with a Value of 11.5 and a Parameter of approximately 72.9. This will make the edges of the object more reflective.

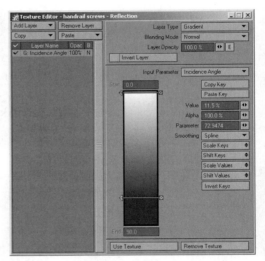

Figure 26-11: Reflection gradient

22. For the "steps sides" surface, make the base color burgundy to create a good contrast with the beige walls, something like 138, 38, 12. Click on the "T" button to add some texture layers to the surface. Make the first layer a red Crumple procedural texture. Change the Blending Mode to PShop Multiply; this will multiply the color information with the base color, resulting in a slightly darker color. Remember, subtlety is key. Having this in mind, use the following values:

Layer Opacity: 5%
Texture Color: 204, 10, 1
Frequencies: 2
Small Power: 0.536
Scale X: 5m, Y: 5m, Z: 5m

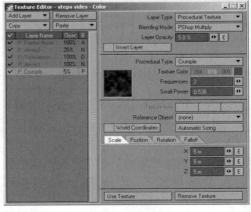

Figure 26-12: Crumple color layer

23. To add some tear and wear discoloration, add a Dented texture layer with the following settings, as seen in Figure 26-13:

Layer Opacity: 100%
Texture Color: 255, 255, 255 (white)
Scale: 2.5
Power: 5
Frequency: 0.75
Octaves: 3
Noise Type: Perlin Noise
Scale X: 20m, Y: 1m, Z: 1m

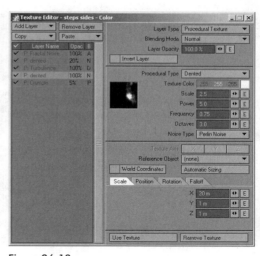

**Figure 26-13**

24. To make this texture more interesting and natural, add a Turbulence layer to the stack. Leave all the settings at their defaults with the exception of Contrast, which should be set to 49%. Also change the Blending Mode to Texture Displacement; this will disturb the texture that sits right above it. Add another Dented texture to the stack (Figure 26-14); this will be the texture that will be displaced by the Turbulence layer. Change the following:

Layer Opacity: 20%
Texture Color: 255, 198, 174
Scale: 1.71
Power: 5
Frequency: 0.75
Octaves: 3
Noise Type: Perlin Noise
Scale X: 50mm, Y: 50mm, Z: 200mm

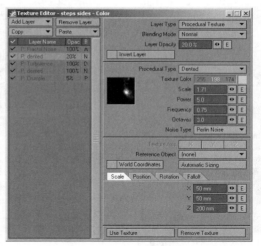

**Figure 26-14**

**597**

25. Now we have some nice streaks caused by the Turbulence layer underneath. The only problem with this as it stands right now is that it covers the whole surface equally and is thus a dead give-away of the procedural pattern. To correct this, add a Fractal Noise layer to the stack, and change the Blending Mode to Alpha and the Contrast to 1.45. Now the Dented texture below will fade in some areas and therefore eliminate the too even pattern.

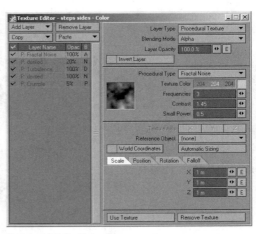

Figure 26-15: Alpha layer

26. For the Diffuse channel, lower the amount to 95%, click on its "T" button to open the Texture Editor, and add a couple of Tur-bulence layers to add variation to the diffuse values, as shown in Figures 26-16 and 26-17.

Layer Opacity: 15%
Texture Value: 80%
Frequencies: 3
Contrast: 0%
Small Power: 0.5
Scale X: 10mm, Y: 7mm, Z: 4mm

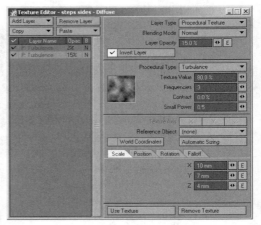

Figure 26-16

Layer Opacity: 3%
Texture Value: 80%
Frequencies: 3
Contrast: 78%
Small Power: 0.92
Scale X: 2m, Y: 2m, Z: 2m

27. Back in the Surface Editor change the Specularity channel value to 10% and Glossiness to 17.5%. Sometimes you can get away with just fine-tuning these values, but it depends on the surface and the look you are going for. In this case, leave

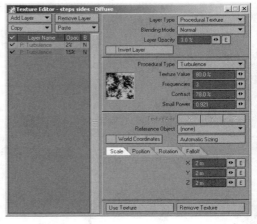

Figure 26-17

Glossiness as is but add a simple Turbulence layer to the Specularity channel:

Layer Opacity: 15%
Texture Value: 80%
Frequencies: 3
Contrast: 0%
Small Power: 0.5
Scale X: 10mm, Y: 7mm, Z: 4mm

28. Almost done with this surface... it just needs some bumps and dents. Go to the Specular channel and click on its "T" button to open the Texture Editor and copy the Turbulence layer. Go back to the Bump Texture Editor by clicking on its "T" button and replace the default layer with the one that we just copied. On top of that create a Dented texture to add imperfections to the surface:

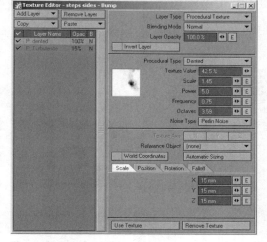

Figure 26-18: Dented bump layer

Texture Value: 42.5%
Scale: 1.45
Power: 5
Frequency: 0.75
Octaves: 3.6
Noise Type: Perlin Noise
Scale X: 15mm, Y: 15mm, Z: 15mm

29. We have two of the main surfaces left to do: the "wainscoting" and "steps tops" surfaces. Copy the "handrail wood" surface and paste it on the wainscoting surface. Since this surface doesn't see as much traffic as a handrail would, let's change the Specularity channel to 20%, the Glossiness channel to 15%, and Reflection to 5% to make it a little glossier looking than the handrail.

30. The surface called "steps tops" is probably the most challenging one of the bunch. Let's start with the Color channel; copy the base color texture layer, Cyclone, from either the handrail wood or wainscoting surface, then click on the steps tops surface and click on the Color channel "T" button and replace the default layer with this one to make it the base texture as well. Now, create a Turbulence layer to be used as a displacement, just like we did before, with the following settings:

Layer Opacity: 100%
Texture Color: 204, 204, 204 (light gray)
Frequencies: 3
Contrast: 87.5%
Small Power: 0.505
Scale X: 2m, Y: 2m, Z: 2m

31. Add a Dented procedural texture layer to the stack and change the following:

Layer Opacity: 15%
Texture Color: 138, 38, 12
Scale: 4
Power: 5
Frequency: 0.75
Octaves: 3
Noise Type: Perlin Noise
Scale X: 40m, Y: 20mm, Z: 20mm

32. Let's add some color variation to the surface using a gradient. Add the gradient to the stack, then change the Blending Mode to PShop Multiply and the Layer Opacity to 35%. The model contains a weight map called "steps." Use this map to drive the gradient by changing the gradient Input Parameter to Weight Map, and selecting the map from the pull-down menu. Figure 26-21 shows the "steps" weight map.

Figure 26-19: Displacement texture

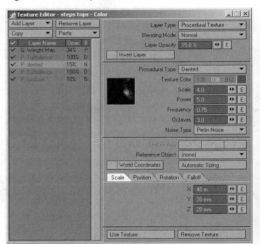

Figure 26-20: Dented layer

You can also load the model into Modeler and take a look at the map there. We need three keys in this gradient with the following values from top to bottom (see Figure 26-22):

Key 1
Color: 000, 000, 000 (black)
Alpha: 36%
Parameter: –100%

Key 2
Color: 255, 245, 213
Alpha: 44%
Parameter: 21%

**600**

Key 3
Color: 146, 121, 71
Alpha: 34.5%
Parameter: 100%

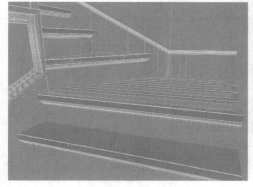

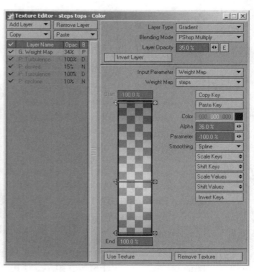

Figure 26-21: "Steps" weight map          Figure 26-22

33. To finish the Color channel, copy the Turbulence displacement layer and paste it below the gradient so it too gets displaced.

34. For the Diffuse channel, just lower the amount to 90%.

35. Let's jump to the Bump channel — lots to do there. You know what's next… click on the Bump channel's "T" button and paste the same Cyclone texture that you used before. Add a Dented procedural to the stack (Figure 26-23), and change the following values:

Texture Value: –42%
Scale: 2.5
Power: 5
Frequency: 0.75
Octaves: 3
Noise Type: Perlin Noise
Scale X: 20m, Y: 10mm, Z: 10mm

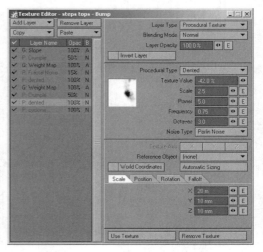

Figure 26-23

36. This surface should show
heavier wear and tear than the
rest of the surfaces of the room,
so let's add some bumps and
dents to the edges of the steps.
Add a Crumple texture, change
the Opacity to 50%, and change
these attributes (see Figure
26-24):

Texture Value: 80%
Frequencies: 4
Small Power: 0.75
Scale X: 20mm, Y: 500mm,
Z: 20mm

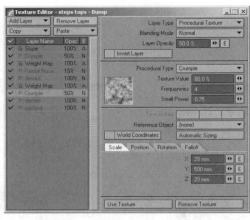

Figure 26-24

37. In order to isolate this texture to the edges of the steps, we can reuse
the weight map that we already have available, so create a gradient with
the Blending Mode set to Alpha and the Input Parameter set to Weight
Map, and pick the "steps" map from the pull-down menu. You can load
the object in Modeler and see what this weight map looks like to get a
better idea of what areas you are isolating with it. We need the following
keys in the gradient:

Key 1
Value: 0%
Alpha: 100%
Parameter: –100%

Key 2
Value: –10%
Alpha: 100%
Parameter: 0%

Key 3
Value: 0%
Alpha: 100%
Parameter: 54%

Key 4
Value: 100%
Alpha: 100%
Parameter: 100%

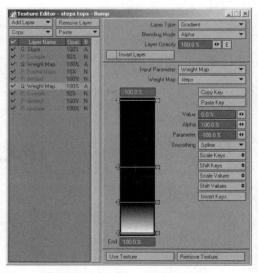

Figure 26-25: Weight alpha gradient

38. Copy the Dented layer already on the stack and paste it to add a copy, keeping everything the same with the exception of the Scale tab values set to X: 40m, Y: 20mm, and Z: 20mm. Let's add another layer of bumps to the edges of the steps. Add a Fractal Noise texture to the stack, change the Opacity to 15%, and change these values:

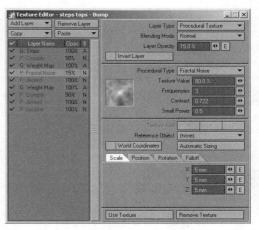

Texture Value: 80%
Frequencies: 3
Contrast: 0.7
Small Power: 0.5
Scale X: 5mm, Y: 5mm, Z: 5mm

Figure 26-26: Fractal Noise texture

39. Since we also want to isolate this texture to the edges, copy the weight map gradient and paste it on top of the Fractal Noise. To finish the bump map, create a Crumple texture (Figure 26-27) with the Opacity at 50%. Also change the following:

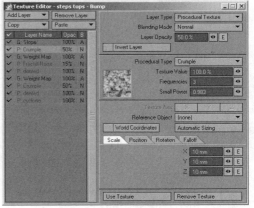

Texture Value: 100%
Frequencies: 3
Small Power: 0.98
Scale X: 10mm, Y: 10mm, Z: 10mm

Figure 26-27: Crumple texture

40. This texture also needs to be isolated, but this time to the sides of steps; to do this use a gradient with the Blending Mode set to Alpha and the Input Parameter set to Slope (Figure 26-28) with the following key values:

Key 1
Value: 0%
Alpha: 100%
Parameter: 0

**603**

Key 2
Value: 77.3%
Alpha: 100%
Parameter: 0.11

Key 3
Value: 100%
Alpha: 100%
Parameter: 0.5

Key 4
Value: 80.3%
Alpha: 100%
Parameter: 0.85

Key 5
Value: 0%
Alpha: 100%
Parameter: 1

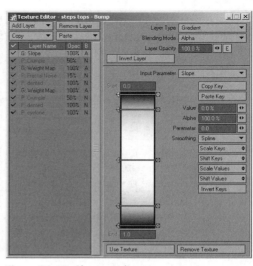

Figure 26-28: Slope gradient

41. The other channels are easy.
Change the Specularity channel
value to 60% and click on the
Specular channel's "T" button.
Change the default texture to a
gradient. Since this is a simple
white to black gradient, just
change the Input Parameter to
Bump. For the Glossiness channel, just change its Value to 40%.
The Reflectivity channel needs
to be at 5% to 8%. It also needs a
Turbulence layer with the Opacity at 25% (Figure 26-29) and the
following settings:

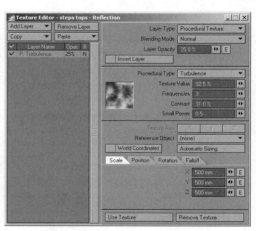

Figure 26-29

Texture Value: 92.5%
Frequencies: 3
Contrast: 31%
Small Power: 0.5
Scale X: 500mm, Y: 500mm, Z: 500mm

You can make a test render or you can use FPrime to see the progress of the
texturing work thus far.

42. Back in the Surface Editor, right-click on the "steps tops" surface and
copy it; paste this surface to the "chipped wood" surface. All we need to
do here is change its color slightly and delete some unneeded texture
layers. Make the base color something like 248, 241, 229 to make it look

**604**

like the geometry dents were at some point painted with the steps, or you can texture them like wood so it looks like the chipped wood is recent. Open the Color texture layers and get rid of the gradient and the Turbulence layer on top of the layer stack; then open the bump layers and get rid of these (bottom to top): the first Crumple and its gradient and the Slope gradient. You should have what's shown in Figure 26-30.

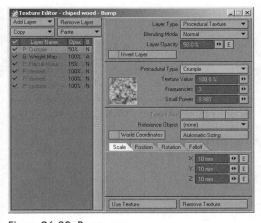

Figure 26-30: Bump map

43. The "foot guard" surface basically follows the same process as we have done before with a slight difference in color and pattern. Copy the surface "steps tops" and paste it into the "foot guard" surface. Change the color to a light gray, something like RGB 223. The Specularity value should be 30%, Glossiness 40%, and Reflection 3%.

44. Open the Texture Editor for the Color channel and delete the weight map gradient. Select the Dented layer and change its Blending Mode to PShop Multiply, then set the texture color to 138, 129, 117. Copy this layer and paste it on top of the Turbulence layer; since the turbulence texture is set to Displacement, the dented texture will get disturbed and thus make smears and scratches on the surface. Change the Dented layer (Figure 26-31) values to the following:

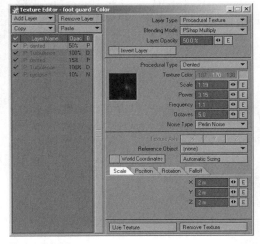

Figure 26-31

Texture Color: 187, 170, 138
Scale: 1.19
Power: 3.15
Frequency: 1.1
Octaves: 5
Noise Type: Perlin Noise
Scale X: 2m, Y: 2m, Z: 2m

Now open the Bump channel's Texture Editor to remove some of the unneeded layers. Remove or turn off (from top to bottom) the Slope gradient, Fractal Noise, the weight map gradient, and the other Fractal Noise layer. The Texture Editor should look like the one in Figure 26-32.

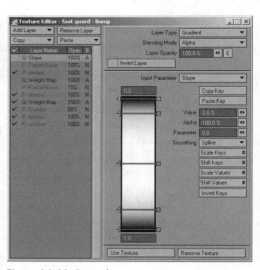

Figure 26-32: Bump layers

As I mentioned at the beginning of the chapter, I added a couple of toys to have a little nostalgic and playful feeling in the image. These objects are hidden in the scene; just open the Scene Editor and unhide them, then activate them so the renderer can see them. If you happen to have Worley's Sasquatch you can load the scene called bear fur.lws included on the companion CD. You can render this pass separately and compose it on top of the finished stairway image. If you don't have Sasquatch, you can use Saslite, which is included with LightWave. Figure 26-33 shows the final composite I created using Photoshop.

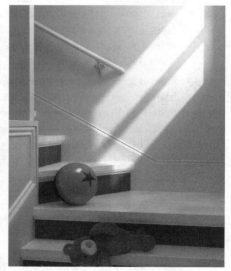

Figure 26-33: Final composite

# Commonly Used Words, Terms, and Phrases

Here is a guide to words, terms, and phrases mentioned within this book, as well as common terms used in the industry.

**alpha channel** — A fourth channel (after RGB) that can be included with 32-bit image formats and contains transparency information. See Appendix B for a list of image formats that can use alpha channels. The alpha channel within a render determines the manner in which it will blend with underlying layers when the render is put in the compositing phase of production.

**CG** — Used as shorthand for "computer-generated." Also, any images, films, or clips created using computers.

**compositing** — The process whereby different elements, either filmed or created digitally, are combined to form visual effects. Popular compositing packages include Adobe After Effects, Discreet Flame, Shake, and many others. Compositing is an extremely critical part of the production process, since it is up to the compositor to ensure that the different elements and plates blend together realistically. Often referred to simply as "comping."

**fractal** — A geometric entity characterized by a pattern that is repeated at ever-decreasing sizes. Fractal patterns form the basis for many procedural textures.

**grunge mapping** — A method of quickly creating dirt in texture maps involving the use of high-contrast and detailed gritty images that are used as overlaid blending layers or used to make selections from other layers to create new gritty-looking texture layers.

**image map** — Any image that is used as a texture on a 3D model.

**image resolution** — In printing terms, the resolution refers to the actual dots per inch ratio, but in broadcast production terms, the resolution of an image usually refers to the actual pixel dimensions of the frame or image being used.

**interpolation** — The process of estimating values between specific points. For example, UV maps use interpolation to calculate the map values across polygons since the actual set values are only initially determined at the vertices where the polygons end.

**node** — Nodes are basically data containers with inputs, outputs, or both inputs and outputs. You can connect two or more of these containers to create what's called a network to describe the final look of the surface or light.

**normal** — *see* surface normal

**Phong shading** — Phong is the shading model that LightWave uses when rendering if it isn't changed through the Node Editor. In order to create the illusion of shapes being smooth, Phong shading interpolates the vertex normals across the surface of the polygon and illuminates the pixel at each point.

**pixel** — A tiny picture element that contains red, green, and blue information for color rendering on a monitor.

**procedural texture** — A mathematical algorithm that creates fractal patterns that can be used as textures on a surface. Procedural textures include Fractal Noise, Turbulence, Grid, and many others.

**projection** — The specific manner in which an image is placed onto a model.

**raster images** — Bitmap images formed by arrays of pixels, such as those made within image editing applications like Adobe Photoshop.

**shader** — In LightWave, a mathematical algorithm that affects the way in which light reacts to a surface as a whole. LightWave's shaders include the BRDF and Fresnel shaders, among others. Shaders can also refer to a surface as a whole or shading models.

**stylus** — A computer artist's alternative to the mouse. A stylus is a pen-like computer input device used with its accompanying tablet for painting and drawing.

**subsurface scattering (SSS)** — This is the phenomenon of light diffusion through a semi-translucent object where light comes in and bounces within the volume of the object before it exits through a different point of the surface. A couple of good examples of this are wax and skin. LightWave has two different SSS shading models to help you simulate this effect in your work: Kappa, which is commonly called "fake SSS," and Omega, which is an accurate, real-world model. Both of these models were written exclusively for LightWave 3D.

**surface normal** — A line emanating from the surface of a polygon that always lies perfectly perpendicular to the polygon. You can see the surface normals by choosing the option in your viewport display options.

**texture map** — *see* image map

**vector images** — Images made from lines and curves defined by mathematical objects called vectors. Commonly used vector programs include Adobe Illustrator and CorelDRAW. Because vectors are not rasterized, they can be scaled up to any size without any degradation of quality.

# A Guide to Image Formats

Due to the vast number of image formats that we have available today, it is a good idea to have a basic understanding of what each format offers and which formats are the most appropriate for you to use in your day-to-day work.

The following guide is a basic introduction to some of the most popular image formats that you may find yourself encountering or working with in the process of creating textures and rendering, as well as a number of formats that you may find useful for optimizing images intended for web output.

## Microsoft Bitmap (.bmp, .dib, .rle)

Recommended for saving textures: No
Recommended for web: No
Recommended for saving renders: Sometimes (for Windows wallpaper images)

The Windows bitmap file format is the standard file format used by Microsoft Paint (Windows Paint program), and is also supported by a number of DOS applications. Bitmap files can contain either 2 (black and white), 16, 256, or 16.7 million colors. Most Windows bitmap files are not compressed, although it is possible to save 16- and 256-color images in a compressed format using *run-length encoding* (RLE), but some applications (notably Windows Paintbrush) are not able to read the compressed files. The RLE compression is a lossless compression scheme, meaning that the image quality is not compromised.

Generally, you do not use this format when creating textures, but you may encounter this when searching for reference. Use this format when saving images that you wish to use as wallpaper images in Windows.

Most bitmap images have the .bmp extension, although you may occasionally encounter some with the .dib (device-independent bitmap) extension, which are sometimes used in computer multimedia systems.

## Encapsulated PostScript (.eps)

Recommended for saving textures: Not applicable
Recommended for web: Not applicable
Recommended for saving renders: Not applicable

The encapsulated PostScript format is purely an interapplication format to allow files to be traded from one software application to another with ease. This includes programs such as QuarkXPress, Adobe Illustrator, Corel-DRAW, and many other graphics and graphics-related software packages. This format is specifically designed to save object-oriented graphics, such as you would find in any vector-based drawing program, intended for printing to a PostScript device. What it does is *rasterize* the vector shapes to create bitmap images for transfer.

LightWave is able to export different viewports from Modeler into EPS files, which is useful for exporting UV maps and such for use in other programs like Adobe Photoshop.

## CompuServe Graphics Interchange Format (.gif)

Recommended for saving textures: No
Recommended for web: Yes
Recommended for saving renders: No

Never used in creating textures, the GIF format is primarily for images that require a small file size for exchange over modems (which is what it was originally designed for), and obviously for uploading onto the web. This format uses LZW compression (Lempel-Ziv-Welch, the same compression scheme as TIFF), but is further optimized by limiting the image to a maximum of 256 colors.

There are two types of GIF, each of which utilize a slightly different codec. The first type is GIF87a, which supports only opaque pixels. The second type, GIF89a, allows transparency via an alpha channel.

# Radiance High Dynamic Range Images (.hdr, .hdri, .pic)

Recommended for saving textures: Not applicable
Recommended for web: Not applicable
Recommended for saving renders: Not applicable

A relatively new image format, HDR images have the ability to contain information that is beyond the range of other file formats. These images can be used as sources of illumination within 3D scenes, and are usually in the form of *light probe images*, which are compiled photographs taken of chrome spheres that reflect a 360° environment.

# Amiga Interchange File Format (.iff)

Recommended for saving textures: No
Recommended for web: No
Recommended for saving renders: No

You may well encounter programs that still (often accidentally) produce IFF files (IFF is Maya's native render format, actually), but generally you do not actually work with them. This format was the common graphics format for Commodore's Amiga computers, which are no longer really used.

Programs like Adobe Photoshop allow you to open and save IFF files, as do some older programs like Electronic Arts DeluxePaint. If you encounter these files, you should save them in a different format, as many applications are unable to read them. Some UV mapping plug-ins, especially the slightly older ones, export the UV maps to IFF files by default.

# Joint Photographic Experts Group (.jpg, .jpeg)

Recommended for saving textures: Yes
Recommended for web: Yes
Recommended for saving renders: Sometimes

Possibly the most widely used graphic file format on the web and in the office, JPEG is one of the most efficient and versatile compression formats currently available for images.

One thing to be aware of is that the JPEG format uses a *lossy* compression scheme, which means that it sacrifices image quality in order to decrease file size. Thus, when saving textures in this format, it is best to leave the quality on maximum to avoid a loss of quality. The advantage to using JPEG is that the file sizes of the textures are considerably smaller than TGA or TIFF formats, thereby reducing rendering time.

The JPEG format is a great choice for images that you wish to upload to the web, as you can compress the images quite substantially without a devastating loss of quality.

Too much compression, however, results in the image becoming very blocky. It is not recommended for images with high contrast or line drawings, as these tend to lose a lot of their definition.

JPEG can be a useful format for saving renders; however, since the file format does not support alpha channels, you lose that information. If you are saving the render so that you can upload it to the web, then this is a good choice. Use a program such as Adobe Photoshop or any other decent image application to adjust the amount of compression on the image.

## Apple Macintosh Picture (.pict, .pct)

Recommended for saving textures: Yes, if you are using a Mac
Recommended for web: No
Recommended for saving renders: Yes, if you are using a Mac

Just as Microsoft Windows has its native BMP format, the Macintosh platform has the PICT (Macintosh Picture) image format. PICT is an extremely versatile format, as it can handle both vector and bitmapped images, and also supports 32-bit image depth, meaning that it can contain alpha channels.

Although this format is a great choice for a number of different uses for Mac users, it is not really ideal for PC users, and TGA and JPEG formats can be used instead.

## Portable Network Graphics (.png)

Recommended for saving textures: Yes
Recommended for web: Yes
Recommended for saving renders: Sometimes

Pronounced *ping*, the PNG format has been until recently primarily a web-oriented image format that enables you to save images in 16 million color without compression quality loss. Another benefit of this format over JPEG, for example, is its ability to contain alpha channel data. Even though PNG has its origins in web graphics, it has been steadily gaining popularity in the CG industry with some studios switching to this format exclusively mostly due to its lossless color compression efficiency.

## Tagged Image File Format (.tif, .tiff)

Recommended for saving textures: No
Recommended for web: No
Recommended for saving renders: Sometimes (especially for print)

Originally developed by Aldus in the early days of the Macintosh, the TIFF format is still one of the most widely used image formats in the printing industry, especially since it is compatible with both PC and Mac platforms. TIFF files can be imported and exported by most 2D and 3D applications.

It is a good choice for saving renders that are intended for the print medium, but not really a useful choice for texture maps.

You can optionally compress TIFF images using the LZW (Lempel-Ziv-Welch) compression scheme, which is a lossless compression. LZW compresses the file size to about half of the uncompressed size without any loss of image quality.

## Truevision Targa (.tga)

Recommended for saving textures: Yes, if an alpha channel is required
Recommended for web: No
Recommended for saving renders: Yes

The best choice for rendering image sequences intended for compositing and broadcast, the TGA format offers 16-bit, 24-bit, and 32-bit images, the latter including alpha channels.

Targa files are uncompressed, which means that their file sizes are rather large, but their quality is perfect, making them an ideal choice for renders and images.

Texture maps that require alpha channels can be saved as 32-bit TGA files, which include the alpha, thus preventing you from having to create a separate image to act as the alpha when the texture is applied to the model.

**614**

# Refraction Index Chart

| Substance | Index of Refraction | Substance | Index of Refraction |
|---|---|---|---|
| Acetone | 1.36 | Diamond | 2.417 |
| Agate | 1.544 | Dolomite | 1.503 |
| Air | 1.0002926 | Emerald | 1.576 |
| Alcohol | 1.329 | Ethanol | 1.36 |
| Aluminum | 1.44 | Ethyl alcohol | 1.36 |
| Amber | 1.546 | Fluoride | 1.56 |
| Amethyst | 1.544 | Formica | 1.47 |
| Aquamarine | 1.577 | Glass | 1.51714 |
| Asphalt | 1.635 | Glycerine | 1.473 |
| Benzene | 1.501 | Gold | 0.47 |
| Bromine (liquid) | 1.661 | Helium | 1.000036 |
| Bronze | 1.18 | Hydrogen (gas) | 1.000140 |
| Calcite | 1.486 | Hydrogen (liquid) | 1.0974 |
| Carbon dioxide (gas) | 1.000449 | Hypersthene | 1.670 |
| Chalk | 1.510 | Ice | 1.309 |
| Chlorine (gas) | 1.000768 | Iodine crystal | 3.34 |
| Chlorine (liquid) | 1.385 | Iron | 1.51 |
| Cobalt blue | 1.74 | Ivory | 1.540 |
| Cobalt green | 1.97 | Jade | 1.610 |
| Cobalt violet | 1.71 | Lapis lazuli | 1.61 |
| Copper | 1.10 | Lead | 2.01 |
| Copper oxide | 2.705 | Mercury | 1.62 |
| Coral | 1.486 | Methanol | 1.329 |
| Crystal | 2.00 | Nitrogen (gas) | 1.000297 |

| Substance | Index of Refraction |
|-----------|---------------------|
| Nitrogen (liquid) | 1.2053 |
| Nylon | 1.53 |
| Onyx | 1.486 |
| Opal | 1.450 |
| Oxygen (gas) | 1.000276 |
| Oxygen (liquid) | 1.221 |
| Pearl | 1.530 |
| Plastic | 1.460 |
| Plexiglas | 1.50 |
| Polystyrene | 1.55 |
| Quartz | 1.544 |
| Rock salt | 1.544 |
| Rubber | 1.5191 |
| Ruby | 1.760 |
| Sapphire | 1.760 |

| Substance | Index of Refraction |
|-----------|---------------------|
| Silicon | 4.24 |
| Silver | 0.18 |
| Sodium chloride | 1.544 |
| Steel | 2.50 |
| Styrofoam | 1.595 |
| Sulphur | 1.960 |
| Teflon | 1.35 |
| Tiger eye | 1.544 |
| Topaz | 1.620 |
| Turpentine | 1.472 |
| Turquoise | 1.610 |
| Water (gas) | 1.000261 |
| Water (100°C) | 1.31819 |
| Water (35°C) | 1.33157 |

# APPENDIX D

# Web Links

Of course, no book is complete without some handy links to relevant sites and possible further reading. So here are my recommendations.

## Community, News, and Tutorial Web Sites

http://www.cgsociety.org — Keep up to date with all the latest CG news and interviews with studios. Loads of information, artwork, and the largest online CG-related forum.

http://www.newtek.com — NewTek's own forum for LightWave and other NewTek products. The site has a lot of tutorials as well as extensive forums for the community.

http://www.flay.com — A great resource for LightWave plug-ins and news.

http://www.lwg3d.org — LightWave Group, a site for LightWave-related news, along with a bustling forum community.

http://www.spinquad.com — LightWave and industry news, and a very active forum community.

http://www.simplylightwave.com — Great LightWave resource with loads of tutorials and a forum.

www.cgfocus.com — Industry news, articles, interviews, and a forum.

www.subdivisionmodeling.com — Not specifically directed to texturing but useful if you like to model. Cool wire gallery useful for reference and a forum.

http://members.shaw.ca/lightwavetutorials — One of the largest collections of LightWave tutorial links on the web. Fantastic for beginners especially.

http://www.thegnomonworkshop.com — Not LightWave at all, but Gnomon Workshop has a fantastic range of digital painting DVDs available that I would recommend to anyone who wishes to enhance and improve their painting knowledge and technique.

## Software Web Sites

http://www.maxon.net — Maxon, developer of BodyPaint 3D.

http://www.righthemisphere.com — Right Hemisphere, developer of Deep Paint 3D and the extraordinarily useful Deep Exploration, the ultimate browser for all file types, including 3D models, video files, images, sound clips, archive files, etc.

http://www.adobe.com — Adobe, developer of Photoshop and a variety of other popular production packages.

http://www.worley.com — Worley Labs, developer of incredible LightWave plug-ins such as Sasquatch, G2, and a number of others.

http://www.shaders.co.uk — IFW2 Procedural Textures web site; be sure to check out the demos on the companion CD.

http://perso.orange.fr/dpont/plugins/nodes/Additionnal_Nodes.html — A collection of fantastic extra nodes for LightWave by Denis Pontonnier.

## Texture Collections

http://www.ransomactive.com — Fabulous range of texture collection CDs that are extremely useful for photographic references as well as photos to incorporate into your textures.

http://www.realtexture.com/ — Another awesome texture collection on CD and DVD. Real Texture also offers collections of high-quality HDR images for sale. Highly recommended.

http://www.mayang.com/textures — Great resource of textures for free download.

http://www.cgtextures.com — Huge online texture collection; the Animals section has great reference material as well.

## Recommended Further Reading

*LightWave v9 Lighting* — Nicholas Boughen, published by Wordware Publishing (1-59822-039-X). Fantastic book for learning lighting principles and sharpening your lighting skills in LightWave. Highly recommended for texturing artists.

# Index

**619**

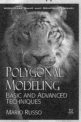
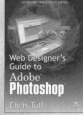

# About the Companion CD

The companion CD-ROM includes trial versions of LightWave, tutorial files, models, demo software, and the book's images, organized into the following directories:

**LightWave Trial Versions** — Demo versions of LightWave v9 as well as pre-created materials from NewTek. The 30-day demos are available for Macintosh (for use with Mac OS X) and Windows (32-bit for Windows 2000/XP and 64-bit for Windows XP Pro x64). Additionally, the Content file contains a variety of royalty-free objects, scenes, and animations to give you a jump start on your LightWave learning experience. Unzip the Content file to your hard drive. Then in each project folder, locate the scene folder and double-click or load the .lws file into LightWave Layout.

**Tutorials** — All of the necessary tutorial files as well as completed examples of the tutorials. Simply copy the folders into an appropriate working folder on your hard drive and set that folder as your Content Directory within LightWave.

**Models** — A number of models from various artists for your own use — go wild with them! Thanks to the artists who so generously contributed some awesome models.

**Software** — Demo version of IFW Procedural Textures from The Graphics Factory. You can expand LightWave nodes with this amazing collection.

**Book Images** — All of the images from this book in color.

**Surface Presets** — Many of the surfaces used throughout the book, including the surfaces used for the cover image. Just load them up into your surface presets folder and enjoy!

**SNoWs_ZBrush_alphas** — A collection of images designed to work as ZBrush alpha brushes. You can use them to add detail, mask, paint, etc., to your models.

 **Warning:**   By opening the CD package, you accept the terms and conditions of the CD/Source Code Usage License Agreement on the following page.

Additionally, opening the CD package makes this book nonreturnable.

# CD/Source Code Usage License Agreement

Please read the following CD/Source Code usage license agreement before opening the CD and using the contents therein:

1. By opening the accompanying software package, you are indicating that you have read and agree to be bound by all terms and conditions of this CD/Source Code usage license agreement.

2. The compilation of code and utilities contained on the CD and in the book are copyrighted and protected by both U.S. copyright law and international copyright treaties, and is owned by Wordware Publishing, Inc. Individual source code, example programs, help files, freeware, shareware, utilities, and evaluation packages, including their copyrights, are owned by the respective authors.

3. No part of the enclosed CD or this book, including all source code, help files, shareware, freeware, utilities, example programs, or evaluation programs, may be made available on a public forum (such as a World Wide Web page, FTP site, bulletin board, or Internet news group) without the express written permission of Wordware Publishing, Inc. or the author of the respective source code, help files, shareware, freeware, utilities, example programs, or evaluation programs.

4. You may not decompile, reverse engineer, disassemble, create a derivative work, or otherwise use the enclosed programs, help files, freeware, shareware, utilities, or evaluation programs except as stated in this agreement.

5. The software, contained on the CD and/or as source code in this book, is sold without warranty of any kind. Wordware Publishing, Inc. and the authors specifically disclaim all other warranties, express or implied, including but not limited to implied warranties of merchantability and fitness for a particular purpose with respect to defects in the disk, the program, source code, sample files, help files, freeware, shareware, utilities, and evaluation programs contained therein, and/or the techniques described in the book and implemented in the example programs. In no event shall Wordware Publishing, Inc., its dealers, its distributors, or the authors be liable or held responsible for any loss of profit or any other alleged or actual private or commercial damage, including but not limited to special, incidental, consequential, or other damages.

6. One (1) copy of the CD or any source code therein may be created for backup purposes. The CD and all accompanying source code, sample files, help files, freeware, shareware, utilities, and evaluation programs may be copied to your hard drive. With the exception of freeware and shareware programs, at no time can any part of the contents of this CD reside on more than one computer at one time. The contents of the CD can be copied to another computer, as long as the contents of the CD contained on the original computer are deleted.

7. You may not include any part of the CD contents, including all source code, example programs, shareware, freeware, help files, utilities, or evaluation programs in any compilation of source code, utilities, help files, example programs, freeware, shareware, or evaluation programs on any media, including but not limited to CD, disk, or Internet distribution, without the express written permission of Wordware Publishing, Inc. or the owner of the individual source code, utilities, help files, example programs, freeware, shareware, or evaluation programs.

8. You may use the source code, techniques, and example programs in your own commercial or private applications unless otherwise noted by additional usage agreements as found on the CD.

 **Warning:** By opening the CD package, you accept the terms and conditions of the CD/Source Code Usage License Agreement.
Additionally, opening the CD package makes this book nonreturnable.